SELECTIONS FROM MUHAMMADAN TRADITIONS

SELECTIONS FROM MUHAMMADAN TRADITIONS

Being a Carefully Chosen and Thoroughly
Representative Collection of the
Most Authentic Traditions
from the Celebrated

MISHKATU'L-MASABIH

Translated from the Arabic

by the

REV. WILLIAM GOLDSACK

GYAN

Published by

Gyan Publishing House
5, Ansari Road
Daryaganj, New Delhi-110002
Phone: 011-47034999, 9811692060
E-mail: books@gyanbooks.com

Distribution Network
gyanbooks.com
India, USA, Canada, UK, Australia, France

ISBN : 978-81-212-6316-0 (PB)
First Published, 1923

2nd Impression 2022

Printed at: Gyan Press, Delhi.

SELECTIONS FROM MUHAMMADAN TRADITIONS
Translated: REV. WILLIAM GOLDSACK

SELECTIONS

FROM

MUḤAMMADAN TRADITIONS

Being a Carefully Chosen and Thoroughly Representative Collection of the Most Authentic Traditions from the Celebrated

MISHKÁTU'L-MAṢÁBÍH

Translated from the Arabic

by the

REV. WILLIAM GOLDSACK

1923

PREFACE

In the system of Islám the Traditions occupy a place second only in importance to the Qur'án itself. They are described as a record of 'the words of the Prophet and his actions and what he permitted.' Their importance is derived from the Muslim belief that Muḥammad, in all he said and did, was divinely guided. The Traditions are technically known as *waḥi ghairu'l-matlú*, unrecited revelation, in contradistinction to the revelation of the Qur'án which is said to have been recited word for word by Gabriel to the Prophet. Thus it will be seen that whilst the Qur'án, according to Muslims, is a purely objective revelation, in the Traditions the inspiration is subjective only.

In Islám the Traditions are used both in the formation of canon law and also in the exegesis of the Qur'án; whilst not a little of what we know of the life and character of Muḥammad is derived from the same source. As every word and act of the Prophet is for the Muslim a divine rule of faith and practice, the influence of the Traditions on the lives of millions, all over the world, is difficult to over-estimate.

A Tradition is technically divided by Muslim theologians into two parts. There is first, the *isnád*, the support or authority on which the Tradition rests. This consists of the names of the succession of reporters by whom the particular Tradition was handed down. This *isnád*, to be complete, must begin with the name of the original person who actually heard the words spoken by Muḥammad, and must continue in an unbroken chain up to the name of the last reporter from whom the written record was made, when, of course, oral transmission automatically ceased. In a genuine Tradition (Ḥadíthu'ṣ-Ṣaḥíḥ) each narrator in the *Isnád* must be a pious man, of unblemished character. Traditions in which there is a break in the chain of narrators are of slight value.[1] The second part of a Tradition

[1] For a list of these see, *The Faith of Islám*, Chapter iv, pp. 120-2.

consists of the actual text of what Muḥammad is reported to have said or done. This is called the *matn* or text.

The Traditions were at first handed down orally from one generation to the next, and it was not until more than a century had passed away after the death of Muḥammad that any attempt was made to collect and reduce them to writing. Since that time, however, very numerous collections of Traditions have been made, amounting, according to the *Ithâfu'n-Nubala*, to no less than 1465 different collections. By general consent six collections have come to be accepted as of paramount authority and value amongst Sunni Muslims. These are the collections of Al-Bukhárí who died in 256 A.H., Muslim who died in 260 A.H., Abú Dáud who died in 275 A.H. Ibn Májah who died in 273 A.H., At-Tirmidhí who died in 299 A.H., and An-Nasá'i who died in 303 A.H. These six great collections are known to-day as the *Al-Kutubu's-sitta*, 'the six (correct) books', and are universally revered by Sunnis all over the world. They are not all regarded as of equal authority, however, for the first two are considered as of pre-eminent authority and are known as *ṣaḥiḥ*, sound or authentic, whilst the others are simply called *sunan*, usages, or *ḥasan*, good.

As hundreds of Traditions are found repeated in more than one of the above-mentioned collections, efforts have been made from time to time to eliminate repetition and at the same time secure a trustworthy and thoroughly representative collection of Traditions by compiling, from these six, one standard and authoritative collection. One of the most famous of such compilations, or reductions, is that known as the *Mishkátu'l-Maṣábiḥ* from which the present selection has been drawn. This work, originally called the *Maṣábiḥ*, was compiled by Imám Abú Muḥammad al-Ḥusain ibn Mas'úd al-Firái' of Baghdad, who died in 516 A.H. It contained 4,484 Traditions, of which 2,434 were *ṣaḥiḥ* and the rest *ḥasan*. The compiler, besides making use of the 'six (correct) books' mentioned above, also used a few other well-known collections such as those of Al-Dáraqutni, Al-Baihaqi, Al-Dárimi and Razín. In the year 737 A.H. Shaikh Waliyu'd-Dín Abú 'Abdu'lláh Maḥmúd revised and enlarged the *Maṣábiḥ*, adding another chapter to each section. He also added much to the value of the original compilation by quoting the authorities whence the various Traditions were derived. This revised edition is now known as the *Mishkâtu'l-Maṣâbîḥ*.

The *Mishkât* was translated into English, with many omissions however, by Captain Matthews in 1809. That work is long since out of print, and now unobtainable. Matthews' translation suffers by being paraphrastic to a degree, and loses in value by its omission of the names of the authorities from whose compilations the various Traditions have been taken.

Some slight variations exist in different editions of the *Mishkât* in the headings to books and sections. The present translation of selections was made from a Lahore edition of 1321 A.H.

No attempt is here made to discuss the question of the authenticity and integrity of the Traditions. The reader will find the whole subject critically discussed in the translator's *The Traditions in Islám*, and to that work he is referred.

It is hoped that this book of Selections will enable the English reader to form an adequate idea of the general character and scope of Muslim Tradition, and will help missionaries in particular to a more sympathetic approach to the followers of the Arabian Prophet.

For typographical reasons diacritical letters such as dh th have not been used.

I have not dealt with the question of the authenticity and genuineness of the Traditions.[1] In modern days, intelligent Muslims place less reliance on many of them. It is known that in the first century of Islám Traditions were forged for political and religious reasons. The late Sir Sayyed Aḥmad accepted very few as genuine ones. The Hon'ble Sir 'Abdu'r-Raḥím says: 'Nothing has been a more fruitful source of conflicting opinions in matters of law among the Sunni jurists than the question whether a particular tradition is to be regarded as genuine or not, though it may be one for whose authority one

---

[1] For a statement on this subject see Appendix A in Sell's *Faith of Islám* (Fourth Ed.)

or more of these writers (Bukhári and Muslim) may have vouchsafed "[1]

The study of the Traditions ('Ilmu'-l-Ḥadíth) is an important part of the curriculum of Muslim Theological Schools. Traditions are of varying value. A Tradition of the highest class is called Ḥadíthu'l-Mutawátir. In this case the *isnád* must be perfect, that is, the chain of narrators must be continuous, and each narrator must have been a man of unblemished conduct. These Traditions are few in number. Next to them come Traditions known as Ḥadíthu'ṣ-Ṣaḥíḥ or genuine Traditions. Those in the collections made by Bukhári and Muslím are generally placed in this class. Traditions known as Ḥadíthu'l-Ḥasan, are accepted as good, though inferior to the other two classes. Weak Traditions, Ḥadíthu'ḍ-Ḍa'íf, are those, amongst the narrators of which were men of doubtful reputation, or who committed the crime of introducing innovations (bid'at) in belief or in worship. A Ḥadíthu'l-Mu'allaq is a Tradition in which there is a break in the chain of narrators, that is, the *isnád* is not perfect. If the Tradition does not come from a Companion of the Prophet, but from a Tábi', a man of the next generation, it is called a Mursal. In some cases there are other defects: these have to be taken note of by the Muslim student, but we may pass them by. A Tradition must not be contrary to a statement in the Qur'án and it can be abrogated by a verse of the Qur'án. The place of the Traditions in Islám theology and law is a very important one. They form the basis of the Sunna, 'To an orthodox Muslim, the Book and the Sunnai, God's word direct and God's word through the mind of the Prophet, recorded in the Traditions, are the foundation and sum of Islám.' The great collectors of the Traditions were ignorant of the sound canons of historical research: they lacked the spirit of the 'higher criticism': they paid little attention to internal evidence. The subject of a Tradition might be foolish, or improbable: that did not matter, if the *isnád* was sound. Like

---

[1] *Muḥammadan Jurisprudence*, p. 31; see also Maulavi Cheragh 'Alí, *Critical Exposition of Jihád*, pp. 65, 67, 73 and his *Reforms Under Muslim Rule*, p. 19; for Mírzá Ghulám Aḥmad's view see Walter, *The Aḥmadiyya Movement*, p. 39. Marglionth's *The Early Development of Muḥammadanism*, Chapter iii, is a valuable contribution to the subject.

so much else in Islám, the procedure was purely mechanical and this accounts for the changed attitude of many modern intelligent Muslims to the whole question of the authenticity, genuineness and authority of many Traditions.

In conclusion the translator desires to thank Mr. A. T. Upson, the talented Superintendent of the Nile Mission Press, for much valuable help received in the interpretation of obscure passages and the Rev. L. Bevan Jones, B.A., B.D., for valuable assistance in reading the proofs.

Jessore, Bengal, 1923. W. G.

CONTENTS

SELECTIONS
FROM
MUHAMMADAN TRADITIONS

I

THE BOOK OF FAITH

It is related from 'Omar binu'-l-Khuṭṭáb that, 'On a certain day when we were near the Prophet, there appeared before us a man dressed in white apparel. His hair was extremely black, and no marks of travel could be seen upon him, and none of us recognized him. At length he sat down beside the Prophet. Then he placed his two knees near the Prophet's knees, and placed the palms of his hands on his thighs and said, "O Muḥammad, teach me about Islám." He replied, "Islám is that thou bear witness that there is no God but Alláh, and that Muḥammad is the Apostle of Alláh, and that thou observe prayer, and that thou give alms, and that thou keep the fast in the month Ramaḍán, and that thou make the pilgrimage to the House (i.e., the temple at Mecca), if thou art able to provide for the journey." He said, "Thou hast spoken truly." At that we wondered at his questioning the Prophet and telling him he had spoken truly. Then he said, "Teach me about faith." The Prophet replied, "It is that thou believe in God and His angels and His books and His apostles and in the last day, and that thou believe in predestination, both of good and evil." He said, "Thou hast spoken truly." Then he said, "Teach me concerning the best action." He replied, "It is that thou worship God as if thou didst see Him; for if thou dost not see Him, yet He sees thee." The man said, "Teach me concerning the hour of resurrection." He replied, "Concerning this matter the questioned is no wiser than the questioner." He said, "Teach me concerning its signs." He replied, "It is that a female slave will give birth to her master, and that thou wilt see the barefooted and the naked and the indigent and shepherds possessing houses." After that the man departed, and I remained sitting for some time. Then the Prophet said to me, "O 'Omar, dost thou know who the questioner was?" I said, "God and His Apostle know best." He replied, "It was Gabriel. He came to teach you your religion."'—*Muslim.*

It is related from 'Abdu'lláh bin 'Omar that, 'The Apostle of God said, "A Muslim is he from whose tongue and hands Muslims are safe. And one who flees for religion is he who flees from what God has forbidden."'—*Muslim, Al Bukhárí.*

It is related from Anas that, 'The Apostle of God said, "None of you will believe until I become more precious to him than his father and his son and all men together."'—*Muslim, Al Bukhárí.*

It is related from 'Abbás bin Abdu'l-Muṭṭalib that, 'The Apostle of God said, "He has tasted the food of faith who is pleased with Alláh as his Lord and with Islám as his religion and Muḥammad as his Apostle."'—*Muslim.*

It is related from Abú Hurairah that, 'The Apostle of God said, "By Him in whose hand is the life of Muḥammad! no one of this people, whether Jew or Christian, shall have heard of me, and shall afterwards die without believing in that with which I am sent, but shall become of the companions of the fire (of hell)."'—*Muslim.*

It is related from Abú Músa Al-Asha'ri that, 'The Apostle of God said, "There are three classes of people who will obtain a double reward: the man of the people of the Book who believes in his own prophet and in Muḥammad; the slave when he does his duty both to God and his masters; and the man who possesses a female slave and, after having connection with her, teaches her good manners and improves them, and gives her instruction and betters it, and then emancipates and marries her."'—*Muslim, Al Bukhárí.*

It is related from Ibn 'Omar that, 'The Apostle of God said, "I am ordered to make war on men until they bear witness that there is no God but Alláh and that Muḥammad is the Apostle of Alláh; and until they observe the prayers and give alms. And if they do that, then their blood and their property will be safe from me, except what is due to me according to the laws of Islám; and their account is with God."'—*Muslim,*

Al Bukhárí, with the exception that Muslim makes no mention of the words "except what is due to me according to the laws of Islam."

It is related from Abú Musa Al-Asha'ri that, "The Apostle of God said, "There is no one more patient than God at the sins which He hears. They attribute a son to Him, yet, after that, He preserves them from evil and provides their daily food."'—*Muslim, Al Bukhárí.*

It is related from Abú Dharr that he said, 'I came to the Prophet, and he had a white cloth over him and was sleeping. Later on I came to him after he had awakened. Then he said, "There is no servant who shall say, 'There is no God but Alláh,' and shall afterwards die relying on that, but will enter heaven." I said, "Although he commit adultery or steal!" He replied, "Although he have committed adultery and theft." I said, "Although he commit adultery and theft!" He replied, "Although he commit adultery and theft." I said, "Although he commit adultery and theft!" He replied, "Although he commit adultery and theft, and in spite of Abú Dharr."'—*Muslim, Al Bukhárí.*

It is related from 'Ubádah bin Aṣ-Ṣámit that, 'The Apostle of God said, "Whoever bears witness that there is no God but Alláh alone, and that He has no partner, and that Muḥammad is His servant and His Apostle, and that Jesus is the servant of God and His Apostle and the son of His handmaid and His word which He cast into Mary and a spirit from Him; and (bears witness) that heaven and hell are true, God will take him into paradise in spite of what his works may have been."'—*Muslim, Al Bukhárí.*

It is related from Abú Umámah that, 'The Apostle of God said, "He who loves for God's sake, and hates for God's sake, and gives for God's sake, and withholds for God's sake, has perfected the faith."'—*Abú Dáud.*

It is related from Anas that he said, 'The Apostle of God scarcely ever addressed us without saying, "He who is not true to his trust has no faith, and he who does not keep his promise has no religion."'—*Al Baihaqi.*

It is related from Abú Hurairah that he said, 'We were sitting around the Apostle of God, and with us in the party were Abú Bakr and 'Omar. And the Apostle of God stood up in our midst and went out from us and delayed (his return) to us. And we feared that, being separated from us, some calamity might befall him ; so we rose up, and I was the first to be afraid and I went out seeking the Apostle until I came to a wall belonging to the Helpers, the Bani Nazzár, and I walked round it to see whether I could find a door to it, but I found none. And behold! a drain which entered a cavity of the wall from a well outside.' Abú Hurairah said, 'So I squeezed myself through and went in to the Apostle. He said "Is it Abú Hurairah?" I said, "Yes, O Apostle of God." He said, "What is the matter with thee?" I replied, "Thou wert in our company, but didst rise up, and delayed to return to us; therefore we feared that, being separated from us, some calamity might happen to thee; and I was the first to be afraid; and I came to this wall, and squeezed myself through like a fox, and these men are following me." The Prophet said, "O Abú Hurairah—and he gave me his shoes—take these shoes of mine, and whoever meets thee behind this wall and bears witness that there is no God but Alláh, affirming it from his heart, then give that one the good tidings of heaven." And the first whom I met was 'Omar, and he said, "What are these shoes, O Abú Hurairah?" I replied, "These are the Apostle's shoes. He has sent me with them that whomsoever I meet, who bears witness from the heart that there is no God but Alláh, to him I should give the good tidings of heaven." Then 'Omar struck me between the breasts and I fell down on my back. And he said, "Return, O Abú Hurairah." So I returned to the Apostle of God with loud weeping. And 'Omar followed closely in my tracks. Then the Apostle of God said, "What is the matter with thee, O Abú Hurairah?" I replied, "I met 'Omar, and informed him of the message with which thou sentest me, but he struck me between my breasts, so that I fell on my back. Then he told me to return." Then the Apostle of God said, "What, O 'Omar, incited thee to act as thou didst?" He replied, "O Apostle of God, by my father and my mother, didst thou send Abú Hurairah with thy shoes to inform whomsoever he met, and that bare witness from the heart that there is no God but

Alláh, that he should give him good tidings of heaven?" He said, "Yes." 'Omar said, "Then do not do so; for I fear that men will depend upon this alone. Therefore leave them alone to perform their works." Then the Apostle of God said, "Leave them alone."'—*Muslim.*

It is related from Abú Umámah that, 'A man asked the Apostle of God, "What is faith?" He replied, "When your good actions give you pleasure, and your evil actions give you pain, then you are a believer." He said, "O Apostle of God, then what is sin?" He replied, "When anything pricks your conscience, then forsake it."'—*Aḥmad.*

It is related from Mu'ádh bin Jabal that, 'He asked the Apostle of God as to what was the best part of faith. He replied, "That you love for the sake of God and hate for the sake of God, and that you employ your tongue in the mention of God." He said, "And what else, O Apostle of God?" He replied, "And that you love for men what you love for yourself, and hate for them what you hate for yourself."'—*Aḥmad.*

On Mortal Sins and the Signs of Hypocrisy

It is related from 'Abdu'lláh bin 'Omar that, 'The Apostle of God said, "The greatest sins are the associating anything with God, and being disobedient to one's parents, and the taking of life, and making a false oath."'—*Muslim, Al Bukhárí.*

It is related from Abú Hurairah that, 'The Apostle of God said, "Avoid seven destructive things." They said, "O Apostle of God, and what are they?" He replied, "The associating anything with God, magic, the taking of life—which God has forbidden—except for a just cause, the taking of interest, taking the property of an orphan, turning back in the day of battle, and charging with adultery good women who are believers and ignorant of sin."'—*Muslim, Al Bukhárí.*

It is related from Abú Hurairah that, 'The Apostle of God said, "The signs of a hypocrite are three"—and Muslim adds the words, "If he fasts and prays and pretends that he is a Muslim," afterwards the two (Muslim and Bukhárí) agree—"That when he relates anything, he relates falsely, and when he makes a promise he breaks it, and when he is entrusted with anything he is false to his trust."'—*Muslim, Al Bukhárí.*

It is related from Ṣafwán bin 'Assál that, 'A Jew said to a companion of his, "Go with us to this Prophet." His companion said to him, "Do not call him a Prophet, for if he hears thee, he will be pleased." Then they came to the Apostle of God and asked him about the nine clear signs. Then the Apostle of God said, "Do not associate anything with God, do not steal, do not commit adultery, do not take life—which God has forbidden—except for a just cause, do not take an innocent person before one having authority in order to kill him, do not practise magic, do not take interest, do not accuse a good person of adultery, do not turn to flee in the day of battle, and it is specially obligatory on you Jews that ye do not hunt on the sabbath." Then they kissed the Apostle's hands and feet and said, "We bear witness that thou art a Prophet." He replied, "Then what forbids you from following me?" They replied, "Verily David prayed to his Lord, that there should never lack a Prophet in his descendants, and we fear that if we follow thee, the Jews will kill us."'—*Tirmidhí; Abú Dáud, An Nasá'i.*

It is related from Mu'ádh that he said, 'The Apostle of God commanded me ten things: He said, "Associate not anything with God, although thou art killed or burnt, do not disobey thy parents although they command thee to go out from thy family and thy possessions, do not wilfully forsake the prayers which are written down (as obligatory), for verily he who wilfully forsakes the prayers which are written down, from him will be withdrawn the protection of God, and do not drink wine, for it is the root of all evil. 'Beware of disobedience, for by disobedience is set loose the anger of God, and beware of fleeing from battle although men are destroyed, and when death approaches men (in pestilence) and thou dwellest among them, then remain there, and spend for thy family according to thine ability, and do not spare the rod upon them in order to teach them good manners and instruct them in the fear of God."'—*Aḥmad.*

On the Whisperings of Satan

It is related from Ibn Mas'úd that, 'The Apostle of God said, "There is no one of you but has appointed over him a companion from the genii and a companion from the angels." They said, "And what of thee, O Apostle of God?" He replied, "And for me also, but God has aided me against him, and I resign myself to Him, and He only commands me that which is good."'—*Muslim.*

It is related from Abú Hurairah that, 'The Apostle of God said, "There is no son of Adam born, except Mary and her son, but Satan touches him when he is born, and he cries out from the touch of Satan."'—*Muslim, Al Bukhárí.*

It is related from Abú Hurairah that, 'The Apostle of God said, "The cry of a new-born babe at the time of its birth is from the touch of Satan."'—*Muslim, Al Bukhárí.*

It is related from 'Othmán bin Abú'l-'Áṣ that he said, 'I said, "O Apostle of God, verily Satan intruded himself between me and my prayers, and between me and my reading, and confused me in them." The Apostle of God replied, "That is a Satan called Khinzib, therefore when thou realize his presence, then take protection with God from him and spit over thy left side three times." Therefore I did that, and then God drove him away from me.'—*Muslim.*

On Belief in Predestination

It is related from 'Abdu'lláh bin 'Omar that, 'The Apostle of God said, "God wrote the fate of all creation fifty thousand years before He created the heavens and the earth." He said, "And His throne was upon the waters."'—*Muslim.*

It is related from Abú Hurairah that, 'The Apostle of God said, "Adam and Moses debated near their Lord, and Adam prevailed over Moses. Moses said, 'Thou art Adam whom God created by His hand and breathed into from His spirit; and He made the angels to bow down to thee, and He caused thee to dwell in His garden. Afterwards thou, by thy sin, didst cause men to fall to the earth.' Adam said, 'Thou art Moses whom God chose with His message and His word, and He gave thee the tables (of stone) in which were an explanation of all matters, and He brought thee near and taught thee His secrets. Then how long didst thou find that God wrote the Taurát before I was created?' Moses replied, 'Forty years.' Adam said, 'Then didst thou find therein that "Adam disobeyed his

Lord and went astray"?' He said, 'Yes.' He said, 'Then dost thou blame me for doing actions which God wrote concerning me that I would do them forty years before He created me?' The Apostle of God said, "Adam defeated Moses in this argument."'—*Muslim.*

It is related from 'Áyesha that, 'The Apostle of God was called to the funeral of a young child of one of the Helpers; and I said, "O Apostle of God, this one is blessed. He is one of the birds of paradise, for he has neither done evil nor thought it." He replied, "O 'Áyesha, it may be otherwise, for verily God created a people for paradise when they were yet in their fathers' loins, and He created a people for the fire when they were yet in their fathers' loins."'—*Muslim.*

It is related from Abú Hurairah that he said, 'I said, "O Apostle of God, I am a youth, and I fear lest I commit adultery, and I have not the means wherewith to marry a wife"—as if he were seeking permission from him to become an eunuch—but the Apostle of God remained silent. Then I said the same thing again, but he remained silent. Then I repeated it, but he remained silent. Then I repeated the same words, and the Apostle of God said, "O Abú Hurairah, the pen has already dried (after registering) what you will be worthy of; therefore become an eunuch or refrain."'—*Al Bukhárí.*

It is related from 'Abdu'lláh bin 'Omar that, 'The Apostle of God said, "The hearts of the sons of Adam are all between two fingers of the Merciful, like one heart. He turneth them as He wills." Then the Apostle of God said, "O God, turn our hearts to obey thee."'—*Muslim.*

It is related from 'Ubádah binu'ṣ-Ṣámit that, 'The Apostle of God said, "Verily the first thing which was created was a pen. And He said to it, 'Write.' It said, 'What shall I write?' He replied, 'Write down the divine decrees.' So it wrote down all that was and all that will be to eternity."'—*At Tirmidhí*

It is related from Muslim bin Yasár that he said, ''Omar binu'l-Khaṭṭáb was asked concerning this verse (of the Qur'án), "And when thy Lord brought forth their descendants from the backs of the sons of Adam."[1] 'Omar said, "I heard the Apostle of God questioned concerning this verse, and he replied, 'Verily

[1] Qur'án, Súratu'l-A'ráf (vii) 171.

God created Adam and then stroked his back with His right hand and brought out from it certain descendants and said, "I have created these for paradise, and they will do the actions of the people of paradise." Then He stroked Adam's back with His hand and brought forth (other) descendants and said, "These I have created for the fire, and they will do the actions of the people of the fire."' Then a man said, 'Of what use, then, are works, O Apostle of God?' The Apostle of God replied, 'Verily when God creates a servant for paradise, He causes him to do the actions of the people of paradise, until he dies doing the actions of the people of paradise, and then He causes him to enter paradise thereby; and when He creates a servant for the fire, He causes him to do the actions of the people of the fire, until he dies doing the actions of the people of the fire. Then He causes him to enter the fire thereby.'"'—*Málik, At Tirmidhí, Abú Dáud.*

It is related from Abú Khizámah from his father that he said, 'I said, "O Apostle of God, inform me about the charms which I use, the medicine which I swallow, and the shields which I use for protection, whether they will prevent anything of that which is predestined by God." He replied, "These are amongst the things predestined by God."'—*Aḥmad, At Tirmidhí.*

It is related from Abú Hurairah that he said, 'The Apostle of God came out to us when we were debating about fate. Then he became so angry that his face became red to such a degree that it seemed as if the seed of a pomegranite had been split open on his two cheeks. Then he said, "Is it this you have been commanded to do? or was it for this that I was sent to you? Those who preceded you were destroyed when they debated about this matter. I adjure you! I adjure you! not to argue about it."'

It is related from 'Áyesha that she said, 'I said, "O Apostle of God, what becomes of the children of believers?" He replied, "They are as their fathers." I said, "O Apostle of God, even without works?" He replied, "God knows best what they would have done." I said, "And what of the children of the polytheists?" He replied, "They will be as their fathers." I said, "Without works?" He replied, "God knows best what they would have done."'—*Abú Dáud.* 2

It is related from 'Álí that he said, 'Khadíjah asked the Prophet concerning her two children who had died in the time of ignorance (i.e., before Islám). The Apostle of God replied, "They are both in the fire." 'Álí said, When Muhammad saw displeasure in her face he said, "If thou hadst but seen their place (in hell) thou wouldst certainly be displeased with them both." She said, "O Apostle of God, then what of the son (now dead) which I had of thee?" He replied, "It is in paradise." Afterwards the Apostle of God said, "Verily believers and their children are in paradise, and polytheists and their children are in the fire." Then the Apostle of God recited (the verse) "And to those who have believed, whose offspring have followed them will we again unite their offspring."[1]'—*Ahmad.*

It is related from Abú Hurairah that, 'The Apostle of God said, "When God created Adam he stroked his back, and there fell from his back all the men whom He was creating from his descendants until the day of resurrection. And He placed before the eyes of each man of them a flash of light. Afterwards He brought them to Adam. Adam said, 'O my Lord, who are these?' He replied, 'They are thy descendants.' And he saw a man amongst them whose flash of light between his eyes astonished him. He said, 'O my Lord, who is this?' He replied, 'David.' Then he said, 'O my Lord, how long hast Thou fixed his life?' He replied, 'Sixty years.' Adam said, 'My Lord, increase it from my life by forty years.'" The Apostle of God said, "When the life of Adam was completed except forty years, the angel of death came to him. And Adam said, 'Are there not yet forty years of my life remaining?' He replied, 'Didst thou not give them to thy son David?' Then Adam denied, and his descendants have denied, and Adam forgot and ate of the tree, and his descendants have forgotten, and Adam sinned, and his descendants have sinned."'
—*At Tirmidhí.*

ON THE PUNISHMENTS OF THE GRAVE

It is related from Anas that, 'The Apostle of God said, "Verily when a servant is placed in his grave and his com-

[1] Qur'án, Súratu't-Túr (lii) 21.

panions return from him, he certainly hears the noise of their shoes. Then two angels come to him and make him sit up, and they say to him, 'What didst thou say concerning this man Muḥammad?' As to the believer, he will reply, 'I bear witness that he is a servant of God and His Apostle.' Then it will be said to him, 'Look at thy resting-place in the fire which God has changed for thee to a place in paradise.' Then he will look at them both. But as for the hypocrite and the unbeliever, it will be said to him, 'What didst thou say with respect to this person?' Then he will reply, 'I do not know; I used to say what men said.' Then it will be said to him, 'Didst thou neither know nor read?' Then he will be struck forcibly with an iron hammer; and he will call out with a loud cry; and all near him will hear it except men and genii."'—*Muslim*, *Al Bukhárí.*

It is related from 'Áyesha that, 'A Jewess came in to her and mentioned the punishment of the grave, and said to her, "May God protect thee from the punishments of the grave." Then 'Áyesha asked the Apostle of God concerning the punishments of the grave. He replied, "Yes, the punishments of the grave are true." 'Áyesha said, "I never saw the Apostle of God after repeating the prayers, but what he took refuge with God from the punishments of the grave."'—*Muslim*, *Al Bukhárí.*

It is related from Abú Hurairah that, 'The Apostle of God said, "When a dead person is placed in the grave, then two black angels with blue eyes come to him, one of whom is called Munkar and the other Nakír. And they say, 'What didst thou say concerning this person (Muḥammad)?' Then, if he be a believer, he will say, 'He is the servant of God and His Apostle. I bear witness that there is no God but Alláh and that Muḥammad is His servant and His Apostle.' Then the two angels will say, 'We knew that thou wouldest speak thus.' After that his grave will be enlarged for him seventy cubits by seventy cubits. Then the grave will be illuminated for him, after which it will be said to him, 'Sleep on.' And he will say, 'Let me return to my family and inform them'; but the angels will say, 'Sleep on like the sleep of the bridegroom when no one can awaken him but the loved ones of his family, until God raises him up from his place of sleep.' And if the man be a hypocrite he will say, 'I heard men saying a certain thing, and I said the same; I do not know.' Then the angels will say, 'We knew that thou wouldst speak thus.' And it will be said to the earth, 'Close in upon him,' and it will close in upon him, and its sides will change about; and he will continue therein suffering punishment until God raises him up from his resting-place."'—*Al Tirmidhí.*

It is related from 'Othmán that, 'When the Prophet completed the interment of a corpse he stood over it and said, "Do ye ask forgiveness for your brother, and then pray for him that he continue firm, for verily he is now being questioned."'—*Abú Dáud.*

It is related from Abú Sa'íd that, 'The Apostle of God said, "There are certainly appointed over the infidel in his grave ninety-nine serpents to bite and sting him until the hour (of resurrection) comes. If one of such serpents should breathe upon the earth, no green thing would bud forth."'—*Al Dárimi. At Tirmidhí* relates the same, but substitutes 'seventy' for 'ninety-nine'.

On Relying upon the Book and the Traditions

It is related from Jábir that, 'The Apostle of God said, "Verily the best word is the Book of God, and the best guidance is the guidance of Muḥammad; and the worst thing is a new invention, and all innovation is a going astray."'—*Muslim.*

It is related from Ráfi' bin Khadíj that, 'The Prophet of God came to Madína when they were artificially pollenising the dates. Therefore he said, "What are you doing?" They replied, "We were wont to do this (before the coming of Islám)." He said, "Perhaps it would be better if you did not do it." So they abandoned it; but the crops grew less. Then they mentioned the matter to him. He replied, "I am only a man. When, therefore, I command you anything concerning your religion, then accept it; but when I command you anything as a matter of my own opinion then—verily I am only a man."'—*Muslim.*

It is related from Abú Hurairah that he said, 'The people of the Book were reading the Taurát in Hebrew and explaining it in Arabic to the people of Islám. Then the Apostle of God said, "Do not say that the people of the Book are telling the truth, and do not accuse them of falsehood, but say, 'We believe in God and in what has been sent down upon us,'" '—*Al Bukhárí.*

It is related from Al Miqdám bin Ma'díkarib that, 'The Apostle of God said, "Have I not been given the Qur'án, and with it that which is like it! Will not some arrogant person say to you concerning the Qur'án, 'Consider that lawful which you find made lawful in it, and consider that unlawful which you find made unlawful in it.' Verily what the Apostle of God has made unlawful is like what God has made unlawful. Beware, the flesh of the tame ass is not made lawful for you, nor that of beasts of prey, nor is the thing lawful which is dropped by any one with whom you have made a compact, except its owner is in no need of it. And whosoever alights amongst a company, it is their duty to entertain him; and if they do not give him hospitality, then he may take food sufficient for his requirements."'—*Abú Dáud.*

It is related from 'Irbáḍ bin Sáriyah that he said, 'The Apostle of God stood up and said, "Doth any one of you in his arrogance suppose that God has not forbidden anything except what is in the Qur'án? By God! I have commanded and taught and prohibited things which are certainly like the Qur'án or more (than it). Verily God has not made it lawful for you that ye enter the houses of the people of the Book, except by permission, or that ye beat their women, or that ye eat their fruit, when they give you what they are obliged to (as tax)."' —*Abú Dáud.*

It is related from 'Irbáḍ bin Sáriyah that he said, 'On a certain day the Apostle of God said prayers with us; then he drew near to us and gave us eloquent instruction that brought tears to our eyes and by which our hearts were affected. A man said, "O Apostle of God, this is as if it were a farewell address, therefore give us a command." He replied, "I command you the fear of God, and giving ear and obedience (to my successor) although he be an Abyssinian slave; for those of you who will live after me will see many schisms. Therefore it is your duty to follow my rule of faith and the rule of faith of the rightly guided Khalífas. Seize it and hold it fast. Beware of new things, for all new things are an innovation, and all innovation is a going astray." '—*Aḥmad, Abú Dáud, At Tirmidhí. Ibn Majah;* except that the last two do not mention the prayer.

It is related from 'Abdu'lláh bin 'Omar that, 'The Apostle of God said, "There will certainly happen to my followers such as happened to the Bani Israel, as one shoe is to another, so that if any of them commit incest openly with his mother, there will certainly be some of my followers who will do the same. Verily the Bani Israel are divided into seventy-two sects, and my followers will be divided into seventy-three sects, all but one of whom will enter the fire." They said, "O Apostle of God, which is that one?" He replied, "That which I and my followers follow." '—*At Tirmidhí.*

It is related from Jábir from the Prophet that, 'When 'Omar came to him and said, "Verily we hear stories from the Jews which excite our admiration; dost thou wish that I should write some of them down?" He replied, "Are ye bewildered like the Jews and Christians! Verily I have brought you something white and pure. If Moses had been alive, he would have been nothing but a follower of me." '—*Aḥmad.*

It is related from Abú Hurairah that, 'The Apostle of God said, "The Qur'án came down embodying five different features: things lawful, things unlawful, positive precepts, hidden mysteries and parables. Therefore make the lawful lawful, and make the unlawful unlawful, obey the positive precepts, believe in the hidden mysteries, and take warning from the parables." '

It is related from Málik bin Anas that, 'The Apostle of God said, "I have left amongst you two things, and you will never go astray so long as you hold them fast. The one is the word of God, and the other is the practice of His prophet." '—*Al Muwaṭṭa.*

It is related from Jábir that, 'Omar binu'l-Khaṭṭáb came to the Apostle of God with a copy of the Taurát and said, "O Apostle of God, this is a copy of the Taurát." But he remained silent. Then 'Omar began to read; but the countenance of the Apostle of God changed, and Abú Bakr said, "Mothers bereft of their children weep for thee! Dost thou not see what has happened to the Apostle's countenance!" Then 'Omar looked at the Apostle's face and said, "I take refuge with God from the anger of God and His Apostle. We are satisfied with Alláh as our Lord, with Islám as our religion, and with Muḥammad as our Prophet." Then the Apostle of God said, "By Him in whose hand is the life of Muḥammad! if Moses had appeared to you, ye would have followed him and would have forsaken me, and would have gone astray from the straight path. But were Moses alive and had received my prophecy, he would certainly have followed me." '—*Al Dárimi.*

It is related from Jábir that, 'The Apostle of God said, "My words do not abrogate the words of God, but the words of God abrogate mine, and some of the words of God abrogate others." '

II

THE BOOK OF KNOWLEDGE

It is related from 'Abdu'lláh bin 'Amru that, 'The Apostle of God said, "Transmit from me, though it be but one verse, and relate from the children of Israel. There is no fault in that, but whoever wilfully relates from me falsely, let him find his resting-place in the fire."'—*Al Bukhárí.*

It is related from Samurah bin Jundub and Al Mughírah that, 'The Apostle of God said, "Whoever relates a tradition from me knowing it to be false, verily he is one of the liars."' —*Muslim.*

It is related from Abú Hurairah that, 'The Apostle of God said, "When a man dies, then his actions, except three, are dissociated from him, namely, his alms, which continue, or his knowledge by which men are benefited, or a good son who prays for him."'—*Muslim.*

It is related from Abú Hurairah that, 'The Apostle of God said, "Verily the first person who will be judged on the day of resurrection will be a man who died a martyr; and he will be brought and will be shown the benefits (he formerly received) and he will recognize them. And God will say, 'What didst thou with regard to these?' He will reply, 'I fought for Thee until I died a martyr.' God will say, 'Thou hast lied, rather thou foughtest in order that it might be said of thee, "A hero!" and all this has been said.' Then the order will be given concerning him, and he will be dragged on his face until he is cast into hell. Then a man will be brought who acquired knowledge and then taught it to others, and read the Qur'án. And he will be brought and will be shown the benefits (he formerly received) and he will recognize them. And God will say, 'What didst thou with regard to these?' He will reply, 'I acquired knowledge and taught it to others, and I read the Qur'án in Thy name.' God will say, 'Thou hast lied, rather thou acquiredst knowledge in order that it might be said to thee, "Thou art a learned man," and thou didst read the Qur'án in order that it might be said of thee "He is a Qur'án reader," and all this has been said. Then the order will be given concerning him, and he will be dragged on his face until he is cast into hell. Then a man will be brought whom God had enriched, and had given various kinds of wealth. And he will be brought and will be shown the benefits (he formerly received), and he will recognize them. Then God will say, 'And what didst thou with regard to these?' He will reply, 'I neglected not to spend in Thy name and in those ways in which Thou lovest things to be spent.' God will say, 'Thou hast lied, rather thou didst that in order that it might be said, "He is most generous," and all this has been said.' Then the order will be given concerning him, and he will be dragged on his face, and afterwards will be cast into hell." '—*Muslim.*

It is related from Kathír bin Qais that he said, 'I was sitting with 'Abú'l-Dardái in the mosque of Damascus when a man came to him and said, "O Abú'l-Dardái, verily I have come to thee from the city of the Apostle of God for a certain tradition which, I have been informed, thou dost relate from the Apostle of God. I have come for no other purpose." He replied, "Verily I heard the Apostle of God say, 'He who walks a road, seeking knowledge therein, God will cause him to walk on one of the roads of paradise; for verily the angels spread their wings with pleasure for the seeker of knowledge, and verily whatsoever is in the heavens and on the earth and the great fishes in the bosom of the waters will pray for the forgiveness of his sins. And verily the pre-eminence of a learned man over a worshipper is equal to the pre-eminence of the moon at the night of full-moon over all the stars. And verily the learned men are the heirs of the prophets, and the prophets did not inherit a single *dinar* or a single *dirham*, but they only inherited knowledge; and whoever takes that takes an abundant portion." '—*Aḥmad, At Tirmidhí, Abú Dáud, Ibn Májah.*

It is related from Abú Umámahu'l-Báhili that he said, 'Two men were mentioned to the Apostle of God: one of them a worshipper, and the other a learned man. Then the Apostle of God said, "The pre-eminence of the learned man over the worshipper is like my pre-eminence over the meanest of you." After that the Apostle of God said, "Verily God and His angels and the inhabitants of the heavens and the earth, even the ants in their holes, and even the great fishes certainly pray for the teacher of good to men."'—*At Tirmidhí.*

It is related from Anas that, 'The Apostle of God said, "The search after knowledge is an incumbent duty on every male and female Muslim; but the placing knowledge before one who does not appreciate it is like placing a necklace of pearls, jewels and gold on the necks of swine."'—*Ibn Májah.*

It is related from Abú Hurairah that, 'The Apostle of God said, "He who is asked a question concerning knowledge which he possesses, and then hideth it, will, on the day of resurrection, be bridled with a bridle of fire."'—*Aḥmad, Abú Dáud, At Tirmidhí.*

It is related from Ibn 'Abbás that, 'The Apostle of God said, "Whoever speaks concerning the Qur'án from his own opinion, let him find his resting-place in the fire."'—*At Tirmidhí.*

It is related from Ibn Mas'úd that, 'The Apostle of God said, "The Qur'án was sent down in seven readings. In every verse of them are clear and hidden sentences, and for every boundary there is height."'

It is related from Abú Hurairah that he said, 'Amongst the things which I learned from the Apostle of God is that he said, "Verily God, the Exalted and Magnified, will send for the people at the end of every hundred years one who will rejuvenate for them their religion."'—*Abú Dáud.*

It is related from Abú Hurairah that, 'The Apostle of God said, "Verily amongst the things which reach the believer with rewards after his death from his works and good actions are knowledge which he acquired and dispensed to others, a good son which he left behind, or a Qur'án which he bequeathed to others, or a mosque which he built, or a rest-house for travellers which he built, or a canal which he caused to flow, or alms which he bestowed out of his goods whilst in health and during his life-time."'—*Ibn Májah.*

It is related from Abú'l-Dardái that, 'The Apostle of God was asked, "What is the degree of knowledge, which, if a man attains, he becomes a learned man?" The Apostle of God replied, "Whoever preserves for my followers forty traditions concerning their religion, God will raise him up as a learned man, and I will be for him, on the day of resurrection, both intercessor and witness." '

It is related from Al A'masha that, 'The Apostle of God said, "The danger of knowledge is forgetfulness, and the loss of knowledge is that thou speak of it to one who does not appreciate it." '—*Al Dárimi.*

It is related from Sufyán that 'Omar binu'l-Khaṭṭáb said to Ka'b, "Who are the possessors of learning?" He replied. "They who practise what they know." He said, "And what removes learning from the hearts of the learned?" He replied, "Avarice." '—*Al Dárimi.*

It is related from Abú Hurairah that, 'The Apostle of God said, "Take refuge with God from the pit of sorrow." They replied, "O Apostle of God, what is the pit of sorrow?" He replied, "A valley in hell from which hell itself seeks refuge four hundred times a day." It was said, "O Apostle of God, and who will enter it?" He replied, "Those readers of the Qu'rán who are hypocrites in their behaviour." '—*At Tirmidhí.*

It is related from 'Alí that, 'The Apostle of God said, "The time is near which will come to man, when nothing of Islám will remain but its name, and nothing will remain of the Qur'án but a trace of it. At that time mosques will be (used as) dwelling-places, and men will be devoid of guidance. Their learned men will be the most wicked under the surface of the heavens, for from them will go forth contention, and to them it will return." '—*Al Baihaqi.*

It is related from Ziyád bin Labíd that, 'The Prophet mentioned something and said, "That will take place at the time when knowledge will disappear." I said, "O Apostle of God, how will knowledge disappear when we are reading the Qur'án and teaching the reading of it to our children, and our children are teaching the reading of it to their children till the day of resurrection?" He replied, "May thy mother weep for thee, Ziyád! Verily I thought thou wast one of the wisest men in Madína. Are not these Jews and Christians reading the Taurát and Injíl, but they observe nothing of what is in them." '—*Aḥmad, Ibn Májah.*

III

THE BOOK OF PURIFICATIONS

It is related from Abú Hurairah that, 'The Apostle of God said, "Shall I not point you to that by which God blots out sins and raises (your) rank?" They replied, "Yes, O Apostle of God." He said, "The completion of ablutions in a time of difficulty, and the going a long distance to the mosques, and the waiting for another prayer after the completion of one. This is a protection for you."'—*Muslim.*

It is related from 'Othmán that, 'The Apostle of God said, "He who performs his ablutions and does them well, his sins go out from his body, so that they even go out from under his finger nails."'—*Muslim, Al Bukhárí.*

It is related from 'Othmán that he performed his ablutions and poured water on his hands three times, then he washed his mouth, and then cleansed his nose. After that he washed his face three times, then he washed his right arm to his elbow three times, then he washed his left arm to his elbow three times. After that he wiped his hand over his head, then he washed his right foot three times, then the left three times. After that he said, 'I saw the Apostle of God perform his ablutions like these ablutions of mine.' Then he said, 'Whoever performs his ablutions like these ablutions of mine, and then prays two sets of prayers, whilst his mind speaks nothing the while, all his preceding sins will be forgiven him.' —*Muslim, Al Bukhárí.*

It is related from Jábir that, 'The Apostle of God said, "The key of paradise is prayer, and the key of prayer is purification."'—*Aḥmad.*

It is related from Shabib bin Abi Rauḥ from one of the companions of the Apostle of God that, 'The Apostle of God prayed the morning prayer and recited (the chapter) Rúm, when he become confused. Then when he had prayed, he said, "What is the matter with the people that they recite the prayers with us, but do not perform the ablutions properly! These people only confuse the Qur'àn for us."'—*An Nasái.*

WHAT ACTS NECESSITATE ABLUTIONS

It is related from Abú Hurairah that, 'The Apostle of God said, "Prayer will not be accepted from the one who is impure until he performs his ablutions." '—*Muslim, Al Bukhárí.*

It is related from Buraidah that, 'The Prophet prayed the prayers on the day of the conquest (of Mecca) with one ablution, and he wiped his hands over his shoes (instead of washing his feet). Then 'Omar said to him, "Verily thou hast done a thing today which thou never didst before." He replied, "I did it intentionally, O 'Omar." '—*Muslim.*

It is related from Suwaid bin Al-Na'mán that, 'He went out with the Apostle of God in the year of (the conquest of) Khaibár until, when they came to Ṣahbái, which is near Khaibár, he prayed the afternoon prayer. Then he called for food, and nothing was brought but parched grain. Then he gave orders with regard to it, and it was moistened. Then the Apostle of God ate, and we ate. After that he rose up for the evening prayer, and he rinsed out his mouth and we rinsed out our mouths. Then he prayed, but he did not perform the ablutions.'—*Al Bukhárí.*

It is related from Umm Salamah, that she said, 'I placed near the Prophet a roasted shoulder of mutton, and he ate part of it. After that he rose up for prayers, but he did not perform the ablutions.'—*Aḥmad.*

RULES REGARDING NATURAL EVACUATIONS

(The traditions in this section are unfit for translation. We content ourselves with one only.)

It is related from Salmán that, 'One of the polytheists said, as he ridiculed the Prophet, "Verily I see that your companion (Muḥammad) gives you instruction even regarding the voiding of excrement." '—*Muslim, Aḥmad.*

ON THE USE OF THE TWIG FOR CLEANING THE TEETH

It is related from Abú Hurairah that, 'The Apostle of God said, "Were it not that it would inflict hardships on my followers, I would certainly order them to prolong the evening prayer, and to use a twig for cleaning the teeth with every prayer." '—*Muslim, Al Bukhárí.*

It is related from Shuraih bin Háni that he said, 'I asked 'Áyesha what the Apostle of God began to do first when he entered his house. She replied, "(He began) with a twig for cleaning his teeth."'—*Muslim.*

It is related from 'Áyesha that, 'The Apostle of God said, "That prayer for which a twig for cleaning the teeth has been used is seventy times more excellent than the prayer for which it has not been used,"'—*Al Baihaqi.*

Laws Regarding Purification with Water

It is related from Abú Hurairah that, 'The Apostle of God said, "When any one of you awakes from his sleep and performs his ablutions, then let him cleanse his nose three times, because verily Satan takes up his abode in his nose."'—*Muslim, Al Bukhárí.*

It was said to 'Abdu'lláh bin Zaid bin 'Áṣim, 'How did the Apostle of God perform his ablutions?' Then he called for water for ablutions, and poured it on his hands and washed his hands twice. Then he rinsed out his mouth and nose three times, then he washed his face three times, then he washed his hands twice to the elbows; then he wiped his head with his hands, beginning from the forehead to the back of the head and back again until they returned to the place whence they began. Then he washed his feet.—*Málik, An Nasá'i.*

It is related from 'Abdu'lláh bin 'Abbás that he said, 'The Apostle of God only performed his ablutions once (for each member of the body). He did not do it more than this.'—*Al Bukhárí.*

It is related from 'Abdu'lláh bin Zaid that, 'The Prophet performed each ablution twice.'—*Al Bukhárí.*

It is related from 'Abdu'lláh bin 'Omar that he said, 'We returned with the Apostle of God from Mecca to Madína, until when we came to some water by the roadside, a party hastened to afternoon prayers and they performed their ablutions. And they hurried over them; and we overtook them, and the soles of their feet shone, the water not having touched them. Then the Apostle of God said, "Woe to the soles of your feet! for they are in the fire. Complete your ablutions."'—*Muslim.*

It is related from 'Áyesha that she said, 'The Prophet loved (to begin with) the right hand side, so far as it was possible, in all matters, whether in ablutions or combing his hair or in putting on his shoes.'—*Muslim*, *Al Bukhárí.*

It is related from Sa'íd bin Zaid that, 'The Apostle of God said, "There can be no ablutions for him who does not mention the name of God."'—*At Tirmidhí*, *Ibn Májah.*

It is related from Laqít bin Ṣabirah that he said, 'I said, "O Apostle of God, inform me in what ablution consists." He replied, "Complete the ablutions, and draw your fingers between your toes, and inhale water through the nose, unless you are fasting."'—*Abú Dáud*, *At Tirmidhí.*

It is related from Al Mistaurid bin Shaddád that he said, 'I saw the Apostle of God, when he performed his ablutions, draw his little finger between his toes.'—*Abú Dáud*, *At Tirmidhí*, *Ibn Májah.*

It is related from Anas that, 'When the Apostle of God performed his ablutions he took a handful of water and placed it under his chin and therewith combed his beard, and said, "Thus hath my Lord commanded me."'—*Abú Dáud.*

On Bathing

(The traditions in this section are almost entirely devoted to sexual matters, and are quite unfit for translation).

On Intercourse with the Unclean

(Most of the traditions in this section are unfit for translation).

It is related from 'Alí that, 'The Apostle of God said, "The angels will not enter that house in which there is a picture, or a dog, or an unclean person."'—*Abú Dáud An Nasái.*

It is related from 'Abdu'lláh bin Abú Bakr bin Muḥammad bin 'Amru bin Ḥazm that, 'In the letter which the Apostle of God wrote to 'Amru bin Ḥazm (it was written that) "No one should touch the Qur'án, except the pure."'—*Málik.*

Orders Concerning Different Waters

It is related from As Sáib bin Yazíd that he said, 'My aunt took me to the Prophet and said, "O Apostle of God, verily the son of my sister is suffering from pain." Then he stroked my head, and supplicated a blessing for me. After that he performed ablutions, and I drank from the water with which he had performed the ablutions, and then stood up behind his back. And I saw the seal of prophecy between his shoulders like the tassel of a bride's canopy.'—*Muslim*, *Al Bukhárí.*

It is related from Abú Zaid from 'Abdu'lláh bin Mas'úd that, 'The Apostle of God said to him on the night in which the genii (accepted Islám), "What is that in thy dish?" I replied, "The juice of dates." He said, "Dates are good, and water is pure."'—*Abú Dáud.* Aḥmad and At Tirmidhí add to this the words, 'Then he performed his ablutions with it (the date juice).' And Tirmidhí says that Abú Zaid is in error; and the truth is that received from 'Alqamah from 'Abdu'lláh bin Mas'úd who said, "I was not with the Apostle of God on the night when the genii (accepted Islám.)"'—*Muslim.*

It is related from 'Omar binu'l-Khaṭṭáb that he said, 'Do not bathe in water warmed by the sun, because it induces leprosy.'—*Al Dáraqutni.*

On the Cleansing of Impurities

It is related from Abú Hurairah that, 'The Apostle of God said, "When a dog drinks from a vessel of any one of you, then let him wash it seven times."'—*Muslim*, *Al Bukhárí.*

It is related from 'Abdu'lláh bin 'Abbás that, 'A sheep was given in alms to a freed woman of Al Maimúnah, and it died. And the Apostle of God passed by and said, "Have you not taken its skin and tanned it and made some profit by it?" They replied, "But it died!" He said, "Only the eating of it was unlawful (for you)."'—*Muslim*, *Al Bukhárí.*

It is related from Al Miqdám bin Ma'díkarib that he said, 'The Apostle of God prohibited the wearing of skins of beasts of prey and the riding upon them.'—*Abú Dáud*, *An Nasái.*

On Touching the Boots

It is related from Shuraih bin Háni that he said, 'I asked 'Álí bin Abú Ṭálib about wiping the hands on the boots (in place of removing them and washing the feet before prayer). He replied, "The Apostle of God fixed three days and nights (as a limit) for travellers, and one day and one night for those residing in a fixed place."'—*Muslim.*

It is related from Al Mughírah bin Shu'báh that he said, 'I waited upon the Prophet in the battle of Tabúk, and he wiped his hands on the top and bottom of his shoes.'—*Abú Daud, Al Tirmidhí, Ibn Májah.*

It is related from Al Mughírah bin Shu'báh that he said, 'The Apostle of God wiped his hands on his shoes, so I said, "O Apostle of God, thou hast forgotten." He replied, "Rather thou hast forgotten. My Lord, the Exalted and Magnified, has commanded me to do this." '—*Aḥmad, Abú Dáud.*

On the Use of Earth for Purification

It is related from 'Imrán that he said, 'We were with the Prophet on a journey; and he prayed with the people. When he had finished his prayer, behold! a man sitting apart who had not prayed with the company. The Prophet said, "What prevented thee, O so and so, from praying with the company?" He replied, "I was impure and could get no water." He said, "Thou shouldst have used some earth, for verily that would have sufficed for thee." '—*Muslim, Al Bukhárí.*

It is related from Abú Dharr that, 'The Apostle of God said, "Verily clean earth is ablution for the Muslim, although he does not obtain water for ten years. But if he finds water, then let him touch his whole body with it; for verily that is better." '—*Abú Dáud, Aḥmad, At Tirmidhí.*

On Obligatory Washings

It is related from Ibn 'Omar that, 'The Apostle of God said, "When any one of you comes to the Friday prayers, then let him wash himself all over." '—*Muslim, Al Bukhárí,*

It is related from Abú Hurairah that, 'The Apostle of God said, "He who washes a dead body must (afterwards) wash himself all over." '—*Ibn Májah.* Aḥmad and At Tirmidhí and Abú Dáud have added the words "And whoever lifts up (a dead body) let him perform ablutions."

It is related from 'Áyesha that, 'The Apostle of God washed his whole body for four things: for personal impurity, for the Friday prayers, after being cupped, and after washing a corpse.'—*Abú Dáud.*

On the Menses.

(The traditions under this section are quite unfit for translation.)

IV

THE BOOK OF PRAYER

It is related from Abú Hurairah that, 'The Apostle of God said, "The five daily prayers, and the Friday prayer to the next Friday prayer, and the fast of Ramaḍán to the next fast of Ramaḍán are an expiation (for all sins committed) between them so long as the mortal sins are avoided." '—*Muslim.*

It is related from Anas that he said, 'A man came and said, "O Apostle of God, I have done something worthy of punishment, therefore execute the punishment for it upon me." But the Prophet did not ask him what it was. And the time for prayer arrived, and he prayed with the Apostle of God. And when the Prophet had finished prayer the man stood up and said, "O Apostle of God, I have done something worthy of punishment, therefore execute my punishment as it is laid down in the Book of God." He replied, "Hast thou not said prayers with us?" The man replied, "Yes." He said, "Then God has forgiven for thee thy sins or thy punishment." '—*Muslim, Al-Bukhárí.*

It is related from Ibn Mas'úd that he said, 'I asked the Prophet, "Which work is the most pleasing to God most high?" He replied, "Prayer at its proper times." I said, "After that, which?" He replied, "The honouring of parents." I said, "And after that, which?" He replied, "Religious warfare in the way of God." ' Ibn Mas'úd said, 'He related this to me, and if I had asked him for more, he would certainly have mentioned them to me.'—*Muslim, Al-Bukhárí.*

It is related from Abú Umámah that, 'The Apostle of God said, "Perform your five stated prayers, and fast your stated months, and give alms of your substance, and obey the one who has rule over you, and you will enter paradise with your Lord." '—*Aḥmad, At Tirmidhí.*

It is related from 'Amru bin Shu'aib from his father from his grandfather that, 'The Apostle of God said, "Command your children to say the prayers when they are seven years old, and beat them for dereliction of duty therein when they are ten years of age ; and separate between (the sexes) in their beds (at the latter age)." '—*Abú Dáud.*

CONCERNING THE TIMES OF PRAYER

It is related from 'Abdu'lláh bin 'Omar that, 'The Apostle of God said, "The time for the midday prayer is when the sun declines, and a man's shadow becomes equal to his height, and the afternoon prayer has not arrived. And the time for the afternoon prayer is so long as the sun has not become yellow ; and the time for the evening prayer is so long as the ruddy light of twilight has not disappeared ; and the time of the night prayer is to the first half of the night ; and the time for the morning prayer is from the breaking of the dawn until the sun rises. When the sun rises, then withhold from the morning prayer, for verily it rises between the two horns of Satan." '—*Muslim.*

ON PROMPTITUDE IN PRAYER

It is related from Anas that he said, 'When we said the midday prayers behind the Prophet, we prostrated upon our clothes in order to escape the heat.'—*Muslim*, *Al Bukhárí.*

It is related from Abú Hurairah that, 'The Apostle of God said, "When the heat is excessive, then say your prayers when it gets cooler." '

It is related from Anas that, 'The Apostle of God said, "He who forgets a prayer, or goes to sleep without saying it, then the expiation of his fault is that he repeat the prayer when he remembers it." And in some traditions it runs, "There is no expiation for it except this." '—*Muslim*, *Al Bukhárí.*

It is related from Abú Hurairah that, 'The Apostle of God said, "If it were not that it would be distressing to my followers, I would certainly command them to prolong the evening prayer to one third of the night, or to one half of it." '—*Aḥmad*, *At Tirmidhí*, *Ibn Májah.*

ON THE EXCELLENCIES OF PRAYER

It is related from 'Umárah bin Ruwaibah that he said, 'I heard the Apostle of God say, "No one will enter the fire who prays before the rising of the sun, and before its setting, that is (who prays) the morning and afternoon prayers." '—*Muslim.*

On the Call to Prayer

It is related from Anas that he said (when the question of calling to prayer was being discussed), 'Some mentioned a fire and a bell. They also mentioned (the customs) of the Jews and Christians. Then Bilál was ordered to make the call to prayer twice, and to repeat the words "Prayer is now ready," once.'—*Muslim, Al Bukhárí.*

It is related from Abú Maḥdhurah that, 'The Apostle of God himself placed on me the duty of calling to prayer and said, "Say, 'God is great, God is great, God is great, God is great. I bear witness that there is no God but Alláh, I bear witness that there is no God but Alláh; I bear witness that Muḥammad is the Apostle of God, I bear witness that Muḥammad is the Apostle of God.' Then repeat it and say, 'I bear witness that there is no God but Alláh, I bear witness that there is no God but Alláh; I bear witness that Muḥammad is the Apostle of God, I bear witness that Muḥammad is the Apostle of God. Come to prayers, come to prayers. Come to salvation, come to salvation. God is great, God is great. There is no God but Alláh."'—*Muslim.*

It is related from Ibn 'Omar that he said, 'When the Muslims came to Medina they used to come together and draw near for prayer; and there was no one (appointed) to call them to it. And on a certain day they were discussing the matter, and some of them said, "Let us take something like the bell of the Christians," and others said, "Let us take a horn like the horn of the Jews." And 'Omar said, "Why do ye not appoint a man to call to prayers?" Then the Apostle of God said, "O Bilál, rise up and call to prayers."'—*Muslim, Al Bukhárí.*

It is related from 'Abdu'lláh bin Zaid that he said, 'When the Apostle of God ordered a bell to be rung for calling the people to come together for prayers, there came to me a person as I slept, carrying a bell in his hand. I said, "O servant of God, wilt thou sell the bell?" He replied, "And what wilt thou do with it?" I said, "With it I will call the people to prayers." He replied, "Shall I not point thee to something better than that?" I said to him, "Yes." He said, "Say, God is great"—to the end of the call, and thus with the announcement of being ready for prayers. And when I arose in the morning, I came to the Apostle of God and informed him of what I had seen. He said, "Verily this is a true vision, if God will; therefore stand up with Bilál and teach him what thou hast seen, and let him make the call to prayer in accordance with it, for he is of stronger voice than thou." So I stood up with Bilál, and began to teach him; and he made the call to prayer in that way. And 'Omar binu'l-Khaṭṭáb heard of that when he was in his house, and he came out, dragging his mantle and saying, "O Apostle of God, by Him who hath sent thee with the truth, verily I have seen (a vision) similar to that which was shown him." Then the Apostle of God said, "Praise be to God."'—*Abú Dáud, Al Ḍárimi, Ibn Májah.*

It is related from Málik that information reached him that; the one who called to prayers went to 'Omar to call him to the morning prayer and found him sleeping. So he said, 'Prayer is better than sleep.' Then 'Omar ordered him to include these words in the call to morning prayer.—*In Al Muwaṭṭa.*

It is related from 'Abdu'r-Ráḥmán bin Sa'd bin 'Ammár bin Sa'd the caller-to-prayer of the Apostle of God that he said, 'My father informed me that he heard his father say from his grandfather that the Apostle of God ordered Bilál to put his fingers in his ears, and said, "It will raise thy voice."'—*Ibn Májah.*

On the Excellence of the Call to Prayer

It is related from 'Abdu'lláh bin 'Amru binu'l-'Áṣ that, 'The Apostle of God said, "When ye hear the caller-to-prayer, then say the same as he says. Then pray for blessings on me, for verily, whoever prays for blessings on me, God will bless him ten times for it. Then ask God for favour for me, and that is a station in paradise. This is not fitting for any but one of the servants of God, and I hope that I shall be that one. And whoever asks (this) favour for me, intercession will be available for him."'—*Muslim.*

It is related from Anas that he said, 'The Prophet used to go in quest of plunder, and when the morning dawned he used to listen for the call to prayer; and if he heard the call to prayer he would withhold, otherwise he plundered. And he heard a man calling, "God is great, God is great," and the Apostle of God said, "(He) is in the true religion." After that the man said, "I bear witness that there is no God but Alláh." And the Apostle of God said, "Thou hast come out from the fire." And they looked at him and, behold! he was a goatherd.'—*Muslim*.

It is related from Jábir that he said, 'I heard the Apostle of God say, "Verily when Satan hears the call to prayer, he goes away to the place called Al Rauḥái: a place distant thirty-six miles from Madína." '—*Muslim*.

On Delaying the Call to Prayer

It is related from Ibn 'Omar that, 'The Apostle of God said, "Verily Bilál calls to prayer in the night, therefore eat and drink until Ibn Umm Maktúm makes the call." Ibn 'Omar said, 'Ibn Maktúm was a blind man and did not call to prayers until it was said to him, "The morning has come! the morning has come!" '—*Muslim, Al Bukhárí*.

On Mosques and Places of Prayer

It is related from Ibn 'Abbás that, 'When the Prophet entered the House (i.e., the temple at Mecca) he made his extempore prayers in every side of it; but he did not repeat the canonical prayers until he came out of it. And when he came out he prayed in two rak'ahs[1] in front of the mosque and said, "This is the direction to face in prayer." '—*Muslim, Al Bukhárí*.

It is related from Abú Hurairah that, 'The Apostle of God said, "One prayer in this mosque of mine (i.e., the mosque of Madína) is better than a thousand prayers in any other, except the holy mosque (of Mecca)." '—*Muslim, Al Bukhárí*.

It is related from Abú sa'ídu'l-Khudri that, 'The Apostle of God said, "Let not men bind themselves to visit mosques other than these three: the holy mosque (of Mecca), the distant mosque (at Jerusalem) and this mosque of mine (at Madína)." '—*Muslim, Al Bukhárí*.

It is related from 'Othmán that, 'The Apostle of God said, "He who builds a mosque for God, God will build a house for him in paradise." '—*Muslim, Al Bukhárí*.

---

[1] The *rak'ah* is a term used to cover one complete performance of the Muslim liturgical prayers, and ending with the *takbir*, 'God is great', which is repeated standing. If the form of prayer be repeated a second time, it ends with the repetition of the Muslim confession of faith. The five obligatory prayers are generally said in either two or four *rak'ahs*.

It is related from Abú Hurairah that, 'The Apostle of God said, "The prayers of a man said in an assembly are (worth) double the prayers said in his house, and twenty-five times more than those said in the bazaar. That is because when he performs his ablutions, and does them well, and then goes out to a mosque, nothing sends him out but the prayers. He does not walk a step but what there is raised for him thereby a high position, and his sins are removed from him thereby; and when he prays, the angels continue to pray for him so long as he is in the place of prayer (saying), 'O God, bless him, O God, have mercy upon him.' And one of you will continue in prayer so long as he waits for it."'—*Muslim, Al Bukhárí.*

It is related from Ibn 'Abbás that, 'The Apostle of God said, "I was not commanded to build high mosques." Ibn 'Abbás said, "You may certainly adorn them as the Jews and Christians do theirs."'—*Abu Dáud.*

It is related from Fáṭimah bintu 'l-Husain from her grandmother Fáṭimahu 'l-Kubra, that she said, 'When the Apostle of God entered a mosque he used to ask for peace and blessings on Muḥammad, and said, "My Lord, forgive me my sins, and open for me the gates of Thy mercy." And when he went out he would ask for peace and blessings on Muḥammad, and would say, "My Lord, forgive me my sins, and open for me the gates of Thy favour."'—*Ibn Májah, At Tirmidhí.*

It is related from Abú Sa'íd that, 'The Apostle of God said, "The whole earth is a mosque except a graveyard and a bath."'—*Abú Dáud, At Tirmidhí.*

It is related from Ibn 'Abbás that, 'The Apostle of God cursed the female visitors to tombs, and the builders of mosques thereon, and the (maker of) places for lamps thereon.' —*Abú Dáud, At Tirmidhí.*

It is related from Mu'ádh bin Jabal that he said, 'The Apostle of God, on a certain day, hindered us from the morning prayers until we were nearly seeing the sun. And he came out quickly, and the call to prayer was made, and the Apostle of God prayed and hastened in his prayers; and when he had made the salutation (at the end of the prayers) he called out and said, to us, "Stay in your ranks as you are." Then he came out to us, and afterwards said, "I will inform you what it was that hindered me from coming to you this morning. Verily I rose whilst it was yet night and performed my ablutions and prayed the prayer appointed for me, and I became drowsy in my prayers, so much so that I was overcome with sleep, and behold! my blessed Lord, the most High, in a most lovely form! And He said, 'O Muḥammad.' I said, 'At Thy service, my Lord.' He said, 'Concerning what do the highest angels dispute?' I said, 'I know not.' He said, 'They are three.'" Then Muḥammad said, "I saw Him place the palm of His hand between my two shoulders, until I felt the cold of His finger-tips between my breasts. Then everything appeared clear to me, and I knew. Then He said, 'O Muḥammad.' I said, 'At Thy service my Lord.' He said, 'Concerning what do the highest angels dispute?' I said, 'They dispute concerning atonement of sins.' He said, 'And what are they?' I replied, 'The going on foot to the assembly, and sitting in mosques after the prayers, and completing the ablutions under circumstances of difficulty.' He said, 'After that, concerning what do they dispute?' I replied, 'Concerning high ranks.' He said, 'And what are they?' I replied, 'The giving of food, the using of mild language, and prayers at night whilst people sleep.' He said, 'Ask!' I said, 'O God, I supplicate of Thee good actions and the abandonment of evil actions, and love of the poor, and that Thou forgive me and have mercy on me, and when Thou desirest a trial amongst the people, that Thou take me without being tried; and I pray Thee for Thy love and the love of those who love Thee, and I pray for the love of those actions which will bring me near to Thy love.'" Then the Apostle of God said, "Verily it (the dream) is true, therefore do ye study it and afterwards teach it."'—*Aḥmad, At Tirmidhí.*

It is related from Anas bin Málik that, 'The Apostle of God said, "The prayer of a man in his house is equal to one prayer, and his prayer in an adjacent mosque is equal to twenty-five prayers, and his prayer in a mosque in which men assemble is equal to five hundred prayers, and his prayer in the distant mosque (at Jerusalem) is equal to fifty thousand prayers, and his prayer in my mosque (at Madína) is equal to fifty thousand prayers, and his prayer in the holy mosque (at Mecca) is equal to one hundred thousand prayers."'—*Ibn Májah*

It is related from Abú Dharr that he said, 'I said, "O Apostle of God, which mosque was built first on the earth?" He replied, "The holy mosque (at Mecca)." I said, "And after that, which one?" He replied, "The distant mosque (at Jerusalem)." I said, "How long was it between (the building of) the two?" He replied, "Forty years." Then he said, "The earth is a mosque for thee, therefore wherever the time of prayer reaches thee, there pray."'—*Muslim, Al Bukhárí.*

On Covering Oneself

It is related from Abú Hurairah that, 'The Apostle of God said, "Let not any one of you pray in a single cloth, some portion of which does not cover both his shoulders."'—*Muslim, Al Bukhárí.*

It is related from 'Uqbah bin 'Ámir that he said, 'The Apostle of God was presented with a silk garment. This he put on, and then said his prayers. Afterwards he departed and threw it off with force, as if it were distasteful to him. Then he said, "This is not fitting for those who fear God."'—*Muslim, Al Bukhárí.*

It is related from Abú Hurairah that he said, 'Whilst a man was praying in long trousers, the Apostle of God said to him, "Go and perform ablutions." So he went and performed his ablutions and then returned. And a certain man said, "O Apostle of God, what was the reason that you ordered him to perform ablutions?" He replied, "Verily he was praying in long trousers. Verily God does not accept the prayer of a man clothed in long trousers."'—*Abú Dáud.*

It is related from Shaddád bin Aus that, 'The Apostle of God said, "Do the opposite to what the Jews do, for they do not say prayers in their boots or shoes."'—*Abú Dáud.*

It is related from Abú Sa'ídu'l-Khudri that he said, 'Whilst the Apostle of God was praying with his companions, behold he took off his shoes and placed them on his left side. And when the people saw that, they too threw off their shoes. And when the Apostle of God had finished his prayers he said, "What induced you to throw off your shoes?" They replied, "We saw thee cast off thy shoes, therefore we cast ours off." The Apostle of God said, "Verily Gabriel came to me and informed me that on them (my shoes) there was some impurity. When any one of you comes to the mosque, then let him look, and if he sees any impurity on his shoes, then let him wipe them and then pray in them." '—*Abú Dáud, Al Dárimi.*

It is related from 'Amru biṇ Shu'aib from his father, from his grandfather, that he said, 'I saw the Apostle of God praying barefooted and also in his shoes.'—*Abú Dáud.*

On That Which Conceals

It is related from Abú Hurairah that, 'The Apostle of God said, "When any one of you prays, let him place something in front of him; and if he cannot find anything, then let him set up his stick; and if he has no stick with him, then let him draw a line on the ground. Then nothing that passes in front of him will do him any harm." '—*Abú Dáud, Ibn Májah.*

It is related from Abú Sa'íd that, 'The Apostle of God said, "When any one of you prays towards anything placed in front of him as a cover from men, and anyone wishes to pass in front of him, then let him turn him back; and if he refuses, then let him fight him, for he is none but Satan." '—*Muslim, Al Bukhárí.*

It is related from Ka'bu'l-Aḥbár that he said, 'If the one who passes before one engaged in prayer had but known the punishment that awaits him! It would have been better for him that he were swallowed up by the earth, than that he should pass before him.'—*Málik.*

On the Nature of Prayer

It is related from 'Áyesha that she said, 'The Apostle of God used to begin the prayers by repeating the words, "God is great"; and by the recitation of (the chapter beginning with the words) "Praise be to God, the Lord of the worlds"; and when he used to bow down he did not raise his head, nor bend it low, but midway between. And when he used to raise his head from the bowing, he did not prostrate himself until he had stood erect; and when he used to raise his head from the prostrations, he did not prostrate again until he had sat up erect. And he used to repeat the salutation in every two sections of prayers; and he used to spread out his left foot and raise his right foot. And he used to forbid sitting with the buttocks resting on the heels. And he used to forbid men stretching out their limbs when sitting down as wild animals stretch their limbs; and he used to complete his prayer with the salutation.'—*Muslim.*

It is related from Sa'íd binu'l-Ḥárith binu'l-Mu'alli that he said, 'Abu Sa'ídu'l-Khudri prayed (that is, acted as leader) for us and said, "God is great," when he raised his head from the prostrations, and when he prostrated himself, and when he raised himself from bowing down, and he said, "Thus I saw the Prophet do."'—*Al Bukhárí.*

It is related from Abú Hurairah that he said, 'The Apostle of God prayed the midday prayer with us, and in the back part of the rows (of worshippers) there was a man who said his prayer badly. When, therefore, he had said the salutation, the Apostle of God called him and said, "O so-and-so, dost thou not fear God, and dost thou not observe how thou prayest? Do ye imagine that anything of what ye do is hidden from me? By God! I certainly see behind me as I see before me."' —*Aḥmad.*

On What should be Repeated after the Words, 'God is Great'

It is related from Abú Hurairah that he said, 'The Apostle of God used to remain silent between the repetition of the words "God is great" and the recital (of a portion of the Qur'án). Therefore I said, "May my father and mother be sacrificed for thee, O Apostle of God, what sayest thou when silent between the repetition of the words 'God is great' and the recital?" He replied, "I say, 'O God, place a distance between me and my sins as Thou hast placed a distance between East and West. O God, cleanse me from my sins as a white garment is cleansed from impurities. O God, wash away my sins with water and snow and hail.'"'—*Muslim, Al Bukhárí.*

It is related from 'Alí that he said, 'When the Prophet stood up to prayer—or, according to another tradition, 'When he opened his prayer'—he said, "God is great." Then he said, "I turn my face as a Hanif to Him who created the heavens and the earth; and I am not a polytheist. Verily, my prayers and my worship and my life and my death are for God, the Lord of the worlds. He has no partner, and to that was I ordered, and I am one of the Muslims. O God, Thou art the King. There is no God but Thee. Thou art my Lord, and I am Thy servant. I have offended against mine own soul, and I confess my sins; therefore forgive me all my sins, for none can forgive sins but Thou. Guide Thou me to the best disposition, for none can guide to the best but Thou; and turn Thou away from me its evil, for none can turn away evil from me but Thou. I am ready for Thy service and to assist Thee. And every good is in Thy hands, and no wickedness can be ascribed to Thee. I am (strong) in Thee, and to Thee (I shall return). Thou art blessed and exalted. I ask forgiveness of Thee, and I repent towards Thee." And when the Apostle of God bowed down he said, "O God, to Thee have I bowed down, and in Thee have I placed my trust, and to Thee I resign myself. My ears and my eyes, my brain, my bones and my nerves humble themselves before Thee." And when he raised his head he said, "O God, our Lord, to Thee be praise to the full of the heavens and the earth and what is between them and to the full of whatever Thou mayest desire hereafter." And when he prostrated himself he said, "O God, to Thee have I prostrated myself, and in Thee have I placed my trust, and to Thee am I resigned. My face has prostrated itself to Him who created it and formed it and divided its ears and its eyes. Blessed be God, the best of Creators!" After that he used to say at the end, what he said between the bearing witness and the salutation, "O God, forgive me the sins I have committed before, and those I shall commit hereafter, and those I have concealed, and those I have committed openly, and those I have committed to excess, and those which Thou knowest better than I. Thou art the beginning and Thou art the end. There is no God but Thee." '—*Muslim.*

On Reciting the Qur'an in Prayer

It is related from 'Ubádah binu'ṣ-Ṣámit that, 'The Apostle of God said, "There can be no prayer for the one who does not recite the opening chapter of the Book." '—*Muslim, Al Bukhárí.*

It is related from Anas that, 'The Prophet and Abú Bakr and 'Omar used to begin the prayers with the words, "Praise be to God, the Lord of the worlds." '—*Muslim.*

It is related from Abú Hurairah that, 'The Apostle of God said, "When the leader of the prayers says 'Amen,' then do ye say 'Amen' likewise; and whoever says 'Amen,' the amen of the angels, the sins which he committed previously are forgiven." '—*Muslim, Al Bukhárí.*

It is related from 'Abdu'lláh binu's-Sáib that he said, 'The Apostle of God said the morning prayers for us (as leader) at Mecca, and he began the recital of the chapter, "The Believers," until he came to the mention of Moses and Aaron or the mention of Jesus, when he was seized with a fit of coughing. Then he bowed down.'—*Muslim.*

It is related from Ibn 'Abbás that he said, 'The Apostle of God used to begin his prayers with the words, "In the name of God, the merciful, the compassionate." '—*At Tirmidhí.*

It is related from 'Uqbah bin 'Ámir that he said, 'I used to lead the female camel of the Apostle of God when on a journey; and he said to me, "O 'Uqbah, shall I not teach thee what are the two best chapters (of the Qur'án) to be recited?" Then he taught me, "Say, I take refuge with the Lord of the daybreak," and "Say, I take refuge with the Lord of men.[1]"' 'Uqbah said, 'The Prophet did not see me very pleased with these two chapters, and when he alighted for the morning prayers, he prayed those two for the morning prayers for the people; and when he had finished he turned to me and said, "O 'Uqbah, how dost thou like them?" '—*Ahmad, Abú Dáud, An Nasáí.*

It is related from Ubádah binu'ṣ-Sámit that he said, 'We were behind the Prophet at the morning prayers, and he recited (a portion of the Qur'án), but the recital became difficult for him. And when he had finished, he said, "Perhaps you recited after your leader?" We said, "Yes, O Apostle of God." He said, "Do not do it, except for the opening chapter of the Book; for he who does not recite that chapter, does not say prayers at all." '—*Abú Dáud, At Tirmidhí.*

It is related from Ibn 'Omaru'l-Bayáḍi, that he said, 'The Apostle of God said, "Verily the one who prays communes secretly with his Lord, therefore let him take heed as to what he says to Him; and let not some of you raise their voices above the voices of others in (reciting) the Qur'án." '—*Aḥmad.*

---

[1] Chapters cxiii and cxiv.

It is related from 'Abdu'lláh bin abi Awfi that he said, 'A man came to the Prophet and said, "I am not able to remember any portion of the Qur'án, then teach me that which is proper for me to say (in place thereof)." He replied, "Say, 'Glory be to God!' and, 'Praise be to God!' and, 'There is no God but Alláh' and, 'God, is great, there is no power and no strength but in God.'" He said, "O Apostle of God, this all has reference to God, but what is there which has reference to me?" The Prophet replied, "Say, 'O God, have mercy on me, and forgive me, and guide me, and give me my daily bread.'" The man spoke thus (beckoning) with his hands and then closed them. Then the Apostle of God said, "Verily this man has filled his two hands with good."'—*Abú Dáud.*

ON THE GENUFLECTION CALLED RUQÚ'[1]

It is related from Anas that, 'The Apostle of God said, "Perform the bowing and the prostrations,[2] for by God! I certainly see you from behind me."'—*Muslim, Al Bukhárí.*

It is related from Ibn 'Abbás that, 'The Apostle of God said, "Have I not been forbidden to recite the Qur'án whilst bowing down and prostrating; and as for the bowing down magnify God therein, and in the prostrations be diligent in supplication. It is fitting that they should be granted to you."' —*Muslim.*

It is related from Abú Mas'údu'l-Anṣari that, 'The Apostle of God said, "The prayer of a man will not be accepted until he straightens his back in the bowing and in the prostrations."'—*Abú Dáud, Al Tirmidhí, An Nasái, Ibn Májah.*

It is related from Auf bin Málik that he said, 'I stood up with the Apostle of God; and when he bowed he stayed in that position for a time equal to that occupied in the recital of chapter Baqarah[3]; and he said in his bowing, "Praise be to God, the One endued with power and royalty and majesty and greatness."'—*An Nasái.*

---

[1] It is made by bending the head forward with the palms of the hands resting upon the knees. Here translated 'bow.'

[2] The *Sajdah*, here translated 'prostration' is made by bowing down on the knees until the forehead touches the ground.

[3] This chapter of the Qur'án contains two hundred and eighty-five verses.

It is related from Abú Qatádah that, 'The Apostle of God said, "The worst man for thieving is he who steals from his prayers." They said, "O Apostle of God, and how does he steal from his prayers?" He replied, "He does not complete it in its bowing down or its prostrations."'—*Aḥmad.*

On Prostration and its Excellence

It is related from Ibn'Abbás that, 'The Apostle of God said, "I was commanded to prostrate in seven members of my body: on my forehead, my two hands, my two knees, and the extremities of my two feet, and that we should not tuck up our clothes or hair."'—*Muslim, Al Bukhárí.*

It is related from Al Barái bin 'Ázib that, 'The Apostle of God said, "When thou makest a prostration then place the palms of thy hands (on the ground), but raise up thine elbows."'—*Muslim.*

It is related from Abú Hurairah that, 'The Apostle of God said, "A servant is nearest to his Lord when he is making the prostration, therefore multiply your supplications."'—*Muslim.*

It is related from Abú Hurairah that, 'The Apostle of God said, "When a son of Adam recites the chapter entitled 'Prostration'[1] and prostrates himself, Satan betakes himself away weeping and saying, 'Woe is me! the son of Adam was commanded to prostrate, and he prostrated, and for him is paradise; and I was ordered to prostrate, but I refused, and for me is the fire.'"'—*Muslim.*

It is related from Wáil bin Ḥujr that he said, 'I saw the Apostle of God when he prostrated himself, place his knees (on the ground) before his hands, and when he rose up from prostration he raised his hands before (he got up from) his knees.'—*Abú Dáud, At Tirmidhí.*

On Bearing Witness

It is related from Ibn 'Omar that he said, 'When the Apostle of God used to sit in the act of bearing witness (concerning the unity of God and the apostleship of Muḥammad) he used to place his left hand upon his left knee, and his right hand upon his right knee, and used to clasp his fingers together and make a sign with the fore-finger.'—*Muslim.*

[1] Chapter xxxii of the Qur'án.

It is related from Jábir that he said, 'The Apostle of God used to teach us the (method of) bearing witness in the same way that he taught us a chapter of the Qur'án. (He used to say) "In the name of God. Salutations are for God, together with prayers and alms. Peace be on thee, O Prophet, and the mercy of God and His blessing, and peace be on us and on the virtuous servants of God. I bear witness that there is no God but Alláh, and I bear witness that Muḥammad is His servant and His Apostle. I supplicate God for paradise, and I take refuge with God from the fire." '—*An Nasái.*

On Asking Blessings on the Prophet

It is related from 'Abdu'r-Raḥmán bin abú Laila that he said, 'Ka'b bin 'Ujrah met me and said, "Shall I make thee a present of that which I heard from the Prophet?" I replied, "Yes, make me a present thereof." He said, "We asked the Apostle of God, and said, 'O Apostle of God, how are blessings to be asked for you, the people of the house, for verily God has taught us how we should pray for thee?'" He replied, "Say, 'O God, bless Muḥammad and the family of Muḥammad, as Thou hast blessed Abraham and the family of Abraham. Verily Thou art praised and glorified. O God, bless Muḥammad and the family of Muḥammad, as Thou hast blessed Abraham and the family of Abraham, verily Thou art praised and glorified.'"' —*Muslim, Al Bukhárí.*

It is related from Anas that, 'The Apostle of God said, "Whoever prays a single prayer for blessings on me, God will send on him ten blessings, and ten sins will be taken away from him, and there will be raised for him ten steps in rank."' —*An Nasái.*

It is related from Ibn Mas'úd that, 'The Apostle of God said, "Verily God has angels who move about on earth and bring greetings to me from my followers."'—*An Nasái, Al Dárimi.*

It is related from Faḍálah bin 'Ubaid that he said, 'Whilst the Apostle of God was sitting, behold a man entered and prayed and said, "O God, forgive me, and have mercy on me." Then the Apostle of God said, "Thou hast hastened, O thou that prayest. When thou prayest and sittest down, then praise God in a manner of which He is worthy, and ask blessings on me. Afterwards, present thine own supplications to Him."' Faḍálah said, 'Then, after that, another man prayed, and praised God, and asked blessings on the Prophet. Then the Prophet said to him, "O thou that prayest, ask and it shall be given thee."'—*At Tirmidhí.*

It is related from Abú Hurairah that, 'The Apostle of God said, "Whoever wishes to fill up the measure of his desires, when he asks blessings on us, the Prophet's family, then let him say, 'O God, bless Muḥammad, the ignorant Prophet, and his wives, the mothers of the faithful, and his descendants, and the people of his family, as Thou hast blessed the family of Abraham; for verily Thou art praised and glorified.'"'—*Abú Dáud.*

It is related from Ruwaifa' that, 'The Apostle of God said, "He who prays for blessings on Muḥammad, and says, 'O God, appoint him a sitting-place near Thee on the day of resurrection,' my intercession will be available for him."'—*Aḥmad.*

It is related from 'Omar binu'l-Khaṭṭáb that he said, 'Verily supplications are kept stationary between heaven and earth, and nothing of them ascends until thou pray for blessings on thy Prophet.'—*At Tirmidhí.*

On Supplication at the Time of Bearing Witness

It is related from 'Áyesha that she said, 'The Apostle of God used to make supplication in prayer and say, "O God, I take refuge with Thee from the punishments of the grave, and I take refuge with Thee from the sedition of the false Messiah, and I take refuge with Thee from the seditions of life and death. O God, I take refuge with Thee from sins and from debt." Then a certain person said to him, "It is very strange that Thou shouldest take refuge from debt." He replied, "Verily when a man falls into debt, he talks and lies, and makes promises, and then acts contrary to them."'—*Muslim, Al Bukhárí.*

It is related from Abú Hurairah that, 'The Apostle of God said, "When any one of you finishes the repetition of the bearing witness, then let him take refuge with God from four things: from the punishment of hell, from the punishment of the grave, from the seditions of life and death, and from the wickedness of the false Messiah."'—*Muslim.*

It is related from Umm Salamah that she said, 'Verily, in the time of the Apostle of God, when women repeated the salutation in the obligatory prayers, they used to rise up, but the Apostle of God and those men who prayed remained sitting so long as God wished; and when the Apostle of God rose up, then the men rose up also.'—*Al Bukhárí.*

It is related from Mu'ádh bin Jabal that he said, 'The Apostle of God took me by the hand and said, "I certainly love thee, O Mu'ádh." I replied, "And I love thee, O Apostle of God." He said, "Never omit to say at the end of every prayer, 'O my Lord, assist me to remember Thee and to give Thee thanks, and to render Thee fitting worship.'"'—*Aḥmad, Abú Dáud, An Nasái.*

It is related from Shaddád bin Aus that he said, 'The Apostle of God used to say in his prayer, "O God, I supplicate from Thee firmness in the works (of religion) and determination in the right way; and I supplicate from Thee gratitude for Thy favours, and worthiness in Thy worship; and I supplicate from Thee a sincere heart and a truthful tongue; and I supplicate from Thee the good that Thou knowest; and I take refuge with Thee from the evil that Thou knowest; and I ask pardon of Thee for (the sins) which Thou knowest."' —*An Nasái.*

CONCERNING THINGS TO BE MENTIONED AFTER PRAYER

It is related from Ibn 'Abbás that he said, 'I used to know the conclusion of the prayers of the Apostle of God by the words "God is great."'—*Muslim, Al Bukhárí.*

It is related from 'Abdu'lláh bin Zubair that he said, 'The Prophet of God, when giving the salutation in the prayers, used to say with a loud voice, "There is no God but Alláh alone. He has no partner. His is the dominion, and His is the praise, and He is powerful over all things. There is no power and no strength but in God. There is no God but Alláh, and we worship none but Him. His is the grace, and for Him is the excellence, and for Him is the excellent praise. There is no God but Alláh. We exhibit for Him the sincerity of our religion, although the unbelievers abhor it."'—*Muslim.*

It is related from Abú Hurairah that he said, 'The poor people of those who fled from Mecca to Madína came to the

Apostle of God and said, "The rich (among us) have attained to a high station and permanent favour." He replied, "And what is that?" They said, "They pray as we do, and fast as we do, and they give alms, which (by reason of our poverty) we do not, and they free slaves which we (having none) do not do." The Apostle of God replied, "Shall I not teach you something by which you will reach (in rank) those who preceded you and will precede those who follow you; and none will be more excellent than you, except he who shall do as ye do?" They said, "Yes, O Apostle of God." He replied, "Then at the end of each prayer repeat the adoration of God, and magnify Him and give voice to His praises thirty-three times." Abú Ṣálih said, "Then the poor who had fled from Mecca to Madína returned to the Apostle of God and said, 'Our brethren, the rich, heard what we did, and they did the same.'" The Apostle of God said, "That is the grace of God. He gives to whom He wills."'—*Muslim, Al Bukhárí.*

It is related from Abú Hurairah that, 'The Apostle of God said, "Whoever repeats the adoration of God thirty-three times at the end of each prayer, and gives voice to the praise of God thirty-three times, and magnifies God thirty-three times, that is ninety-nine times, and whoever completes the hundred by saying, 'There is no God but Alláh alone. He has no partner. His is the dominion and His the praise, and He is powerful over all things,' his sins will be forgiven, although they be as the foam of the sea."'—*Muslim.*

It is related from 'Alí that he said, 'I heard the Apostle of God say on the wood of this pulpit that, "He who recites the verse of the throne[1] at the end of each prayer, nothing will prevent him from entering paradise but death; and whoever recites it when he retires to his bed, God will keep him safe in his house, and in the house of his neighbour, and in the houses of the people round about him."'—*Al Baihaqi*

Concerning What Is or Is Not Permitted to be Done in Prayer

It is related from 'Abdu'lláh bin Mas'úd that he said, 'We used to salute the Prophet whilst he was saying his prayers, and

[1] Qur'án, Súratu'l-Baqarah (ii) 254.

he used to return our salutation; but when we returned from Abyssinia we saluted him, but he did not return our salutation. So we said, "O Apostle of God, we used to salute thee during prayer, and thou wert wont to return our salutation!" He replied, "Verily in prayer there is labour."'—*Muslim, Al Bukhárí.*

It is related from Abú Hurairah that, 'The Apostle of God said, "Verily a demon from the genii escaped yesterday in order to obstruct my prayers; but God enabled me to overcome him; and I seized him, and wished to tie him to one of the pillars of the mosque in order that ye all might see him. But I remembered the supplication of my brother, Solomon, 'O Lord, give me a dominion which it is not proper for any to possess after me.' Therefore I sent him away humiliated."'—*Muslim, Al Bukhárí.*

It is related from Ṭalq bin 'Alí that, 'The Apostle of God said, "When any one of you breaks wind during prayer, then let him depart and perform the ablutions, and then let him return to his prayers."'—*Abú Dáud, At Tirmidhí.*

It is related from Abú Hurairah that, 'The Prophet came out to the prayers, and when he had said, "God is great," he departed and motioned to them to remain as they were. And then he went out and bathed himself. Then he came again, and his head was dripping, and prayed with them. And when he had prayed he said, "Verily I was impure, and I had forgotten to bathe myself."'—*Aḥmad.*

On Forgetting in Prayer

It is related from Abú Hurairah that, 'The Apostle of God said, "When any one of you stands up to pray, then Satan comes to him and confuses him, so that he does not know how many times he has prayed. Therefore when any one of you finds it thus, let him make two prostrations whilst he is sitting."'—*Al Bukhárí.*

It is related from 'Abdu'lláh bin Mas'úd that, 'The Apostle of God prayed the midday prayer in five *rak'ahs.*[1] So it was said to him, "Have the prayers been increased?" He replied, "What is that?" They said, "Thou hast prayed in five

[1] See note on p. 30.

rak'ahs." Then he made two prostrations, after he had given the salutation.'—And in another tradition it runs, 'He said, "I am only a man like you. I forget as ye do. Therefore if I forget, do ye remind me; and if any one of you doubts in his prayers, then let him act on a correct opinion, and complete the prayers according to that. Then let him give the salutation, and then prostrate himself twice."'—*Muslim, Al Bukhárí.*

It is related from Ibn Sírín from Abú Hurairah that he said, 'The Apostle of God prayed with us one of the afternoon prayers—Ibn Sírín said, "Abú Hurairah named the prayer, but I have forgotten it"—and he prayed with us two *rak'ahs.* Then he gave the salutation and stood up by a piece of wood placed in the mosque, and leaned upon it as if he were angry. And he placed his right hand upon his left, and put his fingers through each other, and placed his right cheek on the back of his left hand. And the people hastened out by the doors of the mosque, and said, "The prayers have been shortened." And amongst them were Abú Bakr and 'Omar, but they feared to speak to the Prophet about it. And amongst the people was a man with long hands, called "The one of the two hands." He said, "O Apostle of God, didst thou forget, or have the prayers been shortened?" He replied, "I neither forgot, nor have the prayers been shortened." Then the Apostle of God asked (the people) "Is it as 'The one of the two hands' says?" They replied, "Yes." Then he went forward and prayed what he had omitted. Then he made the salutation and then said, "God is great." Then he prostrated as was his wont, or made the prostration longer. After that he raised his head and said, "God is great." Then he again said, "God is great," and prostrated as was his wont, or longer. Then he raised his head and said, "God is great." And perhaps they asked him (Ibn Sírín), "After that did he give the salutation?" He said, "I have been informed that 'Imrán bin Husain said, 'After that he gave the salutation.'"'—*Muslim, Al Bukhárí.*

On the Prostrations to be Made when Reciting the Qur'an

It is related from Ibn 'Abbás that, 'The Prophet prostrated when reciting the chapter entitled "The Star," and the Muslims and the polytheists and the genii and the people prostrated with him.'—*Al Bukhárí.*

It is related from 'Amr binu'l-'Áṣ that he said, 'The Apostle of God taught me fifteen prostrations during the recital of the Qur'án. Of these, three were for various subjects, and two prostrations were for the chapter entitled "Pilgrimage."' —*Abú Dáud, Ibn Májah.*

It is related from 'Uqbah bin 'Ámir that he said, 'I said, "O Apostle of God, the chapter entitled 'Pilgrimage' is superior to others, for during its recital two prostrations are required." He replied, "Yes, and whosoever does not make the two prostrations, has not recited the two (verses for which they are prescribed)."'—*At Tirmidhí.*

It is related from Ibn 'Abbás that he said, 'Verily the Prophet prostrated himself, when reciting the chapter entitled "Ṣad" and said, "David made this prostration as a sign of repentance, and we make it out of gratitude."'—*An Nasái.*

On the Times when Prayer is Forbidden

It is related from Ibn 'Omar that, 'The Apostle of God said, "Let not any one of you seek to repeat the prayers at the rising or the setting of the sun." And in another tradition it runs, he said, "When the edge of the sun rises, then leave the prayers until it (fully) appears. And when the edge of the sun sets, then leave the prayers until it disappears; and draw not near to your prayers at the rising of the sun or at its setting, for verily it rises between the two horns of Satan."'—*Muslim, Al Bukhárí.*

It is related from Jubair bin Muṭ'im that, 'The Prophet said, "O Bani 'Abd Manáf, do not forbid anyone from walking round this house (i.e., the temple at Mecca) and from praying at any hour of the night or day they please."'—*At Tirmidhí, Abú Dáud, An Nasái.*

On Praying in an Assembly, and the Excellence thereof

It is related from Ibn 'Omar that, 'The Apostle of God said, "The prayers said in an assembly excel the prayers said alone by twenty-seven degrees."'—*Muslim, Al Bukhárí.*

It is related from Abú Hurairah that he said, 'A blind man came to the Prophet and said, "O Apostle of God, I have no guide to lead, me to the mosque." And he begged of the Apostle of God that a concession might be made for him, so that he might pray in his house. So the Apostle of God made a concession for him; and when he turned his back, the Apostle called him and said, "Dost thou hear the call to prayer?" He replied, "Yes." He said, "Then do thou answer it."'—*Muslim.*

It is related from Ibn 'Omar that, 'He made the call to prayer on a cold and windy night. Then he said, "Beware! pray in your houses." After that he said, "Verily the Apostle of God used to order the one who called to prayers, when it was a cold and rainy night, to say 'Beware! pray in your houses.'"' —*Muslim, Al Bukhárí.*

It is related from Ibn 'Omar that, 'The Apostle of God said, "When the wife of any one of you asks permission to go to the mosque, then let him not forbid her."'—*Muslim, Al Bukhárí.*

It is related from Ibn 'Omar that, 'The Apostle of God said, "Do not forbid your wives the mosques, but their houses are better for them."'—*Abú Dáud.*

It is related from Abú Hurairah that he said, 'Verily I heard my beloved Abú'l-Qásim say, "The prayer of that woman will not be accepted who comes perfumed to the mosque, until she washes herself with the washing prescribed for impurity."' —*Abú Dáud.*

It is related from Abú'l-Dardái that, 'The Apostle of God said, "There are no three persons in a village or desert who do not perform the prayers amongst themselves, but Satan prevails over them. Pray in an assembly, for the wolf only eats the one that has strayed from the flock."' —*Aḥmad, Abú Dáud, An Nasái.*

It is related from Abú Hurairah that, 'The Prophet said, "If it were not that there were women and children in the houses, I would have performed the evening prayers and commanded my young men to burn with fire whatever was in the houses (of those who do not attend prayers in the mosque.)"' —*Aḥmad.*

It is related from 'Abdu'lláh bin Umm Maktúm that he said, 'O Apostle of God, in the city are many venomous reptiles and rapacious animals, and I am blind. Wilt thou, therefore, obtain a concession for me (to say prayers at home)?' He replied, 'Dost thou hear the call, "Come to prayers! come to salvation!"' He said, 'Yes.' The Prophet replied, 'Then come at once.' And he did not give him a concession. —*Abú Dáud, An Nasái.*

It is related from Abú Músáu'l-Ash'ari that, 'The Apostle of God said, "Two people, or any greater number, constitute an assembly for prayers."'—*Ibn Májah.*

On Dressing Ranks for Prayer

It is related from Nu'mán bin Bashír that he said, 'The Apostle of God used to dress our ranks so that they looked as if he had made them straight as arrows. This he did until he saw that we had understood the matter. After this he came out on a certain day and stood up until it was near the time for repeating the words, "God is great." Then he saw a man whose breast projected from the rank, and said, "O servants of God, you must keep your ranks even, otherwise God will certainly make a difference in your faces."'—*Muslim.*

It is related from Abú Hurairah that, 'The Apostle of God said, "The best rank of men is the first of them, and the worst of them is the last. And the best rank of women is the last of them, and the worst of them is the first rank."'—*Muslim.*

It is related from Anas that, 'The Apostle of God said, "Arrange your ranks, and keep close together between them. Keep the necks in line, for, by Him in whose hand is my life! I certainly see Satan enter through an opening in the ranks, as if he were a kid."'—*Abú Dáud.*

On the Places for Standing in Prayer

It is related from Samurah bin Jundub that he said, 'The Apostle of God commanded us that when we were three persons (for prayer), one of us should stand in front (as leader).'—*At Tirmidhí.*

It is related from 'Áyesha that she said, 'The Apostle of God prayed in his room, and the people followed him from behind the room.'—*Abú Dáud.*

On the Office of Leader of Prayers

It is related from Abú Mas'úd that, 'The Apostle of God said, "Let him act as leader in the prayers who knows best the recital of the Book of God; and if all be equal in reciting, then the one who knows best the laws of religion; and if they be all equal in knowledge of the laws of religion, then let that one act who was first of them in forsaking his home for the sake of religion; and if they be all equal in that respect, then let the eldest of them lead. And let not any man act as leader in the prayers to a man in the latter's sphere of authority (i.e. where he is the constituted leader); and let him not sit in a seat of honour in his house, except with his permission." '—*Muslim.*

It is related from Abú 'Aṭiyahu'l-'Uqaili that he said, 'Málik binu'l-Ḥuwairith used to come to us to our place of prayer and converse. And one day the time for prayer arrived, so we said to him, "Stand thou in front and act as leader in the prayers." He said to us, "Put a man from amongst yourselves in front to lead the prayers for you, and I will tell you why I did not pray for you (as leader). I heard the Apostle of God say, 'Let not that one who visits a people act as leader of the prayers for them, but let a man from amongst themselves act as leader.' " '—*Abú Dáud, At Tirmidhí, An Nasái.*

It is related from Anas that he said, 'The Apostle of God appointed Ibn Umm Maktum to act as leader of the prayers for the people; and he was blind.'—*Abú Dáud.*

It is related from Ibn 'Omar that, 'The Apostle of God said, "There are three persons whose prayers will not be accepted from them: he who stands before the people as leader of the prayers when he is disliked by the people; the man who comes to prayers at the end—to come at the end is to come when the time is past—and the man who enslaves a free woman." '—*Abú Dáud, Ibn Májah.*

It is related from Abú Hurairah that, 'The Apostle of God said, "Religious warfare is incumbent upon you in company with every prince, whether he be righteous or unrighteous, even though he be guilty of mortal sins. And prayer is incumbent upon you after every Muslim, whether he be righteous or unrighteous, even though he be guilty of mortal sins. And prayer is incumbent over every (dead) Muslim, whether he be righteous or unrighteous, even though he be guilty of mortal sins."'—*Abú Dáud.*

On What is Necessary for the Leader of Prayers

It is related from Abú Hurairah that, 'The Apostle of God said, "When any one of you prays for the people (as leader), then let him be brief, because amongst them are sick and weak and aged persons; and when any one of you prays for himself, then let him be as long as he likes."'—*Muslim, Al Bukhárí.*

It is related from Qais binu'l-abú Ḥázim that he said, 'Abú Mas'úd informed me that a man said, "O Apostle of God, by God! verily I delay to come to the morning prayers on account of so-and-so making the prayers so long for us." Then I never saw the Apostle of God more angry in the place of instruction than he was then. Afterwards the Prophet said, "Verily amongst you are those who cause people to withdraw themselves (from prayers); therefore whoever of you prays (as leader) for the people, let him be indulgent, because there are amongst them, weak and aged and indigent."'—*Muslim, Al Bukhárí*

On the Duties of a Congregation

It is related from Abú Hurairah that, 'The Apostle of God said, "Do not hasten before the leader of the prayers (in reciting). When he says, 'God is great', then do ye say 'God is great', and when he says, 'Nor of those who go astray,' then do ye say, 'Amen,' and when he bows down, then do ye bow down, and when he repeats the words, 'God hears him who praises Him,' then say ye, 'O God our Lord, to Thee be the praise.'"'—*Muslim, Al Bukhárí*; except, that *Al Bukhárí* does not mention the words 'When he says, "Nor of those who go astray."'

It is related from 'Áyesha that she said, 'When the Prophet became oppressed (with the sickness from which he died), Bilál came to call him to prayers, and he said, "Command Abú Bakr to pray for the people (as leader)." So Abú Bakr prayed those days. Afterwards the Prophet felt some alleviation (of his sickness) and rose up and was led between two men, and his feet dragged upon the earth, until he entered the mosque.

And when Abú Bakr heard the low sound (of the Prophet's approach) he began to go to the rear; but the Apostle of God motioned to him not to go to the rear. Then the Prophet came until he sat on the left hand of Abú Bakr. And Abú Bakr was praying standing, but the Apostle of God was praying sitting. Abú Bakr was following the prayer of the Apostle of God, and the people were following the prayer of Abú Bakr.'—*Muslim, Al Bukhárí.*

It is related from Abú Hurairah that he said, 'Whoever raises his head or lowers it before the leader of the prayers does, verily his forelock is in the hands of Satan.'—*Málik.*

Concerning Those Who say the Prayers Twice

It is related from Jábir that he said, 'Mu'ádh used to say the evening prayer with the Prophet, after which he used to return to his family and pray the evening prayer with them. And this was supererogatory for him.'—*Muslim, Al Bukhárí.*

It is related from Busr bin Miḥjan from his father that, 'He was in an assembly with the Apostle of God, and the call to prayer was given; and the Apostle of God stood up and repeated the prayer; and he turned, and Miḥjan was in his seat. Therefore the Apostle of God said to him, "What prevented thee from praying with the people? Art thou not a Muslim?" He replied, "Yes, O Apostle of God, but I had already said my prayers in my family." Then the Apostle of God said to him, "When thou goest to the mosque, having already said thy prayers, and the prayers are being said, then pray with the people, although thou hast already prayed."'—*Málik, An Nasái.*

It is related from Sulaiman, a freed man of Maimúnah, that he said, 'Ibn 'Omar came to us on the pavement (of the mosque) when they were praying. So I said, "Wilt thou not pray with them?" He replied, "I have already prayed, and I heard the Apostle of God say, 'Do not pray one prayer twice in the same day.'"'—*Aḥmad, Abú Dáud, An Nasái.*

On Supererogatory Prayers

It is related from, 'Abdu'lláh bin Shaqíq that he said, 'I asked 'Áyesha concerning the voluntary prayers of the Apostle of God, and she replied that, "He used to pray in four *rak'ahs*[1] in my house before the mid-day prayer; then he used to go out and pray with the people. Then he would enter (my house) and pray in two *rak'ahs.* And he used to pray the sunset prayers with the people, after which he would enter (my house) and pray in two *rak'ahs.* After that he would pray the night prayer with the people, and would then enter my house and pray in two *rak'ahs.* And he used to pray in nine *rak'ahs* at night, amongst which were the *witr*[2] prayers. And he used to pray a long time at night, standing, and a long time at night, sitting. And when he used to recite standing, he performed the bowing and the prostrations whilst he was standing; and when he recited sitting down, he bowed and prostrated himself whilst he was sitting. And when the dawn broke he would pray in two *rak'ahs.*" '—*Muslim.*

It is related from Umm Ḥabíbah that she said, 'I heard the Apostle of God say, "Whoever performs prayers in four *rak'ahs* before the midday prayer and in four after it, God has made the fire prohibited for him." '—*Aḥmad, At Tirmidhí, Abú Dáud, An Nasái, Ibn Májah.*

It is related from Abú Hurairaih that, 'The Apostle of God said, "Whoever prays in six *rak'ahs* after the sunset prayer, and does not between the time of praying them say anything evil, he will be recompensed (with a reward) equal to that of twelve years of worship." '—*At Tirmidhí.*

It is related from Ka'b bin 'Ujraḥ that he said, 'The Prophet came to a mosque of the Bani 'Abdu'l-Ashhal and prayed in it the evening prayers. And when they had finished their prayers he saw them after that praising God, and he said to them, "These are prayers for your houses" '—*Abú Dáud.* According to *At Tirmidhí* and *An Nasái,* the tradition runs thus, 'The people stood up to say supererogatory prayers, and the Prophet said, "You must say these prayers in your houses." '

On Prayers Said at Night

It is related from Masrúq that he said, 'I asked 'Áyesha about the prayers which the Apostle of God used to say at

[1] See note on p. 30.

[2] A *witr* prayer, is one consisting of an odd number of *rak'ahs.* It is said at night, and is said in addition to the obligatory prayers.

night, and she replied, "He used at various times to say them in seven and nine and eleven *rak'ahs*, besides the two *rak'ahs* which he made in the morning."'—*Al Bukhárí.*

It is related from Ibn 'Abbás that, 'He went to sleep near the Apostle of God. Then the Apostle of God awoke and cleaned his teeth and performed the ablutions, saying as he did so, "Verily in the creation of the heavens and the earth," until he finished the chapter. Then he rose up and prayed in two *rak'ahs*, and in these he prolonged the standing and the bowing and the prostrations. After that he turned away and went to sleep until he snored. He did that three times; six *rak'ahs* in all. In each of those he cleaned his teeth and performed the ablutions and recited those verses. Then he repeated the *witr* prayers three times.'—*Muslim.*

It is related from 'Áyesha that she said, 'When the Apostle of God grew corpulent and heavy, most of his prayers were said sitting.'—*Muslim, Al Bukhárí.*

It is related from Abú Hurairah that 'The recital of the prayers of the Prophet at night was sometimes in a loud voice, and sometimes in a low voice.'—*Abú Dáud.*

On What is to be Said in the Night Prayers

It is related from Ibn 'Abbás that he said, 'When the Prophet rose at night to keep the night watch he used to say, "O God, to Thee be the praise. Thou art the Founder of the heavens and the earth and of whatsoever is therein, and to Thee be the praise. Thou art the Light of the heavens and the earth and of whatsoever is therein. And to Thee be the praise. Thou art the King of the heavens and the earth and of whatsoever is therein. To Thee be the praise. Thou art the Truth, and Thy promise is true, and the meeting with Thee is true, and Thy word is true, and paradise is true, and the fire is true, and the prophets are true, and Muḥammad is true, and the hour (of resurrection) is true. O God, to Thee I resign myself, and in Thee I place my faith, and upon Thee I put my trust, and to Thee shall I return, and with Thee (as Helper) do I fight, and to Thee I make my plaint. Therefore, forgive me (the sins) which I have committed heretofore, and those which I shall commit hereafter, and those which I have concealed, and those which I have committed openly, and those which Thou knowest better than I. Thou art the Beginning and the End. There is no God but Thee, and there is no God beside Thee."' —*Muslim*, *Al Bukhárí.*

It is related from 'Áyesha that she said,' When the Apostle of God used to wake at night, he would say, "There is no God but Thee. Adoration and praise be to Thee. O God, I ask pardon of Thee for my sin, and I supplicate Thy mercy. O God, increase me in knowledge, and lead not my heart astray after that Thou hast guided me. And bestow on me mercy from Thyself, for Thou art the Giver."'—*Abú Dáud.*

On Things which Encourage to Prayer at Night

It is related from Abú Hurairah that, 'The Apostle of God said, "Satan ties three knots on the back of the head of each one of you when he goes to sleep, and repeats over each knot the words, 'The night is long for thee, therefore take thy sleep.' And if the man wakes up and remembers God, then one of the knots becomes unloosed; and if he performs the ablutions, another knot becomes unloosed; and if he engage in prayer, the remaining knot becomes unloosed, and he rises from sleep in the morning with gladness and a pure mind; otherwise he rises with an impure mind and void of energy."'—*Muslim*, *Al Bukhárí.*

It is related from Al Mughíra that he said, 'The Prophet stood (at night prayers) until his feet swelled. Therefore it was said to him, "Why dost thou act thus, when the sins thou hast committed heretofore and those thou wilt commit hereafter are all forgiven?" He replied, "Shall I not be a grateful servant?"'—*Muslim*, *Al Bukhárí.*

It is related from 'Abdu'lláh bin 'Omar that, 'The Apostle of God said, "The prayer most precious in the sight of God was the prayer of David, and the fasts most precious to God were the fasts of David. He used to sleep half the night, and then rise for one-third of the night, and then sleep one-sixth of it. And he used to fast a day and then abstain from fasting for a day."'—*Muslim*, *Al Bukhárí.*

It is related from Abú Umámah that, 'The Apostle of God said, "You ought to rise at night (for prayer), for verily that was the practice of the righteous who lived before you. And it is a means of your drawing near to your Lord, and a covering for sins and a preventive of evil." '—*At Tirmidhí.*

It is related from Abú Sa'ídu'l-Khudri that, 'The Apostle of God said, "There are three persons with whom God is well pleased: a man when he rises at night in order to pray, people when they dress their ranks for prayer, and people when they dress their ranks for fighting with the enemy." '—*In Sharḥu's-Sunnah.*

It is related from Abú Hurairah that he said, 'A man came to the Prophet and said, "Verily such an one prays at night, and steals when the dawn breaks." He replied, "That which thou speakest of will prevent him." '—*Aḥmad.*

It is related from Ibn 'Abbás that, 'The Apostle of God said, "The noblest of my followers are those who carry the Qur'án (in their memories), and are companions of the night (by keeping awake for prayer)." '—*Al Baihaqi.*

On Determination in Religious Observances

It is related from 'Áyesha that, 'The Apostle of God said, "Take such works as ye are able to perform, for verily God will not tire (of rewarding) till ye tire (of doing)." '—*Muslim, Al Bukhárí.*

It is related from 'Imrán bin Ḥusain that, 'The Apostle of God said, "Say your prayers standing, but if you are not able, then say them sitting, and if you are not able to do that, then say them reclining on your side." '—*Al Bukhárí.*

It is related from 'Imrán bin Ḥusain that, 'He asked the Prophet concerning the prayer of a man which he said sitting. He replied, "It is better if he pray standing, and he who prays sitting will get half the reward of him who prays standing, and he who prays lying down will get half the reward of him who prays sitting." '—*Al Bukhárí.*

On *Witr*[1]—Prayers

It is related from 'Áyesha that she said, 'The Apostle of God used to pray at night in thirteen *rak'ahs*, five of which were made *witr* prayers. He sat in none of them except the last.'—*Muslim, Al Bukhárí.*

---

[1] See note on p. 52.

It is related from Abú Hurairah that he said, 'My friend (Muḥammad) ordered me three things: to fast three days in each month, to pray in two *rak'ahs* in the early morning before sunrise, and to pray *witr* prayers before going to sleep.'—*Muslim, Al Bukhárí.*

It is related from Ghuḍaif binu'l-Ḥárith that he said, 'I said to 'Áyesha, "Didst thou see the Apostle of God whether, after impurity, he bathed himself in the beginning of the night or the latter part of it?" She replied, "Sometimes he bathed himself in the beginning of the night, and sometimes he bathed himself in the latter part of it." I said, "God is great! Praise be to God, who has established such latitude in this matter." Then I asked, "Did he perform *witr* prayers at the beginning of the night, or at the latter part of it.?" She replied, "Sometimes he performed *witr* prayers at the beginning of the night, and sometimes he performed them at the end of it." I said, "God is great! Praise be to God, who has established such latitude in this matter." Then I asked, "Did he raise his voice in the recitation (of the Qur'án), or lower it?" She replied, "Sometimes he raised it, and sometimes he lowered it." I said, "God is great! Praise be to God, who has established such latitude in this matter."'—*Abú Dáud.*

On Special Forms of Supplication

It is related from Abú Hurairah that, 'When the Apostle of God wished to invoke a curse on anyone, or supplicate (a blessing) on their behalf, he prayed after bowing down, and generally said, when he prayed, "God hears him who praiseth Him. O Lord, to Thee be the praise. O God, free Al Walíd binu'l-Walíd and Salamah bin Hishám and 'Ayyásh bin abi Rabíyah. O God, be severe to (the tribe of) Muḍar, and make it in years (of famine) like unto the years of Joseph." And he used to say in some of his prayers, "O God, curse such and such tribes of Arabs," until God sent down the verse, "Thou hast no part in the matter."'—*Muslim, Al Bukhárí.*

On Standing in Prayer in the Month Ramaḍan

It is related from Zaid bin Thábit that, 'The Apostle of God said, "The prayer of a man in his house is better than his prayer in this mosque of mine, except the obligatory prayers." '—*Abú Dáud, At Tirmidhí.*

— It is related from Áyesha that, 'The Prophet said, "Dost thou know, O 'Áyesha, what (excellence) is in this night, namely the night of the half (month) after Sh'abán (i.e., the fifteenth of Ramaḍán)?" She replied, "What is in it, O Apostle of God?" He said, "In it all those born of the sons of Adam in the current year are written down, and in it all those who are to die of the sons of Adam in the current year are written down, and in it their actions are taken up, and in it their daily subsistence is sent down." She replied, "O Apostle of God, do none enter heaven, except by the mercy of God most High?" He said three times, "None enter heaven, except by the mercy of God most High." I said, "Not even thou, O Apostle of God?" Then he placed his hand on his head and said, "Not even I, except that God cover me with His mercy." This he said three times.'—*Al Baihaqi.*

— It is related from 'Alí that, 'The Apostle of God said, "When it is the night of the half (month) after Sh'abán then remain standing (in prayer) the night thereof, and fast during the day thereof, for verily God most High sends down on that night at the setting of the sun to the heavens surrounding the earth and says, 'Is there no one to ask forgiveness, that I may forgive him; and is there no one seeking food, that I may provide for him; and is there no one in affliction, that I may relieve him? And is there such-and-such?'—until the day breaks." '—*Ibn Májah.*

CONCERNING THE MORNING PRAYERS

It is related from Mu'ádhah that she said, 'I asked 'Áyesha, "How many *rak'ahs* did the Apostle of God perform at the morning prayers?" She replied, "Four *rak'ahs*, and he also exceeded that, according to the will of God." '—*Muslim.*

—It is related from Buraidah that he said, 'I heard the Apostle of God say, "There are three hundred and sixty joints in a man, therefore it is his duty to give alms for each joint of them." They replied, "And who is able to do that, O Prophet of God?" He said, "Bury the phlegm which falls in the mosque, and remove anything from the road, and if thou dost not find anything (impure), then two *rak'ahs* at the morning prayer will suffice thee." '—*Abú Dáud.*

It is related from Anas that, 'The Apostle of God said, "He who performs twelve *rak'ahs* at the morning prayer, God will build for him a palace of gold in paradise." '—*At Tirmidhí, Ibn Májah.*

It is related from Abu Sa'íd that he said, 'The Apostle of God used to pray so long in the morning prayers that we used to say, "He will never leave off." And he used to abstain from them so long that we used to say, "He will never pray them." '—*At Tirmidhí.*

On Voluntary Prayers

It is related from Abú Hurairah that, 'The Apostle of God said to Bilál at the time of the early morning prayers, "O Bilál, inform me of the act which thou hast performed in Islám from which thou hopest most; for verily I heard the noise of thy shoes before me in paradise." He replied, "I never performed any action from which I hoped any thing, with the exception that I never purified myself at any hour of the night or day without praying the prayer laid down for me conformable to that purification." '—*Muslim, Al Bukhárí.*

On the Prayer called *Tasbiḥ*

It is related from Ibn 'Abbás that, 'The Prophet said to 'Abbás bin 'Abdu'l-Muṭṭalib, "O 'Abbás, O my uncle, shall I not give thee, shall I not bestow on thee, shall I not inform thee of ten particular acts which, when thou doest them, God will forgive thee thy sins first and last, old and new, unintentional and intentional, small and great, hidden and disclosed, namely, that thou pray in four *rak'ahs* and recite in every *rak'ah* the opening chapter of the Book and any other chapter, and when thou dost finish the recital in the first *rak'ah* then stand up and say; 'Adoration be to God!' and 'Praise be to God!' 'There is no God but Alláh,' and 'God is great,' fifteen times. Afterwards, that thou perform the bowing down and say the above words whilst bowing ten times. After that thou must raise thy head from the bowings and repeat them whilst thou art bowing ten times. After that thou must raise thy head from the bowings and repeat the words ten times. After that thou must fall down in prostration and repeat them whilst thou art prostrating ten times. After that thou must raise thy head from prostration and repeat them ten times. Then thou must prostrate again and repeat the words ten times. Then thou must raise thy head and say them ten times, that is seventy five times in every *rak'ah*. Thou must do that in four *rak'ahs*. If thou art able to pray thus once every day, then do so; but if thou canst not do this, then once every Friday; and if thou art not able to do this, then once in every month; but if thou canst not do this, then once every year; but if thou canst not do that, then do it once in thy lifetime." *'Abú Dáud, Ibn Májah.*

On Prayers for a Journey

It is related from Anas that he said, 'We went out with the Apostle of God from Madína to Mecca, and he was praying in two *rak'ahs* at each prayer, until we returned to Madína.' It was said to him (Anas), 'Did you stay any time in Mecca?' He replied, 'We stayed in it ten days.'—*Muslim, Al Bukhárí.*

It is related from Ibn 'Abbás that he said, 'When the Apostle of God was on a journey he used to say the midday and afternoon prayers together, and he used to say the sunset and night prayers together.'—*Al Bukhárí.*

It is related from Ibn 'Omar that he said, 'When the Apostle of God was on a journey he used to say his prayers, except the obligatory prayers, on his camel in any direction it turned with him. And he used to make signs for the night prayers, and he used to perform the *witr*[1] prayers on his camel.'—*Muslim, Al Bukhárí.*

It is related from Jábir that he said, 'The Apostle of God sent me on a certain business, and I returned, and he was saying his prayers on his camel towards the East, and he was making his prostrations lower than the bowings'—*Abú Dáud.*

It is related from 'Áyesha that she said, 'Prayers were first ordained in two *rak'ahs*. Afterwards the Apostle of God fled to Madína and four *rak'ahs* were appointed; but the prayers to be said on a journey were according to the first ordinance (two *rak'ahs*). Al Zuhri said, 'I said to 'Urwah, "What is

[1] See note on page 52.

the matter with 'Áyesha, that she says the full prayers?" He replied, "She interprets it as 'Uthmán does."'—*Muslim, Al Bukhárí.*

Concerning the Friday Prayers

It is related from Abú Hurairah that, 'The Apostle of God said, "We the last (in time) will be the first on the day of resurrection although they (the Jews and Christians) were given the Book before us, and it was given to us after them. Then they changed this day of theirs, the observance of which was made obligatory for them, namely Friday, and God guided us to it, and the people follow us in this matter. The Jews observe the morrow, and the Christians the day after the morrow."' And in a tradition from Muslim it runs, 'He said, "We, the last, will be the first on the day of resurrection, and we will be the first who will enter heaven."'

It is related from Abú Hurairah that he said, 'I went out to Mount Tur and I met Ka'b, a learned man of the Jews, and I sat down with him, and he spoke to me about the Taurát, and I told him about the Apostle of God. And it came to pass that when I spoke to him I said, "The Apostle of God said that the best day on which the sun rose was Friday, because on that day Adam was created, and on it he was cast down (out of paradise), and on it he repented, and on it he died, and on it will take place the resurrection, And there is no moving creature, except the genii and men, that does not await Friday from the time it dawns till the sun rises out of fear of the resurrection. And on that day there is an hour in which no servant, being a Muslim, prays and asks God for anything but God gives it to him." Ka'b replied, "That takes place on one day in every year." I said, "Rather it comes on every Friday." Then Ka'b read the Taurát and said, "The Apostle of God spoke truly."' Abú Hurairah said, 'I met 'Abdu'lláh bin Salám, and I spoke to him of my sitting with Ka'b, the learned man of the Jews, and of what I had said to him concerning Friday; and I informed him that Ka'b said, "That takes place on one day in every year." 'Abdu'lláh bin Salám replied, "Ka'b lied." I said to him, "After that Ka'b read the Taurát and said, 'Rather it comes on every Friday.'" Then 'Abdu'lláh bin Salám said, "Ka'b spoke the truth."

Afterwards 'Abdu'lláh bin Salám said, "I have certainly come to know what hour it is." Abú Hurairah said, "Tell me of it, and keep it not to thyself." 'Abdu'lláh bin Salám replied, "It is the last hour of Friday." I said to him, "How can it be the last hour of Friday, when the Apostle of God has said, 'It is an hour in which no servant, being a Muslim, prays and asks God for anything, but God gives it to him?'" 'Abdu'lláh bin Salám replied, "Did not the Apostle of God say, 'He who sits in an assembly waiting for prayer is in prayer until he prays?'" I said, "Yes." He said, "Well it is that hour."'—*Málik, Abú Dáud, At Tirmidhí, An Nasái.*

It is related from Aus bin Aus that, 'The Apostle of God said, "Verily Friday is one of the excellent of your days. In it Adam was born, in it he died, in it will take place the blowing (of the trumpet at the resurrection) and in it (will be heard) the noise of the thunderbolt. Therefore on that day multiply your prayers for blessings on me, for verily your prayers are presented before me." They replied, "O Apostle of God, how will our prayers be placed before thee when thou hast turned to dust?" He said, "Verily God has forbidden to the earth the bodies of the prophets."'—*Abú Dáud, An Nasái, Ibn Májah.*

It is related from 'Abdu'lláh bin 'Omar that, 'The Apostle of God said, "There is no Muslim who dies on Friday or on the night thereof, but God preserves him from the tortures of the grave."'—*Aḥmad, At Tirmidhí.*

ON THE OBLIGATORY FRIDAY PRAYERS

It is related from Samurah bin Jundub that, 'The Apostle of God said, "He who neglects the Friday prayers without excuse, let him give in alms one *dinar*, and if he cannot get it, then half a *dinar*."'—*Aḥmad, Abú Dáud.*

It is related from Ṭáriq bin Shiháb that, 'The Apostle of God said, "The Friday prayers in the assembly are proper and obligatory for every Muslim, except for four persons: a slave, a woman, a child, or a sick person."'—*Abú Dáud.*

ON CLEANSING THE BODY AND HASTENING TO PRAYER

It is related from Náfi' that he said, 'I heard Ibn 'Omar say that the Apostle of God prohibited any man from making another to rise from his seat and sitting therein himself.' It was said to Náfi', 'Does this refer to Friday prayers?' He replied, 'To Friday prayers, and to others also.'—*Muslim, Al Bukhárí.*

It is related from 'Abdu'lláh bin 'Omar that, 'The Apostle of God said, "Three classes of people come to Friday prayers: the man who comes to them indulging in idle talk, and that is his reward therefrom; the man who comes in order to make supplication, and he is a man who asks of God, and if He wills He gives him his request, and if He wills He refuses it; and the man who comes to prayers in quietness and silence, and does not mark the neck of a Muslim nor inconvenience any one, and this is an atonement (for his sins) until the Friday which follows, and for three days longer, because God says, "He who comes with one good action, will receive ten like unto it."'—*Abú Dáud.*

It is related from Ibn 'Abbás that, 'The Apostle of God said, "He who speaks on Friday whilst the leader of the prayers is delivering his address, is like an ass which carries books; and whoever says to him, 'Be silent!' will not have performed acceptable Friday prayers."'—*Aḥmad.*

On the Public Address and Prayers

It is related from Jábir bin Samurah that he said, 'The Prophet made two public addresses (at the Friday prayers), and he used to sit between them and recite the Qur'án and admonish the people. And his prayers were of medium length, and his address was of medium length.'—*Muslim.*

It is related from 'Ammár that he said, 'I heard the Apostle of God say, "Verily the length of a man's prayers and the brevity of his public address are signs of his understanding. Therefore lengthen the prayers, and shorten the public address. Verily in rhetoric is deception."'—*Muslim.*

It is related from Jábir bin Samurah that he said, 'The Prophet used to give the public address standing. Then he would sit down, then he would rise up and deliver the second address standing. Whoever tells thee that he used to deliver the address sitting has lied, for by God! I prayed with the Prophet more than two thousand prayers.'—*Muslim.*

It is related from 'Umárah bin Ruaibah that, 'He saw Bishr bin Marwán standing on the pulpit and raising his hands (when delivering the public address), and he said, "May God curse these two hands! for verily I have seen the Apostle of God, and he did no more than speak with his hand thus"—and he made a sign with his fore-finger.'—*Muslim*.

On Prayers of Alarm

It is related from Salim bin 'Abdu'lláh bin 'Omar, from his father, that he said, 'I went on a military expedition with the Apostle of God towards Nejd, and we faced the enemy and drew up in line to meet them. Then the Apostle of God stood up to lead the prayers for us; and one party stood up with him and one party remained facing the enemy, and the Apostle of God bowed down with those who were with him and prostrated himself in two prostrations. After that, they moved off to the place of those who had not prayed, and they came and the Apostle of God bowed once with them and prostrated in two prostrations. Then he gave the salutation, and every one of them stood up and bowed once for himself and prostrated in two prostrations.' And Náfi' has related the same, but adds, 'And if the danger were more imminent than that, they prayed man by man, standing on their feet or mounted or facing the Qibla or without facing it.' Náfi' says, 'I do not imagine that Ibn 'Omar mentioned that, except he had it from the Apostle of God.'—*Al Bukhárí*.

It is related from Jábir that he said, 'We went forward with the Apostle of God until we came to Dhatu'l-Riqá'; and when we came to a shady tree we left it for the Apostle of God. And a man of the polytheists came, and the Apostle's sword was hanging from the tree, and he took the sword of the Prophet of God and unsheathed it and said to the Apostle of God, "Art thou not afraid of me?" He replied, "No." He said, "Who can protect thee from me?" He replied, "God will protect me from thee." Jábir said, "Then the companions of the Prophet frightened the man, and he returned the sword to its sheath and hung it up. Then we were called to prayers, and the Prophet prayed with one party in two *rak'ahs*, and then they moved behind and he prayed with the other party in two genuflections. Thus the Apostle of God prayed in all, in four *rak'ahs*, but the people prayed in two only." '—*Muslim, Al Bukhárí.*

It is related from Abú Hurairah that, 'The Apostle of God alighted between Ḍajnán and 'Usfán. Then the polytheists said, "Verily prayer is more precious to these people than their fathers and their children—and it was the afternoon prayer—do ye, therefore, join forces and advance upon them in one attack." But verily Gabriel came to the Prophet and commanded him to divide his companions into two parties and to pray with them, and that the other party should stand behind them and remain on guard holding their arms. And they prayed in one *rak'ah*, but the Apostle of God prayed in two *rak'ahs.*'—*At Tirmidhí, An Nasái.*

Concerning the Prayers of the Two Great Festivals

It is related from Jábir bin Samurah that he said, 'I said prayers with the Apostle of God at the two festivals (of sacrifice and of breaking the fast) not only once or twice, (but many times) without the call to prayer or the words "Prayers are now ready." '—*Muslim.*

It is related that Ibn 'Abbás was asked, 'Wast thou present with the Apostle of God at the festival?' He replied, 'Yes, the Apostle of God came out at the festival and said the prayers, after which he gave the address—but Ibn 'Abbás did not mention the call to prayers or the repetition of the words, "Prayer is now ready"—then he came to the women and admonished them and gave them advice and commanded them to give alms. And I saw them put their hands to their ears and throats and throw (their ornaments) to Bilál, after which he and Bilál went away to his house.'—*Muslim, Al Bukhárí.*

It is related from 'Áyesha that she said, 'Abú Bakr entered where she was, and there were two girls with her on the day of Mina, and they were playing the tambourine and beating it.'—And in another tradition it runs, 'They were singing the words which the helpers repeated on the day (of the battle) of Bu'áth—and the Prophet was covered with his cloth. And Abú Bakr rebuked them; but the Prophet uncovered his face and said, "Let them alone, O Abú Bakr, for verily these are days of festival." ' And in another tradition it runs, "O Abú

Bakr, every nation has its festival, and this is ours.'—*Muslim, Al Bukhárí.*

It is related from Al Barái that he said, 'The Prophet addressed us on the day of sacrifice and said, "Verily the first thing we do on this day of ours is that we repeat the prayers. Then we return and offer the sacrifice. And whoever does that has followed our practice; and whoever sacrifices before we pray has merely hurried in providing sheep's flesh for his family, he has in no respect fulfilled his duty towards God." '—*Muslim, Al Bukhárí.*

It is related from Anas that, 'The Prophet came to Madína and the people of Madína had two days on which they used to have sports. And he said, "What are these two days?" They replied, "We used, in the time of ignorance (before Islám) to play on these days." The Apostle of God said, "God has exchanged for you something better than these, namely, the day of sacrifice and the day of breaking the fast."' —*Abú Dáud.*

It is related from Abú'l-Huwairith that, 'The Apostle of God wrote to 'Amru bin Ḥazm when he was in Najrán, "Be quick in the performance of the feast of sacrifice, and delay in the observance of the feast of breaking the fast; and admonish the people." '—*Ash Sháfi.*

It is related from Abú Sa'ídu'l-Khudri that, 'The Apostle of God used to come out on the day of the festival of sacrifice and on the day of the festival of breaking the fast and begin with the prayers. And when he had said his prayers he used to rise up and face the people, whilst they remained sitting in the place in which they said their prayers. And if he had occasion to send (an army anywhere) he used to mention it to the people, or if he had occasion for anything else he commanded them with regard to it. And he used to say, "Give alms! give alms! give alms!" And most of those who gave alms were women. Then he would take his departure. And the practice continued thus until Marwán binu'l-Ḥakam. And I came out by the side of Marwán until we arrived at the place of prayer, and behold! Kathir binu'ṣ-Ṣalt had built a pulpit of mud and unburnt bricks, and Marwán began to push me by the hand as if he would drag me to the pulpit. And I was dragging him towards the prayers. ' And when I saw his design (to have the address before the prayers) I said, "Where is the beginning of prayer?" He replied, "No, O Abú Sa'íd, that which thou knowest has been abandoned." I said, "Never! by Him in whose hand is my life! You will never bring anything better than what I know." This he said thrice and departed.'—*Muslim.*

On Sacrifice

It is related from 'Áyesha that, 'The Apostle of God ordered a ram with horns to be brought that walked in blackness, slept in blackness and looked in blackness (i.e., which had black feet, sides and eyes). And it was brought that he might sacrifice it. He said, "O 'Áyesha, bring me a knife." Then he said, "Sharpen it with a stone," and I did so. Then he took it and took the ram and threw it on its side, then he slew it. After that he said, "In the name of God! O God, accept this from Muḥammad, and the family of Muḥammad, and the followers of Muḥammad." Then he offered the flesh to the poor.'—*Muslim.*

It is related from Jábir that, 'The Apostle of God said, "Do not sacrifice any but a beast of full age; but if that be difficult for you, then sacrifice a female lamb." '—*Muslim.*

It is related from Jábir that he said, 'The Prophet, on the day of sacrifice, killed two black and white, castrated, male sheep with horns; and when he turned them (towards the temple at Mecca) he said, "I turn my face to Him who created the heavens and the earth, according to the religion of Abraham the Hanif; and I am not one of the polytheists. Verily my prayers and my devotions and my life and my death are devoted to God, the Lord of the worlds. He has no partner, and for that I have been commanded, and I am one of the Muslims. O God (this sacrifice) is from Thee and for Thee on behalf of Muḥammad and his people. In the name of God. God is great." Then he sacrified.'—*Aḥmad, Abú Dáud, Ibn Májah.*

It is related from Ḥanash that he said, 'I saw 'Alí sacrifice two male sheep, and I said to him, "What is this?" He replied, "Verily the Apostle of God ordered me to sacrifice for him. Therefore I am sacrificing for him." '—*Abú Dáud.*

It is related from Al Barái bin 'Azib that, 'Verily the Apostle of God was asked what (animals) were unfit for sacrifice. Then he made a sign with his hand and said, "There are four: the lame whose lameness is clearly perceived, the blind whose blindness is manifest, the sick whose disease is manifest, and those very emaciated which are not without blemish." '—*Málik, Aḥmad, At Tirmidhí.*

It is related from 'Áyesha that she said, 'The Apostle of God said, "The sons of Aḍam have done no action on the day of sacrifice more pleasing to God than the shedding of blood, and verily it will come on the day of resurrection with its horns and its hairs and its hoofs, and verily the blood will be accepted of God before it falls to the ground. Therefore rejoice in it." ' —*At Tirmidhí, Ibn Májah.*

It is related from Zaid bin Arqam that he said, 'The companions of the Apostle of God said, "O Apostle of God, what are these sacrifices?" He replied, "They are the practice of your father Abraham." They said, "And what benefit do we derive from them, O Apostle of God?" He replied, "There is benefit in every hair." They said, "And what if it be wool, O Apostle of God?" He replied, "There is benefit in every hair of the wool." '—*Aḥmad, Ibn Májah.*

On Prayers at Eclipses

It is related from Abú Músá that he said, 'There was an eclipse of the sun, and the Prophet rose up in terror, fearing that the hour (of resurrection) was coming. And he came to the mosque and prayed standing and bowing and prostrating himself a long time such as I never saw him do before. And he said, "These signs which God sends are not on account of the death or life of any one; but God frightens His servants therewith. Therefore when ye see any such, flee for refuge by remembering Him and calling upon Him and asking pardon of Him." '—*Muslim, Al Bukhárí.*

It is related from Jábir that he said, 'There was an eclipse of the sun in the time of the Apostle of God on the day on which Abraham, the son of the Apostle of God, died. And he prayed with the people in six *rak'ahs* and with four prostrations.' —*Muslim.*

It is related from Asmá' bint Abú Bakr that she said, 'Verily the Prophet ordered the liberation of a slave at the time of an eclipse of the sun.'—*Al Bukhári.*

It is related from Nu'mán bin Bashír that he said, 'The sun was eclipsed in the time of the Apostle of God, and he began to pray in two *rak'ahs* at a time, and he continued to ask concerning the sun until it became bright again.'—*Abú Dáud.* And in a tradition from An Nasái it runs, 'Verily the Prophet prayed when the sun was eclipsed the same as our (ordinary) prayers. He both bowed down and prostrated himself.'— And in another tradition it is related that, 'The Prophet came out on a certain day, hastening to the mosque, and the sun had become eclipsed. And he prayed until it became bright again. Then he said, "Verily the people of the time of ignorance (before Islám) used to say that the sun and the moon were eclipsed only for the death of some great person of the world. But verily the sun and the moon are not eclipsed for the death of anyone, nor yet for their life; but they are two parts of His creation. God makes new anything of his creation that He wishes. Therefore whichever of these two is eclipsed, pray until it becomes bright again, or God gives some new order." '—*An Nasái.*

On Prostration for Gratitude

It is related from Abú Bakr that he said, 'The Apostle of God, when a pleasing order came to him or one by which he was pleased, used to fall down in prostration as a thanksgiving to God most High.'—*Abú Dáud, At Tirmidhí.*

It is related from Sa'd bin abú Waqqáṣ that he said, 'We went out with the Apostle of God from Mecca, wishing to go to Madína. And when we approached Azwazá he alighted. Then he raised his hands and prayed to God for an hour. Then he fell down in prostration and remained thus for a long time. Then he rose up and raised his hands for an hour. Then he fell down in prostration, and remained thus for a long time. Then he rose up and raised his hands for an hour. Then he fell down in prostration, and he said (to us), "Verily I asked of my Lord and interceded for my followers, and He gave me one-third of my followers. Therefore I fell down in prostration before my Lord in thanksgiving. Then I raised my head and supplicated my Lord for my followers, and He gave me one-third of my followers. Therefore I fell down in prostration before my Lord in thanksgiving. Then I raised my head and supplicated my Lord for my followers, and He gave me the last third. Therefore I fell down in prostration before my Lord." '—*Aḥmad, Abú Dáud.*

On Prayers for Rain

It is related from 'Abdu'lláh bin Zaid that he said, 'The Apostle of God came out with the people to the place of prayer in order to pray for rain, and he prayed with them in two *rak'ahs* which he recited in a loud voice; and he turned towards the temple at Mecca and made supplication, and he raised his hands and drew his garments around him when he faced in the direction of the temple at Mecca.'—*Muslim, Al Bukhárí.*

It is related from 'Umair, a freed slave of Abú Al Laḥm that, 'He saw the Prophet at Aḥjáru'l-Zait near Zawrai standing and supplicating for rain; and he was raising his hands before his face, but he did not raise them above his head.' —*Abú Dáud, At Tirmidhí.*

It is related from Ibn 'Abbás that he said, 'The Apostle of God came out to pray for rain, dressed in poor clothes and in humble mien and with fear and self-abasement.'—*At Tirmidhí, Abú Dáud, Ibn Májah.*

It is related from 'Áyesha that she said, 'The people complained to the Apostle of God concerning the want of rain. Then he ordered the pulpit, and it was placed for him in the place of prayer. And he arranged with the people a certain day on which they should come to it. Then the Apostle of God came out when a part of the sun appeared, and he sat down on the pulpit. Then he said, "God is great!" and he praised God. Then he said, "Verily ye have complained of the drought in your region and of the withholding of the rain from you in its season; and God has commanded you to supplicate Him, and has promised you that He will answer your supplications." After that he said, "Praise be to God, the Lord of the worlds, the Merciful and Compassionate, King of the day of judgement. There is no God but Alláh. He does whatsoever He wills. O God, Thou art God. There is no God but Thee, the self-sufficient; but we are poor, send down upon us the rain, and make that which Thou sendest down for us strength and a sufficient portion for the time." Then he raised his hands, and did not desist from raising them until the white of his armpits were visible. Then he turned to the people, and turned or changed his mantle whilst he was raising his hands. Then he turned towards the people and came down and prayed in two *rak'ahs*. And God brought a cloud, and it thundered and lightened, after which it rained by the permission of God; and he did not come to his mosque until the rain flowed in torrents. And when he saw their haste in making for shelter, he laughed until his teeth appeared. And he said, "I bear witness that God is powerful over all, and that I am the servant of God and His Apostle."'—*Abú Dáud.*

It is related from Anas that 'There was a drought, and 'Omar binu'l-Khaṭṭáb prayed for rain in the name of 'Abbás bin 'Abdu'l-Muṭṭalib and said, "O God, we used to supplicate Thee through our Prophet, and Thou gavest us rain, and now we supplicate Thee through the uncle of our Prophet, therefore do Thou send us rain." Anas said, "Then they were given rain."'—*Al Bukhárí.*

Concerning Winds

It is related from Abú Hurairah that he said, 'I heard the Apostle of God say, "The wind is from the breath of God. It comes in mercy and in punishment. Do not abuse it, but supplicate from God some of its benefits, and take refuge with Him from its evils."'—*Abú Dáud, Ibn Májah.*

It is related from Ibn 'Abbás that, 'A man cursed the wind near the Prophet. He said, "Do not curse the wind, for it has been ordered. And whosoever curses anything which is not deserving thereof, his curses will return upon himself."'—*At Tirmidhí.*

It is related from 'Áyesha that she said, 'When the Prophet saw any creation in the sky as, for example, a cloud, he left his work and turned towards it and said, "O God, I take refuge with Thee from whatever evil may be in it." And if He dispelled it, he would say, "Praise be to God!" And if it rained, he would say, "O God, (give) profitable rain."'—*Abú Dáud, An Nasái, Ibn Májah, As Shafí.*'

V

THE BOOK OF BIERS

On Visiting the Sick, and the Rewards of Sickness

It is related from Abú Musá that, 'The Apostle of God said, "Feed the hungry, visit the sick, and free the captive."'—*Al Bukhárí.*

It is related from Abú Hurairah that, 'The Apostle of God said, "The duties of a Muslim towards fellow-Muslims are five: returning a salutation, visiting the sick, following a bier, accepting an invitation and replying to one who sneezes (by saying 'May God have mercy on thee')."'—*Muslim, Al Bukhárí.*

It is related from Abú Hurairah that, 'The Apostle of God said, "Verily God most High will say on the day of resurrection, 'O son of Adam, I was sick, and thou didst not visit me.' He will say, 'O Lord, how could I visit Thee when Thou art the Lord of the worlds?' He will say, 'Didst thou not know that My servant so-and-so was sick, and thou didst not visit him. Didst thou not know that if thou hadst visited him, thou wouldst certainly have found Me beside him.' And God will say, 'O son of Adam, I asked food of thee, but thou gavest Me no food.' He will reply, 'O Lord, how couldst I give Thee food, when Thou art the Lord of the worlds?' He will say, 'Didst thou not know that so-and-so, a servant of Mine, asked food of thee, and thou gavest him no food. Didst thou not know that if thou hadst given him food, thou wouldst certainly have found that with Me. O son of Adam, I asked drink of thee, but thou gavest Me nothing to drink.' He will reply, 'O Lord, how could I give Thee water to drink, when Thou art the Lord of the worlds?' He will say, 'So-and-so, a servant of Mine, asked water of thee, but thou gavest him nothing to drink. Didst thou not know that, if thou hadst given him to drink, thou wouldst have found that with Me.'"'—*Muslim.*

It is related from Ibn 'Abbás that, 'The Prophet entered in to a desert Arab to visit him—and it was his custom when he visited the sick to say, "There is no fear. It is a purification, if God will"—and he said to him, "There is no fear. It is a purification, if God will." The man replied, "Never! rather it is a fever boiling on an old man, which will send him on a visit to the graves!" The Prophet replied, "Very well, then be it so."'—*Al Bukhárí.*

It is related from Abú Sa'ídu'l-Khudri that, 'Gabriel came to the Prophet and said, "O Muḥammad, art thou ill?" He replied, "Yes." He said, "In the name of God I utter this spell for thee, that He will protect thee from the evil of every person and of every envious eye. May God heal thee. In the name of God I utter this spell for thee."'—*Muslim.*

It is related from Ibn 'Abbás that he said, 'The Apostle of God used to make over Ḥasan and Ḥusain to the protection of God, saying, "I make you over to the protection of the perfect word of God from the evil of every Satan and from every reptile and from every evil eye." And he used to say, "Verily your father (Abraham) used to protect Ishmael and Isaac by these words."'—*Al Bukhárí.*

It is related from 'Abdu'lláh bin Mas'úd that he said, 'I entered in to the Prophet when he was in a fever, and I massaged him with my hand, and said, "O Apostle of God, verily the fever is severe upon thee." He replied, "Yes, I am afflicted with fever equal to that of two other men of you." I said, "That is because thou wilt obtain a double reward." He replied, "Yes." Then he said, "There is no Muslim afflicted with illness or anything else, but God thereby puts away his sins, as a tree sheds its leaves."'—*Muslim, Al Bukhárí.*

It is related from 'Áyesha that she said, 'I never saw anyone suffer such severe pain as the Apostle of God.'—*Muslim, Al Bukhárí.*

It is related from Abú Hurairah that, 'The Apostle of God said, "Martyrs are of five kinds: those who die of pestilence, of stomach troubles, of drowning, of a broken back, and those who die in war for the faith."'—*Muslim, Al Bukhárí.*

It is related from 'Áyesha that she said, 'I asked the Apostle of God about the plague, and he informed me that it was a punishment which God sends upon whomsoever He wills, and that God had made it a mercy for the believers. He said, "There is no one on whom the plague comes who remains in his own country, patiently considering the matter, and knowing that nothing can befall him unless God has written it for him, but he will receive a reward equal to that of a martyr." '—*Al Bukhárí.*

It is related from Usámah bin Zaid that, 'The Apostle of God said, "The plague is a punishment which was sent on one of the tribes of the Children of Israel, or on those who preceded you. Therefore when ye hear of its presence in a country, do not go into it; and when it breaks out in the land in which ye are, then do not flee away from it." '—*Muslim, Al Bukhárí.*

It is related from 'Alí that he said, 'I heard the Apostle of God say, "There is no Muslim who visits a sick Muslim in the morning, but seventy thousand angels pray for blessings upon him until the evening comes. And if he visits him in the evening, seventy thousand angels pray for blessings upon him until the morning dawns; and there will be prepared for him a garden in paradise." '—*Abú Dáud, At Tirmidhí.*

It is related from Abú'l-Dardái that he said, 'I heard the Apostle of God say, "Whoever of you complains of any sickness, or his brother complains of sickness, let him say, 'Our Lord God, who art in heaven, hallowed be Thy name. Thy command is in heaven and on earth. As Thy mercy is in heaven, so make it upon earth. Forgive our sins and our transgressions. Thou art the Lord of the pure. Send down mercy from Thy mercy, and healing from thy healing upon this pain, and it will be healed.' " '—*Abú Dáud.*

It is related from 'Abdu'lláh bin 'Omar that, 'The Apostle of God said, "When a man comes to visit the sick, let him say, 'O God, heal Thy servant, that he may wound for Thee the enemy or go for Thee to a funeral.' " '—*Abú Dáud.*

It is related from 'Áyesha that she said, 'I saw the Prophet when he was dying, and near him was a vessel in which was water; and he put his hand into the vessel, and then wiped his face and then said, "O God, aid me against the evils of death or the agony of death." '—*At Tirmidhí, Ibn Májah.*

It is related from Abú Sa'íd that, 'The Apostle of God said, "When ye enter in to a sick person, then speak hopefully of his condition. That will not avert anything from him, but it will be a solace for his soul." '—*At Tirmidhí, Ibn Májah.*

It is related from Anas that he said, 'A Jewish boy used to wait on the Prophet, and he fell sick. And the Prophet came to visit him and sat down near his head. And he said to him, "Become a Muslim." And the boy looked towards his father, who was near him. He said, "Obey the father of Qásim (i.e. Muḥammad)." Then he embraced Islám. And the Prophet went out saying, "Praise be to God, who has saved him from the fire."'—*Al Bukhárí.*

It is related from Yaḥya bin Sa'íd that he said, 'Verily death came to a man in the time of the Apostle of God. And a certain man said, "He was fortunate. He died without being afflicted with disease." The Apostle of God replied, "Alas on thee! Who told thee? If God had tormented him with disease, it would have made expiation for his sins."'—*Málik.*

It is related from 'Áyesha that, 'The Apostle of God said, "When the sins of a servant (of God) increase, and he has no works wherewith to make expiation for them, then God afflicts him with grief in order to make expiation for him."'—*Aḥmad.*

It is related from Thawbán that, 'The Apostle of God said, "When fever attacks any one of you—and verily fever is a part of the fire—then let him extinguish it with water; and let him immerse himself in a flowing river, and let him face the current and say, 'In the name of God. O God, cure Thy servant and establish the truthfulness of Thine Apostle.' (This should be done) after the morning prayer and before the rising of the sun. And let him plunge himself in it in three immersions for three days. And if he is not well in three, then let him do it for five days; and if he is not cured in five, then let him do it for seven; and if he is not cured in seven, then for nine. For verily it scarcely ever exceeds nine, by the permission of God, the Exalted and Magnified."'—*At Tirmidhí.*

It is related from 'Omar binu'l-Khaṭṭáb that, 'The Apostle of God said, "When thou enterest in to a sick person, command him to pray for thee, for verily his supplication is like the supplication of the angels."'—*Ibn Májah.*

On Wishing for Death

It is related from Abú Hurairah that, 'The Apostle of God said, "Let not any one of you wish for death; the good man because, perchance, (if he live) he may increase in goodness, and the wicked man because, perchance, he may seek the pleasure of God." '—*Al Bukhárí.*

— It is related from 'Abdu'lláh bin 'Omar that he said, 'The Apostle of God seized me by my shoulder and said, "Be in the world as if thou wert a stranger or one passing on a journey." ' —*Al Bukhárí.*

It is related from Abú Umámah that he said, 'We sat near the Apostle of God, and he was reminding us (of death), and he touched our hearts. And Sa'd bin abú Waqqáṣ wept and exceeded in his lamentation, and said, "Would that I had died!" The Apostle of God said, "O Sa'd, near me dost thou wish for death!" This he repeated three times. Then he said, "O Sa'd, if thou hast been created for paradise, then the longer thy life and the better thine actions, the better it will be for thee." '—*Aḥmad.*

On what should be Said, to One approaching Death

It is related from Abú Sa'íd and Abú Hurairah that, 'The Apostle of God said, "Repeat to your dead, 'There is no God but Alláh.' " '—*Muslim.*

It is related from Mu'ádh bin Jabal that, 'The Apostle of God said, "That person whose last words are, 'There is no God but Alláh,' will enter paradise." '—*Abú Dáud.*

On Washing and Shrouding the Dead

It is related from 'Áyesha that, 'The Apostle of God was shrouded in three garments of white cloth of yemen of cotton from Suhuli. There was no shirt and no turban.'—*Muslim, Al Bukhárí.*

It is related from Ibn 'Abbás that, 'The Apostle of God said, "Dress yourselves in white clothes, for they are the best of your clothes; and shroud your dead in them. And the best collyrium for you is *ithmúd*, for it makes the hair grow and brightens the eyes." '—*Abú Dáud, At Tirmidhí.*

— It is related from Abú Sa'lídu'l Khudri that, 'When death drew near to him, he called for new clothes and put them on. Then he said, I heard the Apostle of God say, "The dead will be raised up in the clothes in which he dies." '—*Abú Dáud.*

On Going with a Bier

It is related from Abu Sa'íd that, 'The Apostle of God said, " When a corpse is placed (on a bier), and men carry it on their shoulders, then, if it was a good person, it will say 'Carry me forward.' And if it was not a good person, it will say to its bearers, 'Woe to it! where are you carrying it!' And everything hears its voice except mankind; and if mankind heard it he would swoon away." '—*Al Bukhárí.*

It is related from Jábir that he said, 'A funeral passed by, and the Apostle of God stood up for it, and we stood up with him. And we said, "O Apostle of God, verily it was a Jewess." He replied, " Verily death is a terrible thing, therefore whenever you see a funeral, stand." '—*Muslim, Al Bukhárí.*

It is related from Auf bin Málik that he said, 'The Apostle of God prayed over a corpse, and I memorized a part of his prayer. He said, "O Lord, forgive him, and have mercy on him, and preserve him from evil, and remit his sins for him, and make his resting-place honourable, and expand the (grave) into which he enters, and wash him with water and with snow and with hail, and purify him from sins as Thou cleansest a white robe from impurity, and exchange for his (present) house a better one, and for his people a better people, and for his wife a better wife. Enter him into paradise, and protect him from the punishments of the grave and the punishment of the fire." And in another tradition it runs, "Protect him from the afflictions of the grave and the punishment of the fire." Auf said, (He prayed thus) until I wished that I might become that dead man.'—*Muslim.*

It is related from Ibn 'Omar that, 'The Apostle of God said, " Make mention of the good deeds of your dead, but abstain from their faults." '—*Abú Dáud.*

It is related from 'Ubádah binu'ṣ-Ṣámit that he said, 'When the Apostle of God used to follow a corpse he did not sit down until it was placed in the grave. And a learned man of the Jews approached him and said to him, "O Muḥammad, we do the same as this." ' 'Ubádah said, 'Then the Apostle of God sat down and said, " Do the opposite to what they do." '—*Al Tirmidhí, Abú Ḍáud, Ibn Májah.*

It is related from Abú Músá that, 'The Apostle of God said, "When a corpse passes by thee whether it be of a Jew, a Christian, or a Muslim, then stand up for it, for ye do not rise for it, but ye only rise for the angels who are with it."'—*Aḥmad.*

On Burying the Dead

It is related from Abu'l-Hayyáju'l Asadi that he said, ''Alí said to me, "Shall I not send thee on a business on which the Apostle of God sent me? Namely, that thou do not leave any image without effacing it, or any high tomb without levelling it with the ground."'—*Muslim.*

It is related from Jábir that he said, 'The Apostle of God prohibited tombs from being built with mortar, or from being built over, or from being sat upon.'—*Muslim.*

It is related from 'Áyesha that, 'The Apostle of God said, "The breaking of the bones of a dead person is like breaking them when he is alive."—*Málik, Abú Dáud, Ibn Májah.*

It is related from 'Amru bin Ḥazm that he said, 'The Prophet saw me leaning on a grave, and he said, "Do not annoy the occupant of this grave, or (he said) do not annoy him."'—*Aḥmad.*

On Weeping over the Dead

It is related from Anas that he said, 'We entered in with the Prophet to Abú Saif, the blacksmith, and he was the husband of Abraham's wet-nurse. And the Apostle of God took Abraham (his son) and kissed him and smelt him. After that we entered into him again when Abraham was at the point of death, and the eyes of the Apostle of God were flowing with tears; and 'Abdu'r-Raḥmán bin Auf said to him, "And dost thou (weep also), O Apostle of God?" He replied, "O Ibn Auf, verily they are tears of compassion." Then he followed it with more tears and said, "Verily the eyes shed tears, and the heart is oppressed with grief; and we say nothing but what is pleasing to our Lord; and we, O Abraham, are verily sore grieved at thy separation from us."'—*Muslim, Al Bukhárí.*

It is related from Usámah bin Zaid that he said, 'The daughter of the Prophet sent to him saying, "My son is at the point of death; come to us." And he sent one to give his salutations and to say, "Verily to God belongs what He has taken, and to Him belongs what He has given, and everyone has a fixed time with him. Therefore let her have patience and consider." Then she sent to him adjuring him that he must certainly come to her. And he rose up, and with him were Sa'd bin 'Ubádah and Mu'ádh bin Jabal and Ubai bin Ka'b and Zaid bin Thábit and other men. And the child was lifted up for the Apostle of God, and his life was flickering away. And the Apostle's eyes overflowed with tears, and Sa'd said, "O Apostle of God, what is this!" He replied, "This is compassion which God has placed in the hearts of His servants; and verily God only compassionates those of His servants who are compassionate."'—*Muslim, Al Bukhárí.*

It is related from 'Abdu'lláh bin Mas'úd that he said, 'The Apostle of God said, "That person is not one of us who beats his cheeks and rends the bosom of his garments and cries out with the cries of the time of ignorance."'—*Muslim, Al Bukhárí.*

It is related from Abú Hurairah that, 'The Apostle of God said, "No Muslim loses three children by death and enters the fire, except to expiate the oath (that all must enter hell)."'—*Muslim, Al Bukhárí.*

It is related from Abú Sa'ídu'l-Khudri that he said, 'The Apostle of God cursed the woman who made lamentation (for the dead), and he cursed the one who listened to her.'—*Abú Dáud.*

It is related from Abú Barzah that, 'The Apostle of God said, "He who comforts a woman bereft of her children, will be clothed with the cloak of a derwish in paradise."'—*At Tirmidhí.*

It is related from Al Mughíra bin Shu'bah that he said, 'I heard the Apostle of God say, "He over whom lamentation is made will be punished at the day of resurrection for the lamentation made over him."'—*Muslim, Al Bukhárí.*

It is related from 'Amrah bint 'Abdu'r-Raḥmán that she said, 'I heard 'Áyesha say—when it was mentioned to her that 'Abdu'llah bin 'Omar had said that the dead would certainly be punished for the lamentations of the living over them—"God forgive the father of 'Abdu'r-Raḥmán. Beware! he did not lie, but he forgot or he made a slip. The facts were these; the

Apostle of God only passed by a Jewish woman over whom lamentation was being made, and he said, 'Verily these are lamenting over her, and she is certainly being punished in her grave.' " '—*Muslim, Al Bukhári.*

On Visiting Graves

It is related from Buraidah that, 'The Apostle of God said, " I prohibited you from visiting graves, but (now) visit them; and I prohibited you from meat which had been offered in sacrifice above the space of three days, but (now) retain it as long as you like; and I prohibited you from unfermented wine, except in a leathern bag, but now drink it from all kinds of drinking vessels; but do not drink anything intoxicating." ' —*Muslim.*

It is related from Abú Hurairah that he said, 'The Prophet visited his mother's tomb and wept, causing those around him to weep also. And he said, " I sought permission of my Lord to pray for forgiveness for her, but permission was not given me; and I asked His permission to visit her tomb, and permission was given me. Therefore visit the tombs, for they remind of death." '—*Muslim.*

VI

THE BOOK OF ALMS

It is related from Ibn 'Abbás that, 'The Apostle of God sent Mu'ádh to Yemen and said, "Verily thou art coming to a community of the People of the Book (i.e., Jews and Christians), therefore call on them to bear witness that there is no God but Alláh and that Muḥammad is the Apostle of Alláh. And if they agree to that, then teach them that God has made obligatory on them five prayers in the day and night; and if they submit to that, then teach them that God has made obligatory for them the giving of alms, to be taken from the rich among them and given to their poor; and if they submit to that, then beware and refrain from taking the best of their property, and be on thy guard against the complaints of the oppressed, for verily there is no veil between them and God."' —*Muslim, Al Bukhárí.*

It is related from Abú Hurairah that, 'The Apostle of God said, "He to whom God has given wealth and does not give alms thereof, his wealth on the day of resurrection will be changed into the form of a serpent, having two black spots over its eyes, which will be hung like a necklace around his neck. Then on the day of resurrection it will seize him by the jaws, and after that will say, 'I am thy property. I am thy treasure.'" Then the Prophet repeated the verse, "And let not those who are niggard of what God hath vouchsafed them in His bounty (imagine that their avarice is better for them; nay, rather, it is worse for them[1])."'—*Al Bukhárí.*

It is related from Jábir bin 'Abdu'lláh that he said, 'Some people of the desert Arabs came to the Apostle of God and said, "Verily some people of those who collect the alms come to us and oppress us." He replied, "Satisfy your collectors of alms." They said, "O Apostle of God, although they oppress us?" He replied, "Satisfy your collectors of alms, even though you are oppressed."'—*Abú Dáud.*

---

[1] Qur'án. Súratu Áli 'Imrán (iii) 180.

It is related from 'Amru bin Shu'aib from his father, from his grandfather that, 'The Prophet addressed the people and said, "Are there those among you who are guardians of orphans who possess property? Then let them trade therewith, and not leave it (uninvested), so that the alms due on it do not swallow it up."'—*At Tirmidhí.*

It is related from Abú Hurairah that he said, 'When the Prophet died and Abú Bakr succeeded him as Khalífa, and certain of the Arabs became infidels, 'Omar binu'l-Khaṭṭáb said to Abú Bakr, "How is it that thou dost fight with the people when the Apostle of God has said, 'I was commanded to fight with the people until they say, "There is no God but Alláh," and whoever says, "There is no God but Alláh," makes his goods and his person safe from me, except what is due (as alms); and his account is with God?'" Then Abú Bakr replied, "By God! I will certainly fight with those who make a distinction between prayers and alms; for alms are due from property. By God! if they had denied me a lamb, such as they used to give to the Prophet of God, I would certainly have fought with them because of such refusal." 'Omar said, "By God! I saw nothing, except that God had opened the heart of Abú Bakr to fight. Then I knew it was right."'—*Muslim, Al Bukhárí.*

Concerning the Things on which Alms are Obligatory

It is related from Abú Sa'ídu'l-Khudri that, 'The Apostle of God said, "There are no alms required for less than five camel-loads of dates, and no alms are required for less than five *uqiyas*, (i.e. three hundred drams) of silver, and no alms are required for less than five camels."'—*Muslim, Al Bukhárí.*

It is related from Abú Hurairah that, 'The Apostle of God said, "A Muslim is not obliged to give alms for his slave or his horse."—And in another tradition it runs, "There is no alms for his slave, except the alms for the feast of the breaking the fast."'—*Muslim, Al Bukhárí.*

It is related from Mu'ádh that he said, 'Verily the Prophet when he sent him to Yemen, commanded him to take one yearling heifer or bull from every thirty, and one full-grown cow from every forty.'—*Abú Dáud, At Tirmidhí.*

It is related from 'Áyesha that she said, 'The Prophet used to send 'Abdu'lláh bin Rawáḥah to the Jews, and he used to compute the dates when they became sweet, and before they were eaten from.'—*Abú Dáud.*

It is related from Zainab the wife of 'Abdu'lláh that she said, 'The Apostle of God addressed us and said, "O assembly of women, give alms, although it be of your ornaments, for verily you will compose the majority of the inhabitants of hell on the day of resurrection." '—*At Tirmidhí.*

Concerning the Alms to be Given at the Festival of the Breaking of the Fast

It is related from Ibn 'Omar that he said, 'The Apostle of God made the alms obligatory for the feast of the breaking of the fast: a measure of dates, or a measure of barley to be given by a slave or a free man, a male or a female, the young and old of all Muslims; and he ordered that it should be given before coming out to the prayers.'—*Muslim, Al Bukhárí.*

Concerning Those for Whom Alms are Unlawful

It is related from 'Abdu'l-Muṭṭalib bin Rabí'ah that, 'The Apostle of God said, "Verily these alms are only the impurities of men, and they are not lawful for Muḥammad or the family of Muḥammad." '—*Muslim.*

It is related from Abú Ḥurairah that he said, 'When food was brought to the Apostle of God, he used to ask about it; whether it was a present or alms. And if it was said, "It is alms," he would say to his companions, "You eat," but would not eat it himself. But if it was said, "It is a present," he would stretch out his hand and eat with them.'—*Muslim, Al Bukhárí.*

It is related from 'Abdu'lláh bin 'Omar that, 'The Apostle of God said, "Alms are not lawful for the rich, nor for the strong and healthy." '—*At Tirmidhí.*

It is related from Zaid bin Aslam that he said, ''Omar binu'l-Khaṭṭáb drank some milk which delighted him, and he asked the one who gave him to drink, "Whence came this milk?" He informed him that he arrived at a watering-place, which he named, and (said he), "Behold some camels which had been given in alms; and they were watering them. And they milked some of them, so I placed it in my leathern bag, and that is the milk which thou hast drunk." Then 'Omar put his hand into his mouth, and caused himself to vomit.'—*Málik.*

Concerning Those for Whom Begging is not Lawful, and for Whom it is

It is related from Abú Hurairah that, 'The Apostle of God said, "He who begs from men their wealth in order to increase his own, only asks live coals, whether he ask little or much." '—*Muslim.*

It is related from Sahal binu'l-Ḥanzaliyyah that, 'The Apostle of God said, "He who begs, when he has what makes him independent of it, is only asking for an increase of the fire." Al Nufail, who was one of the reporters of traditions, said, in another tradition, "What are the riches, having which it is not right to beg?" He replied, "That amount which suffices for the morning and evening meal." And he said in another place, "That he have enough to satisfy him for a day or a night and a day." '—*Abú Dáud.*

It is related from Anas that, 'A man of the helpers came to the Prophet to beg from him. He said, "Is there nothing in thy house?" The man said, "Yes, there is a blanket, with a part of it we cover ourselves, and a part of it we spread on the floor. And there is a large drinking-bowl from which we drink water." The Prophet said, "Bring them to me." Then he brought them. Then the Apostle of God took them in his hand and said, "Who will buy these two?" A man said, "I will take them for one *dirham.*" He replied twice or thrice, "Who will give more than one *dirham*?" A man said, "I will take them for two *dirhams.*" Then the Prophet gave them to him, and he took the two *dirhams* and gave them to the helper and said, "Buy with one of them food and give it to thy family, and with the other buy a hatchet and bring it to me." So he brought it to him. Then the Apostle of God fitted a handle to it with his own hands, and after that said, "Go and cut firewood and sell it, and let me not see thee for fifteen days." So the man went to cut firewood and sell it. Then he came back to him, and he had gained ten *dirhams,* and with a portion of it he had bought clothes, and with a portion of it he bought food. Then the Apostle of God said to him, "This is better for thee than that thy begging should come on the day of resurrection as marks on thy face. Verily begging is not lawful except for three persons: a poor man who lives in miserable circumstances, or one who is excessively in debt, or one who has a bleeding sore."'—*Abú Dáud.*

On Spending and Bring Niggardly

It is related from Abú Hurairah that, 'The Apostle of God said, "If I possessed gold equal to the mountain of 'Uḥud, it would delight me that nothing of it should remain with me after three nights had passed over me, except something I might keep for debt."'—*Al Bukhárí.*

It is related from Abú Hurairah that, 'The Apostle of God said, "God most High has said, 'Spend, O son of Adam, and I will spend on thee.'"'—*Muslim, Al Bukhárí.*

It is related from Abú Hurairah that, 'The Apostle of God said, "The liberal man is near to God, near to paradise and near to men, and far removed from the fire; but the miser is far from God, far from paradise and far from men, and near the fire; and the ignorant (but) liberal man is more beloved of God than the miserly worshipper."'—*At Tirmidhí.*

It is related from Abú Sa'íd that, 'The Apostle of God said, "Verily that a man give one *dirham* in alms in his lifetime, is better for him than that he should give one hundred in alms at his death."'—*Abú Dáud.*

It is related from 'Áyesha that, 'Some of the wives of the Prophet said to him, "Who of us will be quickest in joining thee (after death)?" The Prophet replied, "The one of you who has the longest arm." Then they took a rod and began to measure their arms, and Saudah had the longest arm of them all. But afterwards we came to know that the length of the arm signified almsgiving, and the quickest of us in joining the Prophet was Zainab, and she used to love almsgiving.'—*Al Bukhárí.*

It is related from a freed slave of 'Othmán that he said, 'A present of a piece of meat was sent to Umm Salamah, and the meat was relished by the Prophet; and she said to a servant, "Put it in the house, perhaps the Prophet will eat it." So she placed it in a recess in the wall. And a beggar came and stood at the door and said, "Give me alms, and may God bless you." And they replied, "And may God bless thee." Then the beggar went away, and the Prophet entered and said, "O Umm Salamah, hast thou anything for me to eat?" She replied, "Yes," and said to the servant, "Go and bring the Apostle of God that meat." So she departed, but found nothing in the recess except a piece of stone. Then the Prophet said, "Verily that meat has turned to stone, because you did not give it to the beggar."' —*Al Baihaqi.*

It is related from 'Áyesha that she said, 'There were, during the illness of the Apostle of God, six or seven *dinars* belonging to him in my keeping. And the Apostle of God ordered me to distribute them. But the pain of the Prophet of God kept me busy. Afterwards he asked me about them as to what the six or seven *dinars* had accomplished. She said, "No by God! thy pain kept me busy." And he called for them and placed them in the palm of his hand and said, "What would the Prophet of God think if God, the Exalted and Magnified, met him whilst these were still with him?"' —*Aḥmad.*

On Obligatory Alms

It is related from Abú Músáu'l-Ash'ari that, 'The Apostle of God said, "Alms are obligatory on every Muslim." They said, "And if he has nothing?" He replied, "Then let him work with his hands, and gain something for himself, and give alms." They said, "And if he is not able to work, or has not done so?" He replied, "Then let him assist those who are in need and in distress." They said, "And if he does not do that?" He replied, "Then let him order people to do right." They said, "And if he does not do that?" He replied, "Then let him withhold himself from evil; and verily that will be alms for him."' —*Muslim, Al Bukhári.*

It is related from Anas that, 'The Apostle of God said, "There is no Muslim who plants a tree or sows a field, and men or birds or beasts eat therefrom, but it becomes alms for him."' —*Muslim, Al Bukhári.*—And in another tradition from Muslim the words are added, 'And whatever is stolen from him will be counted as alms for him.'

It is related from Abú Hurairah that, 'The Apostle of God said, "An adulteress was forgiven (under the following circumstances): She passed by a dog at the entrance to a well. And its tongue was hanging out, and it was about to die from thirst. And she took off her shoe and tied it to her veil and let it down (to draw) water for it. And for that she was forgiven her sins." It was said, "Is there any reward for us (for doing good) to beasts?" He replied, "For every merciful woman there is a reward."'—*Muslim, Al Bukhárí.*

It is related from Abú Hurairah that, 'The Apostle of God said, "A man passed by the branch of a tree which overhung the road, and he said, 'I will remove this from the road of Muslims, so that it may not incommode them.' Then he was given entrance into paradise."'—*Muslim, Al Bukhárí.*

It is related from Anas that, 'The Apostle of God said, "Verily alms quench the Lord's anger, and put away an evil death."'—*At Tirmidhí.*

It is related from 'Abdu'lláh bin Mas'úd, from the Apostle of God, that he said, 'There are three persons whom God loves: the man who rises at night to recite the Book of God; the man who gives alms with his right hand and, I think, he said, hiding it from his left; the man who, being in a band of soldiers, and his companions being put to flight, continues to face the enemy."'—*At Tirmidhí.*

It is related from Anas that, 'The Apostle of God said, "When God created the earth, it began to tremble, therefore He created the mountains and placed them upon it, and it became firm. And the angels were astonished at the strength of the mountains and said, 'O Lord, is there anything in Thy creation more powerful than the mountains?' He replied, 'Yes, iron.' They said, 'O Lord, is there anything in Thy creation more powerful than iron?' He replied, 'Yes, fire.' They said, 'O Lord, is there anything more powerful in Thy creation than fire?' He replied, 'Yes, water.' They said, 'O Lord, is there anything in Thy creation more powerful than water?' He replied, 'Yes, the wind.' They said, 'O Lord, is there anything in Thy creation more powerful than the wind?' He replied, 'Yes, the son of Adam who gives alms with his right hand, and hides it from his left.'"'—*At Tirmidhí.*

On the Excellence of Almsgiving

It is related from Abú Hurairah that, 'The Apostle of God said, "Of a *dinar* which thou hast spent in the way of God, and a *dinar* which thou hast spent in freeing a slave, and a *dinar* which thou hast spent in giving alms to the poor, and a *dinar* which thou hast spent on thy family, the greatest of them all, in point of reward, is that which thou hast spent on thy family." '—*Muslim.*

It is related from Maimunah bintu'l-Ḥárith that, 'She emancipated a slave-girl in the time of the Apostle of God, and mentioned that to the Apostle of God. He replied, "If thou hadst given her to thy maternal uncles, thy reward would have been greater." '—*Muslim, Al Bukhárí.*

It is related from Abú Hurairah that, 'A man came to the Prophet and said, "I have a *dinar.*" He replied, "Then spend it on thyself." He said, "I have another." He replied, "Then spend it on thy child." He said, "I have another." He replied, "Then spend it on thy family." He said, "I have another." He replied, "Then spend it on thy servant." He said, "I have another." He replied, "Thou knowest best." '—*Abú Dáud, An Nasái.*

It is related from Ibn 'Omar that, 'The Apostle of God said, "Give protection to him who asks protection of thee in the name of God, and give to him who asks alms of thee in the name of God, accept the invitation of him who invites thee, and recompense him who does thee a favour; but if thou hast not wherewith to recompense him, then pray for him until thou consider thou hast recompensed him." '—*Aḥmad, Abú Dáud, An Nasái.*

It is related from Anas that he said, 'Abú Ṭalḥah was the richest of all the helpers in Madína in date trees; and the most treasured of his possessions was Bairḥá'a (a garden) facing the mosque. And the Apostle of God used to enter it and drink from the excellent water therein. And when this verse descended, "Ye will never attain unto righteousness until ye spend in alms of what ye love,[1]" Abú Ṭalḥah rose up and said to the Apostle of God, "O Apostle of God, verily God most High says, 'Ye will never attain unto righteousness until

[1] Qur'án. Súratu Áli 'Imrán (iii) 92.

ye spend in alms of what ye love,' and verily the most treasured of my possessions is Bairḥá'a (the garden), therefore it is given in alms to God most High. I hope for the righteousness thereof, and its provision is with God, therefore, O Apostle of God, bestow it wherever God shows thee." The Apostle of God replied, "Well done! Well done! that is a profitable property. I have heard what thou hast said, and verily I see that the place to bestow it is with thy relations." Abú Ṭalḥaḥ said, "I shall do that, O Apostle of God." Then Abú Ṭalḥaḥ divided it amongst his relations and the sons of his paternal uncle.'—*Muslim, Al Bukhárí.*

On a Woman's Giving Alms from Her Husband's Property

It is related from Abú Hurairah that, 'The Apostle of God said, "When a woman spends in alms from the earnings of her husband, without his orders, then he will get half its reward."'—*Muslim, Al Bukhárí.*

It is related from 'Áyesha that, 'A man said to the Prophet, "Verily my mother died suddenly, and I think that, had she spoken, she would have given alms. Will she, then, obtain the reward if I give alms on her behalf?" He replied, "Yes."'—*Muslim, Al Bukhárí.*

It is related from Abú Umámah that he said, 'I heard the Apostle of God say, in his public address, in the year of the farewell pilgrimage, "Let not a woman spend anything in alms from the house of her husband, except with the permission of her husband." It was said, "O Apostle of God, not even food?" He replied, "That is the best of our property."'—*At Tirmidhí.*

It is related from 'Umair, a freed slave of Abú'l-Laḥm, that he said, 'My master ordered me to dry a piece of meat; and there came to me a poor beggar, and I gave him to eat of it. And my master was made aware of the fact and beat me. Then I came to the Apostle of God and mentioned the matter to him. And he called Abú'l-Laḥm and said, "Why didst thou beat him?" He replied, "He gave away my food without my ordering him to do so." He said, "Its reward is (divided) between the two of you." And in another tradition it is stated that he said, "I was a slave, and I asked the Apostle of God, may I give anything in alms of my master's goods?" He replied, "Yes, and its reward is (divided) equally between the two of you."'—*Muslim*.

CONCERNING THOSE WHO MAY NOT TAKE BACK ALMS ONCE GIVEN

It is related from 'Omar binu'l-Khaṭṭáb that he said, 'I provided a horse for a man in the way of God (i.e. for religious war), but he with whom it was neglected it. Then I wished to buy it back, and imagined that he would sell it cheaply. So I asked the Prophet, and he said, "Do not buy it, and do not take back thine alms, even though he give it thee for a *dirham*; for verily one who takes back his alms is like a dog which returns to its vomit."'—*Muslim*, *Al Bukhárí*.

It is related from Buraidah that he said, 'I was sitting by the Prophet when a woman came to him and said, "O Apostle of God, I gave a slave-girl in alms to my mother, and the latter has died." He replied, "Thy reward (for the alms) is thy proper right, and the inheritance will return her to thee again." She said, "O Apostle of God, my mother had undertaken to fast for a mouth; may I fast on her behalf?" He replied, "Fast on her behalf." She said, "Verily my mother never performed the pilgrimage; may I perform it on her behalf?" He replied, "Yes, perform the pilgrimage on her behalf."'—*Muslim*.

VII

THE BOOK OF FASTING

It is related from Abú Hurairah that, 'The Apostle of God said, " When (the month) Ramaḍán begins, the doors of heaven are opened." And in another tradition it runs, "The doors of paradise are opened, and the doors of hell are closed, and the satans are chained." And in another tradition it runs, "The doors of mercy are opened." '—*Muslim, Al Bukhárí.*

It is related from Abú Hurairah that, 'The Apostle of God said, "He who fasts in the month Ramaḍán, in faith, hoping for a reward, all his past sins will be forgiven him; and he who stands up (to pray) in Ramaḍán in faith, hoping for a reward, all his past sins will be forgiven him; and he who stands up (to pray) in the night of power in faith, hoping for a reward, all his past sins will be forgiven him." '—*Muslim, Al Bukhárí.*

It is related from Abú Hurairah that, 'The Apostle of God said, "The blessed month, Ramaḍán, has come to you. God has made its fast incumbent upon you. In it the doors of heaven are opened, and in it the doors of hell are closed, and in it the rebellious satans are manacled. In it there is a night better than a thousand months. He who is deprived of its benefits is deprived indeed." '—*Aḥmad, An Nasái.*

It is related from 'Abdu'll'áh bin 'Amru that, 'Verily the Apostle of God said, "The fast and the Qur'án intercede for the servant (of God). The fast says, 'O Lord, verily I forbade him food and sensual pleasures by day, therefore accept my intercession for him.' And the Qur'án says, 'I forbade him sleep by night, therefore accept my intercession for him.' Then both their intercessions are accepted.'" '—*Al Baihaqi.*

It is related from Ibn 'Abbás that, 'The Apostle of God used, when the month Ramaḍán arrived, to release all captives, and used to give to all beggars.'

On Seeing the New Moon

It is related from Ibn 'Omar that, 'The Apostle of God said, " Do not fast until ye see the new moon, and do not break the fast until ye see it; and if it be concealed from you by clouds, then compute (the time) for it." And in another tradition it runs, "A month is twenty-nine nights, therefore do not fast until ye see it, and if it be hidden from you by clouds, then complete the full period of thirty." '—*Muslim, Al Bukhárí.*

It is related from Abú Hurairah that, 'The Apostle of God said, "Let none of you fast a day or two days before Ramaḍán, unless he be a man who is in the habit of fasting. In that case, let him fast on that day." '—*Muslim, Al Bukhárí.*

It is related from Umm Salamah that she said, 'I never saw the Prophet fast on two successive months, except in the months Sha'bán and Ramaḍán.'—*Abú Dáud, Ibn Májah, Al Tirmidhí and An Nasái.*

It is related from Ibn 'Abbás that he said, 'A desert Arab came to the Prophet and said, "I have seen the new moon," namely, the new moon of Ramaḍán. The Prophet replied, "Dost thou bear witness that there is no God but Alláh?" He said, "Yes." He replied, "Dost thou bear witness that Muḥammad is the Apostle of God?" He said, "Yes." Then the Prophet said, "O Bilál, proclaim to the people that they keep the fast from to-morrow." '—*Abú Dáud, Al Tirmidhí, An Nasái, Ibn Májah.*

It is related from Anas that, 'The Apostle of God said, "Eat in the early dawn, for verily in the meal taken at early dawn there is a blessing." '—*Muslim, Al Bukhárí.*

It is related from 'Amru binu'l-'Áṣ that, 'The Apostle of God said, "The difference between our fasts and the fasts of the People of the Book is in the meal taken at early dawn." '—*Muslim.*

It is related from Abú Hurairah that he said, 'The Apostle of God forbade fasting continuously for two or more days during the fast Ramaḍán. Then a man said to him, "O Apostle of God, verily thou dost fast continuously for two or more days." He replied, "Which of you is like me? Verily I pass the night, and my Lord gives me food and drink." '—*Muslim, Al Bukhárí.*

It is related from Salmán bin 'Amru that, 'The Apostle of God said, "When any one of you breaks the fast, then let him break it with dried dates, because that is a blessing, but if he cannot find such, then let him break it with water, because it is pure." '—*Aḥmad, At Tirmidhí, Abú Dáud, Ibn Májah.*

It is related from Mu'ádh bin Zuhrah that, 'When the Prophet broke the fast he used to say, "O God, for Thee I have kept the fast, and with food provided by Thee I have broken it." '—*Abú Dáud.*

It is related from Abú Hurairah that, 'The Apostle of God said, "Religion will continue victorious so long as men hasten in breaking the fast, because the Jews and Christians delay (therein)." '—*Abú Dáud, Ibn Májah.*

On What Nullifies the Fast

It is related from Abú Hurairah that, 'The Apostle of God said, "He who does not abandon false words, and acts accordingly, God requires not that he give up his eating and drinking." '—*Al Bukhárí.*

It is related from Abú Hurairah that, 'The Apostle of God said, "The person who has forgotten whilst engaged in the fast, and eaten and drunken, let him complete his fast, for verily it was only God who caused him to eat and drink." '—*Muslim, Al Bukhárí.*

It is related from Abú Hurairah that he said, 'Whilst we were sitting with the Prophet, behold a man came to him and said, "O Apostle of God, I am undone!" He replied, "What has happened to thee?" He said, "I have had connexion with my wife whilst I was observing the fast." The Apostle of God replied, "Hast thou a female slave whom thou canst set at liberty?" He said, "No." He replied, "Art thou able to fast two months in succession?" He said, "No." He said, "Hast thou victuals wherewith to feed sixty poor people?" He said, "No." He said, "Sit down." Then the Prophet waited, and whilst he was waiting there was brought to the Prophet a bag in which were dry dates, and the bag was made of fig-leaves. Then the Prophet said, "Where is the beggar?" He replied, "I am he." He said, "Take this and give alms from it." The man replied, "O Apostle of God, shall I (be able to give to) one poorer than myself! By God! there is no household between the two hills (of Madína) poorer than mine!" Then the Prophet laughed until his teeth were exposed. Then he said, "Give to thine own family to eat."'—*Muslim, Al Bukhárí.*

It is related from Ma'dán bin Ṭalḥah that Abú Dardái' informed him that the Apostle of God vomited and broke his fast. He said, 'Then I met Thaubán in the mosque of Damascus and said, "Verily Abú Dardái' informed me that the Apostle of God vomited and broke his fast." He replied, "He spoke truly, and I poured out water for his ablutions."'—*Abú Dáud, At Tirmidhí.*

It is related from Abú Hurairah that, 'The Apostle of God said, "He who breaks the fast for one day in the month Ramaḍán without permission, or except for sickness, the fasts of all the ages will not atone for it, even though he keep them."'—*Aḥmad, At Tirmidhí, Abú Dáud, Ibn Májah.*

It is related from Abú Hurairah that, 'The Apostle of God said, "How many there are who keep the fast, who receive nothing from their fast but thirst! And how many there are who stand up (to pray at night), who receive nothing from their standing but wakefulness!"'—*Al Dárimí.*

Concerning the Fast of the Traveller

It is related from 'Áyesha that she said, 'Verily Ḥamzah bin 'Amru'l-Aslami said to the Prophet, "Should I fast during a journey?" And he was a great faster. The Prophet replied, "If thou desirest, fast; and if thou desirest, discontinue the fast."'—*Muslim, Al Bukhárí.*

It is related from Abú Sa'ídu'l-Khudri that he said, 'We went on a warlike expedition with the Apostle of God until sixteen days of the month Ramaḍán had passed. And some of us kept the fast, and some of us broke it. And those who fasted did not blame those who broke the fast; and those who broke the fast found no fault with those who fasted.'—*Muslim.*

It is related from Anas bin Máliku'l-Ka'bi that, 'The Apostle of God said, "Verily God has removed half the prayers from the traveller; and He has removed all the fast from the traveller, and from one giving suck, and from one who is pregnant."'—*Abú Dáud, At Tirmidhí, An Nasáí, Ibn Májah.*

It is related from Salamah binu'l-Muḥabbaq that, 'The Apostle of God said, "He who has a beast of burden, which carries him to his destination in comfort, must keep the fast of Ramaḍán wherever it comes to him." '—*Abú Dáud.*

On the Execution of an (Omitted) Duty

It is related from Abú Hurairah that, 'The Apostle of God said, "It is not right for a woman to fast when her husband is present, except with his permission; or for her to allow anyone in his house, except with his permission." '—*Muslim.*

It is related from 'Áyesha that, 'The Apostle of God said, "He who dies leaving a fast unperformed, his heir must fast for him." '—*Muslim, Al Bukhárí.*

It is related from Málik that he heard that Ibn 'Omar was asked, 'May one person fast for another, or may one pray in place of another?' He replied, 'No one may fast for another, and no one may pray in place of another.'—*Al Muwaṭṭa.*

On Voluntary Fasts

It is related from Abú Hurairah that, 'The Apostle of God said, "The best fast, after that of Ramaḍán, is that of the month of God, Muḥarram. And the best prayers, after the five obligatory prayers, are the night prayers." '—*Muslim.*

It is related from Ibn 'Abbás that he said, 'When the Apostle of God fasted on the day of 'Áshura (i.e. the tenth of Muḥarram) they said, "O Apostle of God, verily it is a day held in respect by the Jews and Christians." The Apostle of God said, "If I remain till next year, I will certainly keep the ninth day." '—*Muslim.*

It is related from Abú Qatádah that, 'A man came to the Prophet and said, "How dost thou keep the fast, O Apostle of God?" Then the Apostle of God became angry at his words. And when 'Omar saw his anger, he said, "We are satisfied with Alláh as our Lord, with Islám as our religion, and with Muḥammad as our Prophet. We take refuge with God from the anger of God and the anger of His Apostle." And 'Omar continued to repeat these words until his anger subsided. Then 'Omar said, "O Apostle of God, how is it with the man who fasts the whole of the time?" The Apostle of God replied, "There is (for him) neither fast nor breaking of fast," or he said, "He has neither fasted nor broken the fast." 'Omar said, "How is it with the man who fasts two days, and breaks the fast one day?" He replied, "Is anyone able to do that?"

He said, "How is it with the man who fasts one day, and breaks the fast one day?" He replied, "That was the fast of David." He said, "How is it with the man who fasts one day, and abstains from fasting two days?" He replied, "I wished that I might be able to do that." Then the Apostle of God said, "Three days in each month and the month Ramaḍán (are sufficient) till the next Ramaḍán; and this is the fast of the whole year, and the fast of the day of Arafat. I hope in God that these will atone for the year which precedes it and the year which follows it. And the fast of the day of 'Ashura, I hope in God that it will atone for the year which precedes it." '—*Muslim*.

It is related from Abú Sa'ídu'l-Khudri that he said, 'The Apostle of God forbade fasting on the day of the breaking of the fast and on the day of sacrifice.'—*Muslim*, *Al Bukhárí*.

It is related from Abú Sa'ídu'l-Khudri that, 'The Apostle of God said, "He who fasts one day in the road of God, God removes his face seventy years from the fire." '—*Muslim*, *Al Bukhárí*.

It is related from 'Abdu'lláh bin 'Amru binu'l-'Áṣ that he said, 'The Apostle of God said to me, "O 'Abdu'lláh, have I not been informed that thou dost fast in the day and stand up (in prayer) during the night?" I said, "Yes, O Apostle of God." He replied, "Then do not do it. Keep the fast, and also eat; and stand up to pray, and also sleep; for verily thou hast a duty towards thy body, and thou hast a duty towards thine eyes, and thou hast a duty towards thy wife, and thou hast a duty towards thy guests. He who fasts all the time, does not fast at all. The fast of three days in each month is equal to a constant fast, therefore fast three days in each month, and read the Qur'án in every month." I said, "Verily I am able to do more than that." He replied, "Fast. The best fast is the fast of David, namely to fast one day and eat one day. And recite the (Qur'án) once in every seven nights, and do not do more than that." '—*Muslim*, *Al Bukhárí*.

— It is related from 'Áyesha that, 'The Apostle of G d used to fast on Mondays and Thursdays.'—*At Tirmidhí*, *An Nasái*.

— It is related from Abú Hurairah that, 'The Apostle of God said, "The actions of men are placed before God on Mondays and Thursdays, and I wish that my actions should be placed before Him whilst I am fasting." '—*At Tirmidhí.*

It is related from Ibn 'Abbás that he said, 'Verily the Apostle of God came to Madína and found the Jews fasting on the day of 'Ashura. Therefore the Apostle of God said to them, "What is this day which you are observing by a fast?" They replied, "This is a great day. On it God saved Moses and his people, and drowned Pharaoh and his people; so Moses fasted on that day out of gratitude; and we fast thereon." Then the Apostle of God said, "We are more worthy of and nearer to Moses than ye." Then the Apostle of God fasted on that day, and ordered the people to fast thereon.'—*Muslim, Al Bukhárí.*

It is related from Umm Ṣalamah that, 'The Apostle of God used to fast on Saturdays and Sundays more than on any other day, and used to say, "Verily these two days are festivals of the polytheists, and I like to act contrary to them." '—*Aḥmad.*

It is related from Abú Hurairah that, 'The Prophet used to fast on Mondays and Thursdays, and it was said, "O Apostle of God, thou fastest on Mondays and Thursdays?" He replied, "Verily on Mondays and Thursdays God forgives every Muslim except the two who are alienated from one another. He says, 'Leave them alone until they become reconciled.' " '—*Aḥmad, Ibn Májah.*

It is related from Umm Háni that she said, 'On the day of the conquest of Mecca, Fáṭimah came and sat on the Apostle's left, and Umm Háni sat on his right. Then there came a girl with a vessel containing drink, and she gave it to him, and he drank from it. Then she gave it to Umm Háni, and she drank from it. Then she said, "O Apostle of God, I have broken my fast, for I was fasting." He said to her, "Were you carrying out anything (omitted from a previous fast)?" She said, "No." He said, "Then it will do you no harm, if it was a voluntary fast." '—*Abú Dáuḍ, At Tirmidhí.*—And in another tradition from *Aḥmad* and *At Tirmidhí* it runs, 'She said, "O Apostle of God, beware, verily I was fasting." He replied, "The performer of a voluntary fast is his own master; if he wishes he may fast, and if he wishes he may break the fast." '

Concerning the Night of Power

It is related from 'Áyesha that, 'The Apostle of God said, "Seek the night of power in the odd nights of the last ten days of the month Ramaḍán." '—*Al Bukhárí.*

It is related from Ubádah bin Ṣámit that he said, 'The Prophet came out to inform us of the night of power; and two men of the Muslims were disputing together, and he said, "I came out to inform you of the night of power, and such-and-such an one were disputing together, and it was taken away (from my memory). And perhaps it is better for you; therefore seek it in the ninth and seventh and fifth." '—*Al Bukhárí.*

On Seclusion for Religious Exercises

It is related from Abú Hurairah that, 'The Qur'án was recited to the Prophet once every year, but it was recited twice to him during the year in which he died. And he used to seclude himself each year for ten days; but he secluded himself for twenty days during the year in which he died.'—*Al Bukhárí.*

It is related from Anas that, 'The Prophet used to seclude himself during the last ten days of Ramaḍán; but one year he did not seclude himself, and when the following year came round he secluded himself twenty days.'—*At Tirmidhí.*

It is related trom 'Áyesha that she said, 'It is the rule that they who seclude themselves should not visit the sick, nor be present at funerals, nor touch a woman, nor live with her, nor go out for any purpose except what is indispensably necessary. And there is no seclusion apart from fasting, and there is no seclusion except in a mosque.'—*Abú Dáud.*

VIII

THE BOOK OF THE EXCELLENCIES OF THE QUR'ÁN

It is related from 'Othmán that, 'The Apostle of God said, "The best of you is he who learns the Qur'án and teaches it."' —*Al Bukhárí.*

It is related from Abú Sa'ídu'l-Khudri that Usaid bin Ḥuḍair said, 'On a certain night when he was reading Súratu'l Baqara, and his horse was tethered near him, behold! the horse wheeled round. Then he became silent, and it also became steady. Then he read (again), and it wheeled round. Then he became silent, and it ceased wheeling round. He again read, and the horse wheeled round as before. Then he turned away, and his son Yaḥyá was near it, and he feared that it would injure him. And when he moved the child away he raised his head to the heavens, and behold! something like a cloud and in it objects resembling lamps. And when the morning came he informed the Prophet. He replied, "Read, O Ibn Ḥuḍair, read of Ibn Ḥuḍair." He replied, "I feared, O Apostle of God, that it would tread on Yaḥyá who was near it, and I moved near to him, and raised my head to the heavens, and behold! something resembling a cloud, in which were objects like lamps, and I went out in order that I should not see them." He replied, "And dost thou know what that was?" He said, "No." He said, "Those were angels which came near at the sound of thy voice, and if thou hadst continued to read, they would have remained until the morning, and men would have seen them. They would not have remained hidden."'—*Muslim, Al Bukhárí.*

It is related from Abú Umámah that he said, 'I heard the Prophet say, "Read the Qur'án, for verily it will come on the day of resurrection as an intercessor for those who read it. Read the two bright chapters : chapter Baqara and chapter Áli 'Imrán, for verily they will come on the day of resurrection as if they were clouds, or two canopies or two flocks of birds in ranks arguing on behalf of those who read them. Read chapter

Baqara, because memorising it is a blessing, and neglecting it a grief. The slothful cannot memorise it." '—*Muslim.*

It is related from Ubai bin Ka'b that, 'The Apostle of God said, "O Abú Al Mandhar, dost thou know which verse from the Book of God most High which is with thee is the greatest?" I said, "God and His Apostle know best." He said, "O Abú Al Mandhar, dost thou know which verse from the Book of God which is with thee is greatest?" I said, "God, there is no God but He, the Living, the Self-subsisting.[1]"' Ubai said, 'And he struck me on my breast and said, "O Abú Al Mandhar, may knowledge be welcome to thee."' —*Muslim.*

It is related from Ibn 'Abbás that he said, 'Whilst Gabriel was sitting near the Prophet he heard a sound above him, and raised his head. And Gabriel said, "This is a door of heaven which has been opened to-day. It was never opened before to-day." And an angel came down from it. And he said, "This is an angel who has come down to the earth. He never came down except to-day." Then he saluted him and said, "Be glad in the two lights which have been given thee, and which were not given to any Prophet before thee, namely the chapter opening the Book and the last sections of Súratu'l Baqara. Thou wilt never recite a single letter from them without being given (its reward.)"' —*Muslim.*

It is related from Abú'l-Dardái that, 'The Apostle of God said, "Is any one of you unable to recite one third of the Qur'án in one night?" They replied, "How can he recite one third of the Qur'án?" He said, "Say, 'He is Lord alone.'[2] It will equal one third of the Qur'án."' —*Muslim.*

It is related from Anas that a man said, 'O Apostle of God, I love this chapter (beginning with the words) "Say, He is God alone." He replied, "Verily thy love for it will take thee to paradise."' —*At Tirmidhí.*

It is related from Ibn 'Abbás that, 'The Apostle of God said, "Verily he in whose heart there is nothing of the Qur'án is like a deserted house."' —*At Tirmidhí.*

It is related from Abú Sa'íd that, 'The Apostle of God

---

[1] Súratu'l-Baqara (ii) 256.

[2] That is, repeat the chapter of the Qur'án beginning with these words, viz. Súratu'l-Ikhláṣ (cxii).

said, "The Blessed and most High Lord says, 'He whom (the reciting of) the Qur'án diverts from the remembrance of me and from praying to me, I will give him better than what I give those who pray. And the superiority of the Word of God over other words is like the superiority of God over His creation.'" '—*At Tirmidhí.*

It is related from Al Hárithu'l-A'war that he said, 'I passed into the mosque, and behold the people were engaging in conversation; so I went in to 'Alí and informed him. He said, "Have they done so?" I said, "Yes." He replied, "Verily I heard the Apostle of God, say, 'Beware! for there will be strife.'" I said, "O Apostle of God, what is the way out of such strife?" He replied, "The Word of God in which is the history of what happened before you, and information of what will come after you, and a command concerning the things which are amongst you. It is a separator between (true and false). It is not a vain utterance. He who is proud and abandons it, God will break him in pieces, and he who desires guidance apart from it, God will lead him astray. And it is the strong rope of God, and it is a wise admonition, and it is a straight road, and it is that by which men do not go astray, and by which the tongue does not become entangled. And the wise do not become satiated thereby. It does not become worn out by much repetition, and its wonders do not cease. It is a Book which, when the genii heard it, they said, 'Verily we have heard a wonderful Qur'án. It guides to the straight path, and we have believed in it.' Whoever speaks by it will speak the truth, and whoever acts according to it will be rewarded, and he who judges by it will judge justly, and whoever invites men to it, will himself be guided to the straight path." '—*At Tirmidhí.*

It is related from 'Uqbah bin 'Ámir that he said, 'I heard the Apostle of God say, "If the Qur'án were placed in a leathern skin and cast into the fire, it would not be burned." '—*Al Dárimi.*

It is related from 'Alí that, 'The Apostle of God said, "He who reads the Qur'án and remembers it, and makes lawful the lawful in it, and considers unlawful what is unlawful in it, God will bring him into paradise, and will accept his intercession for ten people of his household, for each of whom the fire was fitting." '—*Aḥmad, At Tirmidhí, Ibn Májah.*

It is related from Abú Hurairah that, 'The Apostle of God said to Ubai bin Ka'b, "How dost thou recite in prayer?" Then he recited the "Mother of the Qur'án" (viz. Súratu'l-Fátiḥa). The Apostle of God said, "By Him in whose hands is my life, there has not been sent down in the Taurát, or the Gospel, or the Psalms, or in the Furqán the like of it. Verily it is the seven (verses) twice repeated, and the great Qur'án which was given to me." '—*At Tirmidhí.*

It is related from Abú Hurairah that, 'The Apostle of God said, "Learn the Qur'án and recite it, for verily the likeness of the Qur'án for him who learns and recites it, and stands up for it, is like that of a leathern bag filled with musk which diffuses its scent in every place. And the likeness of him who learns it, and goes to sleep, although it is in his heart, is like that of a bag of musk with its mouth tied." '—*At Tirmidhí, An Nasái.*

It is related from An Nu'mán bin Bashír that, 'The Apostle of God said, "Verily God wrote a book two thousand years before He created the heavens and the earth, and sent down two verses from it with which He ended Súratu'l-Baqara. Satan approaches near to that house in which they are not recited for three nights." '—*At Tirmidhí, Al Dárimi.*

It is related from Anas that, 'The Apostle of God said, "Everything has a heart, and the heart of the Qur'án is (the chapter entitled) Yá Sín[1]. And he who recites the chapter Yá Sín, God will, for its recital, write down for him (the reward) for reading the whole Qur'án ten times." '—*At Tirmidhí, Al Dárimi.*

It is related from Ibn 'Abbás and Anas bin Málik that, 'The Apostle of God said, "(The chapter beginning), 'When the earth shall quake[2]', equals one half of the Qur'án, and (the chapter beginning), 'Say, He is God alone[3]', equals one third of the Qur'án, and (that beginning), 'Say, O unbelievers[4]', equals one fourth of the Qur'án." '—*At Tirmidhí.*

It is related from Anas that, 'The Apostle of God said, "Whoever recites two hundred times every day (the chapter

---

[1] Chapter xxxvi.
[2] Chapter xcix.
[3] Chapter cxii.
[4] Chapter cix.

beginning with the words), 'Say, He is God alone,' the sins of fifty years will be erased from him, unless he has a debt." ' —*Al Tirmidhí, Al Dárimi.*

It is related from 'Uqbah bin 'Ámir that he said, 'Whilst I was going with the Apostle of God between Al Hajfah and Al Abwái, behold! there overtook us a wind of deep darkness, and the Apostle of God began to seek protection by (reciting the two chapters beginning) "I take refuge with the Lord of the daybreak[1]," and "I take refuge with the Lord of men[2]." And he said, "O 'Uqbah, seek protection by reciting these two chapters, for no one has ever sought protection by anything like these." '—*Abú Dáud.*

It is related from 'Áyesha that, 'The Prophet said, "Verily the recitation of the Qur'án in prayer is better than its recitation at other times, and the recitation of the Qur'án at other times than the time of prayer is better than repeating the praises of God and saying, 'God is great.' And repeating the praises of God is better than alms, and alms are better than fasting, and fasting is a protection from the fire." '

On the Recitation of the Qur'án.

It is related from Ibn Mas'úd that, 'The Apostle of God said, "It is a bad thing for any one of you to say, 'I have forgotten such-and-such a verse.' Rather say, 'I have been caused to forget it.' Remember the Qur'án, because it is quicker in leaving the hearts of men than a quadruped." '—*Muslim, Al Bukhárí.*

It is related from Ibn 'Omar that, 'The Prophet said "The likeness of one who owns (that is memorizes) the Qur'án is like that of the owner of the camel which is tied up. If he pays attention to it, he will retain it; but if he frees it, it will go away." '—*Muslim, Al Bukhárí.*

It is related from Qatádah that he said, 'Anas was asked what the recital of the Prophet was like (when reciting the Qur'án). He replied, "It was drawn out." After that he recited, "In the name of the Merciful, the Compassionate," and he lengthened the words, "In the name of" and, "the Merciful" and, "the Compassionate." '—*Al Bukhárí.*

---

[1] Chapter cxiii.
[2] Chapter cxiv.

It is related from Anas that, 'The Apostle of God said to Ubai bin Ka'b, "Verily God has commanded me to recite the Qur'án to thee." He replied, "Did God mention me by name?" He said, "Yes." He replied, "Then I have been mentioned by the Lord of the worlds!" He said, "Yes." Then Ka'b's eyes flowed with tears.'—*Muslim*, *Al Bukhári.*

It is related from Ibn 'Omar that, 'The Apostle of God forbade travelling with the Qur'án towards the land of an enemy.'—*Muslim*, *Al Bukhári.*—And in another tradition by *Muslim* it runs, 'Do not travel with the Qur'án, for I cannot protect it from being taken by the enemy.'

It is related from Abú Sa'ídu'l-Khudri that he said, 'I sat in a company of the feeble amongst those who had fled from Mecca to Madína, and some of them were covering others on account of nakedness. And a reciter was reciting the Qur'án to us, when, behold! the Apostle of God came and stood beside us. And when the Apostle of God stood, the reciter became silent. And the Prophet saluted and then asked, "What were you doing?" We replied, "We were listening to the Book of God." He said, "Praise be to God, who has appointed amongst my followers a people with whom I am commanded to make my soul patient."' Abú Sa'íd said, 'Then he sat in our midst in order to make himself our equal. After that he beckoned with his hand, (Sit) thus! Then they sat in a circle, and their faces were visible to him. Then he said, "Rejoice, O poor and needy emigrants, for the perfect light on the day of resurrection. You will enter paradise before the rich men by half a day, which is equal to five hundred years."'—*Abú Dáud.*

It is related from Hudhaifah that, 'The Apostle of God said, "Recite the Qur'án in the dialect and tone of the Arabs, and beware of the tones of lovers and the tones of the people of the two Books; for there will come after me a people who will repeat the Qur'án in the tones of singing and wailing. It will not go further than their throats. Their hearts and the hearts of those whose dignity excites their admiration will be involved in faction."'—*Al Baihaqi.*

It is related from Ṭáus that he said, 'The Prophet was asked, "What man has the best voice for the Qur'án, and is the best in reciting it?" He replied, "He who, when thou hearest him recite, appears to fear God."' Ṭáus said, 'Ṭalq was such an one.'—*Al Dárimi.*

On the Various Readings of the Qur'án

It is related from 'Omar binu'l-Khaṭṭáb that he said, 'I heard Hishám bin Ḥakím bin Ḥizám recite Súratu'l-Furqán in a different way from which I recited it, and from which the Apostle of God taught me to recite it. And I wished to hasten upon him, but I gave him respite until he had completed the recital. After that I bound him with his cloak and took him to the Apostle of God and said, "O Apostle of God, verily I heard this man recite Súratu'l-Furqán in a different manner from that in which thou taughtest me to recite it." The Apostle of God replied, "Let him go." (Then he said to him) "Recite." Then he recited in the way in which I had heard him recite. Then the Apostle of God said, "Thus it was sent down." After that he said to me, "Do thou recite." Then I recited. And he said, "Thus it was sent down. Verily this Qur'án was sent down in seven readings. Recite in whichever of them is easy for you."'—*Muslim, Al Bukhárí.*

It is related from Ibn Mas'úd that he said, 'I heard a man reciting the Qur'án, and I heard the Prophet reciting differently from it. Then I brought him to the Prophet and informed him. And I perceived in his face signs of displeasure. Then he said, "Both of you are right, therefore do not contradict each other; for verily those who were before you differed and were destroyed."'—*Al Bukhárí.*

It is related from Ubai bin Ka'b that he said, 'I was in a mosque, and there entered a man to pray. And he recited in a reading of which I disapproved. After that there entered another man, and he recited in a reading different from that of his companion. And when we had finished the prayers we all went in together to the Apostle of God, and I said, "Verily this man recited in a reading of which I disapproved; and this other came in and recited in a reading different from that of his companion." Then the Prophet commanded them both, and they recited. And he commended the reading of both of them. Then there entered my mind a desire to accuse of falsehood such as had not existed when I was in ignorance (of Islám). Then, when the Apostle of God saw what had come to me, he struck me on my breast, at which I broke out into perspiration, as if I were looking at God from fear. Then he said to me, "O Ubai, (orders) were sent to me that I should recite the Qur'án in one reading. Then I took the matter to God that it might be made easy for my followers. Then (orders) were sent back to me a second time, 'Recite it in two readings.' Then I took the matter back to God that it might be made easy for my followers, and (orders) were sent back to me a third time, 'Recite it in seven readings. For thee (O Muḥammad) is every reply which I have sent thee at the request thou didst make.' Then I said, 'O God, forgive my people; O God, forgive my people.' And I delayed a third request for the day when the whole world, even to Abraham, would long for me"'—*Muslim.*

It is related from Ibn 'Abbás that, 'The Apostle of God said, "Gabriel taught me to recite in one reading, but I referred the matter back to him and continued asking him to increase it, and he continued to increase it for me until it ended up in seven readings." Ibn Shiháb said, "I was informed that those seven readings were one in substance. They did not differ in the matter of lawful and unlawful."'—*Muslim*, *Al Bukhárí.*

It is related from Ubai bin Ka'b that he said, 'The Apostle of God met Gabriel and said, "O Gabriel, verily I have been sent to a people who are ignorant. Amongst them are old women and old men, and boys and girls, and men who have never read a book." He replied, "O Muḥammad, verily the Qur'án has been sent down in seven readings."'—*At Tirmidhí.*

It is related from 'Ibn Abbás that he said, 'The Apostle of God did not know the divisions of the chapters (of the Qur'án) until there descended upon him the words "In the name of God, the Merciful, the Compassionate."'—*Abú Dáud.*

It is related from Alqamah that he said, 'We were in Homs, and Ibn Mas'úd recited the chapter entitled "Joseph." And a certain man said, "It was not sent down in this manner." Then 'Abdu'lláh said, "By God! I certainly recited it in the time of the Apostle of God, and he said, 'Thou hast recited well.'" And whilst the man was speaking to Ibn Mas'úd, behold the latter discerned the smell of wine upon him, and he said, "Dost thou drink wine, and falsify the Book!" Then he beat him to the utmost limits of the law.'—*Muslim, Al Bukhárí.*

It is related from Zaid bin Thábit that he said, 'Abú Bakr sent to me at the time of the battle of the people of Yamámah, and behold 'Omar binu'l-Khaṭṭáb was with him. Abú Bakr said, "Verily 'Omar came to me and said, 'Verily the slaughter amongst the reciters of the Qur'án was very severe on the day (of the battle) of Yamámah, and I fear that if the slaughter of reciters in the (surrounding) countries be severe, much will go from the Qur'án. I am therefore of opinion that thou shouldst order the collection of the Qur'án.' I said to 'Omar, 'How canst thou do a thing which the Apostle of God did not do?' 'Omar said, 'By God! this is good.' And 'Omar continued repeating it to me until God opened my mind to (understand) that, and I became of the same opinion about it as 'Omar."' Zaid said, 'Abú Bakr said to me, "Verily thou art a young man and wise, and we do not suspect thee, and thou wert in the habit of writing down the revelations for the Apostle of God. Therefore do thou search out the Qur'án and collect it together." Then by God! if they had imposed upon me the task of removing one of the mountains, it would not have been more difficult for me than what he ordered me regarding the collection of the Qur'án. I said, "How canst thou do a thing which the Apostle of God never did?" He replied, "By God! it is good." And Abú Bakr continued repeating it to me until God opened my mind to understand that which he had opened Abú Bakr's and 'Omar's minds to understand. Then I sought out the Qur'án and collected it together from leaves of dates and white stones and the breasts of men until I found the last part of Súratu't-Tauba with Abú Khazaimahu'l-Anṣári. I found it with none else beside him. (It was this) "There hath come to you an Apostle from amongst yourselves," up to the end of the chapter. And the written pages remained with Abú Bakr until God caused him to die, after that (they remained) with 'Omar during his lifetime. Then (they remained) with Ḥafṣa the daughter of 'Omar.'—*Al Bukhárí.*

It is related from Anas bin Málik that, 'Ḥudhaifa binu'l-Yamán came to 'Othmán; and he had been fighting with the people of Syria in the conquest of Armenia and Adharbíján with the people of 'Iráq. And their differences in reciting (the Qur'án) had made Ḥudhaifa afraid, and he said to 'Othmán, "O Commander of the faithful, assist this people before they differ in the Book, as do the Jews and Christians." Then 'Othmán sent to Ḥafṣa saying, "Send to us the written pages. We will copy them into a number of copies, and then return them to thee." Then Ḥafṣa sent them to 'Othmán, and he commanded Zaid bin Thábit and Abdu'lláh binu'l-Zubair and Sa'íd binu'l-'Áṣ and Abdu'lláh binu'l-Ḥárith bin Ḥishám, and they copied them into a number of copies. And 'Othmán said to the three who were of the tribe of the Quraish, "When you three and Zaid bin Thábit differ in anything from the Qur'án, then write it in the tongue of the Quraish, for it only came down in their tongue." Then they did so until, when they had copied the written pages into a number of copies, 'Othmán returned the pages to Ḥafṣa. And he sent into all regions with a copy of that which they had copied. And he gave orders with respect to all other written pages or complete copies of the Qur'án that they should be burnt. Ibn Shiháb said, "Khárijah bin Zaid bin Thábit informed me that he heard Zaid bin Thábit say, 'I lost a verse from (the chapter entitled) Al Aḥzáb when we copied the Book, and which I used to hear the Apostle of God recite. Then we sought for it and found it with Khuzaimah bin Thábitu'l-Anṣári, namely, "Of the believers there are men who remain true to the covenant which they make with God.[1]" Then we placed it in its chapter in the Book.' " '—*Al Bukhári.*

It is related from Ibn 'Abbás that he said, 'I said to 'Othmán, "What incited thee to give thine attention to Súratu'l-Anfál—and it was one of the twice-sent—and to Súratu'l-Barát, and to join them together? And thou didst not write the words 'In the name of God the Merciful, the Compassionate' (between them). And thou didst place them amongst the seven long chapters. What incited thee to that?" 'Othmán replied, "A time used to come to the Apostle of God when many

---

[1] Súratu'l-Aḥzáb (xxxiii) 23.

chapters descended upon him: and when anything used to descend upon him, he would call some of those who used to write (his revelations) and would say, 'Place these verses in the chapter in which such-and-such things are mentioned.' And when the verses descended upon him, he used to say, 'Place these verses in the chapter in which such-and-such things are mentioned.' And Súratu'l-Anfál was amongst the first chapters which were sent down at Madína, and Súratu'l-Barát was one of the last of the Qur'án to come down. And the subject-matter of the one was the same as the subject-matter of the other. And the Apostle of God was taken, and he never pointed out to us whether the one was a part of the other. And for that reason I joined them together, but did not write the words, 'In the name of God the Merciful, the Compassionate.' And I placed it amongst the seven long chapters."'
—*At-Tirmidhí, Aḥmad, Abú Dáud.*

IX

THE BOOK OF SUPPLICATIONS

It is related from Abú Hurairah that, 'The Apostle of God said, "There is a supplication which is accepted from every prophet. And every prophet hastened to offer his supplication; but I have concealed my supplication, namely intercession for my people, until the day of resurrection; and it will be available, if God will, for whoever of my people dies without associating anything with God."'—*Muslim, Al Bukhárí.*

It is related from Abú Hurairah that, 'The Apostle of God said, "O God, verily I have received a covenant from Thee which Thou wilt never break. But I am only a man, therefore whomsoever of the believers I injure, or revile, or curse, or scourge, do Thou make these for him prayers and alms and a means by which Thou mayest bring him near to Thyself on the day of resurrection."'—*Muslim, Al Bukhárí.*

It is related from Abú Hurairah that, 'The Apostle of God said, "When anyone of you prays, then let him not say, 'O God, forgive me, if Thou wilt; have mercy on me, if Thou wilt;' but let him pray with firm purpose. For He will do what He wishes; there is none who can compel him."'—*Al Bukhárí.*

It is related from Nu'mán bin Bashír that, 'The Apostle of God said, "Supplication is worship." Then he recited (the words) "Your Lord said, 'Call upon me, and I will answer you'"'—*Aḥmad, At Tirmidhí, Abú Dáud, Ibn Majáh, An Nasái.*

It is related from Ibn Mas'úd that, 'The Apostle of God said, "Pray to God for his favours, for verily God loves to be supplicated. And the best part of worship is waiting for relief."'—*At Tirmidhí.*

It is related from Abú Hurairah that, 'The Apostle of God said, "He who would be pleased by God's answering his prayer in times of distress, let him multiply his prayers in times of abundance."'—*At Tirmidhí.*

It is related from Abú Hurairah that, 'The Apostle of God said, "Pray to God when you are certain that it will be answered; for know ye that God will not answer the prayer of a proud and negligent heart." '—*At Tirmidhí.*

It is related from 'Omar binu'l-Khaṭṭáb that he said, 'I asked permission of the Prophet to make the lesser pilgrimage, and he gave me permission.' And he said, "O dear brother, make us partners in thy supplications, and do not forget us." He said a thing than which the whole world in exchange would not have pleased me more.'—*Abú Dáud, At Tirmidhí.*

It is related from Anas that, 'The Apostle of God said, "Let each one of you supplicate his Lord for all his needs, even to asking him for his bootlaces when they are broken." ' And in a tradition from Thábitu'l-Bunáni it is added, 'Even to asking Him for salt, and to asking Him for his boot-lace when it is broken.'—*At Tirmidhí.*

On Remembering God, and Approaching Near to Him

It is related from Abú Hurairah and Abú Sa'íd that, 'The Apostle of God said, "No people sit remembering God, but the angels encompass them about, and mercy covers them over, and there comes down upon them the *Sakinah*, and God remembers them amongst those who are near Him." '—*Muslim.*

It is related from Abú Músá that, 'The Apostle of God said, "The likeness of him who remembers his Lord, and of him who remembers Him not, is as the living and the dead." '—*Muslim, Al Bukhárí.*

It is related from Abú Dharr that, 'The Apostle of God said, "God most High says, 'He who comes with one good action will get ten (rewards) like unto it and more. And he who comes with one evil action, its punishment is one evil equal thereto, or I will forgive him. And he who approaches near to me one span, I will approach near to him one cubit; and he who approaches near to me one cubit, I will approach near to him one fathom; and whoever approaches me walking, I will come to him running; and he who meets me with sins equivalent to the whole world, but does not associate anything with me, I will greet him with forgiveness equal to it.' " '—*Muslim.*

It is related from Abú Hurairah that, 'The Apostle of God said, "Verily God has certain angels who go round the roads seeking people who remember Him; and when they find a peo-

ple who remember God, they cry out, 'Come ye to what ye seek.'" He said, "Then they surround them on all sides with their wings, even to the skies of the world. Then their Lord asks them—and He knows better than they—'What say My servants?' They reply, 'They adore Thee and magnify Thee and praise Thee and glorify Thee.' Then He says, 'Have they seen Me?' They reply, 'No, by God! they have not seen Thee.' He says, 'How would it be if they had seen me?' They reply, 'If they had seen Thee, they would have worshipped Thee still more earnestly and glorified Thee still more earnestly and praised Thee still more.' He says, 'And what do they ask?' They say, 'They ask of Thee paradise.' He says, 'And have they seen it?' They say, 'No, by God! O Lord, they have not seen it.' He says, 'How would it be if they had seen it?' They say, 'If they had seen it, they would have longed still more for it, and would have searched still more for it, and would have desired it still more.' He says, 'From what do they seek protection?' They say, 'From the fire.' He says, 'Have they seen it?' They say, 'No by God! O Lord, they have not seen it.' He says, 'Then how would it be if they had seen it?' They say, 'If they had seen it, they would have fled from it still more, and would have feared it still more.' He says, 'I call you to witness that verily I have forgiven them.' Then one of the angels says, 'Such an one amongst them is not (really) of them. He only came of necessity.' He says, 'They are sitting (with those who remember me). Their sitting will not render them unhappy.'"'
—*Al Bukhári.*

It is related from Ḥanzalah bínu'l-Rubai'ul-Usaidi that he said, 'Abú Bakr met me and said, "How art thou, O Hanzalah?" I said, "Hanzalah has become a hypocrite." He replied, "Praise be to God! What sayest thou?" I said, "We stay with the Apostle of God when he reminds us of the fire and paradise, and it seems as if we see them with our eyes; but when we go out from the Apostle of God we become busy with our wives and children and cultivated lands, and we forget much." Abú Bakr said, "By God! verily we meet (difficulties) like this." Then Abú Bakr and I departed until we entered in to the Apostle of God. And I said, "O Apostle of God,

Ḥanzalah has become a hypocrite." Then the Apostle of God said, "What is that?" I said, "O Apostle of God, we stay with thee when thou dost remind us of the fire and paradise, and it seems as if we see them with our eyes. But when we go out from thee, we become busy with our wives and children and cultivated lands, and forget much." The Apostle of God said, "By Him in whose hand is my life! if you had continued in that state in which you were with me, and in remembrance of me, verily the angels would have taken you by the hand on your beds and in your journeys; but O Ḥanzalah, give an hour (to religion) and an hour (to worldly duties)." This he said three times.'—*Muslim.*

It is related from Thawbán that he said, 'When the verse descended, "To those who treasure up gold and silver," we were with the Prophet in some of his journeys. And some of his companions said, "The revelation came down concerning gold and silver. If we had known what property was better, we would have taken it." He replied, "Better than these is a remembering tongue and a grateful heart, and a believing wife who helps him in his faith."'—*Aḥmad, At Tirmidhí, Ibn Májah.*

X

THE BOOK OF THE NAMES OF GOD

It is related from Abú Hurairah that, 'The Apostle of God said, "Verily God Most High has ninety-nine names. Whoever counts them will enter paradise. He is Alláh, than whom there is no other God, the Merciful, the Compassionate, the King, the Holy, the Peace, the Faithful, the Protector, the Mighty, the Compeller, the Proud, the Creator, the Maker, the Fashioner, the Forgiver, the Dominant, the Bestower, the Provider, the Opener, the Knower, the Restrainer, the Speaker, the Abaser, the Exalter, the Honourer, the Destroyer, the Hearer, the Seer, the Ruler, the Just, the Subtle, the Aware, the Clement, the Grand, the Forgiving, the Grateful, the Exalted, The Great, the Guardian, the Strengthener, the Reckoner, the Majestic, the Generous, the Watcher, the Approver, the Comprehensive, the Wise, the Loving, the Glorious, the Raiser, the Witness, the Truth, the Advocate, the Strong, the Firm, the Patron, the Laudable, the Counter, the Beginner, the Restorer, the Quickener, the Killer, the Living, the Subsisting, the Finder, the Glorious, the One, the Eternal, the Powerful, the Prevailing, the Bringer-forward, the Deferrer, the First, the Last, the Evident, the Hidden, the Governor, the Exalted, the Righteous, the Accepter of Repentance, the Avenger, the Pardoner, the Kind, the Ruler of the Kingdom, the Lord of majesty and liberality, the Equitable, the Collector, the Independent, the Enricher, the Giver, the Withholder, the Distresser, the Profiter, the Light, the Guide, the Incomparable, the Enduring, the Inheritor, the Director, the Patient." '—*At Tirmidhí.*

It is related from Asmá' bint Yazíd that, 'The Prophet said, "The greatest name of God is in these two verses, 'Your God is one God; there is no God but He, the Merciful, the Compassionate,' and the opening verse of Súratu Áli 'Imrán, 'Alláh, there is no God but He. He is the Living, the Self-subsisting.'" '—*At Tirmidhí, Abú Dáud, Ibn Májah.*

It is related from Sa'd that, 'The Apostle of God said, "The supplication of the man of the fish (Jonah) when he called upon his Lord, when he was still in the belly of the fish, was this, 'There is no God but Thee. Praise be to Thee. Verily I was of the unjust.' No man, being a Muslim, prays this prayer in regard to anything, but it is granted to him."'—*Aḥmad, At Tirmidhí.*

On the Rewards of Magnifying and Praising God

It is related from Samurah bin Jundub that, 'The Apostle of God said, "The best words are four: 'Glory be to God,' 'Praise be to God,' 'There is no God but Alláh,' and 'God is Great.'" And in another tradition it runs, "The words most loved of God are four: 'Glory be to God,' 'Praise be to God,' 'There is no God but Alláh,' and 'God is great.' It will bring you no injury if you begin with any one of them."'—*Muslim.*

It is related from Abú Hurairah that, 'The Apostle of God said, "Whoever says, 'Glory be to God,' and, 'In His praise,' one hundred times in a day, his sins will be put away from him though they be as the foam of the sea."'—*Muslim, Al Bukhárí.*

It is related from Abú Hurairah that, 'The Apostle of God said, "Whoever says, 'There is no God but Alláh alone. He has no partner. For Him is the Kingdom and for Him the praise; and He is powerful over all,' one hundred times in a day, there will be for him a reward equal to the freeing of ten slaves; and one hundred good actions will be written for him, and one hundred evil actions will be erased for him; and they will be a protection for him against Satan on that day until the evening. And no one will come with anything better than what he brings except the man who has done more than he."'—*Muslim, Al Bukhárí.*

It is related from Abú Músáu'l-Ash'ari that he said, 'We were with the Apostle of God on a journey, and the men began to repeat the words, "God is great" in a loud voice. And the Apostle of God said, "O men, be easy on yourselves. Verily ye are not calling upon One who is deaf or absent. Ye are calling upon One who hears and sees; and He is with you. And He whom ye call upon is nearer to one of you than the neck of his camel," Abú Músá said, "When I was behind him,

I was saying to myself, 'There is no power and no strength, except in God,' and he said, 'O 'Abdu'lláh bin Qais, shall I not point thee to one of the treasures of paradise?' I said, 'Yes, O Apostle of God.' He said, 'It is (the phrase), There is no power and no strength, except in God.'"'—*Muslim, Al Bukhári.*

It is related from Abú Sa'ídu'l-Khudri that, 'The Apostle of God said, "Moses said, 'O my Lord, teach me something by which I can remember Thee and call upon Thee.' God replied, 'O Moses, say, "There is no God but Alláh."' He replied, 'O my Lord, all Thy servants say this. I only wish for something by which Thou wilt specialize me.' He said, 'O Moses, verily if the seven heavens and their inhabitants—omitting me—and the seven earths were placed in one scale, and the words, "There is no God but Alláh" in the other scale, that in which the words, "There is no God but Alláh" are placed would go down.'"'—In *Sharḥu's-Sunnah.*

It is related from Ibn Mas'úd that, 'The Apostle of God said, "I met Abraham on the night on which I made the journey to heaven, and he said, 'O Muḥammad, give my salutation to thy followers, and inform them that paradise has good earth and sweet water, and it is level, and its vegetation is, Glory be to God, Praise be to God, and There is no God but Alláh, and God is great.'"'—*At Tirmidhí.*

On Asking Pardon and Repentance

It is related from Abú Hurairah that, 'The Apostle of God said, "By God! I certainly ask pardon of God and repent towards Him more than seventy times a day."'—*Al Bukhárí.*

It is related from Agharu'l-Muzanni that, 'The Apostle of God said, "O men, repent towards God; for verily I repent towards Him one hundred times in a day."'—*Muslim.*

It is related from Abú Hurairah that, 'The Apostle of God said, "Verily a servant (of God) committed a sin and said, 'My Lord, I have sinned, therefore forgive me.' His Lord said, 'Doth My servant know that he has a Lord who forgives sins and punishes on account of them. I have forgiven My servant.' Then he remained as long as God wished, and then he committed a sin and said, 'My Lord, I have committed a sin, therefore forgive me.' He said, 'Doth My servant know that he has a Lord who forgives sins, and punishes on account of them. I have forgiven My servant.' Then he remained as long as God wished, and afterwards he committed a sin and said, 'My Lord, I have committed another sin, therefore forgive it for me.' He said, 'Doth My servant know that he has a Lord who forgives a sin and punishes on account of it. I have forgiven My servant. Therefore let him do what he likes.'" '—*Muslim, Al Bukhárí.*

It is related from Abú Bakru'ṣ-Ṣiddíq that, 'The Apostle of God said, "That person who asks pardon, does not remain immersed in sin, although he returns to it seventy times a day."'—*At Tirmidhí, Abú Dáud.*

It is related from Ṣafwán bin 'Assál that, 'The Apostle of God said, "Verily God Most High has placed in the West a door for repentance whose width is seventy years journey. It will not be shut so long as the sun does not rise before it (i.e. in the West). And that is the word of God Most High in the day when certain signs of thy Lord shall appear, 'The faith of no soul shall benefit it, which has not believed before that.'"'—*At Tirmidhí, Ibn Májah.*

It is related from Abú Hurairah that, 'The Apostle of God said, "Verily there were two men of the Children of Israel who were friends together. One of them was intent on worship, but the other used to proclaim himself a sinner. And the first began to say, 'Give up that in which thou art (entangled).' His companion said, 'Leave me and my Lord,' until one day he found him engaged in grievous sin. Then he said, 'Forsake it.' He replied, 'Leave me and my Lord. Hast thou been sent as a guardian over me!' He said, 'By God! God will never forgive thee, nor enter thee into paradise.' Then God sent an angel to them both, who took both their souls, and they were brought together near to God. He said to the sinner, 'Enter paradise by My mercy.' And He said to the other, 'Art thou able to forbid My servant My mercy?' He replied, 'No, O God.' He said (to the angels) 'Take him away to the fire.'"' —*Aḥmad.*

It is related from Abú Hurairah that, 'The Apostle of God said, "Verily God, the Exalted and Magnified, most certainly raises the rank of the good servant in paradise. And the latter will say, 'O Lord, why is this (dignity) for me?' He will reply, 'On account of the prayers of thy son for thee for My forgiveness.'"'—*Aḥmad.*

It is related from 'Abdu'lláh bin 'Abbás that, 'The Apostle of God said, "There is no dead person in the grave, but he is like one immersed in water and crying for help. He expects the prayer of his father or mother or brother or friend may reach him; and when it reaches him, it is more pleasant to him than the world and all that is therein. And verily God Most High certainly causes to enter the tombs, on account of the prayers of the people of the earth, (rewards) like mountains. Verily the gifts of the living to the dead are asking forgiveness for them."'—*Al Baihaqi.*

It is related from 'Áyesha that, 'Verily the Prophet used to say, "O God, make me one of those who, when they do good, rejoice; and when they do evil, pray for forgiveness."'—*Ibn Májah.*

It is related from Al Ḥárith bin Suaid that he said, ''Abdu'lláh bin Mas'úd related to us two traditions; one of them from the Apostle of God, and the other from himself. He said, "Verily a believer sees his sins as if he were sitting beneath a mountain, and fearing that it would fall upon him. And the sinner sees his sins as if they were a fly that had passed over his nose; and he says concerning it, 'Thus!' that is, he drives it away from him with his hand." After that (Ibn Mas'úd) said, 'I heard the Apostle of God say, "God rejoices at the repentance of one of His believing servants more than a man who alights on the ground in a destructive desert, with whom is his camel laden with his food and water. And he lays down his head and sleeps for a while, and then awakes to find that his camel has gone. Then he searches for it, until when the heat and thirst oppress him—or whatever else God wills—he says, 'I will return to the place where I was, and there I will sleep until I die.' Then he places his head upon his forearm in order that he may die. And he awakes, and lo! his camel stands beside him, and on it his food and drink. Verily God rejoices more at the repentance of a believing servant, than this man at the return of his camel and food."'—*Muslim.*

It is related from Abú Dharr that, 'The Apostle of God said, "Verily God Most High will certainly forgive His servant, so long as a veil does not intervene." They said, "O Apostle of God, what is the veil?" He replied, "That a soul expires whilst associating something with God."'—*Aḥmad.*

On the Abundance of God's Mercy

It is related from Abú Hurairah that, 'The Apostle of God said, "When God completed the work of creation, He wrote a book which is with Him above His throne; 'Verily my mercy outruns my anger.' And in another tradition it runs 'overcomes my anger.'"'—*Muslim, Al Bukhárí.*

It is related from 'Omar binu'l-Khaṭṭáb that he said, 'Some captives appeared before the Prophet. And, lo! a woman of the captives, whose breasts were flowing with milk, when she found her child amongst the captives, took it and clasped it to her breast and suckled it. Then the Prophet said to us, "Do you think that this woman would throw her child into the fire?" We replied, "No, not if she be able to do otherwise." He said, "God is more merciful towards His servants than this woman towards her child."'—*Muslim, Al Bukhárí.*

It is related from Jábir that, 'The Apostle of God said, "The actions of none of you will take him into paradise, or protect him from the fire. Not even I, except by the mercy of God."'—*Muslim.*

It is related from Abú Dardái that, 'He heard the Prophet repeat from the pulpit, when he was speaking, these words; "For him who fears the standing before his Lord are two paradises." I said, "O Apostle of God, although he commit adultery and steal?" He replied a second time, "For him who fears the standing before his Lord are two paradises." I said a second time, "O Apostle of God, although he commit adultery and steal?" He replied a third time, "For him who fears the standing before his Lord are two paradises." I said a third time, "O Apostle of God, although he commit adultery and steal?" He replied, "Even though Abú Dardái's nose be humiliated thereby."'—*Aḥmad.*

It is related from 'Ámiru'r-Rám that he said, 'When we were with the Prophet, behold a man drew near to him, dressed in an upper garment, and on his head was something which he had wrapped up (in a cloth). And he said, "O Apostle of God,

I passed by a thicket of trees, and I heard therein the sound of young birds. Then I took them and placed them in my upper garment, and their mother came and circled round my head. Then I uncovered them for her, and she descended upon them. Then I again wrapped them up in my garment, and they are these with me." The Prophet replied, "Put them down." Then I put them down, but their mother refused to leave them. Then the Apostle of God said, "Art thou surprised at the kindness of the mother of the young birds towards them? By Him who sent me with the truth! God is more merciful to His servants, than the mother of the young birds to her young. Return with them until thou replace them whence thou didst take them, and their mother with them." Then he returned with them.'—*Abû Dâud.*

It is related from 'Abdu'lláh bin 'Omar that he said, 'We were with the Prophet in certain warlike expeditions when he passed a band of people, and asked "Who are these people?" They said, "We are Muslims." And a woman was lighting a fire under her pot, and her son was with her. And when the heat of the fire rose up, she moved him away from it. Then she came to the Prophet and said, "Art thou the Apostle of God?" He replied, "Yes." She said, "May my father and my mother be sacrified for thee! Is not God the most merciful of the merciful?" He replied, "Certainly." She said, "Is not God more merciful towards His servants than a mother towards her child?" He replied, "Certainly." She said, "Verily a mother would not cast her child into the fire!" Then the Apostle of God bowed his face to the ground weeping; afterwards he raised his head towards her and said, "Verily God does not punish any of His servants, except the rebellious one who rebels against him, and refuses to say, 'There is no God but Allah.'"'—*Ibn Mâjah.*

On What should be Said in the Morning, the Evening, and the Time of Sleep

It is related from 'Abdu'lláh that he said, 'When the evening came the Apostle of God used to say, "We have reached the evening, and God's kingdom has reached the evening. Praise be to God! There is no God but Alláh alone.

He has no partner. His is the kingdom, and His is the praise, and He is powerful over all. O God, I ask of Thee the good of this night, and the good that is in it; and I take refuge with Thee from its evil, and the evil that is in it. O God, verily I take refuge with Thee from negligence and from the weakness of old age and from the evils of old age, and from the calamities of the world, and the punishments of the grave." And when the morning dawned he used to repeat that again (saying), "We have reached the morning, and God's kingdom has reached the morning." And in another tradition it runs, "My Lord, verily I take refuge with Thee from the punishment of the fire and the punishment of the grave."'—*Muslim.*

It is related from Ḥudhaifa that he said, 'When the Prophet lay down at night he used to place his hand under his cheek. Then he would say, "O God, in Thy name I die and live." And when he awoke he would say, "Praise be to God who gives us life after that He caused us to die; and to Him is the resurrection."'—*Muslim, Al Bukhárí.*

It is related from Abú Hurairah that, 'The Apostle of God said, "When anyone of you retires for rest to his bed, then let him dust his bed with the inner side of his drawers; for he does not know what may have fallen upon it. After that let him say, 'In Thy name, O my Lord, I have laid down on my side, and in Thy name I will raise it up. If Thou takest my soul, then have mercy upon it; and if thou send it back (after sleep), then guard it with that by which Thou guardest Thy victorious servants.'" And in another tradition it runs, "Then let him lie down on his right side, and after that let him say, 'In Thy Name.'" And in another tradition it runs, "Then let him dust it with the border of his garment three times," and "If Thou takest my soul, then forgive it."'—*Muslim, Al Bukhárí.*

It is related from Abú Hurairah that, 'Abú Bakr said, "I said, O Apostle of God, command me something which I can say when I reach the morning and when I reach the evening." He replied, "Say, 'O God, the Knower of the hidden and the revealed, the Creator of the heavens and the earth, Lord of all things and Master thereof, I bear witness that there is no God but Thee; and I take refuge with Thee from the evil of my own soul, and from the evil of Satan and his associating partners (with Thee).' Say this when thou reachest the morning, and when thou reachest the evening, and when thou takest to thy bed."'—*At Tirmidhí, Abú Dáud, Al Dárimi.*

It is related from Abú 'Ayyásh that verily, 'The Apostle of God said, "He who says, when morning dawns, 'There is no God but Alláh alone. He has no partner. For Him is the kingdom, and for Him is the praise; and He is powerful over all,' will receive a reward equal to that for emancipating a slave of the sons of Ishmael. And ten good deeds will be written down for him, and ten evil deeds will be taken away from him; and ten degrees of eminence will be accredited to him, and he will be protected from Satan until the evening comes. And if he repeats these words when the evening comes, he will receive the same (rewards) until the morning." Then a certain man saw the Apostle of God in his sleep, when he was dreaming, and he said, "O Apostle of God, verily Abú 'Ayyásh relates concerning thee in such-and-such a way." He replied, "Abú 'Ayyásh has told the truth." '—*Abú Dáud, Ibn Májah.*

It is related from Thawbán that, 'The Apostle of God said, "There is no Muslim servant who says three times, when evening comes and morning comes, 'I am satisfied with Alláh as Lord, and with Islám as a religion, and with Muḥammad as a Prophet,' but it becomes incumbent on God to be satisfied with him on the day of resurrection."'—*Aḥmad, At Tirmidhí.*

It is related from Abú Sa'íd that, 'The Apostle of God said, "Whoever says, when he seeks rest upon his bed, 'I ask pardon of God, beside whom there is no God, the Living, the Self-subsisting; and I repent towards Him three times,' God will forgive him his sins, though they be as the foam of the sea, or in number like the sands of the desert, or in number like the leaves of the trees, or in number equal to the days of the world."'—*At Tirmidhí.*

It is related from Shaddád bin Aus that, 'The Apostle of God said, "There is no Muslim who goes to bed reciting a chapter from the Book of God, but God appoints an angel over him as guard, so that nothing approaches him to hurt him until he awakes, whenever that may be."'—*At Tirmidhí.*

Concerning Prayer on Special Occasions

It is related from Sulaimán bin Ṣurad that he said, 'Two men were abusing each other near the Prophet, and we were sitting near him. And one of the two was reviling his companion in anger, until his face became red. Then the Prophet said, "Verily I know a word which, had he spoken it, that (anger) which he has would have gone from him, namely, 'I take refuge with God from the accursed Satan.'" Then they said to the man, "Dost thou not hear what the Prophet says?" He replied, "Verily I am not mad."'—*Muslim, Al Bukhárí.*

It is related from Abú Hurairah that, 'The Apostle of God said, "When you hear the crow of a cock, then supplicate God for a portion of His grace; for verily it has seen an angel. And when you hear the bray of an ass, then take refuge with God from the accursed Satan; for verily it has seen Satan."' —*Muslim, Al Bukhárí.*

It is related from Ibn 'Omar that, 'When the Apostle of God used to mount his camel in order to set out on a journey, he would say, "God is great" three times, and then say, "Praise be to Him who has made this (animal) to work for us; for we were not able to do it; and verily to our Lord do we return. O God we ask of Thee in this journey of ours virtue and abstinence and actions with which Thou wilt be pleased. O God, make this journey easy for us, and shorten for us its length. O God, Thou art the Companion on a journey, and the substitute in our families. O God, I take refuge with Thee from the difficulties of the journey, and from evil sights, and from an inauspicious return to my property and my family." And when he returned, he would repeat these words, and add to them (the words), "We return, we repent, we worship, we praise our Lord."'—*Muslim.*

It is related from Abú Hurairah that, 'A man came to the Apostle of God and said, "O Apostle of God, how much I have suffered from a scorpion which bit me yesterday!" He replied, "If thou hadst said, when thou reachedst the evening, 'I take refuge in the perfect word of God from the evil of what He has created,' it would not have injured thee."'—*Muslim.*

It is related from 'Abd'ulláh bin abi Awfi that he said, 'The Apostle of God invoked a curse against the polytheists on the day (of the battle) of Ahzáb, and said, "O God, the Sender-down of the Book, the Quick in taking account, O God, put to rout the confederates. O God, put them to rout, and cause them to tremble."'—*Muslim, Al Bukhárí.*

It is related from Mu'ádh bin Jabal that he said, 'The Prophet heard a man praying and saying, "O God, verily I supplicate of Thee complete favours." (The Prophet) said, "What are complete favours?" He replied, "This is a prayer by which I hope for good." (The Prophet) said, "Verily complete favours give an entrance into Paradise and escape from the fire." And he heard a man saying, "O Lord, to Thee be glory and honour." Then he said to him, "Thy prayer has been answered for thee; therefore ask." And the Prophet heard a man saying, "O God, verily I ask of Thee patience." The Prophet said, "Thou hast asked God for calamity; but ask Him for health."'—*At Tirmidhí.*

It is related from 'Abdu'lláhu'l-Khaṭmi that he said, 'When the Apostle of God wished to bid farewell to the army, he used to say, "I commit to the care of God your religion and your safety and the results of your actions."'—*Abú Dáud.*

It is related from Ibn 'Omar that, 'When the Apostle of God was on a journey and night drew near, he used to say, "O earth, my Lord and thy Lord is Alláh. I take refuge with God from thy evil, and from the evil that is in thee, and from the evil that is created in thee, and from the evil that moves over thee. And I take refuge with God from lions and black snakes and serpents and scorpions, and from the evil of the inhabitants of the land, and from the father and what he begets."'—*Abú Dáud.*

It is related from Anas that, 'When the Apostle of God went on a warlike expedition, he used to say, "O God, Thou art my support and my help. In Thee I devise stratagems, and in Thee I spring to the assault, and in Thee I fight."'—*At Tirmidhí, Abú Dáud.*

It is related from Abú Máliku'l-Ashári that, 'The Apostle of God said, "When a man enters his house, then let him say, 'O God, I ask Thee for a favourable entrance and a favourable exit. In the name of God we enter, and on God our Lord we lean.' After that let him salute the people of the house."'—*Abú Dáud.*

It is related from Abú Bakr that, 'The Apostle of God said, "The prayer of a person in grief is this, 'O God, for Thy mercy I hope. Do not leave me to myself for a single instant, and make all my condition favourable. There is no God but Thee.'"'—*Abú Dáúd.*

It is related from 'Áyesha that she said, 'When the Apostle of God sat in an assembly or prayed, he used to repeat certain words. So I asked him concerning the words. He replied, "If good words have been spoken, they will be a seal upon them till the day of resurrection; but if bad words have been spoken, they will be an atonement for them. (They are these), 'Glory be to Thee, O God, and praise be to Thee. There is no God but Thee. I ask pardon of Thee, and I repent towards Thee.'"'—*An-Nasáí.*

It is related from Abú Sa'ídu'l-Khudri that he said, 'On the day of (the battle of) the ditch we said, "O Apostle of God, is there anything which we can say, for our hearts are in our throats (from fear)." He replied, "Yes, (say) O God, guard us from our faults, and protect us from our fear." Abú Sa'íd said, 'Then God struck the faces of His enemies with a wind, and put them to rout with the wind.'—*Aḥmad.*

On Seeking Refuge

It is related from 'Áyesha that, 'The Prophet used to say, "O God, I take refuge with Thee from laziness and from the weakness of old age and from debt and from that which causes me to sin. O God, verily I take refuge with Thee from the punishment of the fire and the calamity of the fire, and from the calamity of the grave and the punishment of the grave, and from the evil of the seduction of riches, and from the evil of the affliction of poverty, and from the evil of the sedition of the (false) Messiah, Dajjal. O God, wash my sins in snow-water and hail-water, and purify my heart as a white garment is cleansed from impurity, and place a distance between me and my sins, as thou hast placed a distance between the East and the West."'—*Muslim, Al Bukhárí.*

It is related from 'Áyesha that, 'The Apostle of God used to say, "O God, verily I take refuge with Thee from the evil which I have done, and from the evil which I have not done."'—*Muslim.*

It is related from Ibn 'Abbás that, 'The Apostle of God used to say, "O God, for Thee I have become a Muslim, and in Thee I trust, and upon Thee I lean, and to Thee I return, and by Thee I fight. O God, verily I take refuge in Thy honour—there is no God but Thee—lest Thou lead me astray. Thou art the Living, who dieth not; but the genii and men die."'—*Muslim, Al Bukhári.*

It is related from Abú Hurairah that he said, 'The Apostle of God used to say, "O God, I take refuge with Thee from four things: from knowledge which does not benefit, and from a heart which is not submissive, and from a soul that is not satisfied, and from a supplication which is not heard."'—*Áḥmad, Abú Dáud, Ibn Májah.*

It is related from 'Imrán bin Ḥuṣain that he said, 'The Prophet said to my father, "O Ḥuṣain, how many gods hast thou worshipped to-day?" My father replied, "Six on earth and one in heaven." He said, "Then which of them dost thou count upon (to satisfy) thy desires, and which dost thou fear?" He replied, "He who is in heaven." The Prophet said, "O Ḥuṣain, beware! If thou hadst been a Muslim, I would have taught thee two words, which would have benefitted thee."' 'Imrán said, 'When Ḥuṣain became a Muslim, he said, "O Apostle of God, teach me the two words which thou promised me." He replied, "Say, O God, inspire me with regard to my proper road, and give me protection from the evil of my inner self."'—*At Tirmidhí.*

It is related from Abú Sa'íd that he said, 'I heard the Apostle of God say, "I take refuge with God from infidelity and debt." Then a man said, "O Apostle of God, dost thou make infidelity equal to debt?" He replied, "Yes." And in another tradition it runs, "I take refuge from infidelity and poverty." A man said, "Are these two equal?" He replied, "Yes."'—*An Nasái.*

On Comprehensive Prayer

It is related from Abú Músáu'l-Ash'ari from the Prophet, that he used to pray this prayer, "O God, forgive me my sins and my ignorance and my extravagance in my affairs, and what thou knowest better than I. O God, forgive my (wrong) intentions and my jesting and my unintentional sins and my intentional sins; for all these are with me. O God, forgive me those sins I have committed before, and those I shall commit hereafter, and those I have committed in secret, and those I have committed openly, and those which Thou knowest better than I; for Thou art the Setter-forward and the Holder-back, and Thou art powerful over all things." '—*Muslim, Al Bukhárí.*

It is related from 'Abdu'lláh bin Ma'súd that, 'The Prophet used to say, "O God, verily I ask of Thee guidance and piety and chastity and riches." '—*Muslim.*

It is related from Abú Máliku'l-Ashja'i from his father that he said, 'When a certain man became a Muslim, the Prophet taught him the prayers and then commanded him to offer supplication in these words, "O God, forgive me and have mercy on me and guide me and give me health and my daily food." '—*Muslim.*

It is related from Ibn 'Abbás that he said, 'The Prophet used to pray and say, "My Lord, help me, but do not help (others) against me; and give me the victory, but do not give (others) the victory over me; deceive on my behalf, but do not deceive against me; and guide me, and make the guidance easy for me; and aid me against those who oppress me. My Lord, make me grateful to Thee, and a remembrancer of Thee, and one who fears Thee. Make me obedient to Thee and humble before Thee, and one who returns to Thee with crying. My Lord, accept my repentance, and wash away my sins, and answer my prayers, and strengthen my proofs. Direct my tongue and guide my heart and take out the blackness of my heart." '—*At Tirmidhí, Abú Dáud, Ibn Májah.*

It is related from 'Omar binu'l-Khaṭṭáb that he said, 'When revelations were sent down to the Prophet, a confused sound was heard near his face like the hum of bees. And, on a certain day, revelation was sent down upon him. Then we stayed an hour, and it ceased from him. Then he turned towards the temple at Mecca and raised his hands and said, "O God, increase us, and do not diminish us; honour us, and do not abase us; give to us, and do not disappoint us; give us the precedence, and do not give others the precedence over us; satisfy us, and do Thou be satisfied with us." Then he said, "Ten verses have been sent down upon me. Whoever obeys them will enter paradise." Then he recited, "Now are the believers happy,[1]" to the end of the ten verses.'—*Aḥmad, At Tirmidhí.*

It is related from 'Othmán bin Ḥunaif that he said, 'Verily a blind man came to the Prophet and said, "Pray to God that He would cure me." He replied, "If thou desirest it, I will pray, and if thou desirest, thou mayest have patience, for that is better for thee." He said, "Pray to Him." ('Othmán) said, "Then he ordered him to perform ablutions thoroughly and to pray this prayer, 'O God, I supplicate Thee, and turn to Thee through Thy Prophet Muḥammad, the Prophet of mercy. Verily I turn to Thee: to my Lord that He may satisfy for me these my wants. O God, accept his intercession on my behalf.' "'—*At Tirmidhí.*

It is related from Abú Dardái that, 'The Apostle of God said, "One of the prayers of David was this. He used to say, 'O God, I ask of Thee Thy love and the love of him who loveth Thee, and the action which will secure Thy love for me. O God; make Thy love more precious to me than mine own soul and my property and my family and than cold water.'" Abú Dardái said,' When the Apostle of God mentioned David, he used to speak of him and say, "He was the greatest worshipper amongst men."'—*At Tirmidhí.*

[1] Súratu'l-Mú'minúñ (xxiii) 1-10.

XI

THE BOOK OF THE RITES OF PILGRIMAGE

It is related from Abú Hurairah that he said, 'The Apostle of God addressed us and said, "O men, the pilgrimage hath been made incumbent upon you; then perform it." A man asked, "(Shall we perform it) every year, O Apostle of God?" He remained silent until the man repeated the question three times. Then he replied, "If I had said, 'Yes,' it would certainly have become obligatory, but ye are certainly not able (to perform it every year)." Then he said, "Leave me alone, so long as I leave you alone. Those who were before you were destroyed simply because of their many questions and their contradicting their prophets. Therefore, when I command you anything, perform what you are able of it, and when I forbid you anything, then leave it alone."'—*Muslim.*

It is related from Abú Hurairah that, 'The Apostle of God said, "He who makes a pilgrimage for God, and abstains from sexual intercourse, and does not forsake the path of righteousness, returns like he was on the day when his mother gave him birth."'—*Muslim, Al Bukhárí.*

It is related from Ibn 'Abbás that, 'A woman of (the tribe of) Khash'am said, "O Apostle of God, it is a duty imposed by God on His servants that they perform the pilgrimage. My father is an old man and cannot sit firmly on his camel; then shall I perform the pilgrimage on his behalf?" He replied, "Yes." That occurred during the farewell pilgrimage.'—*Muslim, Al Bukhárí.*

It is related from Ibn 'Abbás that, 'A man came to the Prophet and said, "Verily my sister made a vow to perform the pilgrimage, but she died." The Prophet said, "If she had been in debt, wouldst thou have redeemed it?" He replied, "Yes." He said, "Then redeem the debt of God, for that is the most worthy of redemption."'—*Muslim, Al Bukhárí.*

It is related from 'Áyesha that she said, 'I asked the Prophet's permission to join in the religious wars. He replied, "Thy religious war is pilgrimage."'—*Muslim, Al Bukhárí.*

It is related from 'Alí that, 'The Apostle of God said, "He who possesses food for the journey and a camel to carry him to the House of God (at Mecca), and does not perform the pilgrimage; then if he dies, there is no difference between him and a Jew or a Christian. That is because God Most High says, 'The pilgrimage for God to the House is incumbent upon men who are able to perform the journey.'"'—*At Tirmidhí.*

It is related from Ibn 'Abbás that, 'The Apostle of God heard a man saying, "I am ready to serve Thee on behalf of Shubrumah." He said, "Who is Shubrumah?" He replied, "My brother," or (he said) "Some relation." He said, "Hast thou performed the pilgrimage for thyself?" He replied, "No." He said, "Perform the pilgrimage for thyself, and then perform it for Shubrumah."'—*As Shafi, Abú Dáud, Ibn Májah.*

It is related from Ibn 'Abbás that, 'The people of Yemen were performing the pilgrimage, but had not provided themselves with food for the journey, and they said, "We put our trust (in God)." Then when they reached Mecca, they begged of the people. Then God sent down the revelation, "Provide yourselves with necessary food; and verily the best of food is piety."'—*Al Bukhárí.*

It is related from 'Áyesha that she said, 'I said, "O Apostle of God, is religious war incumbent upon women?" He replied, "Yes, religious war is incumbent upon them in that in which there is no fighting. It is the pilgrimage and the lesser pilgrimage."'—*Ibn Májah.*

It is related from Abú Umámah that, 'The Apostle of God said, "He whom evident needs or a tyrannical king or restraining disease does not prevent from performing the pilgrimage, and yet dies without performing it; let him die, if he wishes, a Jew, or if he wishes, a Christian."'—*Al Dárimi.*

It is related from Abú Hurairah that, 'The Apostle of God said, "Whoever sets out to perform the pilgrimage or the lesser pilgrimage, or to wage religious war, and then dies in the road thereof, God writes for him the reward of a fighter and a pilgrim and a performer of the lesser pilgrimage."'—*Al Baihaqi.*

CONCERNING THE PILGRIM GARB AND CRY

It is related from 'Áyesha that she said, 'I used to perfume the Apostle of God for the pilgrim garb before he put it on, and for putting off the pilgrim garb before he went round the House. There was musk in the perfume. It was as if I saw the light of the musk in the part of the Apostle's hair whilst he was performing the ceremonies of the pilgrimage.' —*Muslim, Al Bukhárí.*

It is related from Ibn 'Omar that he said, 'I heard the Apostle of God profess the unity of God with matted hair and say, "Here I am at Thy service, O God. Here I am at Thy service. Here I am at Thy service. Thou hast no partner. I am at Thy service. Verily praise and power and dominion are for Thee. Thou hast no partner." He did not add to these words.'—*Muslim, Al Bukhárí.*

It is related from Ibn 'Omar that, 'The Prophet matted his hair with a decoction of mallow and myrtle leaves.'—*Abú Dáud.*

It is related from Khallád binu's-Sáib that, 'The Apostle of God said, "Gabriel came to me and ordered me to command my companions to raise their voices in the declaration of the unity and in repeating the words, 'Here I am at Thy service.'"' —*Málik, At Tirmidhí, Abú Dáud, An Nasái.*

It is related from Sahl bin Sa'd that, 'The Apostle of God said, "No Muslim repeats the words, 'Here I am at Thy service,' but whatever is on his right hand and on his left repeats the same, whether it be stones or trees or clods of earth, until the earth is shaken from one end to the other."'—*At Tirmidhí, Ibn Májah.*

It is related from 'Abbás that, 'The polytheists used to say, "Here I am at Thy service. Thou hast no partner." Then the Apostle of God used to say, "Woe to you! Enough! Enough! ('no partner') except the partners which ye own, and which rule you!" They used to say this when they went round the House.'—*Muslim.*

Concerning the Farewell Pilgrimage[1]

It is related from Jábir bin 'Abdu'lláh that, 'The Apostle of God remained at Madína for nine years, and did not make the pilgrimage. Afterwards, in his tenth year, he announced

[1] The last pilgrimage performed by the Prophet, who died a few months later.

amongst the people news of a pilgrimage (saying), "Verily the Apostle of God goeth on pilgrimage." Then many men came to Ma'dína, and we went out with him until we reached Dhu'l-Ḥudaifah. Then Asmá bint 'Umais gave birth to a son, Muḥammad bin Abú Bakr. And she sent to the Apostle of God (saying), "How shall I manage?" He replied, "Bathe, and bind thy loins with a cloth, and put on the pilgrim garb." Then the Apostle of God prayed in the mosque, and afterwards mounted (his camel) Al Qaswá, until, when his camel arrived with him at Baidái, he made the declaration of the unity, saying, "Here I am at Thy service, O God. Here I am at Thy service. Here I am at Thy service. Thou hast no partner. Here I am at Thy service. Verily praise and favour and dominion are for Thee. Thou hast no partner."' Jábir said, 'We had not intended any more than the pilgrimage. We had not known of the lesser pilgrimage, until, when we came to the House (of God at Mecca) with him, he kissed the (black) stone and ran round the house quickly three times, and walked round it four times. Then he approached the place of Abraham and recited, "Then take the place of Abraham as a place of prayer."[1] And he fixed the place between it and the House.' And in another tradition it runs, 'He recited in two *rak'ahs*, "Say, He is one God" and, "Say, O unbelievers." Then he returned to the stone, and kissed it. Then he came out from the door to (Mount) Ṣafá, and when he drew near to (Mount) Ṣafá, he recited, "Verily, Al Ṣafá and Al Marwah are of the signs of God. I begin with what God began." Then he began with Al Ṣafá and ascended it until he saw the House. Then he faced the temple of Mecca and repeated the declaration of the unity and said, "God is great! There is no God but Alláh alone. He has no partner. For Him is the dominion, and for Him is the praise, and He is powerful over all things. There is no God but Alláh alone. He has kept his promise and helped His servant, and alone put to rout the confederate enemy." After that he prayed in the midst of it and said similar words three times. Then he descended and walked to (Mount) Marwah until his feet went down into the bottom of the valley. Then he ran until, when ascending, he walked until he came to Al

[1] Súratu'l-Baqara (ii) 126.

Marwah. Then he did on Al Marwah as he had done on Al Ṣafá, until when he came to the last circumambulation of Marwah he called out whilst still on Marwah and the people beneath him. He said, "If I had known before what I knew afterwards, I would not have brought the sacrifice and would have made it a lesser pilgrimage. And whoever of you has not a sacrifice with him, let him put off the pilgrim garb, and let him consider it as the lesser pilgrimage." Then Suráqah bin Sálik bin Ju'shum stood up and said, "O Apostle of God, is this for this year only or for always?" Then the Apostle of God entwined his fingers in one another and said twice over, "The lesser pilgrimage has entered into the pilgrimage not (for this year only) but for always." Then 'Ali came from Yemen with the Prophet's victims for sacrifice. The Prophet said, "What didst thou say when thou imposed upon thyself the pilgrimage?" He replied, "I said, O God, verily I put on as the pilgrim garb what Thine Apostle put on." He said, "Verily the victims for sacrifice are with me, therefore do not put off thy pilgrim garb."' (Jábir) said, 'All the victims for sacrifice which 'Alí had brought from Yemen, and those which the Prophet had brought numbered one hundred.' He said, 'Then all the people put off their pilgrim garb and shortened their hair, except the Prophet and those with whom were victims for sacrifice. Then when the day of Tarwiyah came they set their faces towards Mina and put off the pilgrim garb. And the Prophet rode to it, and performed the midday, afternoon, evening, night and morning prayers. Then he remained a little until the sun rose, and then he ordered a tent of hair to be pitched for him in Namirah. Then the Apostle of God went on, and the Quraish did not doubt but that he would stop at Al Masha'ru'l-Ḥarám, as the Quraish used to do in the times of ignorance. But the Apostle of God passed on until he came to Arafat. And he found that a tent had been pitched for him in Namirah, so he dismounted and entered it until, when the sun had declined, he ordered his camel, Al Qáswah, and it was brought to him, and he came to the bottom of the valley. Then he addressed the people and said, "Verily your blood and your goods are forbidden you, as this day in this month in this land is forbidden. Are not the commands of the time of ignorance placed under my feet (that is, abrogated)? And the blood of the time of ignorance is so placed. And verily the first of our blood shed was the blood of Nádam bin Rabiya binu'l-Ḥárith. Verily he was brought up amongst the Bani Sa'd, and Hudhail killed him. And the taking of interest in the time of ignorance is abrogated. And the first interest taken amongst us was that taken by 'Abbás bin 'Abdu'l-Muṭṭalib, and it is totally abrogated. And fear God in the matter of your wives, for ye have taken them with the protection of God and have made them inviolate by the Word of God. Their duty towards you is (to see) that no one is brought to your bed whom ye despise; and if they do that, then beat them, though not severely. And your duty to them is to give them sustenance and their clothing with kindness. And verily I have left amongst you that by which ye will never stray after (receiving) it, if ye protect yourselves by it, that is the Word of God. And ye will be asked concerning me (on the judgement day). Then what will ye say?" They replied, "We will bear witness that thou hast brought us news and carried out thy commission and given us instruction." Then he said, raising his forefinger towards heaven, and turning it towards the people, "O God, be Thou witness; O God, be Thou witness." This he said three times. After that Bilál gave the call to prayers and repeated the affirmation of the intention to pray. And he prayed the midday prayer. After that he gave the call to prayer and said the afternoon prayer. And he never prayed any prayer between these two. After that he mounted his camel, and came to the place of standing. Then he placed the breast of his camel, Al Qáswah, in the direction of As Ṣakhrat, and placed the Ḥablu'l-Mashát in front of him and faced the temple of Mecca. And he continued standing until the sun sank in the West and the yellow tints faded away and the sun set. Then he took up Usámah behind him, and returned until he came to Al Muzdalifah, where he prayed the evening prayer and the night prayer with one call to prayer, but with two announcements of the intention to pray. And he did not praise God between the two. After that he lay down upon his side until the morning dawned. Then he prayed the morning prayer when the morning was announced to him by the call to prayer and the announcement of the intention to pray. Then he rode Al Qáswah until he came to Al Mash'aru'l-Ḥarám, and he faced the temple of Mecca and prayed and repeated the words, "God is great. There is no God but Alláh" and "God is one." And he continued standing until the sky became very red, after which he returned before the sun rose. Then he mounted behind him Al Faḍl bin 'Abbás until he came to the bottom of the valley Muḥassir. There he hastened a little. Afterwards he took the middle road, which comes out at Al Jamrahu'l-Kubra, until he came to Al Jamra, which is near a tree. There he threw seven pebbles, similar to the small stone pebbles which he threw in the bottom of the valley, and with each pebble he repeated the words, "God is great." After that he returned to the place of sacrifice and sacrificed sixty-three camels with his own hand. After that he gave what remained to 'Alí and he sacrificed them. Thus he made 'Alí a partner in his sacrifice. Then he ordered a small piece from each camel, and they were placed in a cooking vessel and were cooked. And they both ate of their flesh and drank the soup. After that he mounted his camel and hastened to the House (of God), and prayed in Mecca the midday prayer. Then he came to the sons of 'Abdu'l-Muṭṭalib as they were giving the people to drink of the water of (the well) Zamzam. And he said, "Draw, ye sons of 'Abdu'l-Muṭṭalib, for had it not been that the people would have gained possession of your right to draw, and would have given this water to drink, verily I would have drawn with you." Then they gave him a bucket, and he drank from it.'—*Muslim.*

It is related from 'Áyesha that she said, 'The Prophet of God arrived (at Mecca) on the fourth or fifth night of (the month) Dhu'l-Hajj, and came in to me, and he was angry. I said to him, "Who has angered thee, O Apostle of God; may God put him in the fire!" He replied, "Dost thou not know that I ordered the people a certain thing, and behold, they hesitate (to do it). If I had known before what I have learned since of my affairs, I would not have brought the sacrifice with me, until I had bought it (in Mecca). Then I would have taken off the pilgrim garb as they have done."'—*Muslim.*

On Entering Mecca and Going Round the Mosque

It is related from 'Áyesha that, 'When the Prophet came to Mecca, he entered it from its high side, and left it by its lower side.'—*Muslim, Al Bukhárí.*

It is related from 'Urwah binu'l-Zubair that he said, 'The Prophet performed the pilgrimage, and 'Áyesha informed me that the first thing he did when he arrived at Mecca was to perform ablutions. Then he went round the House. And it was the lesser pilgrimage. After that Abú Bakr performed the pilgrimage, and the first thing he did was to go round the House. And it was not the lesser pilgrimage. After that 'Omar and 'Othmán did the same.'—*Muslim, Al Bukhárı.*

It is related from Jábir that, 'When the Apostle of God arrived at Mecca, he came to the (black) stone and kissed it. After that he walked on its right, and he ran three times and walked four times (round the Ka'bah).'—*Muslim.*

It is related from Ibn 'Omar that he said, 'I did not see the Prophet kiss anything in the House, except the two pillars of Yemen.'—*Muslim, Al Bukhárí.*

It is related from Ibn 'Abbás that, 'The Prophet of God went round the mosque at the farewell pilgrimage mounted on a camel, and he kissed the pillar by means of a hooked stick.' —*Muslim, Al Bukhárí.*

It is related from Abú Hurairah that he said, 'Abú Bakr sent me, in the pilgrimage over which the Prophet ordered him (to preside), before the farewell pilgrimage, on the day of sacrifice amongst a small company of people. He commanded him to proclaim amongst the people, "Beware! After the present year no polytheist must make the pilgrimage, and none must make the circuit of the Ka'bah naked."'—*Muslim, Al Bukhárí.*

It is related from Ibn 'Abbás that, 'The Prophet said, "Making the circuit round the House (of God) is the same as saying the prayers, except that you may converse during it. Then let him who converses in it speak nothing but good words."'—*At Tirmidhí, An Nasái.*

It is related from Ibn 'Abbás that, 'The Apostle of God said, "The black stone came down from paradise. It was whiter than milk, but the sins of the children of Adam have made it black."'—*Aḥmad, At Tirmidhí.*

It is related from Ibn 'Abbás that, 'The Apostle of God said with regard to the stone, "By God! God will certainly raise it up on the day of resurrection; and it will have two eyes by which it will see, and a tongue by which it will speak, and it will bear witness concerning those who have kissed it in truth."'—*At Tirmidhí, Ibn Májah.*

It is related from Ṣafiyah bint Shaibah that she said, 'Bint Abi Tujrah informed me and said, "I entered with other women of the Quraish into the house of the family of Abú Ḥusain, and we were watching the Prophet as he ran between Aṣ Ṣafa and Al Marwah. And I saw him run, and verily his garments were turning about from the intensity of his running. And I heard him say, 'Run, for verily God has written the running as a duty incumbent upon you.'"'—*Sharaḥu's-Sunnah.*

It is related from Qadámah bin 'Abdu'lláh bin 'Ammár that he said, 'I saw the Apostle of God hastening between Aṣ Ṣafa and Al Marwah on a camel. There was no striking or driving away or saying, "Get out of the way! Get out of the way!"'—*Sharaḥu's-Sunnah.*

It is related from 'Abís bin Rabi'ah that he said, 'I saw 'Omar kiss the (black) stone, and heard him say, "Verily I certainly know that thou art a stone which can neither benefit nor injure. And if I had not seen the Apostle of God kiss thee, I would not kiss thee."'—*Muslim, Al Bukhárí.*

On Stopping at Mount Arafat

It is related from 'Ayesha that, 'The Apostle of God said, "There is no day on which God redeems a servant from the fire more than on the day of (the visitation of) Arafat. And verily He draws near to them, and then boasts of them to the angels and says, 'What do these want?'"'—*Muslim.*

It is related from Khálid bin Hawdha that he said, 'I saw the Prophet addressing the people on the day of Arafat, mounted on his camel, and he was standing up in his stirrups.' —*Abú Dáud.*

It is related from Jábir that, 'The Apostle of God said, "When the day of Arafat comes, verily God comes down to the skies of the world and boasts of them to the angels and says, 'Look at my servants, who have come to me with dishevelled hair, dusty, and crying out from the long journey. I call you to witness that I have forgiven them?' The angels say, 'O God, such an one used to tyrannise over men, and so and so and such and such a woman did so and so.'" He said, "God, the Exalted and Magnified, will reply, 'I have forgiven them.'" The Apostle of God said, "There is no day on which more are redeemed from the fire, than on the day of Arafat." '—*Sharaḥu' s-Sunnah.*

It is related from 'Abbás bin Mirdás that, 'Verily the Apostle of God asked forgiveness for the sins of his people on the night of Arafat, and he was answered, "Verily I have forgiven them, with the exception of oppressors, and I will take from them an account of the oppressed." He replied, "O Lord, if thou wilt, Thou canst give paradise to the oppressed and forgive the oppressors." But he was not answered that night. And when it dawned at Al Muzdalifah he repeated his supplication, and he was answered as he had asked.' 'Abbás said, 'Then the Apostle of God laughed, or he said, He smiled. Then Abú Bakr and 'Omar said to him, "May our fathers and mothers be sacrificed for thee! Verily this is a time in which thou hast not been wont to laugh. Then what is it which caused thee to laugh? May God cause Thy teeth to laugh!" He replied, "Verily the enemy of God, Iblis (Satan) when he knew that God, the Exalted and Magnified, had answered my prayer and forgiven my people, took up dust and began to throw it on his head, crying out at his misery and misfortune. Then what I saw of his impatient grief made me laugh." '—*Ibn Májah.*

On Returning from Arafat and Muzdalifah

It is related from Ibn 'Abbás that, 'He returned with the Prophet on the day of Arafat, and the Prophet heard behind him loud shouting and beating of camels; and he beckoned with his whip and said, "O men, you ought to go quietly, for verily righteousness is not in haste." '—*Al Bukhárí.*

It is related from 'Abdu'lláh bin Ma'súd that he said, 'I never saw the Apostle of God say the prayers except in their proper times, with the exception of the sunset and night prayers which he said together. And he prayed the morning prayer that day before its time.'—*Muslim, Al Bukhárí.*

Concerning the Throwing the Pebbles

It is related from Jábir that he said, 'I saw the Prophet throw pebbles (whilst seated) on his camel on the day of sacrifice; and he said, "Take note of the rites of your pilgrimage, for I do not know whether, perchance, I shall not perform pilgrimage after this pilgrimage." '—*Muslim.*

It is related concerning 'Abdu'lláh bin Mas'úd that he arrived at Al Jamru'l-Kubra and placed the House (of God) on his left and Mount Mina on his right, and threw seven pebbles and repeated, 'God is great,' with each pebble. Then he said, 'Thus did he throw, upon whom came down Súratu'l-Baqara.'—*Muslim, Al Bukhárí.*

It is related from 'Áyesha from the Prophet that he said, 'Verily the throwing of pebbles and the running between Aṣ Ṣafa and Al Marwah have only been appointed for remembering God.'—*At Tirmidhí.*

On Animals for Sacrifice

It is related from Ibn 'Abbás that he said, 'The Apostle of God prayed the midday prayer at Dhu'l-Hudaifah. Then he called for his female camel and struck it with a lance in the right side of its hump, and then wiped off the blood from it. Then he placed two straps around its neck, after which he mounted his riding camel. Then when it arrived with him at Baidái he repeated the words for pilgrimage; "Here I am at Thy service." '—*Muslim.*

It is related from 'Áyesha that she said, 'The Prophet on a certain occasion sent a sheep for sacrifice to the House of God, and he put a necklace upon its neck.'—*Muslim, Al Bukhárí.*

It is related from Jábir that he said, 'The Prophet sacrificed a cow on behalf of his women during his pilgrimage.'—*Muslim.*

It is related from Ibn 'Abbás that he said, 'The Apostle of God sent sixteen camels for sacrifice with a man and gave him charge of them. Then the man said, "O Apostle of God, how shall I act with that one of them which is unable to travel?" He replied, "Slaughter it, and then colour its feet with its blood and place it on its side; but do not thou or any of thy travelling companions eat of it." '—*Muslim.*

It is related from Jábir that he said, 'We sacrificed with the Apostle of God in the year of Ḥudaibah one camel for seven people and one cow for seven people.'—*Muslim.*

It is related from 'Alí that he said, 'The Apostle of God ordered me to take care of his camels for sacrifice, and to give in alms their flesh and skins and saddles. And (he ordered) that I should not give a portion to the one who killed them. He said, "We will give him something from ourselves." '—*Muslim, Al Bukhárí.*

It is related from Ibn 'Abbás that, 'The Apostle of God sent for sacrifice in the year of Ḥudaibah, in the sacrifice for the Apostle of God, a camel which formerly belonged to Abú Jaḥl. It had a silver ring in its head (nose)—and in another tradition it has "golden"—and the polytheists were angered thereat.'—*Abú Dáud.*

It is related from Salamah binu'l-Akwa' that, 'The Prophet said, "Whoever of you offers a sacrifice, let him not rise after the third day with any of it still in his house." Then when the next year came round they said, "O Apostle of God, must we do (this year) as we did last year." He replied, "Eat ye of it and give others to eat and put by in store; for verily in that year there was want amongst the people, and I wished that ye should help them." '—*Muslim, Al Bukhárí.*

On Shaving the Head

It is related from Ibn 'Omar that, 'Verily the Apostle of God shaved his head in the farewell pilgrimage, and some of his companions (did the same). And some of them cut their hair short.'—*Muslim, Al Bukhárí.*

It is related from Anas that, 'Verily the Prophet came to Mina. After that he came to all Jamrah and threw pebbles there. After that he came to his lodging at Mina and sacrificed his victims. Then he called a barber and turned to him the right side (of his head), and he shaved it. Then he called Abú Ṭalḥa, the helper, and gave it to him. After that he offered the left side of his head and said, "Shave!" Then he shaved it. And he gave it to Abú Ṭalḥa and said, "Divide it amongst the people." '—*Muslim, Al Bukhárí.*

It is related from 'Alí and 'Áyesha that they said, 'The Apostle of God forbade women to shave the head.'—*At Tirmidhí.*

It is related from Usámah bin Sharík that he said, 'I came out with the Apostle of God to perform the pilgrimage. And the people were coming to him, and some were saying, "O Apostle of God, I performed the running (between Aṣ Ṣafa and Al Marwah) before going round the Ka'bah" or "I delayed to perform something" or "I did something before its time." And he was saying in reply, "There is no sin, except for the man who takes away the reputation of a Muslim and is an oppressor; for that is he who commits a sin and is destroyed."' —*Abú Dáud.*

On the Public Address on the Day of Sacrifice, and Throwing the Pebbles, and Taking Farewell

It is related from Ráfi' bin 'Amru'l-Muzanni that he said, 'I saw the Apostle of God addressing the people at Mina, when the early morning approached (seated) on his black and white mule. And 'Alí was explaining it; and some of the people were standing and some sitting.'—*Abú Dáud.*

It is related from 'Áyesha that, 'The Prophet said, "When any one of you throws pebbles at Jamrahu'l-'Aqabah, then everything has become lawful for him except women."'—*Sharḥu's-Sunnah.*

Concerning Those Things Which Pilgrims Must Abstain From

It is related from 'Abdu'lláh bin 'Omar that, 'A man asked the Apostle of God what clothes a pilgrim must wear. He replied, "Do not wear shirts nor turbans nor trousers nor the dress called *burnús* nor shoes, except one cannot obtain sandals, when he may wear shoes; but in that case let him cut them down below the heels. And do not wear any clothes which saffron or the dye called *waras* have touched."'—*Muslim, Al Bukhárí.* And Bukhárí has added the words, 'And let not a woman on pilgrimage veil her face, and let her not wear gloves.'

It is related from 'Othmán that, 'The Apostle of God said, "Let not one performing the pilgrimage, marry or give in marriage or effect a betrothal."'—*Muslim.*

It is related from Ibn 'Omar that he heard the Apostle of God forbid women who were performing the pilgrimage from wearing gloves or veils and whatever the dye *waras* and saffron had touched, 'but let them (said he), after that, wear whatever they like of yellow-coloured clothes or the cloth called *khazz* or ornaments or long drawers or a chemise or shoes.'—*Abú Dáud.*

On Abstaining from Hunting During Pilgrimage

It is related from Aṣ Ṣa'b bin Jathámah that he brought a present of an ass to the Apostle of God when he was at Abwái or Waddán; but he returned it to him. Then when the Apostle of God saw what (displeasure) was in his face, he said, 'Verily I would not have returned it to thee, except that we had put on the pilgrim garb.'—*Muslim, Al Bukhárí.*

It is related from Abú Qatádah that he went out with the Apostle of God, but he lingered behind with some of his companions. And they were engaged in the pilgrimage, but he was not so engaged. Then they saw a wild ass before he did; but when they saw it they left it alone, until at length Abú Qatádah saw it also. Then he mounted his horse and asked them to give him his whip, but they refused. Then he took it and attacked and wounded it. Afterwards he ate of it, and they ate of it. Then they regretted having done so, and when they came up with the Apostle of God they asked him about it. He replied, 'Is there any of it with you?' They said, 'We have a leg of it with us.' Then the Prophet took and ate of it. —*Muslim, Al Bukhárí.* And in another tradition, given by both *Muslim* and *Al Bukhárí*, it runs, 'When they came to the Apostle of God he said, "Did any one of you order him to attack it or point towards it?" They replied, "No." He said, "Then eat what remains of its flesh."'

It is related from Ibn 'Omar from the Prophet that, 'He said, "There are five things which it is no sin to kill on sacred ground and when one is performing the pilgrimage: a mouse, a raven, a hawk, a scorpion and a biting dog."'—*Muslim, Al Bukhárí.*

It is related from Jábir that, 'The Apostle of God said, "The flesh of game is lawful for you when performing the pilgrimage, so long as you do not hunt it yourselves, or it is not hunted on your behalf."'—*Abú Dáud, At Tirmidhí.*

It is related from 'Abdu'r-Raḥmán bin abi 'Ammár that he said, 'I asked Jábir bin 'Abdu'lláh concerning the hyena: whether it was game. He replied, "Yes." I said, "May it be eaten?" He said, "Yes." I said, "Didst thou hear it from the Apostle of God?" He replied, "Yes."'—*At Tirmidhí, An Nasái.*

On Being Prevented from Going on Pilgrimage and Missing the Time for Its Observance

It is related from 'Abdu'lláh bin 'Omar that he said, 'We went out with the Apostle of God, but the unbelievers of the Quraish prevented him from entering the House (of God). Then the Prophet killed his sacrifices and shaved, and his companions cut their hair short.'—*Al Bukhárí.*

It is related from Ibn 'Omar that he said, 'Is not the practice of the Apostle of God sufficient for you? If any one of you is prevented from performing the pilgrimage, he must make the circuit of the House of God, and (run between) Ṣafa and Marwah. After that he will be free from all obligations until he performs the pilgrimage in the following year. And let him offer a sacrifice, or, if he has not wherewith to sacrifice, then let him fast.'—*Al Bukhárí.*

It is related from Al Ḥajjaj bin 'Amru'l-Anṣári that, 'The Apostle of God said, "He whose limb is broken or who is lame has been released from the obligation to perform the pilgrimage; but he must perform the next pilgrimage."'—*At Tirmidhí, Abú Dáud, An Nasái, Ibn Májah.* And Abú Dáud has added in another tradition the words, 'Or is sick.'

Concerning the Sacred Territory of Mecca which God has Guarded

It is related from Ibn 'Abbás that, 'The Apostle of God said on the day of the conquest of Mecca, "There must be no more fleeing, but fighting, and the intention (to do one's duty). Therefore if ye are called on to go out to fight; then go out to fight." And on the day of the conquest of Mecca he said, "Verily God made this city sacred on the day when He created the heavens and the earth. Then it is sacred with the sanctity of God until the day of resurrection. And verily fighting therein is unlawful for any one before me, and it is unlawful for me, except for one hour of the day. Therefore it is sacred with the sanctity of God until the day of resurrection. Its thorns must not be cut, its game must not be hunted, and that which has fallen upon the ground must not be picked up, except that any one makes it known to the people, and its grass must not be cut." Then Al 'Ayyás said, "O Apostle of God, (let it remain) except the (grass called) *idhkhára*, because it is useful for their blacksmiths and for their houses." Then he replied, "Except *idhkhára*."'—*Muslim*, *Al Bukhárí*.

It is related from Jábir that he said, 'I heard the Prophet say, "It is not lawful for any one of you to carry arms in Mecca."'—*Muslim*.

It is related from Anas that, 'The Prophet entered Mecca on the day of its conquest, and on his head was a piece of mail worn beneath the helmet. And when he took it off a man came and said, "Verily Ibn Khatal is clinging to the veil of the Ka'bah." He replied, "Kill him."'—*Muslim*, *Al Bukhárí*.

It is related from 'Áyesha that, 'The Apostle of God said, "An army will come to attack the Ka'bah, and when they come to Baidái the first and last of them will be swallowed up by the earth." I said, "O Apostle of God, how will the first of them and the last of them be swallowed up, when amongst them will be their camp-followers and those who are not of their party." He replied, "The first of them and the last of them will be swallowed up. Then (at the end) they will be raised up according to their intentions."'—*Muslim*, *Al Bukhárí*.

It is related from Abú Hurairah that, 'The Apostle of God said, "A man of Abyssinia, having small legs, will destroy the Ka'bah."'—*Muslim*, *Al Bukhárí*.

It is related from Ibn 'Abbás that, 'The Apostle of God said, addressing Mecca, "How fine thou art amongst cities! and how beloved of me! If it were not that my people turned me out of thee, I would live in none other but thee."'—*At Tirmidhí*.

It is related from Abú Shuraihu'l-'Adwi that he said to 'Amru bin Sa'íd when he sent an army to Mecca, 'Give me permission, O 'Amir, and I will relate to thee something that the Apostle of God said on the day after the conquest of

Mecca. I heard him with my two ears, and my heart remembered it, and my two eyes saw it. When he spake he glorified and praised God, and then said, "Verily God has made Mecca sacred, and it is not man who has made it sacred, therefore it is not lawful for a man who believes in God and the last day to shed blood therein, or to cut down trees therein. And if any one seeks a concession to do so by virtue of the fighting of the Apostle of God therein, then say to him, 'Verily God gave permission to His Apostle, but has not given you permission.' He only gave me permission (to fight) in it for one hour of the day. And its sanctity has remained to-day what it was yesterday. Then let those present inform those who are absent." Then it was said to Abú Shuraih, "What did 'Amru say to thee." He replied, "He said, I know that better than thou, O Abú Shuraih. Verily the sacred land (of Mecca) does not offer a refuge to rebels, or to those that flee after shedding blood, or to those who flee after destroying property."'—*Muslim, Al Bukhárí.*

Concerning the Sacred Territory of Madína

It is related from Sa'd that, 'The Apostle of God said, "Verily I have made sacred all that lies between the two strong plains of Madína, that its trees be not cut nor its game killed." And he said, "Madína is best for them, if they had but known. No one takes leave of it willingly, but God brings to it in exchange one who is better than he; and no one remains constant in the midst of its hardships and afflictions, but I shall be an intercessor or witness on his behalf on the day of resurrection."'—*Muslim.*

It is related from Abú Hurairah that he said, 'The people, when they saw the first fruits, used to bring them to the Prophet; and when he took them he used to say, "O God, bless us in our fruits, and bless us in our city, and bless us in filling up (the grain measures) *ṣá'a* and *mudda.* O God, verily Abraham was Thy servant and Thy friend and Thy Prophet. And I am Thy servant and Thy Prophet. And he prayed to Thee for Mecca, and I pray to Thee for Madína like as he prayed for Mecca, and a (second) equal portion with it." After that (Abú Hurairah) said, he used to call the smallest boy of his household and give him the fruit.'—*Muslim.*

It is related from 'Ámir bin Sa'd that verily Sa'd was riding towards his home in Al 'Aqíq, and he came across a slave cutting trees, or beating off the leaves; so he plundered him. Then when Sa'd returned, the masters of the slave came to him, and spoke to him, saying that he should return to their slave or to them what he had taken from their slave. He replied, 'God forbid that I should return anything which the Apostle of God gave me as booty.' And he refused to return (the things) to them.—*Muslim.*

It is related from 'Áyesha that she said, 'When the Apostle of God came to Madína, Abú Bakr and Bilál were attacked by fever. Then I came to the Apostle of God and informed him. Then he said, "O God, make Madína beloved to us as thou hast made Mecca beloved to us, or even more so; and make it healthy, and bless us in (filling up its grain measures) *ṣa'a* and *mudda*, and take away its fever and put it in Juḥfah."'—*Muslim, Al Bukhári.*

It is related from Abú Hurairah that, 'The Apostle of God said, "I was ordered to (flee to) a city which eats up other cities. They called it Yathreb, which is Madína. It expels men as a blacksmith's bellows expels the dross of iron."'—*Muslim, Al Bukhári.*

It is related from Anas that, 'The Apostle of God said, "There is no city which Anti-Christ will not tread upon, except Mecca and Madína. These have no road upon which angels do not stand in rank to protect them. Then he will come down on marshy ground, and Madína, with the people thereof, will tremble three times. And all unbelievers and hypocrites will go out to him."'—*Muslim, Al Bukhári.*

It is related from Ibn 'Omar that, 'The Apostle of God said, "Whoever is able to die in Madína, let him die therein; for verily I will intercede for whoever dies therein."'—*Aḥmad, At Tirmidhí.*

It is related from Abú Hurairah that, 'The Apostle of God said, "The last of the cities of Islám to be destroyed is Madína."'—*At Tirmidhí.*

It is related from Ibn 'Omar that, 'The Apostle of God said, "Whoever goes on pilgrimage and visits my grave after my death will be as he who visited me in my lifetime."'—*Al Baihaqi.*

XII

THE BOOK OF BUYING AND SELLING

ON EARNING AND SEEKING WHAT IS LAWFUL

— It is related from Al Miqdám bin Ma'díkarib that, 'The Apostle of God said, "No one can ever eat better food than that he eat of the work of his own hands. Verily God's Prophet, David, used to eat of the work of his hands."'—*Al Bukhárí.*

It is related from Abú Hurairah that, 'The Apostle of God said, "A time will come to man when a person will not care whether what he takes be lawful or unlawful."'—*Al Bukhárí.*

It is related from Abú Juḥaifah that, 'The Prophet forbade the price of blood and the price of a dog and the hire of an adulteress. And he cursed the taker of interest and the giver of it, and the woman who tattoes the skin and the woman who is tattoed, and the painter.'—*Al Bukhárí.*

It is related from Jábir that in the year of the conquest of Mecca, when the Prophet was in Mecca, he heard him say, 'Verily God and His Apostle have made unlawful the selling of wine, and that which dies of itself and swine and idols.' Then it was said, 'O Apostle of God, inform us with regard to the fat of what dies of itself, for verily boats are smeared with it and leather is greased with it, and men light their lamps by it.' He replied, 'No! it is unlawful.' Then he said at that time, 'May God destroy the Jews! Verily when God made unlawful their fat they congealed it and afterwards sold it and ate its price.'—*Muslim, Al Bukhárí.*

It is related from Anas that, 'The Apostle of God cursed ten people in connexion with wine: the one who presses it out of the grapes for others, the one who presses it out for himself, the one who drinks it, the one who carries it, the one to whom it is carried, the one who serves it, the one who sells it, the one who takes its price, the one who buys it, and the one for whom it is bought.'—*At Tirmidhí, Ibn Májah.*

It is related from Abú Umámah that, 'The Apostle of God said, "Do not sell singing slave-girls, nor buy them, and do not teach them; and their price is unlawful." And in (a tradition) similar to this it runs, "And, amongst men, the one who sells amusing stories."'—*Aḥmad, Tirmidhí, Ibn Májah.*

It is related from 'Abdu'lláh bin Ma'súd that, 'The Apostle of God said, "It is an obligatory duty to seek to earn a lawful livelihood after (performing) one's religious duties."'—*Al Baihaqi.*

— It is related from Ibn 'Abbás that he was asked about taking remuneration for writing the Qur'án. He replied, 'There is no harm; they are only makers of pictures, and they only eat from the work of their hands.'—*Razín.*

It is related from Náfi' that he said, 'I used to send expeditions to Syria and to Egypt. Then I sent an expedition to 'Iráq. And I came to the Mother of the Faithful, 'Áyesha, and said to her, "O Mother of the Faithful, I used to send expeditions to Syria, and I have (now) sent an expedition to 'Iráq." She replied, "Do not do so. What is wrong with thee and thy merchandise? For verily I heard the Apostle of God say, 'When God provides a means of livelihood for any one of you in a certain way, then let him not give it up until it becomes impossible to him.'"'—*Aḥmad, Ibn Májah.*

It is related from 'Áyesha that she said, 'Abú Bakr had a slave to whom he used to give a certain allowance of food; and Abú Bakr used to eat of his allowance. And he came on a certain day with some food and Abú Bakr ate of it. Then the slave said to him, "Dost thou know what this is?" Abú Bakr replied, "What is it?" He said, "In the times of ignorance I foretold the future for a man; but I did not tell his fortune well, rather I deceived him. And he met me and gave me something; and this is it of which thou hast eaten." ('Áyesha) said, "Then Abú Bakr put his finger down his throat, and vomited up everything that was in his stomach."'—*Al Bukhárí.*

On Gentleness in Mutual Behaviour

It is related from Ḥudaifah that, 'The Apostle of God said, "Verily there was a man of those who were before you: and the angel (of death) came to him to take his soul. And it was said to the man, 'Hast thou done any good thing?' He replied, 'I do not know.' It was said, 'Consider.' He replied, 'I do not know of anything, except that I used to buy and sell to men in the world, and I satisfied them. And I waited for the rich (to pay), and forgave those in straitened circumstances.' Then God took him into paradise."'—*Muslim, Al Bukhárí.* And in another tradition from *Muslim*, as received through 'Uqbah bin 'Ámir and Abú Ma'súdu'l-Anṣári, it runs, 'God said, "I am more worthy to do that (namely, forgive) than thou. (O angels), pass over my servant."'

It is related from Abú Qatádah that, 'The Apostle of God said, "Beware of many oaths in buying and selling; for verily it causes goods to sell well, but afterwards it destroys."' —*Muslim.*

It is related from Abú Sa'íd that, 'The Apostle of God said, "The truthful and trustworthy merchant will be with the prophets and the just and the martyrs."'—*At Tirmidhí, Al Dárimi.*

On Option in Respect of Buying and Selling

It is related from Ḥakím bin Ḥizám that, 'The Apostle of God said, "The buyer and the seller have an option, so long as they do not separate. And if they speak the truth and explain (the defects) there is a blessing for them in their buying and selling; but if they conceal (defects) and lie, the blessing of their buying and selling is destroyed."'—*Muslim, Al Bukhárí.*

On Interest

It is related from Jábir that he said, 'The Apostle of God cursed the taker of interest and the giver of it, and the writer (of the bond) for it, and the witness to it; and he said, "They are all equal."'—*Muslim.*

It is related from Abú Sa'ídu'l-Khudri that, 'The Apostle of God said, "(Give) gold for gold, silver for silver, wheat for wheat, barley for barley, dates for dates, salt for salt, like for like, from hand to hand. He who gives more and asks for more, has given and taken interest. The taker and the giver of it are alike."'—*Muslim.*

It is related from Abú Sa'íd and Abú Hurairah that the Apostle of God appointed a man over Khaibar. And he brought some *janíb* dates to him. The Prophet said, 'Are all the dates of Khaibar like this?' He replied, 'No, by God! O Apostle of God, we take one *ṣá'a* (measure) of these for two *ṣá'as* (of other dates), or two *ṣá'as* for three.' He said, 'Do not do so; but sell the whole for money. After that buy *janíb* dates with money.' And he said, 'In weights it is the same.'—*Muslim, Al Bukhárí.*

It is related from Abú Sa'íd that he said, 'Bilál brought some *barni* dates to the Prophet. The Prophet said to him, "Whence are these?" He replied, "We had some bad dates, and I sold two *ṣá'a* measures of them for one (of these good dates)." He said, "Ah! the very essence of interest! the very essence of interest! Do not do so; but when you wish to buy, then sell the dates by another transaction. After that buy with the proceeds."'—*Muslim, Al Bukhárí.*

It is related from Jábir that he said, 'A slave came and declared fealty to the Prophet, promising to emigrate to Madína; but the Prophet did not know that he was a slave. Then his master came, asking for him. And the Prophet said to him, "Sell him to me." And he bought him for two black slaves. And after him he never accepted the fealty of any one until he had asked him whether he was a slave or a free man.' —*Muslim.*

It is related from Abú Hurairah that, 'The Apostle of God said, "Certainly a time will come to men when not one will remain who will not take interest. And even if he does not take it, its smoke will reach him." And in another tradition it is said, "Its dust" will reach him.'—*Aḥmad, Abú Dáud, An Nasái, Ibn Májah.*

It is related from 'Abdu'lláh bin Ḥanzalah that, 'The Apostle of God said, "One *dirham* of interest which a man takes, knowing it to be so, is more grievous than thirty six adulteries."'—*Aḥmad.*

It is related from Abú Hurairah that, 'The Apostle of God said, "Interest is composed of seventy parts, the least of which is that a man marry his own mother."'

It is related from Ibn Ma'súd that, 'The Apostle of God said, "Although interest brings increase, yet its end tends to scarcity."'—*Ibn Májah.*

It is related from Abú Hurairah that, 'The Apostle of God said, "On the night of my journey to heaven I came to a people whose bellies were like houses in which were snakes. These were seen from outside their bellies. Then I said, 'O Gabriel, who are these?' He replied, 'These are the takers of interest.'" '—*Aḥmad, Ibn Májah.*

It is related from 'Omar binu'l-Khaṭṭáb that, 'The last revelation which came down was the verse about interest; and verily the Apostle of God was taken without having explained it to us. Therefore abandon interest and all doubtful things.' —*Ibn Májah, Al Dárimi.*

It is related from Abú Burdah bin abi Músá that he said, 'I came to Madína, and I met 'Abdu'lláh bin Salám. And he said, "Verily thou art in a land in which the taking of interest is prevalent. Therefore when thou hast a claim upon any man for debt, and he presents thee with a load of straw or a load of barley or a load of *qatt* grass; then do not take it, for verily it is interest." '—*Al Bukhárí.*

CONCERNING SALE

It is related from 'Abdu'lláh bin 'Omar that, 'The Apostle of God prohibited the sale of fruit until its good condition appeared evident. And he prohibited both the seller and the buyer.'—*Muslim, Al Bukhárí.* And in another tradition from Muslim it runs, 'He forbade the sale of dates until they blossomed, and the selling of corn until it became white and safe from blight.'

It is related from Ibn 'Omar that, 'The Apostle of God said, "Whoever buys food must not re-sell it until he has got it into his full possession." '—*Muslim, Al Bukhárí.* And in another tradition from Ibn 'Abbás it runs, 'Until he measures it.'

It is related from Wathila binu'l-Asqa'i that he said, 'I heard the Apostle of God say, "Whoever sells anything with a fault in it which he does not make known will remain hated of God, and the angels will continue to curse him." '—*Ibn Májah.*

It is related from Ibn 'Omar that, 'The Apostle of God said, "Whoever buys a date tree after the pollen has appeared, its fruit belongs to the seller, unless the buyer makes a condition (to the contrary). And whoever buys a slave who possesses property, his property belongs to the seller, unless the buyer makes a condition (to the contrary)." '—*Muslim.*

It is related from 'Áyesha that she said, 'Barirah came and said, "Verily I have written (a bond to pay for my liberty) nine *uqiyas*, one in each year; therefore assist me." 'Áyesha replied, "If thy masters desire, I will count it over to them in one counting and set thee free; but the right to inherit thy property must remain with me." Then Barirah went to her masters, but they refused, unless the right to inherit her property remained with them. Then the Apostle of God said, "Take her and set her free." Afterwards the Apostle of God stood up amongst the people and magnified God and praised Him. Then after that he said, "What will be the condition of those men who make stipulations which are not in the Book of God! Whatever stipulation is not in the Book of God is null and void, even though there be one hundred of them. And the commands of God are more worthy (to be obeyed), and the stipulations of God are more binding. And verily the right to inherit is only for the one who emancipates."'—*Muslim, Al Bukhárí.*

On Payment in Advance and Pledges

It is related from 'Áyesha that she said, 'The Apostle of God bought some food from a certain Jew (to be paid for) in a certain time. And he pledged him his iron coat of mail.'—*Muslim, Al Bukhárí.*

It is related from 'Áyesha that she said, 'The Apostle of God died, and his coat of mail remained in pledge with the Jew for thirty *ṣá'as* of barley.'—*Al Bukhárí.*

It is related from Ibn 'Abbás that, 'The Apostle of God said to the users of measures and weights, "Verily ye have been appointed over two matters in which the people who were before you were destroyed."'—*At Tirmidhí.*

On Monopolies

It is related from Ma'mar that, 'The Apostle of God said, "Whoever holds goods for excessive prices is a sinner."'—*Muslim.*

It is related from 'Omar binu'l-Khaṭṭáb that he said, 'I heard the Apostle of God say, "Whoever stores up the food of Muslims in order to obtain excessive prices, may God smite him with leprosy and bankruptcy."'—*Ibn Májah.*

On Bankruptcy and Delay (in Demanding Payment)

It is related from Abú Sa'íd that he said, 'A man in the time of the Prophet had a misfortune with some fruit which he had bought, and his debts increased. Then the Apostle of God said, "Give him alms." So the people gave him alms; but it did not reach the amount required to liquidate his debts. Then the Apostle of God said to his creditors, "Take what you get; for you will get nothing else beside that."'—*Muslim.*

It is related from Abú Hurairah that, 'The Prophet said, "There was a man who used to lend men money. And he was in the habit of saying to his young man, "When thou comest to one who is reduced to poverty, then forgive him. It may be that God will forgive us." (The Prophet) said, "That man met God, and he was forgiven."'—*Muslim, Al Bukhárí.*

It is related from Salamah binu'l-Akwa' that he said, 'We were sitting near the Prophet when a bier was brought. And they said (to him), "Pray over it." He replied, "Has he any debts?" They said, "No." Then he prayed over him. After that another bier was brought, and he said, "Has he any debts?" It was said, "Yes." He asked, "Has he left anything?" They replied, "Three *dinars.*" Then he prayed over him. After that a third (bier) was brought. He asked, "Has he any debts?" They replied, "Three *dinars.*" He said, "Has he left anything?" They replied, "No." He said, "Then you may pray over your friend." Abú Qatádah said, "O Apostle of God, pray over him, and I will be responsible for his debts." Then he prayed over him.'—*Al Bukhárí.*

It is related from Abú Qatádah that, 'A man said, "O Apostle of God, tell me, if I am killed in the way of God, being patient, hoping for rewards, facing (the enemy), and not turning my back to them, will God expiate my sins?" The Apostle of God replied, "Yes." Then when the man turned away, he called him and said, "Yes, except debt. Thus said Gabriel."'—*Muslim.*

It is related from Al Barái bin 'Ázib that, 'The Apostle of God said, "A man who is in debt is a prisoner to his debt. He will complain to his Lord of loneliness on the day of resurrection."' —In *Sharhu's-Sunnat.* And it is related that Muá'dh was in debt, and his creditors came to the Prophet. Then the Prophet sold everything which Muá'dh possessed in satisfaction of his debts, until Muá'dh stood without a thing.

It is related from Abú Músá that, 'The Prophet said, "Verily the greatest sin in the sight of God, after the mortal sins, is that a servant should meet Him with what God has forbidden, namely, that a man should die in debt, and leave nothing wherewith to redeem it." '—*Aḥmad, Abú Dáud.*

On Partnership and Agency

It is related from Zuhrah bin Ma'bad that his grandfather, 'Abdu'lláh bin Ḥishám, used to take him out to the bazar and buy food. And Ibn 'Omar and Ibn Zubair met him and said to him, "Take us into partnership, for verily the Prophet prayed for a blessing for thee." Then he took them into partnership. And it sometimes happened that he gained a camel's load, and sent it to his lodging. And it was that 'Abdu'lláh bin Ḥishám whose mother had taken him to the Prophet; and he had stroked his head and supplicated a blessing for him.'—*Al Bukhárí.*

It is related from Jábir that he said, 'The sun was eclipsed in the time of the Apostle of God, on the day that Ibrahim, the Apostle's son, died. And the Prophet prayed with the people in six *rak'ahs* and four prostrations, and then turned away. And the sun had returned to its ordinary condition; and he said, "There is nothing which you have been promised which I have not seen in this prayer of mine. Hell fire was certainly brought, and that was when you saw me draw back in fear lest its scorching heat should reach me, till I saw in it a man with a hooked stick dragging his intestines in the fire. And he used to rob pilgrims with his hooked stick. And if he was spoken to about it, he used to say, 'It only got caught in my hooked stick.' And if the people were unaware of his thieving, then he would take the thing away. And I saw in the fire a woman who used to own a cat, which she tied up, and neither fed nor released so that it might eat of the birds and small animals of the earth, until it died of hunger. After that paradise was brought, and that was when you saw me move forward until I stood in my place and stretched out my hand wishing to take some of its fruit that you might look at it. After that it became manifest to me that I should not do so." '—*Muslim.*

It is related from Ḥarám bin Sa'd bin Muḥaiṣah that, 'The camel of Al Barái bin 'Ázib entered a garden and spoiled it. Then the Apostle of God gave judgement that the protection of gardens is the duty of their owners in the daytime; but that which animals destroy by night their owners are responsible for.'—*Málik, Abú Dáud, Ibn Májah.*

It is related from Al Ḥasan from Samurah that, 'The Prophet said, "When any one of you comes to cattle, then if their owner be amongst them, let him ask his permission (to milk them). But if he be not present, then let him call out three times. Then if any one answer him, let him ask his permission; but if no one answer him, then let him milk and drink; but he must take nothing away."'—*Abú Dáud.*

It is related from Ibn 'Omar that, 'The Prophet said, "Whoever enters a garden may eat thereof, but let him not take away anything in his garments."'—*At Tirmidhí, Ibn Májah.*

On the Right of Pre-emption

It is related from Jábir that he said, 'The Prophet gave orders for pre-emption in everything which was not divided. But when the boundaries are delimitated and roads laid out, there is no pre-emption.'—*Al Bukhárí.*

It is related from Jábir that, 'The Apostle of God gave orders for pre-emption in every matter of partnership which had not been divided: lands or gardens. In such cases it is not lawful for a man to sell until he inform his partner. Then, if the latter wish, he may take it, and if he wish, he may leave it. And if he sell and do not inform his partner, then the latter has a prior right to it.'—*Muslim.*

It is related from Abú Hurairah that, 'The Apostle of God said, "Let not a neighbour forbid his neighbour from fixing a beam of wood in his wall."'—*Muslim, Al Bukhárí.*

It is related from 'Abdu'lláh bin Ḥubaish that, 'The Apostle of God said, "Whoever cuts down a lotus tree, God will put down his head into the fire."'—*Abú Dáud.* And he said, 'This tradition is abbreviated (it should be), "Whoever wantonly and injuriously cuts down a lotus tree in the desert, under which the traveller and beasts seek shade, having no right to do so, God will put down his head in the fire."'

CONCERNING PAYMENT IN KIND FOR SERVICES RENDERED

It is related from 'Abdu'lláh bin 'Omar that, 'The Apostle of God handed over to the Jews of Khaibár its date trees and its land, with the stipulation that they should cultivate them at their own expense; but that the Prophet should have half its fruits.'—*Muslim.*

It is related from Ráfi' bin Khadíj that he said, 'We, the majority of the people of Madína, were cultivators. And there was one of our number who used to hire out his land and say, "(The fruit of) this plot will be mine, and of that yours." And something happened, so that the one produced a crop, and the other did not. Then the Prophet prohibited them (acting thus).' —*Muslim, Al Bukhárí.*

It is related from Abú Umámah that he saw a ploughshare and other implements of cultivation and said, 'I heard the Prophet say, "This does not enter the home of any people, but it causes abasement to enter it." '—*Al Bukhárí.*

It is related from Ráfi' bin Khadíj that, 'The Prophet said, "Whoever sows in the lands of a people without their permission, will have nothing of the crop except what he expended on it." '—*At Tirmidhí, Abú Dáud.*

It is related from Qais bin Muslim from Abú Ja'far that he said, 'There were none of the refugees in Madína who sowed the ground, except on the stipulation that they should receive one-third or one-fourth (of the produce). And 'Alí and Sa'd bin Málik and 'Abdu'lláh bin Ma'súd and 'Omar bin 'Abdu'l-Azíz and Al Qásim and 'Urwah and the family of Abú Bakr and the family of 'Omar and the family of 'Alí and Ibn Sírín sowed in partnership. And 'Abdu'r-Raḥmán binu'l-Aswad said, "I was a partner with 'Abdu'r-Raḥmán bin Yazíd in the crop." And 'Omar arranged with the people that if he supplied the seed himself, he should have one half of the crop; and if they supplied the seed they should have the same.'—*Al Bukhárí.*

ON THE LEASE OF REVENUES OR LABOUR

It is related from Abú Hurairah from the Prophet that he said, 'God sent no prophet who did not graze goats.' Then his companions said, 'And thou?' He replied, 'Yes! I used to graze goats for the people of Mecca for a few *karats.*' —*Al Bukhárí.*

It is related from Abú Hurairah that, 'The Apostle of God said, "God Most High said, 'There are three classes of people whose adversary I shall be on the day of resurrection: the man who makes a promise in my name, and afterwards breaks it; the man who sells a free man, and eats his price; and the man who engages a labourer, and receives full labour from him, but does not pay him his wages.'" '—*Al Bukhárí.*

It is related from Ibn 'Abbás that, 'A party of the companions of the Prophet passed by some water, and amongst them (i.e. the people camping there) was one who had been bitten by some poisonous scorpion or snake. And a man from the people living near the water came to them and said, "Have you a charmer amongst you; for amongst those living near the water is a man who has been bitten by some poisonous scorpion or snake." Then a man of their number went and recited the opening chapter of the Book, on condition of receiving some goats in payment. Then the man recovered, and he (who had recited) brought the goats to his companions. But they were displeased thereat, and said, "Thou hast taken a reward for reciting the Book of God," until they came to Madína and said to the Apostle of God, "He took a reward for reciting the Book of God?" The Apostle of God replied, "Verily the most proper thing for which you can take a reward is the Book of God." '—*Al Bukhárí.* And in another tradition it runs, 'You have acted righty. Divide them; and allot me a share with you.'

It is related from Khárija binu'ṣ-Ṣalt, from his paternal uncle, that he said, 'We came from the Apostle of God to some Arabs. They said, "Verily we have been informed that God has brought blessings from this man (Muḥammad). Have you any medicine or charm, for verily we have here a madman in fetters." We replied, "Yes." Then they brought the madman in fetters, and I recited over him morning and evening for three days the opening chapter of the Book, collecting the spittle in my mouth, and then spitting it on him. Khárija said, "And it was as if a rope were unbound from an animal's leg!" Then they gave me payment. But I said, "No, not until I ask the Prophet." He replied, "Take it, for by my life! certainly whoever takes a reward for a false charm (has sinned), but thou hast taken it for a true one." '—*Aḥmad, Abú Dáud.*

It is related from 'Abdu'lláh bin 'Omar that, 'The Apostle of God said, "Give the labourer his wages before his perspiration becomes dry."'—*Ibn Májah.*

It is related from 'Utbah binu'l-Nuddar that he said, 'We were with the Apostle of God when he recited the chapter of the Qur'án entitled "The story." And when he reached the story of Moses he said, "Verily Moses hired himself for eight or ten years on condition that he preserved his continence and received his food."'—*Aḥmad, Ibn Májah.*

On Rejuvenating Dead (Lands) and Water

It is related from 'Urwah that he said, 'Zubair had an altercation with a man of the helpers concerning a place where water flowed from the hot stony plains. And the Prophet said, "O Zubair, do thou use the water, and then afterwards send it on to thy neighbour." Then the helper said, "(This judgement) is because he is the son of thy aunt!" Then the Prophet's face changed colour, and he said, "O Zubair, use the water, and then impound it until it returns to the dam. After that send on the water to thy neighbour." And the Prophet protected the rights of Zubair for him by his plain orders when the helper made him angry. As a matter of fact, he had advised them a course which had in it amplitude for them both.' —*Muslim, Al Bukhárí.*

It is related from Ibn 'Omar that, 'The Prophet gave Zubair land as a fief as far as his horse could go. Then Zubair drove his horse until it stopped. After that he threw down his whip; and the Apostle of God said, "Give him as far as the whip reaches."'—*Abú Dáud.*

It is related from Ibn 'Abbás that, 'The Apostle of God said, "Muslims are partners in three things: in water and herbage and fire."'—*Abú Dáud, Ibn Májah.*

It is related from Ṭáus that, 'The Apostle of God said, "Whoever rejuvenates dead land, it becomes his, and ancient lands belong to God and His Apostle. Afterwards they become yours from me."'—*Ash Sháfi'.*

It is related from Samurah bin Jundub that he had some date trees in a garden belonging to a man of the helpers. And the man had his family with him. And Samurah used to go into the garden, and thereby caused him annoyance. Then the man came to the Prophet and mentioned the matter to him. Then the Prophet requested him (Samurah) to sell to him; but he refused. Then he requested him to exchange them for others; but he refused. Then the Prophet said, "Then give them to him, and thou wilt obtain such-and-such a reward," inspiring him with a desire for it. But he refused. Then the Apostle of God said, "Thou art a troublesome fellow." After that he said to the helper, "Go and cut down his date trees."' —*Abú Dáud.*

On Giving

It is related from Ibn 'Omar that he obtained some land in Khaibár. And he came to the Prophet and said, 'O Apostle of God, I have obtained some land in Khaibár, more valuable property than which I have never possessed. Then what dost thou command me with respect to it?' He replied, 'Thou mayest endow its principal in the name of religion and give in alms of its produce.' Then 'Omar gave it in alms, so that its principal should not be sold, and should not be given away or inherited. And he gave its produce in alms to the poor, and to his relations, and for the emancipation of slaves, and in the road of God, and for travellers and guests. (And he proclaimed) that it should be no fault in those whom he had thus made participators in the produce if they ate of it in a reasonable manner or gave others to eat when in want. Ibn Sírín said, 'And provided they did not hoard up wealth.'—*Muslim, Al Bukhárí.*

It is related from Al Nu'mán bin Bashír that his father brought him to the Apostle of God and said, 'Verily I have given this son of mine as a slave.' He said, 'Hast thou made presents of all thy sons in this manner?' He replied, 'No.' The Prophet said, 'Take him back.' And in another tradition it runs, 'He said, "Would it please thee that they should be equal before thee in righteousness?" He replied, "Yes." He said, "Then do not give him as a slave."' And in another tradition it runs, 'He said, "My father gave me away as a present. And 'Umrah bint Rawáḥah said, 'I shall not be satisfied until thou make the Apostle of God a witness.' Then he came to the Apostle of God and said, 'Verily I have given my son, born of 'Umrah bint Rawáḥah, as a present, and she ordered me to make thee a witness, O Apostle of God.' He replied, 'Hast thou given away the rest of thy sons in this manner?' He said, 'No.' He said, 'Then fear God, and act justly between thy children.' Nu'mán said, 'Then he returned and took back his present.'"' And in another tradition it runs, 'He said, "I shall not be a witness to injustice."'—*Muslim, Al Bukhárí.*

It is related from Anas that he said, 'When the Apostle of God came to Madína, the refugees came to him and said, "O Apostle of God, we do not see any people more generous in great matters or more helpful in small than the people amongst whom we have settled. Of a truth they have sufficed us in trouble and made us their sharers in food, until we fear that they will take all the reward." He replied, "No, not so long as you pray to God for them and praise them."'—*At Tirmidhí.*

It is related from 'Áyesha that, 'The Prophet said, "Make presents to one another; for verily presents dispel hatred."'

Concerning What is Found

It is related from Zaid bin Khálid that he said, 'A man came to the Apostle of God and asked him concerning (a straying animal) that is found. He replied, "Take note of its powers and its halter; then make it known for a year. Then if its owner comes (give it him), otherwise it becomes yours." The man said, "Then what of a goat which has wandered?" He replied, "It is thine, or thy brother's, or the wolf's." He said, "Then what of a camel that has strayed?" He replied, "What is that to thee, when it has with it its supply of water and the soles of its feet! It comes to water, and eats the trees until its master meets it."'—*Muslim, Al Bukhárí.* And in another tradition from Muslim it runs, 'He said, "Make it known for a year. Then take note of its halter and its powers. After that make use of it; and if its owner comes, then hand it over to him."'

It is related from 'Ámru bin Shuaib, from his father, from his grandfather, that the Apostle of God was asked about fruit hanging (on the trees). He replied, 'Whoever has a need of them (and eats them), without carrying any away in his garment, is blameless; but whoever takes any away must give double its value as damage, as well as (suffer) the punishment due. And whoever steals anything from it after that the threshing-floor has provided a place for it, its value being that of a shield, amputation (of the hand) is his punishment.' And 'Amru made a remark with regard to a camel or goat that had strayed as others have mentioned. He said, '(The Prophet) was asked concerning what is found. He replied, "That which is found on a public road, or in a populous village, advertise it for a year. Then if its owner comes, hand it over to him ; but if he does not appear, then thou mayest keep it. And whatever is found in old, abandoned land, of it and of what is hidden therein—one fifth." '—*An Nasái.*

It is related from Jábir that he said, 'The Apostle of God made a concession to us in the matter of walking-sticks, whips, ropes and the like which a man picks up, that he might use it for his own benefit.'—*Abú Dáud.*

On the Division of Inheritance

It is related from Abú Hurairah that, 'The Prophet said, "I am more fit (to aid) Muslims than they themselves, therefore whoever dies in debt, leaving nothing wherewith to liquidate it, its payment rests with me. And whoever leaves property, it is for his heirs." '—*Muslim, Al Bukhári.*

It is related from Usámah bin Zaid that, 'The Apostle of God said, "A Muslim shall not inherit from an infidel, nor an infidel from a Muslim." '—*Muslim, Al Bukhári.*

It is related from Abú Hurairah that, 'The Apostle of God said, "A murderer shall not inherit." '—*At Tirmidhí, Ibn Májah.*

It is related from Buraidah that, 'The Prophet appointed a sixth for a grandmother, when there is besides her no mother.' —*Abú Dáud.*

It is related from Jábir that, 'The Apostle of God said, "When a (new-born) child utters a cry (and then dies), it must be prayed over, and its inheritance is passed on." '—*Ibn Májah.*

It is related from 'Amru bin Shuaib, from his father, from his grandfather, that, 'The Prophet said, "Whatever man commits adultery, either with a free woman or a slave girl, the child is the child of adultery. It shall not inherit, nor be inherited from." '—*At Tirmidhí.*

It is related from 'Áyesha that, 'A freedman of the Apostle died and left some property, but left no relations or child. Then the Apostle of God said, "Give his inheritance to a man of the people of the village."'—*Abú Dáud, At Tirmidhí.*

It is related from 'Alí that he said, 'Ye read this verse (of the Qur'án), "After the legacies which ye bequeath and the debts," but, verily the Apostle of God ordered the (payment) of debts before the (distribution) of the legacies; and he ordered that the sons of the same mother should inherit from one another, but not if they be by different mothers; and that a man should inherit from his brother born of his own father and mother, but not from his brother by his father only.'—*At Tirmidhí, Ibn Májah.*

It is related from Jábir that he said, 'The wife of Sa'd binu'l-Rábi, came to the Apostle of God with her two daughters by Sa'd binu'l-Rábi' and said, "O Apostle of God, these two are daughters of Sa'd binu'l-Rábi'. Their father was killed as a martyr (when fighting) together with thee on the day of (the battle of) 'Uhud. And verily their uncle has taken their property, and left no property for them; and they cannot marry unless they obtain their property." He replied, "God will adjudicate on that matter." Then came down the verse of inheritance. So the Apostle of God sent to their uncle and said, "Give to the daughters of Sa'd two-thirds, and to their mother one-eighth; and what remains over is for thyself."'—*Aḥmad, At Tirmidhí, Abú Dáud, Ibn Májah.*

It is related from Huzail bin Shuraḥbíl that he said, 'Abú Músá was asked concerning (the inheritance of) a daughter, a son's daughter and a sister. He replied, "One half is for the daughter and one half for the sister; but go to Ibn Ma'súd, and he will corroborate me." Then Ibn Ma'súd was asked, and was informed of the words of Abú Músá. He replied, "Then (if I corroborate) I shall go astray, and shall not be of those who are guided aright. I shall pass judgement in the matter as the Prophet passed judgement. For the daughter is one-half, and for the son's daughter one-sixth to complete a full two-thirds, and what remains is for the sister." Then Abú Músá came to us and informed us of the words of Ibn Ma'súd and said, "Do not ask me so long as this wise man remains amongst you."'—*Al Bukhárí.*

It is related from Qabísah bin Dhuwaib that he said, 'A grandmother came to Abú Bakr to ask about her inheritance. He said to her, "There is nothing for thee according to the Book of God, and nothing for thee according to the traditions of the Prophet. Then return until I can ask the people." Then he enquired, and Al Mughírah bin Shu'bah said, "I was present with the Apostle of God when he gave her (i.e. a grandmother) one-sixth." Abú Bakr said, "Was there anyone present with thee besides thyself?" Then Muḥammad bin Maslamah answered in the same terms that Al Mughírah had spoken. Then Abú Bakr sent it to her. After that another grandmother came to 'Omar to ask him about her inheritance. He replied, "It is that one-sixth. If you both agree, then it may be divided between the two of you; or whoever of you remains alone, it is for her."'—*Mâlik, Aḥmad, At Tirmidhí.*

Concerning Wills

It is related from Sa'd bin abi Waqqáṣ that he said, 'I was ill in the year of the conquest of Mecca, and I was nigh unto death. Then the Apostle of God came to me to visit me. And I said, "O Apostle of God, verily I have much wealth, and I have no one to inherit from me except my daughter. May I will away all that I possess?" He replied, "No." I said, "Then two-thirds of my property?" He replied, "No." I said, "Then one-half?" He replied, "No." I said, "Then one-third?" He replied, "Yes, one-third, for that is sufficient; and it is better to leave your heirs rich than indigent and begging, and holding out hands to beg of men. For thou wilt never expend alms, seeking thereby the face of God, but thou wilt be rewarded for it, even to the morsel thou raisest to thy wife's mouth."'—*Muslim, Al Bukhárí.*

It is related from Abú Hurairah that, 'The Prophet said, "Verily a man and his wife acted in accordance with the will of God for sixty years. Then death claimed them. But they did some one an injury in their will, therefore the fire became their rightful portion."'—*Abú Dáud, Ibn Mâjah.*

XIII

THE BOOK OF MARRIAGE

It is related from Abú Hurairah that, 'The Apostle of God said, "A woman may be married for four reasons: for her wealth, for her noble lineage, for her beauty, and for her religion; therefore obtain one with religion, otherwise may your hands be covered with dirt."'—*Muslim, Al Bukhárí.*

It is related from 'Abdu'lláh bin 'Omar that, 'The Apostle of God said, "The whole world is valuable; but the most valuable thing in the world is a good woman."'—*Muslim.*

It is related from Umámah bin Zaid that, 'The Apostle of God said, "I have not left after me any calamity more distressing to man than woman."'—*Muslim, Al Bukhárí.*

It is related from Abú Sa'ídu'l-Khudri that, 'The Apostle of God said, "The world is sweet and green, and verily God has made you inheritors therein; therefore take heed how ye behave, and abstain from the world and from women; for verily the first rebellion of the children of Israel was on account of women."'—*Muslim.*

It is related from Abú Hurairah that, 'The Apostle of God said, "There are three persons whose assistance is incumbent upon God: the freed slave who wishes to discharge his bond of freedom, the one who marries desiring abstinence from what is unlawful, and the one who fights in the way of God."'—*At Tirmidhí, An Nasái, Ibn Májah.*

It is related from Abú Umámah that, 'The Prophet said, "A believer has not benefitted more, after the fear of God, than by a virtuous wife who, if he commands her, obeys him; and if he looks at her, pleases him; and if he swears by her, justifies him; and if he goes away from her, acts sincerely in respect to herself and his property."'—*Ibn Májah.*

It is related from Anas that, 'The Apostle of God said, "When a servant (of God) marries, he has perfected half of religion; then let him fear God for the remaining half."'

On Looking at One Betrothed

It is related from Al Mughíra bin Shu'bah that he said, 'I asked a woman in marriage; and the Apostle of God said to me, "Hast thou looked at her?" I said, "No." He said, "Then look at her, for that is the best thing for arousing love between you." '—*Aḥmad, At Tirmidhí, An Nasái, Ibn Májah.*

It is related from Buraidah that, 'The Apostle of God said, "O 'Alí, O 'Alí, do not follow up one look with another. For verily the first will be forgiven thee, but the last will not." ' —*Aḥmad, At Tirmidhí, Abú Dáud.*

It is related from Umm Salamah that, 'She was with the Apostle of God and Yamúnah when Ibn Umm Maktum drew near and entered in to him. Then the Apostle of God said, "Conceal yourselves from him." I said, "O Apostle of God, is he not blind and unable to see us?" The Apostle of God replied, "Are you two blind? Do you not see him?" '—*Aḥmad, At Tirmidhí, Abú Dáud.*

It is related from Jábir that, 'The Prophet said, "Do not visit those women whose husbands are absent; for verily Satan circulates in every one of you like the circulation of blood." We replied, "And in thee also, O Apostle of God?" He said, "And in me also, but God has aided me against him so that I am secure." '—*At Tirmidhí.*

It is related from Al Ḥasan that he said, 'I was informed that the Apostle of God said, "God cursed the one who looks (on a woman), and He cursed the one looked on." '—*Al Baihaqi.*

Concerning the Guardian, and Asking the Consent of the Woman

It is related from Abú Hurairah that, 'The Apostle of God said, "A widow shall not be married until she be consulted; and a virgin shall not be married until her consent be asked." They said, "O Apostle of God, how shall her permission (be understood)?" He replied, "That she keep silence." '—*Muslim, Al Bukhárí.*

It is related from Khansái bint Khidhám that, 'Her father gave her in marriage when a widow. And it was distasteful to her; so she came to the Apostle of God. And he set aside the marriage.'—*Al Bukhárí.*

It is related from 'Áyesha that, 'The Prophet married her when she was a girl of seven years. And she was taken to her husband's house when a girl of nine years; and her playthings accompanied her. And the Prophet died and left her when she was a girl of eighteen.'—*Muslim.*

It is related from Abú Músá that, 'The Prophet said, "There is no marriage without a guardian."'—*Aḥmad, At Tirmidhí, Abú Dáud, Ibn Májah.*

It is related from Abú Hurairah that, 'The Apostle of God said, "A female orphan shall be consulted (with regard to her marriage), and if she remain silent, that is her consent. But if she refuse, then no compulsion shall be put on her."'—*At Tirmidhí, Abú Dáud, An Nasái.*

It is related from Jábir that, 'The Prophet said, "Whatever slave marries without the consent of his master is an adulterer."'—*At Tirmidhí, Abú Dáud.*

It is related from Ibn 'Abbás that he said, 'Verily a virgin came to the Apostle of God and informed him that her father had given her in marriage against her wish. Then the Prophet gave her her choice.'—*Abú Dáud.*

It is related from Abú Sa'íd and Ibn 'Abbás that, 'The Apostle of God said, "Whoever has a son born to him, let him give him a good name and teach him good manners; and when he reaches puberty let him get him married. And if he reaches puberty, and he does not get him married, and he falls into sin, then the father only is responsible."'

It is related from 'Omar binu'l-Khaṭṭáb and Anas bin Málik that, 'The Apostle of God said, "It is written in the Taurát, that he whose daughter reaches twelve years of age, and he has not given her in marriage, and she falls into sin, he is responsible for that sin."'—*Al Baihaqi.*

On Publishing Marriages, and the Conditions Governing Them

It is related from Rubayyi'bint Mu'awwidh bin Afrái that she said, 'The Prophet came and entered when I was being taken to his house for the first time; and he sat down on my bed as thou art sitting on it near me. And the slave girls began to beat the drums and to eulogize those of my ancestors who were killed on the day of (the battle of) Badr; when one of them said, "There is a Prophet amongst us who knows what will be on the morrow." Then he said, "Leave this, and say what you were saying before."'—*Al Bukhárí.*

It is related from 'Áyesha that she said, 'The Apostle of God married me in (the month) Shawwál, and I was taken to his house as a bride in Shawwál. Then what wife of the Prophet has enjoyed greater favour from him than I?'—*Muslim.*

It is related from 'Alí that, 'The Apostle of God prohibited the temporary marriage of women on the day of (the conquest of) Khaibár; and he prohibited the eating of the flesh of the domestic ass.'—*Muslim, Al Bukhárí.*

It is related from 'Áyesha that, 'The Apostle of God said, "Publish this marriage and perform it in mosques and beat drums for it."'—*At Tirmidhí.*

It is related from 'Áyesha that she said, 'I had a girl of the helpers, and I gave her in marriage. Then the Apostle of God said, "O Áyesha, will you not sing, for verily this tribe of the helpers loves singing."'

It is related from Ibn 'Abbás that he said, 'Temporary marriage was only at the beginning of Islám. A man would come to a town in which he had no acquaintances. Then he would marry a woman for the time it was seen he would stay there, and she would look after his effects for him and cook his food well for him, until the verse came down, "(Who keep themselves from carnal knowledge of any women) except their wives or the captives which their right hands possess."'[1] Ibn 'Abbás said, "Every womb except these is unlawful."'—*At Tirmidhí.*

It is related from Ámir bin Sa'd that he said, 'I entered in to Qarzah bin Ka'b and Abú Ma'súd, the helper, at a wedding feast, and behold! some girls were singing. So I said, "O ye two companions of the Apostle of God and men of Badr, is this done in your presence!" They replied, "Sit if thou wilt, and listen with us, and if thou wilt, depart; for verily enjoyment is permitted us at a wedding feast."'—*An Nasái.*

Concerning Those Whom It is Unlawful to Marry

It is related from 'Áyesha that she said, 'My uncle from my wet-nurse[2] came to me and asked permission to enter where I was. But I refused to give him permission until I had asked

[1] Qur'án, Súratu'l-Mú'minún (xxiii) 6.

[2] That is, the brother of her wet-nurse's husband.

the Apostle of God. Then the Apostle of God came, and I asked him. He replied, "Verily, he is thy uncle, therefore give him permission."' She said, 'Then I said, "O Apostle of God, only the woman nursed me, and not the man!" The Apostle of God replied, "He is thy uncle, therefore allow him to enter where thou art." And that took place after the verse of veiling was promulgated.'—*Muslim, Al Bukhárí.*

It is related from 'Uqbah binu'l-Ḥaríth that, 'He married a daughter of Abú Iháb bin 'Azíz. Then a woman came and said, "I nursed 'Uqbah and the woman whom he has married." 'Uqbah said to her, "I did not know that thou hadst suckled me, and thou didst not inform me." Then he sent to the family of Abú Iháb and asked them. They said, "We did not know that she had suckled our girl." Then he rode to the Prophet at Madína and asked him. The Apostle of God replied, "How (canst thou keep her) when it has been remarked (that you were both suckled by the same woman!)" Then 'Uqbah separated her; and she married another husband.'—*Al Bukhárí.*

It is related from Abú Sa'ídu'l-Khudri that, 'On the day of (the battle of) Hunain, the Apostle of God sent an army to Awtás; and they met the enemy, and fought with them, and won a victory over them, and they took them prisoners. And certain men of the companions of the Prophet withheld themselves from co-habitation with the women (captives) on account of their husbands among the polytheists. Then God sent down respecting the matter (the revelation, "Ye are forbidden to take to wife) free women who are married, except those women whom your right hands shall possess as slaves."[1] That is they are lawful for them when their stated time shall be fulfilled.'—*Muslim.*

It is related from Al Barái bin 'Azib that he said, 'My uncle Abú Burdah bin Niyári passed by me; and he had with him a standard. And I said, "Where art thou going?" He replied, "The Prophet has sent me to a man who has married the wife of his father, in order to bring his head to him."'—*At Tirmidhí, Abú Dáud.* And in another tradition from An Nasái and Ibn Májah it runs, 'He has commanded me to cut off his head and take his property.'

---

[1] Qu'rán, Súratu'n-Nisá' (iv) 42.

It is related from Ibn 'Omar that Ghailán bin Salamahu'l-Shaqafi became a Muslim. And he had ten wives in the times of ignorance, and they became Muslims with him. Then the Prophet said, "Keep four and send away the rest of them."'—*Aḥmad, Al Tirmidhí, Ibn Májah.*

CONCERNING COHABITATION

(The traditions in this section are too obscene for translation.)

It is related from 'Urwah from 'Áyeshá that, 'The Apostle of God said to her with reference to Barírah, "Take her and set her free." And her husband was (also) a slave. Then the Apostle of God gave her her choice, and she chose herself (i.e. freedom from her husband.) But if he had been a free man, the Prophet would not have given her her choice.'—*Muslim, Al Bukhárí.*

It is related from Ibn 'Abbás that he said, 'The husband of Barírah was a black slave called Mughíth. And it is as if I could see him wandering round after her in the streets of Madína weeping and with his tears flowing over his beard. Then the Prophet said to 'Abbás, "O 'Abbás, art thou not surprised at the love of Mughíth for Barírah, and at the aversion of Barírah for Mughith!" After that the Prophet said, "If thou return to him (it will be better)." She said, "O Apostle of God, dost thou order me?" He said, "I only plead for him." She replied, "I have no need of him."'—*Al Bukhárí.*

CONCERNING MARRIAGE DOWRIES

It is related from Sahl bin Sa'd that, 'A woman came to the Apostle of God and said, "O Apostle of God, verily I have given myself to thee." And she stood up for a long time. Then a man rose up and said, "O Apostle of God, marry her to me if thou hast no need of her." He said, "Hast thou anything with which to provide her a dowry?" He replied, "I have nothing except these trowsers of mine." He said, "Then search for something, although it be but an iron ring." Then the man sought, but found nothing. Then the Apostle of God said, "Hast thou anything of the Qur'án?" He replied, "Yes, I have such-and-such a chapter." He said, "I wed her to thee by what thou hast of the Qur'án."' And in another tradition it runs, 'He said, "Depart, for I have wedded her to thee; and do thou teach her the Qur'án."'—*Muslim, Al Bukhárí.*

It is related from Abú Salamah that he said, 'I asked 'Áyesha, "How much was the dowry of the Prophet?" She replied, "His dowry for his wives was twelve *uqíyas* and one *nash.*" She said, "Dost thou know what a *nash* is?" I said, "No." She replied, "It is half an *uqíya*, and that is five hundred *dirhams.*" '—*Muslim.*

It is related from Jábir that, 'The Prophet said, "Whoever gives as a dowry for his wife two handsful of flour or dates has made her lawful for him." '—*Abú Dáud.*

It is related from Anas that he said, 'Abú Ṭalḥah married Umm Sulaim, and the dowry between them was Islám. Umm Sulaim embraced Islám before Abú Ṭalḥah, and he sued her in marriage. And she said, "I have embraced Islám. If thou embrace Islám, I will wed thee." Then he embraced Islám, and that was the dower between them.'—*An Násaí.*

Concerning the Marriage Feast

It is related from Anas that he said, 'The Apostle of God did not make a marriage feast for any of his wives such as he made for Zainab, when he feasted them with a goat.'—*Muslim, Al Bukhárí.*

It is related from Anas that he said, 'Verily the Apostle of God emancipated Safiyah and married her. And he made her emancipation her dowry; and he made a marriage feast with (the sweetmeat) *hais.*'—*Muslim, Al Bukhárí.*

It is related from Abú Hurairah that, 'The Apostle of God said, "The worst of food is the food of a marriage feast to which the rich are invited and the poor left out, and whoever rejects an invitation has disobeyed God and His Apostle." '—*Muslim, Al Bukhárí.*

It is related from Safínah that, 'A man was the guest of 'Alí binu'l-Muṭṭálib, and the latter prepared food for him. Then Fáṭimah said, "If we invite the Apostle of God, and he eat with us (it will be better)." They then invited him. And he came and placed his hands on the sideposts of the door. And he saw a painted cloth which had been placed on the wall of the house; so he returned home. Fáṭimah said, "Then I followed him and said, 'O Apostle of God, what turned thee back?' He replied, It is not for me, or for any Prophet, to enter a house which has been ornamented" '—*Aḥmad, Ibn Májah.*

Concerning the Division of Time Between Different Wives

It is related from Ibn 'Abbás that, 'The Apostle of God died leaving nine wives; and he used to divide (his time) amongst them as for eight persons.'—*Muslim, Al Bukhárí.*

It is related from 'Áyesha that, 'When Saudah became old, she said, "O Apostle of God, I have given my day with thee to 'Áyesha." So the Apostle of God used to set aside two days for 'Áyesha: her own and that of Saudah.'—*Muslim, Al Bukhárí.*

It is related from 'Áyesha that, 'When the Apostle of God wished to go on a journey, he used to cast lots amongst his wives, and would depart taking her with him whose name came out.'—*Muslim, Al Bukhárí.*

It is related from Abú Hurairah that, 'The Prophet said, "When a man has two wives, and does not treat them impartially; he will come on the day of resurrection with half his body fallen off."'—*At Tirmidhí, Abú Dáud, An Nasái, Ibn Májah.*

On Intercourse with Women, and the Rights of Each

It is related from 'Abú Hurairah that, 'The Apostle of God said, "If the Children of Israel had not lived, flesh would not have become putrid: and if Eve had not lived, no woman would ever have deceived her husband."'—*Muslim, Al Bukhárí.*

It is related from 'Áyesha that she said, 'The Apostle of God said to me, "I well know when thou art pleased with me, and when thou art angry with me." I said, "Whence dost thou know that?" He replied, "When thou art pleased with me, thou sayest, 'No, by the Lord of Muḥammad,' and when thou art angry with me, thou sayest, 'No, by the Lord of Abraham.'" She said, "Yes, by God! O Apostle of God, I abandon nothing but thy name."'—*Muslim, Al Bukhárí.*

It is related from Anas that, 'The Apostle of God swore to abstain from his wives for a month; and he had sprained his foot. And he remained in an upper room for twenty-nine nights. Then he came down. And they said, "O Apostle of God, you swore to abstain for a month." He replied, "Verily this month is one of twenty-nine days."'—*Al Bukhárí.*

It is related from Jábir that he said, 'Abú Bakr came and asked permission of the Apostle of God to enter; and he found other people sitting by his door, not one of whom was given permission.' Jábir said, 'Then Abú Bakr was given permission, and he entered. After that 'Omar drew near and asked permission, and it was given him. And he found the Prophet sitting, sad and silent, with his wives around him. He said, "I shall certainly say something to make the Prophet laugh." So he said, "O Apostle of God, if thou couldst have seen Bint Khárijah asking me for money to spend, and I stood up to her and squeezed her neck!" Then the Apostle of God laughed and said, "These women are around me, as thou seest, asking me for money to spend." Then Abú Bakr rose up to 'Áyesha (his daughter) and squeezed her neck; and 'Omar rose up to Hafṣa (his daughter) and squeezed her neck. They both said, "Dost thou ask of the Apostle of God what he has not got!" They replied, "By God! we never ask the Apostle of God for anything which he has not got." After that the Prophet separated himself from them for a month or twenty-nine days. After that the verse came down, "O Prophet, say unto thy wives, 'If ye seek this present life and the pomp thereof, come, and I will make a handsome provision for you, and I will dismiss you with an honourable dismissal; but if ye seek God and His Apostle and the life to come, verily God hath prepared for such of you as work righteousness a great reward.'"[1] Jábir said, "He said this first to 'Áyesha, and said, 'O 'Áyesha, I wish to bring a matter to thy notice, and I wish thee not to hurry in answering it until thou consult thy parents.' She replied, 'And what is that, O Apostle of God?' Then he recited to her the revelation. She said, 'In regard to thee, O Apostle of God, must I consult my parents? Rather I choose God and His Apostle and the last home (in paradise). I ask thee not to inform any of thy wives of what thou hast said.' He replied, 'None of my wives will ask me, but I will tell her of it. Verily God did not send me to cause people distress, but he sent me as a teacher and preacher of good tidings.'"'—*Muslim.*

It is related from 'Áyesha that she said, 'I was reflecting on the women who had given themselves to the Apostle of God,

[1] Qu'rán, Súratu'l-Aḥzáb (xxxiii) 28.

and I said, "Does a woman give herself away!" Then when God Most High sent down (the revelation), "Thou mayest postpone the turn of such (of thy wives) as thou shalt please; and thou mayest take unto thee her whom thou shalt please, and her whom thou shalt desire of those whom thou shalt have rejected; and it shall be no crime in thee,"[1] I said, "I do not see thy Lord except He hastens in (the fulfilment of) thy passionate desires." '—*Muslim, Al Bukhárí.*

It is related from Abú Hurairah that, 'The Apostle of God said, "If I had ordered anyone to prostrate to another, I would certainly have ordered a woman to prostrate before her husband." '—*At Tirmidhí.*

It is related from Ḥakím bin Mu'áwíyahu'l-Quthhairi, from his father, that he said, 'I said, "O Apostle of God, what is the right of the wife of any one of us from her husband?" He replied, "That thou let her eat when thou eatest, and clothe her when thou clothest thyself; and that thou do not strike her face, or treat her with ignominy, or leave her, except in the house." '—*Aḥmad, Abú Dáud.*

It is related from Iyás bin 'Abdu'lláh that, 'The Apostle of God said, "Do not beat the female servants of God." Then 'Omar came to the Apostle of God and said, "The women are presuming over their husbands (in consequence of thy words.)" Then he gave permission to beat them. Then a large number of women assembled around the Apostle's family complaining of their husbands. Then the Apostle of God said, "Many women have collected around the family of Muḥammad, complaining of their husbands. Those of you (who beat their wives) are not good." '—*Abú Dáuḍ, Ibn Májah, Al Dárimi.*

It is related from Jábir that, 'The Apostle of God said, "There are three persons from whom prayer will not be accepted and for whom their good works will not be taken up (to God): a runaway slave until he returns to his masters and places his hand in theirs, a woman whose husband is angry with her, and a drunkard until he reforms." '—*Al Baihaqi.*

Concerning Divorce

It is related from Ibn 'Abbás that the wife of Thábit bin Qais came to the Prophet and said, "O Apostle of God, I do not

[1] Qur'án, Súratu'l-Aḥzáb (xxxiii) 51.

blame Thábit bin Qais with regard to his manners or his religion; but I am displeased with infidelity in Islám." Then the Apostle of God said, "Wilt thou return his garden to Thábit?" She replied, "Yes." The Apostle of God said (to Thábit) "Take the garden, and divorce her with one divorce."' —*Al Bukhárí.*

It is related from 'Áyesha that, 'The Prophet used to stay with Zainab bint Jaḥsh and drink honey with her. Then Hafṣa and I determined together that to whomsoever of us the Prophet entered, she should say, "Verily I detect upon thee the smell of (the bad-smelling gum) *maghâfir.* Thou hast eaten *maghâfir.*" After that he entered in to one of them, and she repeated that to him. He replied, "There is no harm; I drank honey with Zainab bint Jaḥsh. I will never repeat it again. I have sworn. Tell no one of the matter." (This he said) seeking to please his wives. Then came down (the revelation), "O Prophet, why holdest thou that to be prohibited, which God hath allowed thee, seeking to please thy wives?" "[1]—*Muslim, Al Bukhárí.*

It is related from Ibn 'Omar that, 'The Prophet said, "The most hateful thing in the sight of God, of those things that are lawful, is divorce."'—*Abú Dáud.*

It is related from Maḥmúd bin Labíd that he said, 'The Apostle of God was informed of a man who divorced his wife with three divorces all together. Then he arose in anger and after that said, "Do ye play with the Book of God, the Exalted and Magnified, whilst I am still amongst you!" till a man stood up and said, "O Apostle of God, shall I kill him?"'—*An Nasái.*

On Mutual Cursing

It is related from Ibn 'Omar that, 'The Prophet said to a man and his wife who had been called upon to swear (in a dispute) "Your account is with God. One of you is a liar." (To the man he said) "Thou hast no claim over her." He replied, "O Apostle of God (may I claim) my property?" He said, "There is no property for thee. If thou hast spoken the truth regarding her, then it is for the use thou hast had of her; and if thou hast lied, then it is still more remote from thee."'—*Muslim, Al Bukhárí.*

[1] Qu'rán, Súratu't-Taḥrím (lxvi) 1.

It is related from 'Áyesha that, 'The Apostle of God went out from her on a certain night. She said, "And I was jealous of him; and he came and saw what I was doing and said, 'What is the matter with thee, O 'Áyesha; art thou jealous?'" I replied, "What is the matter with me if such an one as I were not jealous of such an one as thee?" The Apostle of God said, "Thy Satan has certainly come to thee." She said, "O Apostle of God, is there a Satan with me?" He said, "Yes." I said, "And with thee, O Apostle of God?" He said, "Yes, but God has aided me against him, so that I am safe."'—*Muslim.*

Concerning the Period of Waiting for a Divorced Woman

It is related from Abú Salamah from Fáṭimah bint Qais that, 'Abú 'Amru bin Ḥafs divorced her absolutely whilst he was absent. And his agent sent some barley to her; and she was angry with him. Then he said, "By God! thou hast no claim upon us whatever." And she came to the Apostle of God and mentioned the matter to him. He replied, "There is no subsistence allowance for thee." And he commanded her to spend her period of waiting in the house of Umm Sharík. After that he said, "That person is a woman whom my companions visit. Spend thy time of waiting with the son of Umm Maktúm, for he is a blind man, and thou couldest take off thy clothes. Then when thy time has expired, inform me." She said, "Then when the time had expired I mentioned to him that Mu'áwiya bin abu Sufyán and Abu'l-Jahm were seeking my hand in marriage." He said, "As for Abu'l-Jahm, he never lays down his stick from his shoulder (that is, he is a wife-beater), and as for Mu'áwiyah, he is a wretched beggar and has nothing. Marry Usámah bin Zaid." But I disliked him. Again the Prophet said, "Marry Usámah." Then I married him. And God has brought forth blessing out of it, and I have attained to a state of felicity.' And in another tradition it runs, 'But as for Abú Jahm, he is a man who beats his wives.'—*Muslim.* And in another tradition it runs, 'Verily her husband divorced her with a threefold divorce; and she came to the Prophet. And he said, "There is no subsistence allowance for thee, unless thou art pregnant."'

It is related from Umm Salamah that she said, 'A woman came to the Prophet and said, "O Apostle of God, verily my daughter's husband has died, and her eyes ache; may she apply salve to them?" The Apostle of God said, "No." Twice or thrice (was he asked), and each time he said, "No." Afterwards he said, "It is only four months and ten days, whereas in the times of ignorance one of you used to throw dung of animals (as a sign of the completion of the time of waiting) at the end of a year."'—*Muslim, Al Bukhárí.*

It is related from Umm Ḥabíbah and Zainab bint Jaḥsh that, 'The Apostle of God said, "It is not lawful for a woman who believes in God and the last day to observe mourning for the dead more than three nights, except for her husband, which is four months and ten days."'—*Muslim, Al Bukhárí.*

On Searching for the Signs of Pregnancy

On Subsistence Allowances, and the Duty of Slaves

It is related from 'Áyesha that, 'Hind bint 'Utbah said, "O Apostle of God, Abú Sufyán is a miserly fellow, and does not give me enough to suffice for me and my child, except what I take from him without his knowledge." The Prophet said, "Take what will suffice for thee and thy child in a proper manner."'—*Muslim, Al Bukhárí.*

It is related from Abú Hurairah that, 'The Apostle of God said, "A slave has a right to his food and clothes; and he must not be distressed with work other than what he is able to perform."'—*Muslim.*

It is related from Abú Dharr that, 'The Apostle of God said, "God has placed your brethren under your hands (as slaves); then let him, under whose hands God has placed his brother, feed him with what he eats himself, and clothe him with what he wears himself. And let him not give him distress by work which is too much for him. But if he does distress him with work which is too much for him, then let him help him."'—*Muslim, Al Bukhárí.*

It is related from Abú Hurairah that he said, 'I heard the father of Qásim (i.e. Muḥammad) say, "Whoever abuses his slave, when he is innocent of what he charges him with, will be scourged on the day of resurrection, unless it be as he has said."'—*Muslim, Al Bukhárí.*

It is related from 'Amru bin Shuaib, from his father, from his grandfather, that, 'A man came to the Prophet and said, "Verily I have money, but my father is in need of my money." He replied, "Thou and thy money belong to thy father. Verily your children are the best of your earnings. Eat of your children's earnings."'—*Abú Dáud, Ibn Májah.*

It is related from Abú Bakr Aṣ Ṣiddíq that, 'The Prophet said, "The one who treaṭs his slave badly will not enter paradise."'—*At Tirmidhí, Ibn Májah.*

It is related from Abú Ayyúb that he said, 'I heard the Apostle of God say, "Whoever separates a mother and her child; God will separate him from his friends on the day of resurrection."'—*At Tirmidhí, Al Dárimí.*

It is related from 'Abdu'lláh bin 'Omar that he said, 'A man came to the Prophet and said, "O Apostle of God, how often shall we forgive our servants?" But he remained silent. Afterwards he repeated the question, but he remained silent. Then when he asked the third time, he replied, "Forgive him seventy times every day."'—*Abú Dáud.*

It is related from Ibn 'Abbas that, 'When the word of God Most High came down, "Mẹddle not with the substance of the orphan, otherwise than for the improving thereof,"[1] and the word of God, "Surely they who devour the possessions of orphans unjustly shall swallow down nothing but fire into their bellies";[2] then the one who had an orphan living with him departed and separated his food from his own and his drink from his own. And when anything was left out from the food of the orphan, he kept it until the latter ate it or drank it, or it went bad. But that became distressing (to the orphans), and they mentioned it to the Apostle of God. Then God Most High sent down (the revelation), "They will ask thee concerning orphans. Say, to deal righteously with them is best; and if ye mix your things with theirs, verily they are your brethren."[3] Then they mixed their food with their own, and their drink with their own.'—*Abú Dáud, An Nasái.*

---

[1] Qu'rán, Súratu'l-An'ám (vi) 152. [2] Súratu'n-Nisá' (iv) 10.
[3] Súratu'l-Baqara (ii) 219.

Concerning the Young Arriving at Puberty, and on Their Up-bringing

It is related from Ibn 'Omar that he said, 'I was brought before the Apostle of God in the year of (the battle of) Uḥud, when I was fourteen years of age; but he sent me back. After that I was presented to him in the year (of the battle) of the ditch, when I was fifteen years of age. Then he permitted me (to fight).' And 'Omar bin 'Abdu'l-Azíz said, 'This (age) is the boundary between those who fight and children.'—*Muslim, Al Bukhárí.*

It is related from Al Barái bin 'Azíb that he said, 'The Prophet made peace on the day of Ḥudaibah on three conditions: that whoever came to him from the polytheists, he would send him back to them; that whoever came to them from the Muslims, they would not send him back; and that he should enter Mecca the next year, and stay in it three days. Then when he entered it, and the time expired, he went out. And there followed him the daughter of Ḥamza, calling out, "O uncle, O uncle." And 'Alí stretched out his hand, and took her by the hand. And 'Alí and Zaid and Ja'far disputed about her (as to who should become her guardian). 'Alí said, "I took her because she is the daughter of my uncle." Ja'far said, "She is the daughter of my uncle, and her aunt is my wife." And Zaid said, "She is the daughter of my brother." Then the Prophet passed judgement in favour of her mother's sister, and said, "A mother's sister is in the place of a mother." And he said to 'Alí, "Thou belongest to me and I to thee." And he said to Ja'far, "Thou dost resemble me in thy build and disposition." And he said to Zaid, "Thou art our brother and our friend." '—*Muslim, Al Bukhárí.*

XIV

THE BOOK OF THE EMANCIPATION OF SLAVES

It is related from Abú Hurairah that, 'The Apostle of God said, "Whoever emancipates a Muslim slave, God will emancipate every member of his body from the fire, in return for the members (of his slave)." '—*Muslim*, *Al Bukhárí*.

It is related from 'Amru bin 'Abasah that, 'The Prophet said, "Whoever builds a mosque in order that God may be remembered therein; a house will be built for him in paradise. And whoever emancipates a person who is a Muslim, it will be his ransom from hell. And whoever grows grey in the way of God, it will be for him a light on the day of resurrection." '—*In Sharḥu's-Sunnah*.

On the Emancipation of a Slave Who is Jointly Owned

It is related from 'Imrán bin Ḥuṣain that, 'A man at his death freed six slaves which belonged to him. He had no other property besides them. Then the Apostle of God called them and divided them into three lots. After that he cast lots amongst them and freed two of them and retained four in slavery. And he spoke severe words about the man.'—*Muslim*. And in another tradition from Nasái it runs, '"I certainly thought not to pray over him." But he spake severe words of him instead.' And in another tradition from *Abú Dáud* it runs, 'He said, "Had I been present before he was buried, he would not have been buried in a Muslim cemetery." '

It is related from Ibn 'Abbás that, 'The Prophet said, "If a female slave bears a son to her master, then she is free at his death or after it." '—*Al Dárimi*.

It is related from Jábir that he said, 'We used to sell the mothers of children in the time of the Apostle of God and in that of Abú Bakr; but when 'Omar (was *Khalíf*) he forbade us doing it; therefore we brought the practice to an end.'—*Abú Dáud*.

CONCERNING OATHS AND VOWS

It is related from Ibn 'Omar that he said, 'The oath which the Prophet used to use most was, "No, by the Turner of hearts!" '—*Al Bukhárí.*

It is related from Ibn 'Omar that, 'The Apostle of God said, "Verily God has forbidden you to swear by your fathers, Whoever takes an oath, let him swear by God, or remain silent." '—*Muslim, Al Bukhárí.*

It is related from 'Imrán bin Ḥuṣain that, 'The Apostle of God said, "There is no performance of a vow requiring disobedience, or regarding anything which the servant does not own." '—*Muslim.*

It is related from Ibn 'Abbás that he said, 'Whilst the Prophet was making an address, behold! a man remained standing, and he asked about him. They replied, "He is Abu Isrá'íl. He has vowed to stand, and to neither sit, nor go into the shade nor speak. And he has vowed to fast, and he is is fasting." The Prophet said, "Order him to speak and go into the shade and sit down and end his fast." '—*Al Bukhárí.*

It is related from Jábir bin 'Abdu'lláh that 'A man stood up on the day of the conquest of Mecca and said, "O Apostle of God, verily I have vowed to God, the Exalted and Magnified, that if He gave thee conquest over Mecca, I would pray in two *rak'ahs* in Jerusalem." The Prophet replied, "Pray here." Then the man repeated what he had said. He replied, "Pray here." Then the man repeated his words. The Prophet said, "Go your own way then!" '—*Abú Dáud, Al Dárimi.*

It is related from 'Abdu'lláh bin Málik that, ''Uqbah bin 'Ámir asked the Prophet about his sister who had vowed to perform the pilgrimage barefooted and unveiled. The Prophet said, "Order her to veil herself and ride, and to fast three days." '—*Abú Dáud, At Tirmidhí, An Nasái, Ibn Májah.*

It is related from Muḥammad binu'l-Muntashir that he said, 'Verily a man made a vow that if God saved him from his enemies, he would sacrifice himself. So he asked Ibn 'Abbás about it. The latter said to him, "Ask Masrúq." So he asked him. He replied, "Do not sacrifice thyself, for if thou art a believer, then thou wilt kill a believer; and if thou art an infidel, that will hasten thee to the fire. Therefore buy a ram and kill it for the poor ; for verily Isaac was better than thou, and he was ransomed by a ram." Then he informed Ibn Abbás ; and he said, " I wished to answer the question in this way." '—*Razín.*

XV

THE BOOK OF RETALIATION

It is related from Al Miqdám binu'l-Aswad that he said, 'O Apostle of God, tell me, if I meet a man who is an infidel, and we fight together, and he strikes one of my hands with a sword and cuts it off, and then takes refuge from me in a tree and says, "I become a Muslim,"—And in another tradition it runs, "And when I come down to kill him, he says, 'There is no God but Alláh,'—Should I kill him after he says that?" He replied, "Do not kill him." The man said, "O Apostle of God, he has cut off one of my hands!" The Apostle of God said, "Do not kill him; for if thou kill him, verily he was in the same rank as thyself (i.e., a believer) before thou killedst him, and then thou wilt be in the position he occupied before he uttered the words which he spoke." '—*Muslim, Al Bukhárí.*

It is related from Abú Hurairah that, 'The Apostle of God said, "Whoever throws himself down from a mountain and kills himself is in the fire of hell, and he will be thrown into it, and will remain there for ever and ever. And whoever takes poison and kills himself, his poison will remain in his hand, and he will take it continually in the fire of hell, and he will remain therein for ever and ever. And whoever kills himself with any iron weapon, his weapon will remain in his hand, and he will continually stab himself in his belly in the fire of hell, and he will remain there for ever and ever." '—*Muslim, Al Bukhárí.*

It is related from Anas that 'a Jew pounded the head of a slave-girl between two stones. And it was said to her, "Who did this to thee? Was it so and so, or so and so?" until the Jew was named. Then she nodded her head. Then they brought the Jew, and he confessed. Then the Apostle of God gave orders concerning him; and his head was pounded with a stone.'—*Muslim, Al Bukhárí.*

It is related from Anas that he said, 'Al Rubaiya, who was the aunt of Anas bin Málik, broke the front teeth of a daughter of one of the Helpers. And they came to the Prophet; and he ordered retaliation. Then Anas bin Nadar, the uncle of Anas bin Málik said, "No by God! O Apostle of God, her front teeth shall not be broken." The Apostle of God said, "O Anas, the Book of God prescribes retaliation." Then the parties came to an agreement, and they accepted money. Then the Apostle of God said, "Verily amongst the worshippers of God are some who, if they swear by God, He will certainly fulfil it." '—*Muslim, Al Bukhárí.*

It is related from Abú Juḥaifah that he said, 'I asked 'Alí, "Hast thou anything which is not in the Qur'án?" He replied, "By Him who cleft the grain and created man! We have nothing besides what is in the Qur'án, except understanding of what has been given in the Book of God, and what is in the volume." I said, "And what is in the volume?" He replied, "The rules regarding blood-money, and the emancipation of captives, and that a Muslim should not be killed (in retaliation) for an infidel." '—*Muslim, Al Bukhárí.*

It is related from Abú Umámah bin Sahl bin Ḥunaif that, ''Othmán bin 'Affán looked down from a high place on the day of (the seige of) his house and said, "I adjure you by God, whether you know that the Apostle of God said, 'The blood of a Muslim is not lawful except for one of three reasons: adultery after marriage with a chaste woman, or apostasy after Islám, or the murder of a soul which God has forbidden.' Then for which of these are you killing me?" '—*At Tirmidhí, An Nasái, Ibn Májah.*

It is related from Al Ḥasan from Ṣamurah that, 'The Apostle of God said, "Whoever kills his slave, we will kill him; and whoever mutilates his slave, we will mutilate him." '—*At Tirmidhí, Abú Dáud, Ibn Májah.*

It is related from 'Amru bin Shu'aib, from his father, from his grandfather, that, 'The Apostle of God said, "Whoever commits murder intentionally, he must be handed over to the relations of the murdered person. And if they wish, they may kill him; and if they wish, they may take blood-money. And it is thirty camels in their fourth year, and thirty camels in their fifth year and forty camels with young. And it is for them to say which they will be reconciled with." '—*At Tirmidhí.*

It is related from Sa'íd binu'l-Musayyib that, ''Omar binu'l-Khaṭṭáb killed a party of five or seven men (in retaliation) for one man whom they had treacherously murdered. 'Omar said, "If the people of Ṣan'á' had attacked him, I would certainly have killed them all."'—*Málik.*

Concerning Various Kinds of Blood-Money

It is related from 'Amru bin Shu'aib, from his father, from his grandfather, that he said, 'The price of blood-money in the time of the Apostle was eight hundred dinars or eight thousand dirhems; and the blood-money for the People of the Book was then half the blood-money of Muslims.' He said, 'And it remained thus until 'Omar became *Khalíf.* And he stood up and made a speech and said, "Verily camels have become very expensive." And he, 'Omar, fixed the blood-money for the possessors of gold at one thousand dinars, and for the people who possessed silver at twelve thousand, and he fixed it for the people owning cattle at two hundred cows, and for those owning goats at two thousand goats; and for those possessing clothes at two hundred garments. And he left the blood-money for Jews and Christians who were under the protection of Muslims (as it was). He did not raise it when he raised the blood-money.'—*Abú Dáud.*

It is related from 'Amru bin Shu'aib, from his father from his grandfather, that, 'The Apostle of God said, "He who poses as a doctor when the science of medicine is not known to him, will be responsible."'—*Abú Dáud, An Nasái.*

Concerning Faults for which there is no Retaliation

It is related from Abú Hurairah that, 'The Apostle of God said, "Wounds from brute beasts, and from falling into mines, and from falling into wells do not entail responsibility (on the owner)."'—*Muslim, Al Bukhári.*

It is related from Abú Hurairah that he said 'A man came and said, "O Apostle of God, tell me, if a man comes and wishes to take my property, (what shall I do?)" He replied, "Do not give it to him." He said, "Tell me, if he fight me, (what shall I do?)" He replied, "Fight him." He said, "Tell me, if he kills me?" He replied, "Then thou art a martyr." He said, "Tell me, if I kill him, (what then?)" He replied, "He is in the fire."'—*Muslim, Al Bukhári.*

It is related from Abú Hurairah that, 'The Apostle of God said, "When any one of you fights, then let him avoid the face; for verily God created Adam in His own likeness."'—*Muslim.*

It is related from Sa'íd bin Zaid that, 'The Apostle of God said, "Whoever is killed in defence of his religion is a martyr; and whoever is killed in defence of his own blood is a martyr; and whoever is killed in defence of his property is a martyr; and whoever is killed in defence of his family is a martyr."' —*At Tirmidhí, Abú Dáud, An Nasái.*

Concerning Oaths

It is related from Ráfi'a bin Khadíj that he said, 'A man of the Helpers was killed at Khaibár. Then his relations departed and came to the Prophet and mentioned the matter to him. He said, "Have you two witnesses who are able to give evidence against the murderer of your friend?" They said, "O Apostle of God, there was no Muslim there, but only Jews; and they venture to do much worse things than that." He said, "Choose fifty of them and make them swear." But the Jews refused (to swear). Then the Apostle of God paid the blood-money himself.'—*Abú Dáud.*

On Killing Apostates and Those Who Hasten in Impiety

It is related from 'Ikrimah that he said, 'Hypocrites were brought to 'Alí, and he burnt them. The news of that reached Ibn 'Abbás, and he said, "If it had been I, I would not have burnt them, because of the prohibition of the Apostle of God, "Do not punish with the punishment of God"; but I would certainly have killed them according to the word of the Apostle, "Whosoever changes his religion, kill him."'—*Al Bukhárí.*

It is related from 'Alí that he said, 'I heard the Apostle of God say, "There will come forth a people at the end of time, young in age and foolish of vision, who will speak the best words in creation; but their faith will not pass their throats. They will pass through religion as an arrow passes through the thing hit. Therefore, whenever ye meet them, kill them; for verily for whoever kills them there is a reward on the day of resurrection."'—*Muslim, Al Bukhárí.*

It is related from Anas that he said, 'A band of men of the 'Ukl tribe came to the Prophet and embraced Islám. But they fell ill at Madína, so the Prophet ordered them to go to the camels given in alms and drink their wine and milk. Then they did so and regained their health. After that they apostatized and killed the keepers of the camels and drove off the camels. Then (the Prophet) sent after them, and they were brought back. Then he cut off their hands and feet and put out their eyes. After that he did not staunch the bleeding until they died.' And in another tradition it runs, 'He drove nails into their eyes.' And in another tradition it runs, 'He ordered nails, and they were made hot; and he pierced them with them. And he cast them out on to the stony plain. And they asked for a drink, but they were not given to drink, until they died.'—*Muslim, Al Bukhárí.*

It is related from Jarír bin 'Abdu'lláh that he said, 'The Prophet sent an army to Khath'am. And some of the people sought safety by prostrating (in Muslim prayer); but we hastened their slaughter. Then news of the matter reached the Prophet, and he ordered on their behalf half the blood-money, and said, " I am free from every Muslim who resides amongst polytheists." They said, " O Apostle of God, why ? " He replied, " Let them not be able to see the fires of each other." ' —*Abú Dáud.*

It is related from 'Alí that 'A Jewess used to revile and insult the Prophet. Then a man strangled her until she died. And the Prophet annulled (payment for) her blood.'—*Abú Dáud.*

It is related from Jundub that, 'The Apostle of God said, " The punishment for a magician is killing by the sword." '—*At Tirmidhí.*

It is related from Usámah bin Sharík that, 'The Apostle of God said, " Whatever man comes out to make divisions between my followers, strike off his head." '—*An Nasái.*

XVI

THE BOOK OF PUNISHMENTS

It is related from Abú Hurairah and Zaid bin Khálid that, 'Two men disputed before the Apostle of God. And one of them said, "Judge between us by the Book of God." And the other said, "Yes, O Apostle of God, judge between us by the Book of God, and give me permission to speak." He replied, "Say on." He said, "My son was a labourer with this man, and he committed adultery with his wife. And they told me that my son should be stoned. But I redeemed him therefrom by one hundred sheep and by a slave-girl which I had. After that I asked the learned, and they told me that my son must be given one hundred lashes, and must be banished the country for a year, and that stoning was only for this man's wife." The Apostle of God said, "By Him in whose hand is my life! I will certainly judge between you by the Book of God. As for thy sheep and thy slave-girl they must be returned to thee; and as for thy son, he must be given one hundred lashes and banished for a year. And as for thee, O Unais, come in the morning to this woman, and if she confesses, then stone her. Then she confessed, and they stoned her."'—*Muslim, Al Bukhârí.*

It is related from 'Omar that he said, 'Verily God sent Muḥammad with truth, and He sent down on him the Book. And amongst what God Most High sent down was the verse of stoning. The Apostle of God stoned, and we stoned after him. And the stoning in the Book of God is proper for whoever commits adultery when married, whether men or women, when proofs are established, whether by pregnancy or confession."'
—*Muslim, Al Bukhârí.*

It is related from 'Abdu'lláh bin 'Omar that some Jews came to the Apostle of God and told him that one of their men and a woman had committed adultery. The Apostle of God said to them, "What do ye find in the Taurát in the matter of stoning?" They said, "Their evil deeds are exposed, and they are scourged." 'Abdu'lláh bin Salám said, "You lie! Verily in it is the command to stone." Then they brought the Taurát and opened it out. But one of them placed his hand over the verse of stoning, and read what preceded it and what followed it. Then 'Abdu'lláh bin Salám said, "Lift up thy hand." And he lifted it up, and behold in it was the verse of stoning. Then they said, "He has spoken truly, O Muḥammad, in it is the verse of stoning." Then the Prophet gave orders concerning them both, and they were stoned.'—*Muslim, Al Bukhárí.*

It is related from 'Amru bin Shu'aib, from his father, from his grandfather, 'Abdu'lláh bin 'Amru binu'l-'Áṣ that, 'The Apostle of God said, "Remit punishments amongst yourselves; for what reaches my knowledge, of (acts deserving) punishments, it is obligatory for me to carry them out."'—*Abú Dáud, An Nasái.*

It is related from 'Áyesha that she said, 'When (the revelation containing) my exoneration (from the charge of adultery) came down, the Prophet stood up in the pulpit and repeated it. And when he came down from the pulpit he gave orders regarding the two men and the woman (who had accused me), and they were beaten according to the legal punishment.'—*Abú Dáud.*

CONCERNING AMPUTATION FOR THEFT

It is related from 'Áyesha that, 'The Prophet said, "The hand of a thief shall not be cut off, except for (theft of the value of) one-quarter of a dinar and over."'—*Muslim, Al Bukhárí.*

It is related from Ibn 'Omar that he said, 'The Prophet cut off a thief's hand for (stealing) armour valued at three dirhams.'—*Muslim, Al Bukhárí.*

It is related from Abú Hurairah that, 'The Prophet said, "God has cursed the thief who steals an egg, and his hand shall be cut off. And the hand of a thief who steals a rope shall be cut off."'—*Muslim, Al Bukhárí.*

It is related from Ráfi' bin Khadíj that, 'The Prophet said, "There is no amputation for (stealing) fruit or date-buds."'—*Málik, Al Tirmidhí, Abú Dáud, An Nasái.*

It is related from Jábir that, 'The Prophet said, "There is no amputation of the hand for one who betrays his trust or for taking from that which has been plundered, or for that which is snatched away clandestinely."'—*At Tirmidhí, An Nasái.* And in the Sharḥu'-s-Sunnah it is related that 'Ṣawfán bin Umayyah came to Madína and slept in the mosque. And he placed his cloak for a pillow; and a thief came and took it. Then Ṣafwán seized him and brought him to the Apostle of God. And he ordered that his hand should be cut off. Then Ṣafwán said, "Verily I did not desire this. I give it to him in alms." But the Apostle of God said, "Why didst thou not give it before thou broughtest him to me!"'

It is related from Abú Salamah from Abú Hurairah that, 'The Apostle of God said concerning the thief, "If he steal, cut off his hand." After that, if he steal again, then cut off his foot. After that, if he steal again, cut off his other hand. After that, if he steal again, then cut off his other foot."'—*Sharḥu's-Sunnah.*

It is related from Jábir that he said, 'A thief was brought to the Prophet, and he said, "Cut off his hand." And it was cut off. After that a second (thief) was brought to him, and he said, "Cut off his hand." And it was cut off. Then a third was brought to him, and he said, "Cut off his hand." And it was cut off. After that a fourth was brought to him, and he said, "Cut off his hand." And it was done. Then a fifth was brought to him, and he said, "Kill him." Then we took him away and killed him." Afterwards we dragged him away and threw him into a well and cast stones upon him.'—*Abú Dáud, An Nasái.*

It is related from Faḍálah bin 'Ubaid that he said, 'A thief was brought to the Apostle of God; and his hand was cut off. Then he gave orders regarding it, and it was hung on his neck.' —*At Tirmidhí, Abú Dáud, An Nasái, Ibn Májah.*

On Intercession for Remission of Punishments

It is related from 'Áyesha that 'The matter of a woman, whose nose was pierced for ornaments and who had stolen, had made the Quraish anxious. And they said, "Who will speak to the Apostle of God on her behalf?" And they said, "Who will dare to go to him but Usámah bin Zaid, the beloved of the

Apostle of God." Then Usámah spoke to him; and the Apostle of God replied, "Dost thou intercede in the matter of one of God's punishments?" After that he stood up and gave an address and said, "Those who lived before you were destroyed simply because, when any honourable person amongst them committed theft, they used to let him off; but when any insignificant one amongst them committed theft, they used to execute the full penalty of the law upon him. By God! Verily if Fáṭimah, the daughter of Muḥammad, had committed theft, I would certainly have cut off her hand." '—*Muslim, Al Bukhárí.*

Concerning the Punishment for Drinking Intoxicants

It is related from Anas that, 'The Prophet of God beat one who drank wine with the branch of a palm-tree stripped of its leaves, and with shoes. And Abú Bakr scourged with forty stripes.'—*Muslim, Al Bukhárí.* And in another tradition from the same person it runs, 'Verily the Prophet used to beat the one who drank wine, with forty blows of a shoe and a branch of a palm-tree stripped of its leaves.'

It is related from Ibn 'Abbás that he said, 'A man drank wine and became intoxicated. And he was met in the road staggering with unsteady gait, and he was taken to the Apostle of God. But when the man arrived opposite the house of 'Abbás he escaped and entered in to 'Abbás and clung to him. Then the matter was mentioned to the Prophet. Then he laughed and said, "Did he do that!" And he did not order anything concerning him.'—*Abú Dáud.*

Concerning What is not Allowed to be Said to Those Punished

It is related from 'Alí that, 'The Prophet said, "Whoever has violated the law, and his punishment is hastened in this world, then God is too just to repeat the punishment upon His servant a second time in the next world. And whoever violates the law, and God conceals it and forgives it, then He is too generous to return to anything which He has forgiven." '—*At Tirmidhí, Ibn Májah.*

Concerning Punishments Undefined by Law

It is related from 'Abú Burdah bin Niyár that, 'The Prophet said, "A man shall not be scourged with more than ten stripes, except in connexion with the punishments prescribed by God."'—*Muslim, Al Bukhárí.*

It is related from Ibn 'Abbás that, 'The Prophet said, "When one man says to another, "O Jew!" then give him twenty stripes. And when he says, "O effeminate one!" then give him twenty stripes. "And whoever commits adultery with a forbidden woman, kill him."'—*At Tirmidhí.*

Concerning Intoxicants, and Threats to the Drinkers thereof

It is related from Ibn 'Omar that he said, 'Omar gave an address (standing) on the pulpit of the Apostle of God, and said, "Verily the revelation concerning the prohibition of intoxicants came down. And they are (produced) from five things: grapes, dates, wheat, barley and honey. And intoxicants are whatever affect the reason."'—*Al Bukhárí.*

It is related from Ibn 'Omar that, 'The Apostle of God said, "Everything which inebriates is an intoxicant; and every intoxicant is unlawful. And whoever drinks intoxicants in this world, and dies whilst still addicted to them, without repenting, will not drink them in the next world."'—*Muslim.*

It is related from Wa'ilu'l-Ḥaḍrami that, 'Ṭáriq bin Suwaid asked the Prophet concerning intoxicants. But he forbade them. Then Wa'il said, "I only make them as medicines." He replied, "They are not medicine, but a disease."'—*Muslim.*

It is related from Jábir that, 'The Apostle of God said, "Even a little of what, when taken in quantity, produces intoxication, is unlawful."'—*At Tirmidhí, Abú Dáud, Ibn Májah.*

It is related from Dailamu'l-Ḥimyari that he said, 'I said, "O Apostle of God, verily we live in a cold country, and we perform hard work therein; and we take wine with this wheat, and we are strengthened by it for our work and against the cold of our country." He said, "Does it intoxicate?" I replied, "Yes." He said, "Then avoid it." I replied, "The people will not give it up." He said, "If they do not give it up, then fight them."'—*Abú Dáud.*

It is related from 'Abdu'lláh bin 'Omar that, 'The Prophet forbade wine and lots and chess and (the liquor called) *ghubairá.* And he said, "All intoxicants are unlawful."'—*Abú Dáud.*

It is related from 'Abú Umámah that, 'The Apostle of God said, "Verily God Most High has sent me as a mercy to all the worlds, and as a guide to all the worlds. And my Lord, the Exalted and Glorious, has commanded me to do away with musical instruments and reed instruments and idols and crosses and the practices of the times of ignorance. And my Lord, the Exalted and Glorious, has sworn (saying) "By my Eminence! None of my servants shall drink a mouthful of wine, but I will make him drink pus like unto it. And none will forsake it out of fear of me, but I will give him to drink from the holy fountains (of paradise)." '—*Aḥmad.*

XVII

THE BOOK OF RULE AND JUDGEMENT

It is related from Abú Hurairah that, 'The Apostle of God said, "He who obeys me, has obeyed God; and he who disobeys me, has disobeyed God. And whoever obeys the ruler, has obeyed me; and whoever disobeys the ruler, has disobeyed me. And the ruler is only a shield behind whom men fight and through whom they are protected. Then if he orders the fear of God and just dealing, then verily he gains rewards thereby; but if he says anything else, then on him will fall its penalty."' —*Muslim, Al Bukhárí.*

It is related from Ummu'l-Ḥuṣain that she said, 'The Apostle of God said, "If a mutilated slave be appointed over you as ruler, and he leads you according to the Book of God; then give ear to him and obey him."'—*Muslim.*

It is related from Ibn 'Abbás that, 'The Apostle of God said, "Whoever sees in his ruler that which he dislikes; let him be patient. There is no one who divides a community by a span, and dies, but dies the death of one in the time of ignorance."'—*Muslim, Al Bukhárí.*

It is related from 'Awf bin Máliku'l-Ashjai that, 'The Apostle of God said, "The best of your rulers are those whom ye love, and who love you; and for whom ye pray, and who pray for you. And the worst of your rulers are those whom ye hate, and who hate you; and whom ye curse, and who curse you." 'Awf said, "We replied, 'O Apostle of God, under such circumstances should we not repudiate them?' He said, 'No, so long as they keep the observance of the prayers amongst you. No, so long as they keep the observance of the prayers amongst you. Beware! whoever has a ruler placed over him, and sees him do something contrary to the law of God; let him feel displeasure at what he does contrary to the law of God, but let him not withdraw a hand from obeying him.'"'—*Muslim.*

It is related from Abú Hurairah that, 'The Prophet said, "The rulers of the Children of Israel were the Prophets.

Whenever a Prophet died, another Prophet succeeded him; but there is no Prophet after me. But there will be *Khalífs*, and they will be many." They said, "Then what dost thou order us?" He replied, "Give allegiance to the first and to the first (after him), and give them their rights, for verily God will ask them for an account of the souls over whom they have been appointed."'—*Muslim, Al Bukhárí.*

It is related from 'Abdu'lláh bin 'Omar that, 'The Apostle of God said, "Beware! Ye are all rulers, and ye will be all asked concerning your subjects. The *Imám* who is placed as a ruler over men will be asked concerning his subjects; and the man who is a ruler over his household will be asked concerning his subjects; and the woman who rules over the house of her husband and his children will be asked about them; and a man's servant who is the keeper of his master's goods will be asked about them. Beware! every one of you is a ruler, and every one of you will be asked concerning the things committed to his charge."'—*Muslim, Al Bukhárí.*

It is related from Abú Bakr that he said, 'When news reached the Apostle of God that the people of Persia had made a daughter of Kisra, queen over them, he said, "The people who make a woman their ruler will never prosper."'—*Al Bukhárí.*

It is related from Abú Sa'íd that, 'The Apostle of God said, "The most beloved of men in the sight of God at the day of resurrection, and the one of them who will sit nearest to Him will be a just ruler. And the most hated of men in the sight of God on the day of resurrection and the one who will receive the severest punishment."—And in another tradition it runs, "The one who will sit farthest from him,"—will be a tyrannical ruler."'—*At Tirmidhí.*

It is related from Ibn 'Omar that, 'The Prophet said, "Verily the king is the shadow of God on earth. Every oppressed person from amongst his servants turns to him; and when he dispenses justice, then he receives a reward, and thanks are due from his subjects. But when he oppresses them, then on him lies the guilt, and the duty of his subjects is patience."'

On the Duty of Rulers in the Matter of Clemency

It is related from 'Omar binu'l-Khaṭṭáb that 'When he used to send out his officers, he laid these conditions upon them. "Do not ride on Turki horses, and do not eat flour, nor clothe yourselves in fine clothes. And do not close your doors at the time of the peoples' needs. And if ye do anything of that, then punishment will be due to you." After that he would bid farewell to them.'—*Al Baihaqi.*

On Acting in Judicial Affairs

It is related from Abú Bakr that he said, 'I heard the Apostle of God say, "A judge must never judge between two litigants when he is angry."'—*Muslim, Al Bukhárí.*

It is related from Mu'ádh bin Jabal that, 'When the Apostle of God sent him to Yeman he said, "How wilt thou execute judgement when a case for trial comes before thee?" He replied, "I will judge by the Book of God." He said, "And if thou do not find (a judgement) in the Book of God?" He replied, "Then (I will judge) according to the customary practice of the Apostle of God." He said, "And if thou do not find (a similar case) in the customary practice of the Apostle of God?" He replied, "I will do my best according to my own judgement and will not slacken effort."' (Mu'ádh) said, 'Then the Apostle of God smote upon his breast, and said, "Praise be to God who has caused the messenger of the Apostle of God to agree with what the Apostle of God likes."' —*At Tirmidhí, Abú Dáud.*

It is related from Sa'íd binu'l-Musayyib that, 'Verily a Muslim and a Jew disputed together before 'Omar. And he saw that the right was with the Jew and gave judgement in his favour. Then the Jew said to him "By God! thou hast certainly given judgement according to justice." Then 'Omar tapped him on the breast and said, "Who told thee that?" The Jew replied, "By God! I have found in the Taurát that there is no judge who judges justly, but one angel stays on his right-hand and one on his left, who direct him and bring him into conformity with justice so long as he judges justly. But when he forsakes justice, then they rise up and leave him."'—*Málik.*

On the Allowances and Presents of Rulers

It is related from Khawlah, the Helper, that she said, 'The Apostle of God said, "Verily there are men who unjustly appropriate part of God's money. For them will be the fire on the day of resurrection."'—*Al Bukhárí.*

It is related from 'Abdu'lláh bin 'Amr that he said, 'The Apostle of God cursed the giver of a bribe and the taker of it.' —*Abú Dáud, Ibn Májah.*

On Judgements and Evidence

It is related from Ibn 'Abbás that, 'The Prophet said, "If men were given according to their claims, they would certainly lay claim to the blood of men as well as their property; but an oath is incumbent upon the defendant."'—*Muslim.*

It is related from Umm Salamah that, 'The Apostle of God said, "I am only a man, and ye dispute with one another before me. And it may be that some of you are cleverer in (presenting) his proofs than others, and I give judgement in his favour according to what I hear from him. Then ye in whose favour I give judgement concerning any of the rights of his brother, let him not take it; for I only cut off for him a piece of the fire."' —*Muslim, Al Bukhárí.*

It is related from 'Amru bin Shu'aib from his father, from his grandfather, that, 'The Prophet said, "It is incumbent on the plaintiff to produce proofs; and the defendant must take an oath."'—*At Tirmidhí.*

It is related from Abú Músáu'l-Ash'ari that, 'Two men laid claim to a camel in the time of the Apostle of God. And each one of them produced two witnesses. Then the Prophet divided it into two halves between the two of them.' And in another tradition from An Nasái, Abú Dáud and Ibn Májah it runs, 'Two men laid claim to a camel, and neither of them had any proof; so the Prophet allotted it between the two of them.'

It is related from Al Ash'ath bin Qais that he said, 'There was a piece of land in the joint ownership of a man of the Jews and myself; and he denied me my right. Then I took him to the Prophet. And the latter said, "Hast thou any proof?" I said, "No." He said to the Jew, "Take thine oath." I said, "O Apostle of God, then he will swear and take away my property." Then God Most High sent down (the revelation) 'Verily those who sell God's covenant and their oaths for a small price, they shall suffer a grievous punishment.[1] " '—*Abú Dáud, Ibn Májah.*

It is related from Khuraim bin Fátik that he said, 'The Apostle of God prayed the morning prayer, and when he had finished he stood up and said, "False evidence has been made equal to associating anything with God." After that he recited (the verse), "Abstain from the pollution of idols, and abstain from falsehood, whilst inclining to God, and not associating anything with Him."[2]

---

[1] Qur'án, Súratu Áli 'Imrán (iii) 76.

[2] Qur'án, Súratu'l-Ḥajj (xxii) 30.

XVIII

THE BOOK OF RELIGIOUS WAR

(JEHÁD)

It is related from Abú Ḥurairah that, 'The Apostle of God said, "By Him in whose hands is my life! If it were not that some of the men of the believers would be unhappy because they were separated from me, owing to the fact that I have not beasts upon which to mount them, I would never absent myself from the battle which they fight in the way of God. And by Him in whose hands in my life! I would certainly love to be killed in the way of God, and then brought to life, and then killed, and then brought to life, and then killed, and then brought to life."' —*Muslim, Al Bukhárí.*

It is related from Salmánu'l-Fársi that he said, 'I heard the Apostle of God say, "To keep guard one day and one night in the way of God is better than a month's fast and remaining awake at night therein. Then if he dies, (the rewards of) his actions which he used to perform flow to him, and his sustenance is appointed for him, and he becomes safe from the seducer."' —*Muslim.*

It is related from Zaid bin Khálid that, 'The Apostle of God said, "He who equips a warrior in the way of God, has fought himself; and he who takes the place of a warrior in his family, has fought himself."' —*Muslim, Al Bukhárí.*

It is related from Jábir bin Samurah that, 'The Apostle of God said, "This religion will never cease to be in force. A band of Muslims will fight for it until the day of resurrection."' —*Muslim.*

It is related from Anas that, 'The Apostle of God said, "There is no one who enters paradise and wishes to return to the earth and what he possessed there, except the martyr who longs to return to the earth and be killed ten times by reason of what he sees of the liberal rewards."' —*Muslim, Al Bukhárí.*

It is related from Sahl bin Ḥunaif that, 'The Apostle of God said, "Whoever supplicates God in truth for martyrdom,

God will bring to him the honour of martyrs, although he die upon his bed." '—*Muslim.*

It is related from Anas that he said, 'The Apostle of God and his companions went on until they drew near to the polytheists at Bedr. And the polytheists advanced. And the Apostle of God said, "Rise up to paradise, the breadth of which is equal to the heavens and the earth." Then 'Umair binu'l-Ḥumám said, "Good! good!" The Apostle of God said, "What led thee to say, Good! good!" He replied, "By God! O Apostle of God, nothing but the hope that I might be amongst its people." He said, "Verily thou art amongst its people." Anas said, 'Then 'Umair took out some dates from his horn and began to eat some of them. After that he said, "If I live until I eat my dates, it will certainly be a long life." Then he threw away what dates remained with him, and fought them until he was killed.'—*Muslim.*

It is related from 'Imrán bin Ḥuṣain that, 'The Apostle of God said, "A band of my people will continue to fight for the truth, and will overcome those that oppose them, until the last of them fights with the false Messiah." '—*Abú Dáud.*

It is related from Ibn 'Abbás that, 'The Apostle of God said, "There are two eyes which the fire will not touch: the eye which weeps from fear of God, and the eye which remains awake keeping watch in the way of God." '—*At Tirmidhí.*

It is related from Abú Miqdám bin Ma'díkarib that, 'The Apostle of God said, "The martyr has six privileges near God: he is forgiven his sins on (the shedding of) the first drop of blood, he is shown his resting-place in paradise, he is redeemed from the punishment of the grave, he is made secure from the great fear (of hell) and a crown of glory is placed on his head, one ruby of which is better than the world and all that is therein, and he will marry seventy-two wives of the *huris* with black eyes, and his intercession will be accepted for seventy of his relations." '—*Tirmidhí, Ibn Májah.*

It is related from 'Abdu'lláh bin 'Omar that, 'The Apostle of God said, "Do not ride on the sea except as a pilgrim, or as the performer of the lesser pilgrimage, or as a warrior in the way of God; for verily under the sea is a fire, and under the fire is a sea." '—*Abú Dáud.*

It is related from Umm Ḥarám that, 'The Prophet said, "The traveller of the sea who is afflicted with vomiting will get the reward of a martyr, and the one who is drowned will receive the rewards of two martyrs." '—*Abú Dáud.*

It is related from Abú Umámah that he said, 'We went out with the Apostle of God on a warlike expedition. And a man passed by a cavern in which were some water and some herbs. And he said to himself that he would stay therein and separate himself from the world. So he asked permission of the Apostle of God in the matter. The Apostle of God replied, "I have not been sent with the Jewish religion or the Christian religion; but I have been sent with the Ḥaníf religion, the easy one. By Him in whose hands is the life of Muḥammad! the marching about in the early morning in the way of God is certainly better than the world and all that is therein. And the standing of one of you in the line of battle is better than his prayers for sixty years." '—*Aḥmad.*

It is related from Abú Músá that, 'The Apostle of God said, "Verily the doors of paradise are under the shade of swords." Then a man with worn-out clothes stood up and said, "O Abú Músá, didst thou hear the Apostle of God say this?" He replied, "Yes." Then the man returned to his companions and said, "I give you my salutations." Then he broke the scabbard of his sword and threw it away, and then went with his sword towards the enemy and smote with it until he was killed.'—*Muslim.*

It is related from Ḥasná' bint Mu'áwiyah that she said, 'My uncle said to us, "I said to the Prophet, Who is in paradise?" He replied, "A prophet is in paradise, and, a martyr is in paradise, and a new-born child is in paradise, and one buried alive is in paradise." '—*Abú Dáud.*

It is related from Ibn'Áyid that he said, 'The Apostle of God went out to attend the funeral of a certain man. And when he was placed (in the grave) 'Omar binu'l-Khaṭṭáb said, "O Apostle of God, do not pray over him, for verily he was a wicked man." Then the Apostle of God turned to the people and said, "Has any one of you seen him engaged in any work of Islám?" A man replied, "Yes, O Apostle of God, he kept watch one night in the way of God." Then the Apostle of God prayed over him and threw earth on him and said, "Thy companions imagine that thou art amongst the people of the fire; but I bear witness that thou art amongst the people of paradise." And he said, "O 'Omar, verily thou wilt not be asked concerning the actions of men, but will be asked concerning their natural religion." '—*Al Baihaqi.*

On Preparing Weapons of War

It is related from Anas that he said, 'Abú Ṭalḥa used to defend himself and the Prophet with one shield. And Abú Ṭalḥa was expert with the bow; and when he used to shoot arrows, the Prophet would rise up and look towards the place (where he shot) his arrows.'—*Al Bukhárí.*

It is related from Abú Najíḥu's-Sulahi that he said, 'I heard the Apostle of God say, "Whoever reaches the mark with an arrow in the way of God, it becomes for him high rank in paradise; and whoever shoots an arrow in the way of God, it becomes for him equal to the emancipation of a slave; and whoever grows old in the way of God, it will be for him a light on the day of resurrection." '—*Al Baihaqi.*

It is related from Uqbah bin 'abd Sulahi that he heard the Apostle of God say, 'Do not cut the forelocks of horses, or their manes, or their tails. For verily their tails keep off flies, and their manes keep them warm, and blessings are bound up in their forelocks.'—*Abú Dáud.*

It is related from As Sáib bin Yazíd that, 'There were two coats of mail on the Prophet on the day of (the battle of) Uḥud. He wore one on top of the other.'—*Abú Dáud, Ibn Májah.*

It is related from Anas that he said, 'There was nothing more beloved of the Apostle of God after women than horses.'—*An Nasái.*

Concerning the Rules of Travelling

It is related from Ka'b bin Málik that, 'The Prophet went out to the battle of Tabúk on a Thursday; and he used to like to go out on Thursdays.'—*Al Bukhárí.*

It is related from Abú Hurairah that, 'The Apostle of God said, "The angels do not accompany that party in which is a dog or a bell." '—*Muslim.*

It is related from Abú Hurairah that, 'The Apostle of God said, "The bell is Satan's musical instrument."'—*Muslim.*

It is related from 'Abdu'lláh bin Ja'far that he said, 'When the Apostle of God used to arrive from a journey, he used to be met by the children of the people of his house. And he arrived from a certain journey, and I was brought to him first, and he carried me in front of him (on his beast), after that one of the sons of Fáṭimah was brought; and he mounted him behind him.' Abdu'lláh said, 'Then he took us into Madína: three of us on the one beast.'—*Muslim.*

It is related from Jábir that he said, 'The Apostle of God used to keep in the rear of a marching army, and help on the weak, and take them up behind him (on his beast); and he used to pray for them.'—*Abú Dáud.*

It is related from 'Abdu'lláh bin Ma'súd that he said, 'On the day of (the battle of) Bedr, we were every three of us on one camel. And Abú Lubábah and 'Alí bin abú Ṭálib and the Apostle of God were together. And when the turn of the Prophet came (to dismount and walk) we said, "We will walk instead of thee." He replied, "You are no stronger than I; nor am I more independent of rewards than you."'

Concerning Letters to Infidels and Inviting them to Islám.

It is related from Ibn 'Abbás that, 'The Prophet wrote to the (Roman) Emperor, inviting him to Islám, and he sent the letter to him by Diḥyahu'l-Kalbi, and commanded him to deliver it to the Governor of Busrah to hand over to the Emperor. And in it (was written) "In the name of God the Merciful, the Compassionate. From Muḥammad the servant of God and His Apostle to Heraclius the Ruler of the Roman Empire. Peace be on whoever follows the guidance. After this I invite thee with the invitation of Islám. Embrace Islám, and thou wilt be safe. Embrace Islám, and God will give thee thy reward twice over. But if thou turn away, then on thee will be the sin of thy subjects. O people of the Book, come to a doctrine equal between us and you, namely that ye do not worship any except God, and do not associate anything with Him; and that some of us take not others as lords besides God. But if ye turn away, then say, O believers, I bear witness that we are Muslims." '—*Muslim, Al Bukhárí.*

It is related from Ibn 'Abbás that, 'The Apostle of God sent a letter to Kisra (King of Persia) with 'Abdu'lláh bin Ḥudháfahu's-Sahimi, and commanded him to deliver it to the Governor of Bahrain. And the Governor of Bahrain handed it over to Kisra. And when the latter read it, he tore it in pieces.' Ibnu'l-Musayyib said, 'Then the Apostle of God invoked a curse upon them (saying) "May they be torn into pieces!" '—*Al Bukhárí.*

It is related from Sulaimán bin Buraidah, from his father, that he said, 'When the Apostle of God appointed a leader over any army or marauding band, he was in the habit of giving him orders regarding his special duties concerning the fear of God and good behaviour towards those Muslims who were with him. After that he would say, "Go forth to war in the name of God in His road: fight with those who disbelieve in God. Go forth to war. Do not use deceit or break a covenant, or mutilate, or kill children. And when thou meetest thine enemy of the polytheists, then invite them to three things: the rights and privileges of Islám or defeat. Then whichever of the three they give an affirmative answer to, accept it from them and withdraw from them. After that invite them to Islám; and if they give an affirmative answer to thee, then accept it from them and withdraw from them. After that invite them to remove themselves from their homes to the homes of the refugees, and inform them that if they do that, then for them is what is given to the refugees; and their duties are the same as those of the refugees. But if they refuse to change from their homes, then inform them that they will remain as the desert Arabs who have embraced Islám. The commands of God will be obligatory upon them which are obligatory upon other believers; but they will get nothing of the plunder and spoils unless they go to fight along with the other Muslims. But if they refuse (to become Muslims) then ask from them the poll-tax. And if they answer thee in the affirmative, then accept it from them, and withdraw from them. But if they refuse (to pay), then seek help from God and fight them. And when thou besiege the people of a fortress, and they express a desire to thee that thou give them a pledge of security from God and His Prophet; then do not give them a pledge of security from God and His Prophet, but give them thine own pledge and the pledge of thy companions; for if ye violate your pledge and the pledge of your companions, it will be easier than if ye violate the pledge of God and the pledge of His Apostle. And if thou besiege the people in a fortress, and they express to thee a desire that thou bring them down on the condition that they agree to the orders of God; then do not bring them down on the orders of God, but bring them down on (the condition that they agree to) thy orders; for verily thou dost not know whether thou wilt receive the orders of God regarding them or not." '—*Muslim.*

It is related from Anas that, 'When the Prophet went with us to fight any people, he would not fight with us until the dawn broke. And he would look towards them, and if he heard the call to prayer he would withdraw from them, but if he did not hear the call to prayer, he would attack them.' Anas said, 'And we went out to Khaibár, and we reached them at night. Then when it dawned, and he did not hear the call to prayer, he mounted, and I mounted behind Abú Ṭalḥa, and verily my feet touched the feet of the Prophet of God. And they came out towards us with their bags (for dates) and their instruments for irrigation. And when they saw the Prophet they said, "Muḥammad, by God! Muḥammad and the army!" And they took refuge in the fortress. And when the Apostle of God saw them he said, "God is great! God is great! Khaibár is ruined! Verily when we come down on the land of any tribe, then bad is the morning of those who have been warned." '—*Muslim*, *Al Bukhárí.*

It is related from Abú Wái'l that he said, 'Khálid binu'l-Walíd wrote to the people of Persia: "In the name of God the Merciful, the Compassionate, Khálid binu'l-Walíd to Rustam and Mihrán the chiefs of Persia. Peace be to him who follows the guidance. After that we invite you to Islám; and if ye refuse, then give the poll-tax out of hand so that ye be rendered contemptible. But if ye refuse, then with me is a people who love death in the way of God, even as the Persians love wine. Then peace be on him who follows the guidance." '—*Sharḥu's-Sunnah.*

On Fighting in Religious War

It is related from Anas that he said, 'The Apostle of God used to go to war taking with him Umm Sulaim and some women of the helpers. When he fought they would give water to drink and administer medicine to the wounded.'—*Muslim.*

It is related from 'Abdu'lláh bin 'Omar that he said, 'The Apostle of God forbade the killing of women and children.'—*Muslim, Al Bukhárí.*

It is related from Ibn 'Omar that, 'The Apostle of God cut down the date-trees of the Baniu'n-Naḍír and burnt them. And in regard to this Ḥuṣain said, "And the burning in Al Buwairah was easy for the leaders of the Bani Luwai." And in regard to it the revelation came down, "What palm-trees ye cut down, or left standing on their roots, was by the permission of God." '[1]—*Muslim, Al Bukhárí.*

It is related from 'Abdu'lláh bin Awn that Náfi' wrote to him and informed him that Ibn 'Omar informed him that, 'The Prophet made a raid on the Baniu'l-Muṣṭaliq in Muraisi when they were off their guard. And he killed those able to fight, and took into captivity those who were dependant upon them.' —*Muslim, Al Bukhárí.*

It is related from Al Muhallab that, 'The Apostle of God said, "If the enemy make a night attack upon you, then let your watchward be 'By (the symbol) H.M., they'll win!' " '—*Al Tirmidhí.*

It is related from 'Urwah that he said, ' 'Usámah related to me that the Apostle of God gave him a charge and said, "Attack Ubna at dawn, and burn it down." '—*Abú Dáud.*

It is related from Thawbán bin Yazíd that, 'The Prophet fixed up a catapult against the people of Táif.'—*Al Tirmidhí.*

On Orders regarding Prisoners

It is related from Salamah binu'l-Akwa' that he said, 'A spy of the polytheists came to the Prophet when he was on a journey, and sat down near his companions and engaged in conversation. Afterwards he departed; and the Prophet said, "Search him out and kill him." And I killed him, and the

---

[1] Qúr'an, Súratu'l-Ḥashr (lix) 5.

Prophet made me a present of the man's things.'—*Muslim, Al Bukhárí.*

It is related from Abú Sa'ídu'l-Khudri that he said, 'When the Bani Quraizah came down (from their fortress), agreeing to abide by the orders of Sa'd bin Mu'ádh, the Apostle of God sent to the latter, and he came on an ass. And when he drew near, the Apostle of God said, "Stand up to your master." And he came and sat down. And the Apostle of God said, "Verily these have come down (in capitulation) stipulating to abide by thy orders." He replied, "Verily, I give orders that those able to fight be killed, and their dependants taken into captivity." The Prophet said, "Thou hast certainly ordered concerning them in conformity with the orders of the angel (Gabriel)." And in another tradition it runs, "In conformity, with the orders of God." '—*Muslim, Al Bukhárí.*

It is related from Qatádah that he said, 'Anas mentioned to us from Abú Ṭalḥa that the Prophet gave orders on the day (of the battle) of Bedr concerning twenty-four who were leaders of the Quraish, and they were thrown into one of the wells of Bedr which was corrupted and corrupting. And when he conquered any tribe, he used to remain in the place conquered for three nights; so when the third day arrived at Bedr he gave orders for his camel to be brought, and its saddle was placed on it. After that he went off, and his companions followed him, until he stood on the brink of the well. And he began to call (the dead men) by their names and the names of their fathers; "O such-and-such a one, son of so-and-so, has it pleased you that ye obeyed God and His messenger? Verily we have received in truth what our Lord promised us. Have ye received in truth what your Lord promised you?" Then 'Omar said, "O Apostle of God, what art thou saying to bodies which have no souls!" The Prophet replied, "By Him in whose hand is the life of Muḥammad! Ye do not hear what I say better than they do." And in another tradition it runs, "Ye do not hear better than they do; but they do not answer." '—*Muslim, Al Bukhárí.*

It is related from 'Ayesha that she said, 'When the people of Mecca sent ransoms for those of their number taken prisoners (at Bedr), Zainab sent in ransom for Abdú'l-'Áṣ some money and she sent with it a necklace of hers which had belonged to Khadíjah, which she put in with the money for Abú'l-'Áṣ. Then when the Apostle of God saw it, he was touched with a great compassion for her, and said (to his companions), "If ye think it right to release her captive for her, and return to her her ransom (it will be better)." They replied, "Yes." And the Prophet took a promise from Abú'l-Áṣ that he would leave a way open for Zainab to come to him. And the Apostle of God sent Zaid bin Ḥárith and a man of the Helpers and said, "Remain in Baṭu Yajij until Zainab comes to you; and then accompany her until ye bring her here."'—*Aḥmad, Abú Dáud.*

It is related from Ibn Ma'súd that, 'When the Apostle of God wished to kill 'Uqbah bin Abi Mu'aiṭ (after the battle of Bedr), the latter said, "Who will (care for my) children?" He replied, "The fire."'—*Abú Dáud.*

It is related from 'Alí from the Apostle of God that, "Gabriel came down to him and said to him, "Give them (the companions of the Prophet) a choice regarding the captives of Bedr: either death, or ransom on this condition, that in the following year a number of you equal in number to those (ye release on ransom) will be killed." They said, "We choose the ransom, and that certain of us be slain."'—*At Tirmidhí.*

It is related from 'Alí that he said, 'Some slaves went out (from Mecca) to the Apostle of God on the day of Ḥudaibah, before the treaty was made. Then their masters wrote to him and said, "O Muḥammad, by God! they did not go out to thee out of a desire for thy religion, but they only went out in order to flee from slavery." And the people said, "These speak truly, O Apostle of God, send the slaves back to them." Then the Apostle of God became angry and said, "O people of the Quraish, I do not see for you (any hope) that you will abstain from meddling until God sends someone to you to cut off your heads." And he refused to send them back, and said, "They are the freedmen of God."'—*Abú Dáud.*

CONCERNING GIVING PROTECTION

It is related from 'Amru that he said, 'I heard the Apostle of God say, "He who assures a man of safety from death, and afterwards kills him, will be given a standard of perfidy on the day of resurrection."'—*Sharḥu's-Sunnah.*

It is related from Abú Ráfi' that he said, 'The Quraish sent me to the Apostle of God; and when I saw him (the desire for) Islám was kindled in my heart and I said, "O Apostle of God, by God! I will not return to them at all." He replied, "Verily, I do not break a promise or detain ambassadors. Return, and if there still remain in thy heart (the desire) which is now there, then come back." He said, "So I went, and afterwards came to the Prophet and embraced Islám."'—*Abú Dáud.*

It is related from Nu'aim bin Ma'súd that, 'The Apostle of God said to two men who had come from Musailamah, "Beware! by God! were it not that ambassadors are not killed, I would have struck off your heads."'—*Aḥmad, Abú Dáud.*

Concerning the Division of Plunder, and Purloining therefrom

It is related from Abú Hurairah that, 'The Apostle of God said, "Plunder was not lawful for anyone before us. That (has been made so for us), because God saw our weakness and helplessness, and so He made it lawful for us."'—*Muslim, Al Bukhárí.*

It is related from Yezid bin Hurmuz that he said, 'Jandahu'l-Ḥaruriyah wrote to Ibn 'Abbás to ask him concerning the slave and the woman who are present at the place where booty is obtained: whether the booty should be shared with them. He said to Yazíd, "Write to him that they should not receive any fixed share; but a little may be given to them."' —*Muslim.*

It is related from Abú Hurairah that a man presented the Apostle of God with a slave called Mid'am. And whilst he was unsaddling the Prophet's beast, behold a stray arrow struck him and killed him. Then the people said, "May it be well with him in paradise!" But the Apostle of God said, "Never! by Him in whose hands is my life! verily the cloak which he took from the plunder on the day of (the conquest of) Khaibár, when ye had not yet divided it, will light a fire upon him." When the people heard that, a man brought one or two thongs to the Prophet and said, "This is a thong or two from the fire."'—*Muslim, Al Bukhárí.*

It is related from Abú Umámah, from the Prophet, that he said, "Verily God has given me pre-eminence over the Prophets." Or he said, "He has given my people pre-eminence over other people, and has made plunder lawful for us." '—*At Tirmidhí.*

It is related from Anas that, 'The Apostle of God said on that day, namely the day of (the battle of) Ḥunain, "Whoever kills an infidel will get his goods." And Abú Ṭalḥah that day killed twenty men and took their effects." '—*At Tirmidhí*

It is related from Mujammi' bin Járiyah that he said, 'The spoils of Khaibár were divided amongst the people who were present at Ḥudaibah. And the Apostle of God divided it into eighteen portions. And the army consisted of fifteen hundred men, of whom three hundred were cavalry. Then he gave each horseman two shares and each footman one share.'—*Abú Dáud.* And he said, 'The tradition of Ibn 'Omar is more correct and the action taken on it, and an error has crept into the tradition of Mujammi' in that he said, "Three hundred cavalry," when there were only two hundred cavalry.'

It is related from 'Abdu'lláh bin 'Amru that he said, 'When the Apostle of God obtained plunder he used to call Bilál, and he used to call the people; and they used to bring their plunder. Then the Prophet used to take his fifth and divide the remainder. And there came a man on a certain day after that bringing a halter made of hair. And the man said, "O Apostle of God, this is a part of that which we took in plunder." He replied, "Didst thou hear Bilál call three times?" He said, "Yes." He said, "Then what prevented thee from bringing it then?" Then the man made some excuse for himself. The Prophet said, "Let be now; for thou wilt bring it on the day of resurrection; for I will never accept it from thee." '—*Abú Dáud.*

It is related from 'Abdu'r-Raḥmán bin 'Awf that he said, 'Verily I was standing in the ranks on the day of (the battle of) Bedr; and I looked on my right hand and on my left, and behold! I was between two youths of the Helpers who were young in years. And I wished to stand between men stronger than they. Then one of them signed to me and said, "O my uncle, dost thou know Abú Jahl?" I replied, "Yes, what dost thou want with him, O son of my brother?" He replied, "I have been told that he abused the Apostle of God, therefore, by Him in whose hands is my life! if I see him my person shall not separate from his until the quickest of us die." Abdu'r-Raḥmán said, "Then I was astonished at that." He said, "Then the other youth made a sign to me in similar terms. And I did not delay to look for Abú Jahl moving round amongst the men. Then I said, 'Do ye not see him. This is your friend whom ye asked me about.' Then they two ran towards him with their swords and smote him until they killed him. After that they went to the Apostle of God and informed him. He said, 'Which of you killed him?' Each one of them replied, 'I killed him.' He said, 'Have you wiped your swords?' They replied, 'No.' Then the Apostle of God looked at the two swords and said, 'You both killed him.' Then the Apostle of God gave orders that the plunder obtained from Abú Jahl should be given to Mu'ádh bin 'Amru binu'l-Jamuḥ. And the two men were Mu'ádh bin 'Amru binu'l-Jamuḥ and Mu'ádh bin 'Afrá.'"'—*Muslim, Al Bukhárí.*

It is related from Anas that on the day of Badr, 'The Apostle of God said, "Who will see for us what Abú Jahl has done?" Then Ibn Ma'súd departed and found that the two sons of 'Afrá' had smitten him and he had become cold (with the approach of death). Anas said, "Then Ibn Ma'súd seized his beard and said, 'Thou art Abú Jahl?' He replied, 'Dost thou do this over (the death agony of) a man ye have stabbed to death!'"' And in another tradition it runs, 'He said, "Would that some other than a cultivator had killed me!"'—*Muslim, Al Bukhárí.*

It is related from Abú Hurairah that, 'The Prophet said, "One of the Prophets went out to fight; and he said to his people, 'Let no man follow me who has married a wife and wishes to take her to his house, but has not yet done so; nor the one who has built a house, but has not yet raised a roof over it; nor yet the man who has bought a sheep or a camel and is expecting its giving birth to young.' Then he went forth to war. And he drew near to a certain village at the time of evening prayer or about that. Then he said to the sun, 'Verily thou art under orders, and I am also under orders. O

God, restrain it for us.' Then it was restrained (from setting) until God gave him the victory. After that he gathered together the plunder; and a fire came to devour it, but it did not consume it. And he said, 'Verily there is deceit amongst you with regard to the plunder; therefore let a man from each tribe pledge his oath.' Then the hand of a certain man stuck to his hand. He said, 'The deceit concerning the plunder is amongst you.' Then they brought a golden head like the head of a cow. Then he set it down and the fire came and devoured it."' And the relater has added in another tradition, 'And plunder was not lawful for any one before us. Afterwards God made plunder lawful for us. He saw our weakness and impotence and made it lawful for us.'—*Muslim, Al Bukhárí.*

Concerning the Poll-tax

It is related from Jabálah that he said, 'I was the secretary of Jaza'bin Mu'wiyah the uncle of Aḥnaf, and there came to us a letter from 'Omar binu'l-Khaṭṭáb a year before his death, (saying) "Separate every person who is forbidden in marriage from amongst the fire-worshippers." And 'Omar did not take the poll-tax from the fire-worshippers until 'Abdu'r-Raḥmán bin 'Awf bore witness that the Apostle of God took it from the fire-worshippers of Hajar.'—*Al Bukhárí.*

It is related from Mu'ádh that when the Apostle of God sent him towards Yeman, he ordered him to take one dinar, or the cloth of Yeman ordered, called *ma'áfiri* to the value of one dinar from every adult, that is from everyone who had reached puberty.'—*Abú Dáud.*

It is related from Anas that he said, 'The Apostle of God sent Khálid binu'l-Walíd to Ukaider (the Christian king) of Dúmah; and they seized him and brought him. Then the Prophet spared his life and made peace with him on condition that he paid the poll-tax.'—*Abú Dáud.*

Concerning Peace

It is related from Al Miswár bin Makhramah and Marwán binu'l-Ḥakam that they said, 'The Prophet went out in the year of Ḥudaibah with a band of a thousand of his companions. And when he came to Dhu'l-Ḥulaifah he garlanded the camel for sacrifice and branded it in token thereof. He there put on the *iḥrám* (the pilgrim garment) for the lesser pilgrimage and went on until when he came to Al Thaniyah, from where they fall upon the people of Mecca, his camel knelt down. And the people said, "Hal! hal! Al Qaṣwa has refused to go on! Al Qaṣwa has refused to go on!" Then the Prophet said, "Al Qaṣwa has not refused to go on; nor is that natural to her; but he who restrained the elephant has restrained her." Then he said, "By Him in whose hand is my life! they shall not supplicate me on any matter in which the honour of the sacred territories of God is concerned, but I will grant it." After that he forbade 'Al Qaṣwa to remain sitting and she rose up. And he turned aside with them until he descended at the extreme limit of Ḥudaibah, at a place where there was a little water, from which the people were drawing sparingly. And the people did not delay until they had drawn the water and complained to the Apostle of God of thirst. Then he took out an arrow from his quiver, and ordered them to place it in the water; and by God! it continued to flow over for them in abundance until they departed from it. And whilst they were in such circumstances, behold! Budail bin Warqá'u'l-Khuza'i came in a party of the Khuzá'h. After that came 'Urwah bin Ma'súd.' And he related the tradition until he said, 'When Suhail bin 'Amru came, the Prophet said, "Write, This is what Muḥammad, the Apostle of God, agrees upon." Then Suhail said, "By God! if we knew that thou wert the Apostle of God, we would not have repelled thee from the House (of God), nor have fought with thee; but write, Muḥammad the son of 'Abdu'lláh." Then the Prophet said, "By God! I am indeed the Apostle of God, although ye make me a liar. Write, Muḥammad the son of 'Abdu'lláh." Then Suhail said, "And on these conditions (write the treaty of peace), that no man, even though he follow thee, shall come to thee from us, but thou shalt send him back to us." And when he had finished writing the treaty, the Apostle of God said to his companions, "Rise and slay the animals for sacrifice, and then shave your heads." After that some women came (confessing themselves) believers. Then God Most High sent down the revelation, "O ye who believe, when there come to you women who believe as refugees (try them. God well knoweth their faith. And if ye know them to be true believers, send them not back to the infidels)."[1] And God Most High forbade them to send them back; and He commanded them to send back their dowries. After that the Prophet returned to Madína. And Abú Başír, a man of the Quraish, came to him. And he was a Muslim. And they sent two men in search of him; and Muḥammad handed him over to the two men, and they went out with him, until, when they arrived at Dhu'l-Ḥulaifah, they alighted in order to eat dates which they had. Then Abú Başír said to one of the two men, "By God! O so-and-so, verily I perceive that this sword of thine is a good one. Show it me that I may examine it." Then he allowed him. Then Abú Başír smote him till he became cold. And the other man fled until he arrived at Madína and entered running into the mosque. Then the Prophet said, "This man has certainly been terrified." The man said, "By God! my companion has been killed, and verily I am in danger of being killed also." Then Abú Başír came, and the Prophet said, "Alas his mother! he is a kindler of war if he had any one (to help him)." And when Abú Başír heard that, he knew that he would hand him back to them, and he went out until he came to the sea-shore. And Abú Jandal bin Suhail escaped and joined himself to Abú Başír. And it came to pass that no man who had embraced Islám went out from the Quraish without joining himself to Abú Başír, until there was gathered together from them a troop of men. And by God! they never heard of a caravan of the Quraish going out to Syria without attacking it and killing them and taking their goods. Then the Quraish sent to the Prophet and adjured him by God and their family ties to remonstrate with Abú Başír, and his companions. And whoever came to him was safe. Then he sent to them.'—*Al Bukhárí*.

It is related from Al Barái bin 'Ázib that he said, 'The Prophet made peace with the polytheists on the day of Ḥudaibah with three stipulations: that whoever came to him from the polytheists, he would send him back to them; but whoever came to them from the Muslims, they would not send him back; and that he (Muḥammad) should enter Mecca the following year and remain in it three days. And he (agreed)

[1] Qur'án, Súratu'l-Mumtaḥina (lx) 10.

that he would not enter it except with their arms, such as swords and bows and such like, in their sheaths. Then Abú Jandal came to him shackled with fetters on his legs, but he sent him back to them.'—*Muslim, Al Bukhárí.*

It is related from 'Áyesha that she said with regard to the oath of fealty taken by women, that, 'The Apostle of God used to test them by this verse of the Qu'rán, "O Prophet, if there come to thee believing women to take the oath of obedience to thee (that they will not associate anything with God, nor steal, nor commit fornication, nor kill their children, nor come with a calumny which they have forged between their hands and their feet, nor be disobedient to thee)." Then whoever of them agreed to these conditions, he said to her, "I have received thine oath of fealty," by the words which he spoke to her. By God! his hand never touched the hand of a woman in the action of accepting her oath of fealty.'—*Muslim, Al Bukhárí.*

It is related from Al Miswár and Marwán that, 'The Meccans agreed upon the cessation of war for ten years, and that the people should be secure during that period, on the condition that all cause of reproach should be abstained from, and that there should be no attacks by bandits and no treachery.'—*Abú Dáud.*

Concerning the Exclusion of the Jews from Arabia

It is related from Abú Hurairah that he said, 'Whilst we were in the mosque, the Prophet came out and said, "Go to the Jews." So we went with him until we came to their school-house. Then the Prophet rose up and said, "O People of the Jews, embrace Islám, that ye may be secure. And know ye that the earth belongeth to God and His Apostle. And verily I wish to expel you from this land, therefore whoever of you has any of his property (unsold), let him sell it."'—*Muslim, Al Bukhárí.*

It is related from Ibn 'Omar that he said, ''Omar stood up and gave the public address and said, "Verily the Apostle of God employed the Jews of Khaibár over their property, and said, 'We will allow you to remain so long as God allows you to remain.'" But 'Omar deemed it expedient to expel them. Then when 'Omar had resolved on that, one of the Bani abu'l-Ḥuqaiq came to him and said, "O Commander of the Faithful, dost thou turn us out, when Muḥammad allowed us to stay and appointed us over the property?" Then 'Omar replied, "Dost thou imagine that I have forgotten the words of the Apostle of God, 'How will it be with thee when thou art turned out of Khaibár, and thy young she-camels run after thee night after night!'" The Jew replied, "This was a jest of the father of Abu'l Qasim." He replied, "Thou liest, O enemy of God!" Then 'Omar banished them; and he gave them the price of what they possessed of fruits in money and camels and fittings of pack-saddles and ropes and other things.'—*Al Bukhári.*

It is related from Ibn 'Abbás that, 'The Apostle of God commanded three things. He said, "Turn the polytheists out of the Island of Arabia; behave towards ambassadors as I was wont to behave towards them." Ibn 'Abbás said, "And he remained silent regarding the third." Or, he said, "I have forgotten it."'—*Muslim, Al Bukhári.*

It is related from Jábir bin 'Abdu'lláh that he said, ''Omar binu'l-Khaṭṭáb informed me that he heard the Apostle of God say, "I will certainly turn the Jews and Christians out of the Island of Arabia, until I do not leave in it any but Muslims."'—*Muslim.* And in another tradition it runs, 'If I live, and God will, I will certainly turn the Jews and Christians out of the Island of Arabia.'

Concerning Spoil taken from Infidels without Fighting

It is related from Málik bin Aws binu'l-Ḥadathání that ''Omar binu'l Khaṭṭáb said, "Verily God has distinguished His Apostle in this spoil taken from infidels by something which He has not given to any besides him." Then he recited the words, "And as to their spoils which God hath granted to His Apostle (ye did not push forward any horses or camels against the same; but God giveth to His Apostles dominion over whom He pleaseth, for God is almighty.)" And this was free to the Apostle of God. He used to spend from this money on his family for their subsistence for one year. Afterwards he used to take what remained and place it in the place where the property belonging to God was kept.'—*Muslim, Al Bukhári.*

XIX

THE BOOK OF HUNTING AND KILLING

It is related from Abú Tha'labahu'l-Khushámi that he said, 'I said, "O Prophet of God, verily we are in a land belonging to a nation, the People of the Book; may we eat from their vessels? And we are in a land of game; and I hunt with bows and with dogs which have not been trained, as well as with those that have. Then what is the right course of conduct for me?" He replied, "As to what thou didst mention of the vessels of the People of the Book; if thou find any others, then do not eat from them; but if thou do not find others, then wash them and eat from them. And what thou huntest with thy bow, and hast mentioned the name of God over, eat. And what thou hast hunted with thy trained dog and hast repeated the name of God over, eat. And what thou hast hunted with thy untrained dog, and hast found it undefiled, eat."'—*Muslim, Al Bukhârí.*

It is related from Abú Ṭufail that he said, ''Alí was asked, "Has the Apostle of God distinguished thee by anything?" He replied, "He did not distinguish us by anything which he did not make universal for all men, except what is in the scabbard of this sword of mine." Then he brought out a paper on which was written, "God has cursed the one who kills without (repeating the name of) God; and God has cursed the one who steals a land mark." And in another tradition it runs, "Whoever changes a land mark." And, "God has cursed whoever curses his father; and God has cursed whoever gives shelter to an innovator."'—*Muslim.*

It is related from 'Adí bin Ḥátim that he said, 'I said, "O Apostle of God, inform us, if one of us takes game, and he has no knife with him, may he kill it with a lump of stone or a piece of stick?" He replied, "Cause the blood to flow with whatever ye like, and mention the name of God."'—*Abú Dáud, An Nasái.*

CONCERNING DOGS

—It is related from Jábir that he said, 'The Apostle of God ordered us to kill dogs, until a certain woman came from the desert with her dog, and we killed it. After that the Apostle of God forbade us to kill them, and said, " It is your duty to kill that one which is black all over with two spots on it ; for it is Ṣatan." '—*Muslim.*

It is related from Ibn 'Omar that, ' The Prophet commanded the killing of all dogs, except dogs for hunting and sheep-dogs, or dogs for cattle.'—*Muslim, Al Bukhârí.*

It is related from Ibn 'Abbás that he said, ' The Apostle of God forbade fighting between four-footed animals.'—*Abú Dáud.*

ON WHAT IS LAWFUL AND UNLAWFUL AS FOOD

It is related from Abú Hurairah that, 'The Apostle of God said, " The eating of all rapacious animals having canine teeth is unlawful." '—*Muslim.*

It is related from Jábir that, ' The Apostle of God, on the day of Khaibár, forbade (eating) the flesh of domestic asses, but he permitted the flesh of horses.'—*Muslim, Al Bukhârí.*

It is related from Ibn abú Awfi that he said, ' We went on seven warlike expeditions with the Apostle of God; and we used to eat locusts with him.'—*Muslim, Al Bukhârí.*

It is related from Abú Hurairah that, 'The Apostle of God said, " When a fly falls into a vessel belonging to any one of you, then let him immerse the whole of it. Afterwards let him throw it out; for verily in one of its wings is healing, and in the other, disease." '—*Al Bukhârí.*

It is related from Abú Hurairah that, 'The Apostle of God said, " An ant bit a certain prophet. So he gave orders regarding the ant-hill, and it was burnt. Then God Most High sent a revelation to him (saying), ' A single ant bit thee; and thou hast burnt a whole colony of peoples who praise God.' " '

It is related from Kḥálid binu'l-Walíd that, ' The Apostle of God forbade eating the flesh of the horse, the mule and the ass.'—*Abú Dáud, An Nasâi.*

It is related from Ibn 'Omar that, ' The Apostle of God said, " Two things which have died of themselves and two bloods have been made lawful for us. The two dead things are fishes and locusts, and the two bloods are the liver and spleen." ' —*Aḥmad, Ibn Májah.*

It is related from 'Abdu'r-Raḥmán bin abú Lailah, that Abú Lailah said, 'The Apostle of God said, "When a snake appears in a dwelling, then say to it, 'Verily we entreat thee by the covenant of Noah and by the covenant of Solomon, son of David, that thou molest us not.' Then if it returns, kill it." '—*At Tirmidhí, Abú Dáud.*

It is related from Abú Th'alabahu'l-Khushámi that, 'The Prophet said, "The genii are of three kinds: one kind has wings and flies in the heavens; one kind is composed of snakes and dogs; and one kind stays in places and goes on journeys." '—*Sharḥu's-Sunnah.*

CONCERNING THE CEREMONY CALLED 'AQIQAH

It is related from Salmán bin 'Amiru'l-Ḍabbi that he said, 'I heard the Apostle of God say, "With the birth of a boy *'aqíqah* must be observed. Then shed blood on his behalf, and remove evil from him." '—*Al Bukhárí.*

It is related from Umm Kurz that she said, 'I heard the Apostle of God say, "Leave birds alone in their places." She said, "And I heard him say, 'For a boy two sheep, and for a girl one sheep; and it will not matter whether it be a male or a female.'" '—*Abú Dáud, At Tirmidhí, An Nasáí.*

It is related from Muḥammad bin 'Alí bin Ḥusain from 'Alí bin abú Ṭálib that he said, 'The Apostle of God performed the *'aqíqah* ceremony on behalf of Ḥasan with one sheep and said, "O Fáṭimah, shave his head, and give in alms silver equal to the weight of his hair." Then we weighed it; and its weight was one dirham or part of a dirham.'—*At Tirmidhí.*

It is related from Buraidah that he said, 'In the time of ignorance when a son was born to any one of us, we used to sacrifice a sheep, and sprinkle his head with its blood. And when Islám came, we used to sacrifice a sheep on the seventh day, and shave his head and sprinkle it with saffron.'—*Abú Dáud.* And Razín has added the words, 'And we used to name him.'

XX

THE BOOK OF FOODS

It is related from Ibn 'Omar that, 'The Apostle of God said, "When anyone of you eats, then let him eat with his right hand; and when he drinks let him drink with his right hand." '—*Muslim.*

It is related from Jábir that he said, 'I heard the Apostle of God say, "Verily Satan is present at everything which anyone of you does, even to being present at his taking food. Then when a morsel falls from anyone of you, let him wipe off anything that may be on it, and afterwards let him eat it; and let him not leave it for Satan; and when he has finished eating, then let him lick his fingers, for verily he does not know in what part of his food lies a blessing." '—*Muslim.*

It is related from 'Amru bin Umayah that he saw the Prophet carving a shoulder of mutton which was in his hand, and he was called to prayers; and he threw it down together with the knife with which he was carving it. Then he stood up and said the prayers; but he did not perform the ablutions.'—*Muslim, Al Bukhárí.*

It is related from 'Áyesha that she said, 'The Apostle of God used to like sweetmeats and honey.'—*Al Bukhárí.*

It is related from Sa'íd bin Zaid that, 'The Prophet said, "Mushrooms are of the manna, and their juice is medicine for the eyes." '—*Muslim, Al Bukhárí.* And in another tradition from Muslim it runs, 'Mushrooms are of the manna which God Most High sent down on Moses.'

It is related from Sa'd that he said, 'I heard the Apostle of God say, "Whoever begins the morning with seven *ajwah* dates, neither poison nor magic will hurt him for that day." '—*Muslim, Al Bukhárí.*

It is related from 'Áyesha that she said, 'A whole month used to pass with us in which we did not light a fire. There were only dates and water (for our food), unless we were given some meat.'—*Muslim, Al Bukhárí.*

It is related from Jábir that, 'The Prophet said, "Whoever has eaten garlic or onions, let him keep himself away from us" or he said, "Let him keep himself away from our mosque," or "Let him sit in his own house." And a cooking-pot was brought to the Prophet in which were green herbs; and he perceived that they had a smell. And he told them to take them to some of his companions, and said, "Eat; for I have secret communications with one with whom ye do not hold secret communications."'—*Muslim, Al Bukhárí.*

It is related from Umámah bin Makhshi that he said, 'A man was eating; and he did not mention the name of God until there remained of his food but a mouthful. Then when he raised it to his mouth he said, "In the name of God, the first of it and the last of it." And the Prophet laughed and then said, "Satan continued eating with him; and when he mentioned the name of God, he (that is, Satan) vomited up what was in his belly."'—*Abú Dáud.*

It is related from Abú Sa'ídu'l-Khudri that he said, 'When the Apostle of God finished his meals he used to say, "Praise be to God who has given us food and drink, and made us Muslims."'—*At Tirmidhí, Abú Dáud, Ibn Májah.*

It is related from Salmán that he said, 'I read in the Taurát that the blessing of food is the ablution after it. And I repeated this to the Prophet. The Apostle of God said, "The blessing of food is in the ablution before it and the ablution after it."'—*At Tirmidhí, Abú Dáud.*

It is related from 'Áyesha that she said, 'The Apostle of God said, "Do not cut meat with a knife, for that is what is done by foreigners; but tear it with the teeth, for that is pleasanter and healthier."'—*Abú Dáud.*

It is related from Nubaishah that, 'The Apostle of God said, "Whoever eats from a large dish and then licks it; the dish asks pardon for him."'—*Aḥmad, At Tirmidhí, Ibn Májah.*

It is related from Abú Ziyyád that he said, ''Áyesha was asked about (the lawfulness of) onions. She replied, "Verily the last meal which the Apostle of God took was of food which had onions in it."'—*Abú Dáud.*

It is related from Nubaishah that, 'The Apostle of God said, "Whoever eats from a large dish, and then licks it, the dish says to him, 'May God free thee from the fire as thou hast freed me from Satan.'"'—*Razín.*

Concerning Hospitality

It is related from Abú Shuraihu'l-Ka'bi that 'The Apostle of God said, "Whoever believes in God and the last day, let him honour his guest. His right of courteous entertainment is one day and one night, and his right to hospitality extends to three days. And what is given after that is alms. And it is not right for (the guest) to take shelter with him so long that he put him into difficulties."'—*Muslim, Al Bukhárí.*

It is related from Al Miqdám bin Ma'díkarib that he heard the Prophet say, 'Whatever Muslim becomes the guest of a tribe, and he rises in the morning having been refused (food), it is the duty of every Muslim to help him to take for himself his entertainment from the money and grain of the host.'—*Abú Dáud, Al Dárimi.* And in another tradition from Al Miqdám it runs, 'Whatever man becomes the guest of a tribe, and they do not entertain him; he has the right to take from them an amount equal to his entertainment.'

It is related from Abu'l-Ahwasu'l-Jushami from his father, that he said, 'I said, "O Apostle of God, inform me, if I pass by a man, and he does not put food before me and does not extend hospitality to me, and afterwards he passes by me, shall I place food before him or requite him (as he treated me)?" He replied, "Rather entertain him with food."'—*At Tirmidhí.*

Concerning Drinks

It is related from Anas that, 'The Prophet forbade a man to drink in a standing attitude.'—*Muslim.*

It is related from Ibn 'Abbás that he said, 'I brought a bucket of Zemzem water to the Prophet, and he drank from it standing.'—*Muslim, Al Bukhárí.*

It is related from Ḥudhaifah that he said, 'I heard the Apostle of God say, "Do not dress in silk or brocade, and do not drink from vessels of gold or silver, and do not eat from large plates of gold or silver; for verily these are for them (the unbelievers) in this world, and for you in the next."'—*Muslim, Al Bukhárí.*

It is related from Ibn 'Abbás that, 'The Apostle of God said, "When anyone of you eats food, then let him say, 'O God, bless us by this food, and give us food better than it.' And when he is given milk to drink, then let him say, 'O God, bless us by this milk, and give us more than it,' for verily there is nothing which suffices in place of both food and drink except milk."'—*Al Tirmidhí, Abú Dáud.*

Concerning Infusions of Grapes and Dates

It is related from 'Áyesha that she said, 'We used to make an infusion of grapes for the Apostle of God in a leathern bag, which was tied at the top and had a hole at the bottom. And we made the infusion of grapes in the morning, and he used to drink it in the evening. And we used to make the infusion in the evening, and he would drink it in the morning.'—*Muslim.*

It is related from Abú Máliku'l-Ash'ari that he heard the Apostle of God say, 'Some people of my followers will certainly drink wine, calling it by a name not its own.'—*Abú Dáud, Ibn Májah.*

On Covering Vessels and Other Things

It is related from Jábir that, 'The Apostle of God said, "When night falls, or ye reach the evening, then prevent your children (from going out); for verily Satan at that time spreads himself about. And when one hour of the night has passed, then let them go. And shut the doors, and mention the name of God, for verily Satan does not open a door which is shut (in the name of God). And tie the mouths of your leathern bags, and mention the name of God; and cover over your vessels, and mention the name of God, even though ye put something upon them; and extinguish your lamps."'—*Muslim, Al Bukhárí.*

It is related from Jábir that he said, 'I heard the Prophet say, "When ye hear the bark of dogs, or the braying of asses at night, then take refuge with God from Satan the stoned; for verily they see what ye do not see. Therefore go out little when ye have to go on foot, for verily God the Exalted and Magnified spreads abroad certain of His creation at night such as He wishes. Therefore shut the doors, and mention the name of God over them; for verily Satan does not open a door when it is shut and the name of God has been mentioned over it. And immerse your water-jars in water, and turn your vessels upside down and tie the mouths of your leathern bags."'—*Sharhu's-Sunnah.*

XXI

THE BOOK OF CLOTHES

It is related from Anas that he said, 'The clothes which the Prophet liked to wear most were of striped cotton of Yeman.'—*Muslim, Al Bukhârî.*

It is related from Al Mughírah bin Shu'bah that, 'The Prophet wore a Grecian coat with tight sleeves.'—*Muslim, Al Bukhârî.*

It is related from Abú Burdah that he said, ''Áyesha brought out to us a patched upper garment and a pair of coarse drawers and said, "The soul of the Apostle of God was taken (when he was) in these two garments." '—*Muslim, Al Bukhârî.*

It is related from Abú Hurairah that, 'The Apostle of God said, "On the day of resurrection, God will not look upon the person who lengthens his trousers from pride." '—*Muslim, Al Bukhârî.*

It is related from Abú Hurairah that, 'The Apostle of God said, "That part of the trousers which is below the two ankles is in the fire." '—*Al Bukhârî.*

It is related from Mu'áwiyah bin Qurrah, from his father, that he said, 'I came to the Prophet in a band of men of the Muzainah (tribe); and they took the oath of fealty to him. And the buttons (of his shirt) were undone, so I put my hand inside the opening of his shirt and touched the seal of prophecy.'—*Abú Dáud.*

It is related from Samurah that, 'The Prophet said, "Dress in white clothes, for verily they are purest and best; and shroud your dead in them." '—*Aḥmad, An Nasâi.*

It is related from Abú Músáu'l-Ash'arí that, 'The Prophet said, "Gold and silk have been made lawful for the women of my followers, but unlawful for the men." '—*At Tirmidhí, An Nasâi.*

It is related from Mu'ádh bin Anas that, 'The Apostle of God said, "Whoever eats food, and afterwards says, 'Praise be to God, who has fed me with this food and given me sustenance thereby, without (the exercise of) strength or power on my part,' all his former sins will be forgiven him." '—*At Tirmidhí*. And Abú Dáud has added the words, 'Whoever puts on clothes and says, "Praise be to God, who has arrayed me in these and provided me therewith, without (the exercise of) strength and power on my part;" all his former sins and later ones will be forgiven him.'

It is related from 'Alí that he said, 'The Apostle of God forbade me (wearing) a gold signet-ring, and from wearing cloth from Qiss, and from (using) a red saddle-cloth.'—*At Tirmidhí, Abú Dáud, An Nasáí.*

It is related from Abú Rimthah of Taimah that he said, 'I came to the Prophet when he was wearing two green cloths. And old age had reduced his hair; and his grey hairs had been

Page 223, line 18, from the top:

For, 'There were two thick Qitra cloths upon the Prophet' read, 'There were two striped cloths (Qiṭriah) upon the Prophet.'

said, "He has lied! He knows that I am the most God-fearing of them, and the most upright of them in respect of trustworthiness." '—*At Tirmidhí, An Nasáí.*

It is related from 'Ubádah that, 'The Apostle of God said, "It is your duty to wear turbans, for they are the covering of the angels. And let them hang down behind your backs." '—*Al Baihaqi.*

It is related from Ibn 'Abbás that he said, 'Eat what you like and wear what you like, so long as they do not drive you to two sins: extravagance and pride.'—*Al Bukhárí.*

Concerning Signet-Rings

It is related from Ibn 'Omar that he said, 'The Prophet took a golden ring.' And in one tradition it runs, 'He put it on his right hand.' 'Then he took it off. Then he took a ring made of silver, on which was engraved "Muḥammad, the Apostle of God." And he said, "No one must engrave like the engraving of this ring of mine." And whenever he put it on, he used to place the stone of the ring towards the palm of his hand.'—*Muslim, Al Bukhárí.*

It is related from Anas that, 'The Prophet wished to write to Kisra (King of Persia), and to the Emperor of Rome and the King of Abyssinia. And it was remarked that they would not receive a letter unless it was sealed. So the Apostle of God made a signet-ring of silver, on which was engraved, "Muḥammad, the Apostle of God."'—*Muslim.* And in another tradition from Bukhárí it runs, 'The engraving of the ring was in three lines: "Muḥammad" in one line, "Apostle" in one line, and "God" in one line.'

It is related from Bunánah, the slave-girl of 'Abdu'r-Raḥmán bin Ḥayyánu'l-Anṣárí, that she was with 'Áyesha when someone came in to her with a girl upon whom was a string of little bells which tinkled. Then 'Áyesha said, "Do not bring her in to me unless thou cut off her bells, for I heard the Apostle of God say, 'The angels do not enter a house in which is a bell."'—*Abú Dáud.*

Concerning Shoes

It is related from Abú Hurairah that, 'The Apostle of God said, "When anyone of you puts on his shoes, then let him begin with the right one; and when he takes them off, let him begin with the left. Let the right-hand side one be the first in the putting on and the last of them to be taken off."'—*Muslim, Al Bukhárí.*

It is related from Ibn Buraidah from his father that, 'The King of Abyssinia sent a present to the Prophet of a pair of black shoes which were without embellishments; and he put them on.'—*Ibn Májah.* And At Tirmidhí has added the words, from Ibn Buraidah from his father, 'After that he performed ablutions, and he wiped over them (without taking them off).'

On Combing the Hair

It is related from Abú Hurairah that, 'The Apostle of God said, "Five things are obligatory: circumcision, removing the hairs of the privates, shortening and clipping the moustache, paring the nails and plucking out the hairs of the armpit."'—*Muslim, Al Bukhárí.*

It is related from Ibn 'Omar that, 'The Apostle of God said, "Do the opposite of the polytheists. Let your beards grow long, and shorten your moustaches."—*Muslim, Al Bukhárí.*

It is related from Abú Hurairah that, 'The Prophet said, "Verily the Jews and Christians do not dye (their hair). Then do ye the opposite to them."'—*Muslim, Al Bukhárí.*

It is related from Ibn 'Abbás that, 'The Prophet used either to clip his moustache or take away a part of it. And Abraham, the Friend of the Merciful, used to do the same.'—*At Tirmidhí.*

It is related from Ibn 'Omar that, 'The Prophet used to wear shoes of tanned leather; and he used to dye his beard yellow with (the dye called) *wars* and saffron. And Ibn 'Omar used to do the same.'—*An Nasái.*

It is related from Ibn 'Abbás that, 'The Prophet said, "Paint your eyes with antimony because it brightens the sight and causes the hair to grow." And he (Ibn 'Abbás) asserted that the Prophet had a vessel containing antimony from which he painted his eyes every night: three times on the one, and three times on the other.'—*At Tirmidhí.*

It is related from Abú'l-Malíḥ that he said, 'Some women of Hems came to 'Áyesha. She said, "Whence come ye?" They replied, "From Syria." She said, "Then probably ye are from the city the women of which go to baths?" They said, "Yes." She said, "Verily I heard the Apostle of God say, 'No woman takes off her clothes in any house except her husband's, but she tears the veil between herself and her Lord.'"'—*At Tirmidhí, Abu Dáud.*

It is related from Thábit that he said, 'Anas was asked concerning the dye used by the Prophet. He replied, "If I had wished to count the grey hairs which were in his head, I could have done so. He did not use dye."'—*Muslim, Al Bukhárí.*

It is related from Ibn 'Omar that he used to dye his beard yellow with saffron, until his clothes became covered with saffron. And it was remarked to him, "Why dost thou dye with saffron?" He replied, "Verily I saw the Apostle of God dye with it; and there was nothing more pleasing to him than it. And he used to dye the whole of his clothes with it, even to his turban."'—*Abú Dáud, An Nasái.*

It is related from Al Walíd bin 'Uqbah that he said, 'When the Apostle of God conquered Mecca, the people of Mecca began to bring their children to him. And he prayed for a blessing for them, and stroked their heads. And I was brought to him when I was dyed with *khalúq;* and he did not touch me on account of the *khalúq.*"'—*Abú Dáud.*

It is related from Yaḥya bin Sa'íd that he heard Sa'íd binu'l-Musayyib say, 'Abraham, the Friend of the Merciful, was the first man who entertained visitors, and he was the first man who was circumcised, and the first man who shortened his moustache, and the first man who saw grey hairs. And he said, "O Lord, what is this!" The Lord Most High replied, "O Abraham, these are a sign of dignity." Abraham said, "O my Lord, increase me in dignity."'—*Málik.*

Concerning Pictures

It is related from Abú Ṭalḥah that, 'The Prophet said, "The angels do not enter the house in which there is a dog or pictures."'—*Muslim, Al Bukhári.*

It is related from 'Áyesha that, 'The Prophet never left anything in his house on which were pictures of a cross, but would break them.'—*Al Bukhárí.*

It is related from 'Áyesha that, 'The Apostle of God said, "The men who will be most severely punished on the day of resurrection are those who draw likenesses of God's creation."'—*Muslim, Al Bukhárí.*

It is related from Ibn 'Abbás that he said, 'I heard the Apostle of God say, "Every maker of pictures is in the fire. God will appoint for him, for every picture which he has drawn, a person who will punish him in hell." Ibn 'Abbás said, "Then if you must make pictures, make them of trees and things in which there is no life."'—*Muslim, Al Bukhárí.*

It is related from Buraidah that, 'The Prophet said, "Whoever plays at backgammon, it is as if he had dipped his hand into the flesh of swine."'—*Muslim.*

It is related from Abú Hurairah that, 'The Apostle of God said, "Gabriel came to me and said, 'I came to thee yesterday, and nothing prevented me from entering except that there were figures upon the door, and in the house there was a coloured cloth with figures upon it. And there was a dog in the house. Therefore give orders regarding the head of the figure which is on the door of the house, and let it be cut off, and it will become like the figure of a tree. And give orders regarding the cloth, and let it be cut, and let there be made two cushions to recline upon. And give orders regarding the dog, and let it be put out.'" Then the Apostle of God did so.'—*At Tirmidhí, Abú Dáud.*

It is related from Abú Hurairah that, 'The Apostle of God saw a man following a dove; and he said, "A Satan following a Satan!"'—*Aḥmad, Abú Dáud, Ibn Májah.*

It is related from 'Áyesha that she said, 'When the Prophet complained (of sickness) some of his wives mentioned a certain church called Máriyah. And Umm Salamah and Umm Ḥabibah had been to the land of Abyssinia. And they mentioned the virtues of the church and the pictures within it. Then he raised his head and said, "When any good man dies from amongst those people, they build a mosque over his grave, after which they paint within the church those pictures. Those people are the worst of God's creation."'—*Muslim, Al Bukhárí.*

XXII

THE BOOK OF MEDICINE AND SPELLS

It is related from Ibn 'Abbás that, 'The Apostle of God said, "Remedies for disease consist of three things: scarification with a cupping instrument, or the drinking of honey, or cauterising with fire. And I forbid my followers to practise cauterising."'—*Al Bukhárí.*

It is related from Jábir that he said, 'Ubayya was wounded in a vein of his arm by an arrow on the day of Ahzáb. Then the Apostle of God cauterised it.'—*Muslim.*

It is related from 'Áyesha and Ráfi' bin Khadíj that, 'The Prophet said, "Fever is from the boiling heat of hell; therefore cool it with water."'—*Muslim, Al Bukhárí.*

It is related from Anas that he said, 'The Apostle of God specially permitted the use of magic (to protect) from the evil eye and from the sting of poisonous reptiles and from the bite of an ant.'—*Muslim.*

It is related from 'Umm Salamah that, 'The Prophet saw a girl in her house in whose face there was a yellowness. And he said, "Use magic for her, for verily it proceeds from a glance of the eye."'—*Muslim, Al Bukhárí.*

It is related from Usámah bin Sharík that they said, 'O Apostle of God, shall we use medicine?" He replied, "Yes, O servants of God, use medicines, for verily God has not created any disease without creating a remedy for it—except one disease, namely, weakness from old age."'—*Aḥmad, At Tirmidhí, Abú Dáud.*

It is related from Salma, the maid-servant of the Prophet, that she said, 'There was no one who complained to the Apostle of God of a pain in his head, but he replied, "Bleed yourself." And there was no one who complained of a pain in his feet, but he said, "Dye them."'—*Abú Dáud.*

It is related from Asmá' bint 'Umais that she said, 'O Apostle of God, verily the sons of Ja'far are soon affected by the evil eye. Shall I use a spell for them?" He replied, "Yes; for verily if there be anything that can overcome fate, the evil eye will certainly do so."'—*Aḥmad, At Tirmidhí, Ibn Májah.*

It is related from Abú Sa'ídu'l-Khudri that he said, 'The Apostle of God used to take refuge (with God) from the genii and the evil eye of men, until there descended the two chapters of the Qur'án on taking refuge.[1] Then when they descended he used to take them and leave all others.'—*At Tirmidhí, Ibn Májah.*

It is related from 'Othmán bin 'Abdu'lláh bin Marhab that he said, 'My family sent me to Umm Salamah with a cup of water. And when anyone used to be affected by the evil eye or anything else, he used to send to her a water vessel; and she used to bring out a hair of the Apostle of God which she used to keep in a silver bell. And she would rinse it for him (in the water), and he would drink from it. And I looked into the bell, and I saw some red hairs.'—*Al Bukhárí.*

It is related from Abú Kabshahu'l-Anmári that, 'The Apostle of God was cupped on the top of his head on account of poisoned mutton. Ma'mar said, "I was cupped in the same way on the head for other reasons than poisoning, and the excellence of my memory went from me to such an extent that the opening chapter of the Book was dictated to me at the prayers." '—*Razín.*

Concerning Omens and Auguries

It is related from Abú Hurairah that 'The Apostle of God said, "There is no such thing as contagion, nor an omen, nor (a bad influence from) the owl, nor (special calamities in the month) Ṣafar." Then a desert Arab said, "O Apostle of God, then what happens to a camel which was living in the sand (of the desert) like a gazelle (for cleanness), and when it is allowed to mix with a camel afflicted with the itch, it gives it the itch." The Apostle of God replied, "Who infected the first one?" '—*Al Bukhárí.*

It is related from 'Urwah bin 'Ámir that he said, 'Omens were mentioned to the Apostle of God, and he said, "The best of them is a good omen; and do not turn back a Muslim (by an omen). And if any one of you see that which he dislikes, let him say, 'O God, no one can bring good but Thee, and no one can remove evil but Thee. And there is no power and no strength except in God.' " '—*Abú Dáud.*

[1] Namely Súratu'l-Falaq (cxiii), and Súratu'n Nás (cxiv).

Concerning Divination

It is related from 'Áyesha that she said, 'I heard the Apostle of God say, "Verily the angels come down in the clouds and mention the matters determined in heaven. And the satans steal a hearing, and hear it and relate it to the diviners; and they repeat from it a hundred falsehoods from themselves."'—*Al Bukhárí.*

It is related from Zaid bin Khálidu'l-Ḥuhanni that he said, 'The Apostle of God prayed for us (as leader) at the morning prayer at Ḥudaibah on marks of rain which had fallen in the night. And when he had finished, he turned to the people and said, "Do ye know what your Lord said?" They replied, "God and His Apostle know best." He said, (God said) "There arose this morning of my servants some who believe in me, and some who are unbelievers. As for those who said, 'Rain has been sent upon us by the bounty and mercy of God,' they are believers in me and disbelievers in the stars. But as for those who said, 'Rain has been sent upon us in such and such a way as the result of the moon being in a certain constellation,' they are disbelievers in me and believers in the stars."'—*Muslim, Al Bukhárí.*

It is related from Ibn 'Abbás that he said, 'A man of the Prophet's companions, one of the Helpers, informed me that whilst they were sitting on a certain night with the Apostle of God, a star shot and emitted a light. Then the Apostle of God said to them, "What used ye to say in the times of ignorance when a star shot in this way?" They replied, "God and His Apostle know best. We used to say, some great man has been born to-night and some great man has died." The Apostle of God said, "Verily this has not shot on account of the death of anyone or the life of anyone; but our Lord, blessed be His name, when He orders a matter, the bearers of the throne sing praises, after which the inhabitants of heaven who are near them sing praises, until the praises reach the inhabitants of this heaven of the world. Then those who are near the bearers of the throne say to them, 'What did your Lord say'? And they inform them what He said. And some of the inhabitants of the heavens ask others for information, until it reaches this heaven of the world. Then the genii steal a hearing and pass it on to their friends (the diviners). So they are shot at (by the stars). And what they bring is true, but they deceive therein and add thereto." '—*Muslim.*

Concerning Visions

It is related from Abú Hurairah that, 'The Prophet said, "He who sees me in sleep, has certainly seen me; for Satan cannot fashion himself into my likeness." '—*Muslim, Al Bukhárí.*

It is related from Abú Qatádah that, 'The Apostle of God said, "A good vision is from God, but a dream is from Satan, therefore when anyone of you sees in a vision something that he likes, let him not relate it to any but one whom he loves; and when he sees what he dislikes, then let him take refuge with God from its evil and from the evil of Satan; and let him spit three times; and let him not tell it to anyone; then it will never harm him." '—*Muslim, Al Bukhárí.*

It is related from Abú Músá that, 'The Prophet said, "I saw in a dream that I was being taken from Mecca to a land in which were date-trees. And my imagination went so far that it appeared to be Yamámah or Hejr, and behold! it was the city of Yathrib (i.e., Madína.) And I saw in this dream of mine that I was brandishing a sword, and the forepart of it was cut off; and behold! it was what befel the believers on the day of (the battle of) 'Uḥud. After that I brandished it a second time, and it returned to me better than it was before; and behold! it was the victory which God gave them, and the bringing together of the believers." '—*Muslim, Al Bukhárí.*

It is related from 'Áyesha that, 'The Apostle of God was asked about Waraqah. Then Khadíja said to him, "Verily he bore witness to the truth of thy mission. But he died before thou appeared (as a Prophet)." The Apostle of God said, "He was shown to me in a dream. And there were white clothes on him; but if he had been one of the inhabitants of the fire, there would certainly have been upon him different clothes from that." '—*Aḥmad, At Tirmidhí.*

XXIII

THE BOOK OF GOOD MANNERS

On Salutations

It is related from Abú Hurairah that, 'The Apostle of God said, "God created Adam in His own image. His height was sixty cubits; and when He created him He said, 'Go and salute those people—and they were a band of angels who were sitting—and listen to what answer they return thee; for verily it is an answer for thee and for thy progeny.' Then he went and said, 'Peace be on you.' And they said, 'Peace and the mercy of God be on thee.'" (The Prophet) said, "They added to it the words, 'And the mercy of God.' Everyone who enters paradise will do so in the image of Adam. His height will be sixty cubits; but the creation has continued to decrease after him until now."'—*Muslim, Al Bukhárí.*

It is related from Abú Hurairah that, 'The Apostle of God said, "Do not salute a Jew or a Christian first; and when ye meet one of them in the road, force him to the side of it."'—*Muslim.*

It is related from Ibn 'Omar that, 'The Apostle of God said, "When a Jew salutes you, he only says, '*As sám 'alaika.*'[1] ('May death come upon thee'). Then do ye say in response, '*Wa 'alaika*' ('And upon thee')."'—*Muslim, Al Bukhárí.*

It is related from 'Áyesha that she said, 'A party of Jews asked permission (to interview) the Prophet. And they said, "May death come upon you." Then I said, "Rather may death and a curse come upon you." Then (the Apostle) said, "O 'Áyesha, verily God is compassionate and loves compassion in all matters." I said, "Didst thou not hear what they said?" He replied, "I said, 'And upon you?'"'—*Muslim, Al Bukhárí.*

It is related from 'Alí that, 'The Apostle of God said, "There are six duties incumbent upon one Muslim toward another: that he should salute him when he meets him; that he

[1] i.e. Instead of saying, '*As salám 'alaika*' ('Peace be upon thee.')

should accept the invitation when he invites him; that he should say "Praise be to God" when he sneezes; that he should visit him when he is ill; that he should follow his bier when he dies; and that he should love for him what he loves for himself."'—*At Tirmidhí.*

It is related from 'Amru bin ṣhu'aib, from his father, from his grandfather that, 'The Prophet of God said, "He is not of us who makes himself like one who does not belong to us. Do not imitate the Jews and Christians. For the salutation of the Jews is a sign with the fingers, and the salutation of the Christians is a sign with the palms of the hand."'—*At Tirmidhí.*

It is related from Zaid bin Thábit that he said, 'I entered into the Prophet when a writer was (sitting) in front of him; and I heard him say, "Put the pen upon your ear, for it helps one to remember the money."'—*At Tirmidhí.*

It is related from Zaid bin Thábit that he said, 'The Apostle of God ordered me to learn Syriac.' And in another tradition it runs, 'He ordered me to learn the correspondence of the Jews; and said, "I put no reliance in the Jews in regard to correspondence." Zaid said, "Then not half a month had passed over me before I had learnt it. And so it came about that whenever he wrote to a Jew, I wrote (for him). And when they wrote to him, I read their letter to him."'—*At Tirmidhí.*

It is related from Abú Hurairah that, 'The Apostle of God said, "When God created Adam and blew a soul into him, he sneezed and said, 'Praise be to God,' and he praised God by His permission. And his Lord said to him, 'May God have mercy on thee. O Adam, go to those angels, to the party of them which is sitting down, and say, "Peace be upon you."' So he said, 'Peace be upon you.' They replied, 'Upon thee be the peace and mercy of God.' After that he returned to his Lord and He said, 'Verily this is thy salutation and the salutation of thy children amongst themselves.' And God said to him, His two hands being tightly closed, 'Choose which of the two thou wishest.' He replied, 'I choose the right hand of my Lord; but both the hands of my Lord are right and blessed.' Then He extended it, and behold! in it, Adam and his descendants. He said, 'O my Lord, what are these?' He replied, 'These are thy descendants; and behold! the age of every man is written down between his two eyes. And behold! amongst them is a man, the brightest of them all, or one of the brightest of them.' He said, 'O Lord, who is this?' He replied, 'This is thy son David, and I have written his age for him, forty years.' He said, 'O Lord, increase his age.' He replied, 'That is what I have written for him.' He said, 'O my Lord, verily I put to his credit, sixty years of my own life.' He said, 'Do what thou wishest.'" (The Apostle) said, "After that Adam dwelt in paradise as long as God wished, and then he was cast down from it. And Adam was in the habit of counting up (his age) for himself. Then the angel of death came to him. And Adam said to him, 'Thou hast come too soon. A thousand years have been written down for me.' The angel replied, 'That is so; but thou hast placed sixty years to the credit of thy son David.' Then he denied; and his descendants have denied; and he forgot, and his descendants have forgotten." (The Prophet) said, "Then from that time it was ordered to be written down with witnesses."'—*At Tirmidhí.*

On Asking Permission (to Enter)

It is related from Kaldah bin Ḥanbal that Ṣafwán bin Umayyah sent some milk and a young deer and some cucumbers to the Prophet when he was at the higher part of the valley. Kaldah said, 'Then I entered into him, and I neither saluted nor asked permission.' And the Prophet said, "Go back! and say, 'Peace be upon you. May I enter?'"'—*At Tirmidhí, Abú Dáud.*

On Shaking Hands and Embracing

It is related from Qatádah that he said, 'I said to Anas, "Was there shaking of hands amongst the companions of the Prophet of God?" He replied, "Yes."'—*Al Bukhárí.*

It is related from Al Bará' bin 'Ázib that, 'The Apostle of God said, "There are no two Muslims who meet and shake hands; but they are forgiven before they separate."'—*Aḥmad, At Tirmidhí.*

It is related from 'Áyesha that she said, 'I never saw anyone resemble the Apostle of God more in manner and habits and good disposition'—and in another tradition it runs 'in conversation and speech'—' than Fáṭimah. When she entered where he was, he used to rise for her and take her by her hand and kiss her and sit her in his seat. And when he entered where she was, she used to rise for him and take him by his hand and kiss him and sit him in her seat.'—*Abú Dáud.*

It is related from 'Afá'l-Kharásáni that, 'The Apostle of God said, "Shake hands with one another in order to remove envy; and give one another presents, and show love to one another, and so take away malice."'—*Málik.*

On Rising Up

It is related from Anas that he said, 'There was no man more beloved by them than the Apostle of God. And when they saw him, they used not to rise for him, because they were aware of his dislike of that.'—*At Tirmidhí.*

It is related from Abú Hurairah that he said, 'The Apostle of God used to sit with us in the mosque conversing with us. And when he rose up, we used to rise and remain standing until we saw that he had entered into some of the houses of his wives.'

On Sitting and Sleeping and Walking

It is related from 'Abbás bin Tamím, from his uncle, that he said, 'I saw the Apostle of God in the mosque lying on his back and placing one of his feet upon the other.'—*Muslim, Al Bukhárí.*

It is related from Jábir that he said, 'The Apostle of God forbade a man from raising one of his legs upon the other whilst he was lying on his back.'—*Muslim.*

It is related from Abú Hurairah that, 'The Apostle of God said, "When any one of you sits in the shade; and the shadow moves away from him, so that a part of him remains in the sun and a part in the shade, then let him get up."'—*Abú Dáud.* And in the Sharḥu's-Sunnah it runs: 'He said, "When anyone of you sits in the shade, and it moves away from him; then let him get up, for verily the sitting of Satan is of this kind."'

It is related from Ibn 'Omar that, 'The Prophet forbade a man to walk between two women.'—*Abú Daúd.*

On Sneezing and Yawning

It is related from Abú Hurairah that, 'The Prophet said, "Verily God loves sneezing and hates yawning. Therefore when anyone of you sneezes and praises God, it is the duty of every Muslim who hears him to say to him, 'May God have mercy on thee.' But as for yawning, it is only from Satan; therefore when anyone of you yawns, let him suppress it as far as he is able. For verily, when anyone of you yawns, Satan laughs at him."'—*Al Bukhárí.*

It is related from Abú Músa that he said, 'The Jews used to make themselves sneeze near the Prophet; hoping that he would say to them, "May God have mercy on you;" but he used to say, "May God guide you and make good your hearts!"'—*At Tirmidhí, Abú Dáud.*

On Laughing

It is related from 'Áyesha that she said, 'I never saw the Prophet laugh heartily, so that I could see the palate of his mouth. He used only to smile.'—*Al Bukhárí.*

It is related from 'Abdu'lláh binu'l-Ḥárith bin Jazi' that he said, 'I never saw anyone smile more than the Apostle of God.'—*At Tirmidhí.*

Concerning Names

It is related from Anas that he said, 'The Prophet was in a bazaar, and a man said, "O Abu'l-Qásim!" And the Prophet turned round to him. But the man said, "I only called this man." Then the Prophet said, "Give (your children) my name; but do not designate them by my epithet (Abu'l-Qásim)."'—*Muslim, Al Bukhárí.*

It is related from Ibn 'Omar that, 'The Apostle of God said, "Verily the most pleasing of your names in the sight of God are ''Abdu'lláh' and ''Abdu'r-Raḥmán.'"—*Muslim.*

It is related from Abú Hurairah that, 'The Apostle of God said, "No one of you must ever say, 'My slave' and 'My female slave.' All of you are slaves of God, and all your women are His female slaves.' But let him say, 'My boy,' 'My girl,' 'My young man,' 'My young woman.' And a slave must not say, 'My Lord'; but let him say, 'My master.'" And in another tradition it runs, "Let not a slave say to his master, 'My Lord'; for verily your Lord is God."'—*Muslim.*

It is related from Abu'l-Dardái' that, 'The Apostle of God said, "You will be called on the day of resurrection by your names and the names of your fathers. Therefore make your names good ones."'—*Aḥmad, Abú Dáud.*

It is related from 'Áyesha that she said, 'Verily the Prophet used to change bad names.'—*At Tirmidhí.*

It is related from 'Abdu'l-Ḥamíd bin Jubair bin Ṣhaibah that he said, 'I sat near Sa'íd binu'l-Musayyib, and he told me that his grandfather Ḥazn went to the Prophet. And the latter said, "What is thy name?" He replied, "My name is Ḥazn." He said, "Rather thou art Sahl." He replied, "I will not change the name which my father gave me." Ibnu'l-Musayyib said, "Ever since that stubbornness has remained amongst us."'—*Al Bukhárí.*

Concerning Rhetoric and Poetry

—It is related from Ibn 'Omar that he said, 'Two men from the East drew near and made speeches. And the people were astonished at their eloquence. Then the Apostle of God said, "There is certainly magic in eloquence."'—*Al Bukhárí.*

It is related from Abú Hurairah that, 'The Apostle of God said, "The truest word a poet has spoken is the word of Labíd, 'Beware! everything except God is vanity.'"'—*Muslim, Al Bukhárí.*

It is related from Al Baṛái' that, 'The Prophet said to Ḥassán bin Thábit on the day of Quraizah, "Lampoon the polytheists, for verily Gabriel is with thee." And the Apostle of God used to say to Ḥassán, "Answer for me." (And he prayed.) "O God, help him with the Holy Spirit."'—*Muslim, Al Bukhárí.*

It is related from 'Áyesha that, 'The Apostle of God said, "Lampoon the Quraish, for it is more trying to them than the shooting of arrows."'—*Muslim.*

—It is related from Anas that, 'The Apostle of God said, "On the night on which I was taken (up to heaven) I passed by a people whose lips were being cut off with scissors of fire. And I said, 'O Gabriel, who are these?' He replied, 'These are those of thy followers who delivered the public address at prayers, and who said what they did not perform.'"'—*At Tirmidhí.*

It is related from 'Áyesha that she said, 'The Apostle of God used to place a pulpit in the mosque for Ḥassán on which to stand. And he used to stand and magnify the Apostle of God or boast of his virtues. And the Apostle of God said, "Verily God assists Ḥassán with the Holy Spirit so long as he boasts concerning the Apostle of God." '—*Al Bukhárí.*

It is related from Abú Sa'ídu'l-Khudri that he said, 'When we were going with the Apostle of God to Al 'Arj, behold! a poet appeared reciting verses of poetry. Then the Apostle of God said, "Take hold of Satan," or "Seize Satan. It is certainly better that the belly of a man should be full of pus than of poetry." '

It is related from Jábir that, 'The Apostle of God said, "Songs cause hypocrisy to arise in the heart, as water causes the crops to spring up." '—*Al Baihaqi.*

It is related from Náfi' that he said, 'I was with Ibn 'Omar in a certain road. And he heard a reed instrument; and he placed his fingers in his ears, and turned off the road in another direction. Then, after going some distance, he said to me, "O Náfi' dost thou hear anything?" I replied, "No." Then he took his fingers out of his ears and said, "I was with the Apostle of God; and he heard the sound of a reed instrument and did as I did." Náfi' said, "When that happened I was young." '—*Aḥmad, Abú Dáud.*

On Keeping the Tongue, and on Calumny and Abuse

It is related from 'Abdu'lláh bin Ma'súd that, 'The Apostle of God said, "Abuse of a Muslim is disobedience to God, and fighting with him is infidelity." '—*Muslim, Al Bukhárí.*

It is related from Abú Hurairah that, 'The Apostle of God said, "It is not right for one who tells the truth that he should be a great curser." '—*Muslim.*

It is related from Abú Hurairah that, 'The Apostle of God said, "You will find that the worst men on the day of resurrection will be those who are two-faced. Who come to some people in one attitude, and to others in another." '—*Muslim, Al Bukhárí.*

It is related from 'Abdu'lláh bin Ma'súd that, 'The Apostle of God said, "It is your duty to speak the truth; for verily the truth leads to righteousness, and righteousness leads to paradise. And a man will continue to speak the truth and hold it fast until he is written down with God as a truth-teller. Then beware of falsehood, for verily falsehood leads to foul deeds, and foul deeds lead to the fire. And a man will continue to lie and hold falsehood fast until he is written down with God as a great liar." '—*Muslim, Al Bukhárí.*

It is related from Al Miqdád binu'l-Aswad that, 'The Apostle of God said, "When ye see flatterers, then throw dust into their mouths." '—*Muslim.*

It is related from Bahz bin Ḥakím, from his father, from his grandfather that, 'The Apostle of God said, "Woe to him who tells stories and lies in order to make people laugh thereby. Woe to him! Woe to him!" '—*Aḥmad, At Tirmidhí.*

It is related from 'Uqbah bin 'Ámir that he said, 'I met the Apostle of God; and I said, "What is (the means of) salvation?" He replied, "Rule thy tongue, let thine house be a sufficient dwelling-place, and weep for thy sins." '—*Aḥmad, At Tirmidhí.*

It is related from Ibn 'Omar that, 'The Apostle of God said, "When a servant (of God) tells a falsehood, the angel removes from him a mile on account of the bad odour which emanates from it." '—*At Tirmidhí.*

It is related from 'Ammár that, 'The Apostle of God said, "He who is two-faced in the world will have two tongues of fire on the day of resurrection." '—*Abú Dáud.*

It is related from Anas that, 'The Apostle of God said, "When a wicked man is praised, thy Lord Most High becomes angry, and the throne trembles on account of it." '—*Al Baihaqi.*

It is related from Anas that, 'The Apostle of God said, "O Abú Dharr, shall I not point you to two good qualities, which will be light on the back, but heavy in the scales?" I said, "Yes." He replied, "Length of silence, and goodness of disposition. By Him in whose hand is my life! there is no action of man like these two." '

It is related from 'Áyesha that she said, 'The Prophet passed by Abú Bakr when he was cursing some of his slaves. Then he turned to him and said, "Cursers and confirmers of the truth![1] Never by the Lord of the Ka'bah!" Abú Bakr at once set free some of his slaves, and afterwards came to the Prophet and said, "I will not do it again."'—*Al Baihaqi.*

It is related from 'Ubádah binu'ṣ-Sámit that, 'The Prophet said, "Be security for me for six things concerning yourselves; and I will be security for paradise for you. Tell the truth when you speak; perform when you promise; be trustworthy when put in trust; keep your private parts; turn away your eyes (from the forbidden); and withhold your hands (therefrom)."'

Concerning Promises

It is related from Jábir that he said, 'When the Apostle of God died, some property came to Abú Bakr from Al 'Alái' binu'l-Ḥaḍrami. Then Abú Bakr said, "Whomsoever the Prophet owed anything, or to whomsoever he made a promise, let him come to us." Jábir said, "Then I said, 'The Apostle of God promised to give me such and such.'" And he held out his hands three times. Jábir said, "Then he filled my hands once. And I counted it, and behold! it was five hundred (dirhams). And he said, 'Take double the amount.'"'—*Muslim, Al Bukhárí.*

It is related from Zaid bin Arqam that, 'The Prophet said, "When a man makes a promise to his brother, and intends to perform it, but does not do so, and does not come to the place appointed; then there is no fault upon him."'—*Abú Dáud, At Tirmidhí.*

Concerning Joking

It is related from Anas that, 'The Prophet said to an old woman, "Verily no old woman will enter paradise." She replied, "Then what will happen to them?"—and she used to read the Qur'án. He said to her, "Dost thou not read the Qur'án? 'Verily we have created them in a certain fashion, and we will make them virgins.'"'[2]—*Razín.*

It is related from Anas that 'A man of the desert Arabs, whose name was Záhir bin Ḥarám, used to bring presents to

[1] Muḥammad had previously conferred upon Abú Bakr the special title, 'Aṣ Ṣiddiq' ('Confirmer of the truth').

[2] Qur'án, Súratu'l-Wáqi'a (lvi) 35.

the Prophet from the desert. And the Apostle of God used to furnish him with all necessaries when he wished to go out (to his people). And the Prophet said, "Verily Záhir provides us from the desert, and we give him something in return." And the Prophet loved him, and Záhir was ugly. And on a certain day the Prophet came, when he was selling his goods, and caught him in his arms from behind, so that he was not able to see him. And (Záhir) said, "Let me go! Who is this?" Then he turned round and recognized the Prophet. And he struck his back against the Prophet's breast as a sign that he had detected him. Then the Prophet began to say, "Who will buy this slave?" He replied, "O Apostle of God, in that case, by God! you will find me goods not easy to sell!" Then the Prophet said, "But in the sight of God thou art not worthless goods."'—*Sharḥu's-Sunnah.*

It is related from Nu'mán bin Bashír that he said, 'Abú Bakr asked the Prophet permission (to enter his house); and he heard 'Áyesha's voice raised (in anger). And when he entered, he seized her in order to box her ears, and said, "Let me never see thee raising thy voice against the Apostle of God." And the Prophet began to prevent him (from slapping 'Áyesha). Then Abú Bakr went out in anger. And when Abú Bakr went out, the Prophet said, "Dost thou see how I saved thee from that man?"' She said, 'Then Abú Bakr stayed away for some days, and afterwards he asked permission (to enter) and found that the two of them had become reconciled. Then he said to them, "Include me in your reconciliation as ye included me in your quarrel." The Prophet said, "We have done so. We have done so."'—*Abú Dáud.*

On Boasting and Partisanship

It is related from Al Barái' bin 'Ázib that he said, 'On the day of (the battle of) Ḥunain Abú Sufyán binu'l-Ḥárith was holding the reins of his mule, that is the mule of the Apostle of God; and when the polytheists surrounded him, he alighted and began to say, "I am the Prophet, there is no falsehood; I am the son of 'Abdu'l-Muṭṭalib." (Al Barái') said, "No man amongst the people was seen to be braver on that day than he."'—*Muslim, Al Bukhárí.*

It is related from Anas that he said, 'A man came to the Prophet and said, "O best of creation." The Apostle of God replied, "That was Abraham." '—*Muslim.*

It is related from 'Omar that, 'The Apostle of God said, "Do not give me exaggerated praise, as the Christians exaggerate in praising the Son of Mary, for I am only His servant. Therefore say, 'The servant of God and His Apostle." '—*Muslim, Al Bukhárí.*

ON FILIAL PIETY AND CHARITY

It is related from Abú Hurairah that a man said, 'O Apostle of God, who of my associates is most worthy of being treated well?". He replied, "Thy mother." He said, "And who after that?" He replied, "Thy mother." He said, "Who after that?" He replied, "Thy mother." He said, "Who after that?" He replied, "Thy father." '—*Muslim, Al Bukhárí.*

It is related from Al Mughírah that, 'The Apostle of God said, "Verily God has forbidden bad behaviour towards mothers, and has forbidden burying daughters alive, and parsimony and begging. And He dislikes loquaciousness in you. And (He has forbidden) excessive questioning, and squandering of money." '—*Muslim, Al Bukhárí.*

It is related from Ibn 'Omar that, 'The Apostle of God said, "Doing one's duty to one's relations does not consist in making recompense for benefits received; but the one who carries out his family duties is he who, when he is not treated well, still does his duty." '—*Al Bukhárí.*

It is related from Abú Hurairah that, 'A man said, "O Apostle of God, I have some relations whom I treat well, but they treat me badly. And I do good to them, but they do evil to me. And I am patient with them, but they are rude to me." (The Prophet) said, "If thou art as thou sayest, then it is as if thou wert casting coals of fire at them; and thou wilt continue to receive assistance from God against them so long as thou behave thus." '—*Muslim.*

It is related from Abú Usaid that he said, 'When we were near the Apostle of God, behold a man of the Bani 'Salimah came to him and said, "O Apostle of God, is there anything remaining undone of duties towards my parents which I might do to them after their death?" He replied, "Yes, prayer for them and asking forgiveness for them, and the execution of their promises after them, and good behaviour towards their relations, such as is not usually given except to them (the parents), and honouring their friends."'—*Abú Dáud, Ibn Májah.*

It is related from Ibn 'Omar that he said, 'I had a woman as my wife whom I loved, but 'Omar disliked her and said to me, "Divorce her." But I refused. Then 'Omar came to the Apostle of God and mentioned the matter to him. And the Apostle of God said to me, "Divorce her."'—*At Tirmidhí, Abú Dáud.*

It is related from Anas that, 'The Apostle of God said, "Verily the servant whose parents die, or one of them dies, and he has certainly been disobedient to them, must continue to pray for them and ask pardon for them, until God writes him down as one who acts with filial piety."'

It is related from Sa'íd binu'l-'Aṣ that, 'The Apostle of God said, "The rights of an elder brother which he may claim from a younger brother are (the same as) the rights which a parent may claim from his child."'—*Al Baihaqi.*

On Compassion and Mercy towards the Creation

It is related from Abú Hurairah that, 'The Apostle of God said, "The one who takes care of widows and poor people, is like one who is active in the way of God." And I imagine he said, "He is like one who stands up (in prayer) without intermission, and keeps the fast without breaking it."'—*Muslim, Al Bukhárí.*

It is related from Anas that, 'The Apostle of God said "By him in whose hand is my life! no servant believes until he loves for his brother what he loves for himself."'—*Muslim, Al Bukhárí.*

It is related from 'Áyesha and Ibn 'Omar that, 'The Prophet said, "Gabriel continued to give me orders concerning (the rights of) neighbours, until I thought that he would make them heirs."'—*Muslim, Al Bukhárí.*

It is related from Ibn 'Abbás that, 'The Apostle of God said, "He is not of us who is not kind to our little ones, and does not honour our elders, and does not command what is lawful and forbid what is unlawful."'—*At Tirmidhí.*

It is related from Abú Umámah that, 'The Apostle of God said, "He who strokes the head of an orphan for no other reason than for the sake of God, shall have a good deed (ascribed to him) for every hair which his hand passes over. And whoever does good to an orphan, male or female, who is in his care, he and I will be in paradise like these two"—and he joined his two fingers together.'—*At Tirmidhí.*

It is related from Ayyúb bin Músá, from his father, from his grandfather, that, 'The Apostle of God said, "No father has given his son a better present than good manners."'—*At Tirmidhí.*

It is related from Ibn Ma'súd that, 'The Apostle of God said, "Verily God Most High has divided among you your natural dispositions, as He has apportioned among you your sustenance. Verily God Most High gives the earth to those whom He loves and to those whom He does not love; but He does not give religion except to those whom He loves. And he to whom God gives religion, him He has certainly loved. And by Him in whose hand is my life! no servant becomes a Muslim until his heart and tongue do so. And he does not believe until his neighbour is safe from his injustices."'

Concerning Love in God and from God

It is related from Abú Hurairah that, 'The Apostle of God said, "Verily when God loves a servant, He calls Gabriel and says, 'Verily I love such an one, therefore do thou love him.' Then Gabriel loves him; after which he makes proclamation in the heavens and says, 'Verily God loves such an one, therefore do ye love him.' Then the inhabitants of heaven love him. After that his acceptance is established upon the earth. And when God hates a servant, He calls Gabriel and says, 'Verily I hate such an one, therefore do thou hate him.' Then Gabriel hates him; after which he makes proclamation amongst the inhabitants of heaven and says, 'Verily God hates such an one, therefore do ye hate him.' Then they hate him. After that hatred for him is established in the earth."'—*Muslim.*

It is related from Anas that, 'A man said, "O Apostle of God, when will the hour (of resurrection) come?" He replied,

"Woe to thee! what provision hast thou made for it?" He said, "I have made no provision for it, except that I love God and His Apostle." He replied, "Thou wilt be with Him whom thou lovest." Anas said, "I never saw the Muslims rejoice more over anything, after Islám, than their joy at this (saying)." '—*Muslim, Al Bukhárí.*

It is related from 'Omar that, 'The Apostle of God said, "Verily amongst the servants of God there will certainly be some men who were neither prophets nor martyrs, but whose felicity the prophets and martyrs will desire on the day of resurrection on account of their position near God." They said, "O Apostle of God, inform us who they are." He replied, "They are those who love one another in the spirit of God, and not on account of blood-relationships existing between them, or for property which they give and take amongst themselves. And by God! verily their faces will be light, and they will certainly be upon (seats of) light. They will not fear when others fear, nor will they be sorrowful when others grieve." Then he recited this verse of the Qur'án, "Beware! verily the friends of God have no fear on them, nor do they grieve," '[1]—*Abú Dáud.*

It is related from Abú Sa'íd that he heard the Prophet say, 'Do not make friends of any, except a believer; and let none eat of your food, but the pious.'—*At Tirmidhí, Abú Dáud.*

On what is Forbidden regarding Breaking off Friendships, and Searching out Defects

It is related from Abú Hurairah that, 'The Apostle of God said, "The actions of men are reported twice every week: on Mondays and Thursdays. And every believing servant is forgiven except the servant between whom and his brother there is enmity. And it is said (to the angels), 'Leave these two until they become reconciled.' " '—*Muslim.*

It is related from Asmá' bint Yazíd that she said, 'The Apostle of God said, "Falsehood is not lawful except in three cases: the falsehood of a man to his wife in order to please her; falsehood in war; and falsehood in order to effect a reconciliation between men." '—*Aḥmad, At Tirmidhí.*

---

[1] Qur'án, Súratu Yúnas (x) 61.

It is related from Ibn 'Omar that he said, 'The Apostle of God ascended the pulpit and cried with a loud voice and said, "O ye people, who have embraced Islám with the tongue, but whose hearts faith has not reached, distress not Muslims, nor reproach them, nor search out their defects; for verily he who seeks out the defects of his brother Muslim, God will seek out his defects. And he whose defects God seeks out, He will expose them although they be (hidden) in the middle of his pack-saddle." '—*At Tirmidhí.*

It is related from 'Áyesha that she said, 'Safiyah's camel was sick. And Zainab had an excess of riding-camels. And the Apostle of God said to Zainab, "Give her a camel." She replied, "Shall I give to that Jewess!" Then the Apostle of God became angry, and he forsook her for (the months of) Dhu'l-Hajj and Muḥarram and part of Ṣafar." '—*Abú Dáud.*

It is related from Abú Hurairah that, 'The Apostle of God said, "Jesus, the Son of Mary saw a man stealing. Then Jesus, the Son of Mary, said to him, 'Thou didst steal.' He replied, 'Never! by Him besides whom there is no other God!' Then Jesus said, 'I believed in God, but spoke falsely to myself.'" '—*Muslim.*

On Caution and Deliberation in Matters

It is related from Sahl bin Sa'du'l-Sa'íd that, 'The Prophet said, "Deliberation is from God, and haste is from Satan." '—*At Tirmidhí.*

It is related from Abú Hurairah that, 'The Prophet said to Abu'l-Haitam binu'l Tabbihán, "Hast thou a servant?" He replied, "No." He said, "When captives come to us, do thou appear also." Then two captives were brought to the Prophet, and Abu'l-Haitam came to him, and the Prophet said, "Choose one of them." He replied, "O Prophet of God, do thou choose for me." Then the Prophet said, "Verily a counsellor is one to be trusted in. Take this one; for verily I saw him praying. And behave well towards him." '—*At Tirmidhí.*

On Kindness and Modesty and Good Dispositions

It is related from 'Imrán bin Ḥuṣain that, 'The Apostle of God said, "Modesty brings nothing but good." And in another tradition it runs, "All kinds of modesty are good." '—*Muslim, Al Bukhárí.*

It is related from Ibn Má'súd that, 'The Apostle of God said, "Verily one of the things which men have understood from the words of former prophecies is this: 'When thou hast no shame, then do whatever thou wishest.'" '—*Al Bukhárí.*

It is related from Sahl bin Mu'ádh, from his father that, 'The Prophet said, "He who suppresses his anger, when he has the power to give vent to it; God will call him to the chiefs of creation on the day of resurrection in order that He may let him choose which of the black-eyed virgins (Huris) of paradise he may wish." '—*At Tirmidhí, Abú Dáud.*

It is related from Ibn 'Omar that, 'The Prophet said, "Verily modesty and faith are joined together. When one of them is taken away, the other is taken also." And in a tradition from Ibn 'Abbás it runs: "When one of them is stolen, the other follows it." '—*Al Baihaqi.*

On Anger and Pride

It is related from Abú Hurairah that, 'The Apostle of God said, "The strong is not he who throws men down. Only he is the strong who exercises the mastery over himself at the time of anger." '—*Muslim, Al Bukhárí.*

It is related from Ibn Ma'súd that, 'The Apostle of God said, "No one will enter the fire in whose heart is faith equal in weight to a single grain of mustard seed. And no one will enter paradise in whose heart is pride equal in weight to a single grain of mustard seed." '—*Muslim.*

It is related from Abú Dharr that, 'The Apostle of God said, "When anyone of you gets angry whilst he is standing, then let him sit down. Then if the anger leaves him (well); otherwise let him lie on his side." '—*Ahmad, At Tirmidhí.*

It is related from Abú Hurairah that, 'The Apostle of God said, "Moses the son of 'Imrán said, 'O my Lord, who is the most highly esteemed in Thy sight of all Thy servants?' (God) replied, 'He who, when he is able, forgives.'" '

Concerning Oppression

It is related from Hudhaifah that, 'The Apostle of God said, "Do not be partial in your behaviour and say, 'If people do good (to us), we will do good (to them); and if they oppress (us) we will oppress them.' But determine within yourselves that if men do good, you will do good, but if they do evil, you will not oppress."'—*At Tirmidhí.*

It is related from Ibn Ma'súd that he said, 'When the revelation came down, "They who believe, and clothe not their faith with injustice, (they shall enjoy security, and they are rightly directed)"[1] that became grievous to the companions of the Apostle of God, and they said, "O Apostle of God, who of us has not done injustice to his own soul!" The Apostle of God replied, "It is not that. It only refers to attributing partners to God. Have you not heard the word of Luqmán to his son, 'O my little son, do not attribute partners to God, for verily attributing partners to God is great injustice.'"'—*Muslim, Al Bukhárí.*

Concerning Things which are Lawful

It is related from Usámah bin Zaid that, 'The Apostle of God said, "A man will be brought on the day of resurrection and cast into the fire. And his intestines will be poured out into the fire and will be ground to powder in it, like the grinding of a mill-stone by an ass. Then the inhabitants of the fire will gather together to him and say, 'Ho such an one! what is the matter with thee? Wast thou not in the habit of ordering us what was lawful, and forbidding us what was unlawful?' He will reply, 'I used to order you what was lawful, but did not do it myself; and I used to forbid you what was unlawful, but I did it myself.'"'—*Muslim, Al Bukhárí.*

It is related from 'Abdu'lláh bin Ma'súd that, 'The Apostle of God said, "When the Children of Israel fell into disobedience, their learned men forbade them, but they did not prevent them. And they sat in company with them in their assemblies, and ate and drank with them. And God mixed the hearts of some of them with others; and He cursed them by the tongues of David and Jesus, the Son of Mary. That He did because they disobeyed and transgressed." (Ibn Ma'súd) said, "Then the Apostle of God sat down; and he was reclining and he said, 'No, by Him in whose hand is my life! (ye will

[1] Qur'án, Ṣúratu'l-An'ám (vi) 82.

not escape the curse) until ye prevent them (from disobeying).' " '—*At Tirmidhí, Abú Dáud.*

It is related from 'Ammár bin Yásir that, 'The Apostle of God said, " A table descended from heaven with bread and meat (for the Children of Israel); and they were commanded to be faithful to their trust and to make no provision for the morrow; but they abused their trust and made provision and took up food for the morrow; and they were transformed into apes and swine." '—*At Tirmidhí.*

It is related from Jábir that, 'The Apostle of God said, "God, the Exalted and Magnified, revealed to Gabriel that he should turn such and such cities upside down, together with their inhabitants. He replied, 'O my Lord, verily amongst them is Thy servant so and so, who has never disobeyed Thee for the twinkling of an eye.' He said, 'Turn it over upon him and upon them, for verily his face has never changed for a single hour.' " '

XXIV

THE BOOK OF KIND WORDS

It is related from Jábir that, 'The Apostle of God passed by a young goat, dead and with its ears cut off. He said, "Which of you wishes to have this for himself for one dirham?" They replied, "We do not wish to have it for ourselves at any price." He said, "By God! certainly the world is more contemptible in the sight of God than this is to to you."'—*Muslim.*

It is related from Abú Hurairah that, 'The Apostle of God said, "The world is a prison for believers, but paradise for infidels."'—*Muslim.*

It is related from 'Amru bin 'Awf that, 'The Apostle of God said, "By God! I do not fear poverty for you, but I fear lest the world should be made comfortable for you as it was made comfortable for those who were before you; and ye seek after it as they sought after it; and it destroy you as it destroyed them."'—*Muslim, Al Bukhárí.*

It is related from Anas that, 'The Apostle of God said, "Three things follow the dead. Two return, and one remains with him. His family and his goods and his works follow him. His family and his goods return, but his actions remain with him."'—*Muslim, Al Bukhárí.*

It is related from Ibn Ma'súd that, 'The Apostle of God said, "Do not enter into possession of lands, lest ye long for the world."'—*Al Tirmidhí.*

It is related from Abú Músá that, 'The Apostle of God said, "He who loves the world will be a loser in the next life; and he who loves the next life, will be a loser in the world. Therefore choose that which will remain rather than that which will vanish away."'—*Aḥmad.*

It is related from 'Othmán that, 'The Prophet said, "The son of Adam has no right to anything except these particular things: a house to live in, a cloth with which to cover his private parts, a crust of bread and some water."'—*Al Tirmidhí.*

It is related from Mu'áwiyah that, 'He entered in to his uncle Abú Háshim bin 'Utbah to visit him in sickness. Then Abú Háshim wept. (Mu'áwiyah) said, "What makes thee weep, O my uncle? Is it pain that troubles thee, or a craving for the world?" He replied, "No, but the Apostle of God imposed a condition upon us which I have not accepted." He said, "And what is that?" He replied, "I heard him say, 'Let it suffice thee to keep property consisting of one servant and one riding animal for (use in) the way of God'; and verily it seems to me that I have accumulated (property)."' — *Aḥmad, Al Tirmidhí, An Nasái, Ibn Májah.*

It is related from Ḥudhaifah that he said, 'I heard the Apostle of God say in his public address, "Wine is the total of all sins, and women are the nets of Satan, and love of the world is the principal fault."' He said, 'And I heard him say, "Put women behind where God has placed them."'—*Razín.*

It is related from Abú Hurairah that, 'The Prophet said, "When a man dies the angels say, 'What has he sent before (of good works)?' And the sons of Adam say, 'What has he left behind him (of property)?'"'—*Al Baihaqi.*

It is related from Málik that he said, 'It was said to Loqmán, the Wise, "What caused thee to attain that which I see, namely eminence?" He replied, "Speaking the truth, and keeping faith, and giving up what did not benefit me."'—*From Al Muwaṭṭa.*

It is related from 'Áyesha that she said, 'We had a curtain, on which were pictures of birds. Then the Apostle of God said, "O 'Áyesha, change it, for verily when I see it I remember the world."'

On the Excellence of Poverty, and Concerning the Prophet's Manner of Life

It is related from Usámah bin Zaid that, 'The Apostle of God said, "I will stand at the door of paradise, and the generality of those who will enter it will be the poor. And the owners of wealth will be held back, except that those who are destined for the fire will be ordered to the fire. And I will stand at the door of hell, and behold! the generality of those who will enter will be women."'—*Muslim, Al Bukhárí.*

It is related from 'Áyesha that, 'The family of Muḥammad was never satisfied with barley bread for two days in succession until the Apostle of God was taken.'—*Muslim, Al Bukhárí.*

It is related from Anas that he took some barley loaves and some mutton-fat to the Prophet. And the Prophet had pawned his coat of mail in the city with a Jew, and had taken from him some barley for his family. And I heard him say, 'There never remained in the evening with the family of Muḥammad a single measure of wheat or a measure of grain although he had nine wives.'—*Al Bukhárí.*

It is related from 'Omar that he said, 'I went into the Apostle of God, and behold! he was lying on his side on a mat made of reeds. There was no bedding between him and it; and the mat had marked his side. And he was reclining on a pillow made of leather stuffed with the rind of dates. And I said, "O Apostle of God, pray to God to give abundance to thy followers, for verily the Persians and the Greeks have been given abundance although they do not serve God." He replied, "Then art thou, O Ibn Khaṭṭáb, still in this condition! Those are a people whose good things have been given them quickly in the life of this world." And in another tradition it runs, "Art thou not satisfied that the world be for them, and the future life for us?" '—*Muslim, Al Bukhárí.*

It is related from Abú Hurairah that, 'The Apostle of God said, "The poor will enter paradise five hundred years before the rich, and that is half a day (with God)." '—*At Tirmidhí.*

It is related from 'Áyesha that she said, 'Three things of the world pleased the Apostle of God: food and women and perfumes. He obtained two of them, but not the third. He obtained women and perfumes, but he did not get food.'—*Aḥmad.*

It is related from Anas that, 'The Apostle of God said, "Perfumes and women have been made beloved of me, and my eye is refreshed in prayer." '—*Aḥmad, An Nasái.*

On Hope and Avarice

It is related from Abú Hurairah that, 'The Apostle of God said, "The heart of the aged remains young in two respects: in love of the world and length of hope." '—*Muslim, Al Bukhárí.*

It is related from Ibn 'Abbás that, 'The Prophet said, "If the son of Adam had two valleys full of money, he would certainly desire a third. And nothing will fill the belly of the son of Adam except the earth (of the grave). And God turns towards whoever repents."'—*Muslim, Al Bukhárí.*

It is related from Ibn 'Omar that he said, 'The Apostle of God took hold of a part of my body and said, "Be in the world as if thou wert a stranger and a passer along the road; and reckon thyself as one of the inhabitants of the grave."'—*Al Bukhárí.*

On the Desire for Wealth and Long Life in Order to Further Obedience

It is related from a man of the companions of the Prophet that he said, 'We were in an assembly and the Apostle of God came to us with the marks of water on his head. And we said, "O Apostle of God, we perceive thee to be cheerful in mind." He replied, "Yes."' (The man) said, 'Then the people propounded the question of riches. And the Apostle of God said, "There is no harm in riches for him who fears God, the Exalted and Magnified; but for him who fears (God) health is better than wealth, and happiness of soul is one of God's favours."' *Aḥmad.*

It is related from Muḥammad bin abú 'Amírah, one of the companions of the Apostle of God, that he said, 'Verily if a servant were to fall on his face in the worship of God from the day he was born until he died in old age in obeying God, he would certainly despise such worship on that day (of resurrection) and would desire that he be sent back to the world in order that he might increase (by his good actions) the compensations and rewards.'—*Aḥmad.*

On Reliance (on God) and Patience

It is related from Ibn 'Abbás that, 'The Apostle of God said, "Seventy thousand of my followers will enter paradise without (rendering any) account. They are those who do not use spells or draw bad omens, and in their Lord put their trust."'—*Muslim, Al Bukhárí.*

It is related from Abú Hurairah that, 'The Apostle of God said. "A God-fearing believer is better in the sight of God and more beloved of him than the believer who is weak; and there is good in everyone. Strive after that which will benefit thee; and seek the aid of God, and be not weak. And if anything befalls thee, say not, 'If I had done (so and so) such and such would have happened,' but say, 'God ordained it,' and 'He has done what He wished'; for verily, 'if' introduces the work of Satan." '—*Muslim.*

It is related from 'Omar binu'l-Khaṭṭáb that he said, 'I heard the Apostle of God say, "If ye put your trust in God, in the way that He should be trusted, He will certainly provide for you as He provides for the birds. They begin the morning hungry, but reach the evening with full stomachs." '—*At Tirmidhí, Ibn Májah.*

It is related from Ibn 'Abbás that he said, 'I was behind the Apostle of God on a certain day, and he said, "O boy, remember God, and He will remember thee. Remember God, and thou wilt find Him before thee. And when thou prayest for anything, ask it of God; and when thou seekest aid, seek it of Him. And know thou that if all the people were gathered together with the purpose of doing thee a benefit in any matter, they would not benefit thee except in that matter which God has already written down for thee. And if they came together with the purpose of doing thee an injury in some matter, they would not do thee any injury except in that matter which God has already written down. The pens have been lifted up, and the pages are dried." '—*Aḥmad, At Tirmidhí.*

It is related from Jábir that he went with the Apostle of God on a military expedition in the direction of Nejd, and when the Apostle of God returned, he returned with him. And the noon overtook them in a valley having many trees. Then the Apostle of God alighted, and the people separated in order to seek the shade of the trees. And the Apostle of God stopped beneath a *samurah* tree; and he hung up his sword upon it; and we slept for awhile. And behold! The Apostle of God suddenly called us, and with him was a desert Arab. And (the Apostle) said, 'Verily this man unsheathed my sword against me when I was sleeping. And I awoke whilst my sword was still in his hand. He said, "Who will protect thee from me?" I replied, "God." This I said three times.' And he did not punish him, and he sat down.—*Muslim, Al Bukhári.* And in another tradition from Abú Bakr Al Isma'íli it runs, 'He said, "Who will protect thee from me?" He replied, "God." Then the sword fell from his hand; and the Apostle of God took the sword and said, "Who will protect thee from me?" And he replied, "Be thou the best of takers." He said, "Dost thou bear witness that there is no God but Alláh and and that I am the Apostle of Alláh?" He said, "No. But I will make an agreement with thee to the effect that I will not fight against thee, nor will I stay with the people who fight against thee." Then the Prophet let him go his way; and he came to his companions and said, "I have come to you from the best of men."'—*Kitábu'l-Ḥumaidi.*

It is related from Abú Hurairah that, 'A man came in to his family, and when he saw that they were in need, he went out to the desert. Then when his wife saw (what he had done) she stood up near the mill-stones and placed them in position, and went to the oven and heated it and then said, "O God, provide for our sustenance." And she looked, and behold! the dish had become full.' (Abú Hurairah) said, 'Then she went to the oven and found it full. And her husband returned and said, "Didst thou manage to procure something after my departure?" His wife replied, "Yes; from our Lord." And he stood up near the mill-stones (and lifted one up to ascertain the cause). And that incident was mentioned to the Prophet. And he said, "If he had not lifted it up, it would have continued to revolve until the day of resurrection."'—*Aḥmad.*

It is related from Ibn Ma'súd that he said, 'It is as if I could see the Apostle of God relating the story of one of the prophets whose people beat him and caused the blood to flow. And he wiped the blood from his face and said, "O God, forgive my people, for verily they know not (what they do)."' —*Muslim, Al Bukhári.*

On Hypocrisy and Ostentation

It is related from Abú Hurairah that, 'The Apostle of God said, "Verily, God does not look on your outward appearance or your possessions, but He looks at your hearts and your actions."'—*Muslim.*

It is related from Shaddád bin Aws that he said, 'I heard the Apostle of God say, "He who prays with hypocrisy has associated another with God; and he who fasts with hypocrisy has associated another with God; and he who gives alms with hypocrisy has associated another with God."'—*Aḥmad.*

It is related from Abú Sa'íd that he said, 'The Apostle of God came out to us when we were talking about the Antichrist to one another. And he said, "Shall I not tell you of something which I fear for you more than the Antichrist." We said, "Yes, O Apostle of God." He said, "It is the secret association with God of something else; namely that a man stands up and says his prayers and lengthens them because he sees a man looking at him."'—*Ibn Májah.*

On Crying Aloud and Fear

It is related from Abú Hurairah that, 'Abú'l-Qásim said, "By Him in whose hand is my life! if ye knew what I know, ye would certainly weep much and laugh little."'—*Al Bukhárí.*

It is related from Ummu'l-'Alái', the Helper, that she said, 'The Apostle of God said, "Although I am the Apostle of God, yet I do not know what will be done to me or to you."'—*Al Bukhárí.*

It is related from Jábir that, 'The Apostle of God said, "The fire (of hell) was shown to me, and I saw therein a woman of the children of Israel who was being punished on account of a cat which she had possessed, and which she had tied up, and neither fed nor allowed to eat of the small birds and creeping things of the earth, until it died of hunger. And I saw 'Amru bin 'Amiru'l-Khuzái' dragging his intestines in the fire. And he was the first one to set free a female camel (in the name of idols)."'—*Muslim.*

It is related from Anas that, 'The Prophet said, "God, great are His utterances! will say (at the last day), take out from the fire whoever has remembered me for one day, or feared me in one place."'—*At Tirmidhí.*

It is related from Abú Sa'id that he said, 'The Prophet came out to prayers, and he saw the people as if they were laughing. And he said, "Verily if ye had remembered often the cutter of delights, namely death, it would have diverted you from what I see. Therefore remember much the cutter of delights; for no day will come to the grave, but the latter will speak and say, 'I am the house of the stranger, and I am the solitary house, and I am the house of the clay, and I am the house of worms.' And when a believing servant is buried the grave says to him, 'Be welcome and at thine ease, for thou art certainly the most beloved to me of those who have walked over me. And since I rule over thee this day, and thou hast returned to me, thou shalt now see what I will do to thee.' Then the grave is made spacious for him as far as the eye can see, and a door of paradise is opened for him. And when a wicked servant or infidel is buried, the grave says to him, 'Thou art not welcome, and will not be at thine ease, for verily thou art certainly the most hateful to me of those who have walked over me. And since I rule over thee this day, and thou hast returned to me, thou shalt now see what I will do to thee.' Then it will press on him until his ribs are displaced."' (Abú Sa'íd) said, 'Then the Apostle of God mentioned with his fingers, and placed some of them between others, and said, "And seventy serpents are ordered for him, one of which, if it breathed on the earth, nothing of what remained on the earth would grow; and they bite him and lacerate him until he is taken to give his account." And the Apostle of God said, "Verily the grave is only one of the gardens of paradise or one of the pits of hill-fire."'—*At Tirmidhí.*

It is related from Abú Hurairah that, 'The Apostle of God said, "My Lord has ordered me nine things: the fear of God in secret and in public; speaking words of justice, whether in anger or in pleasure; moderation in poverty and in affluence; that I should give presents to those who are estranged from me; that I should give to him who denies me; that I should forgive him who oppresses me; that my silence be spent in contemplation, and my speaking in mentioning God's name; that my seeing be in being an example; and that I should command what is good."'—*Razín.*

On the Mutability of Men

It is related from Abú Sa'íd that, 'The Apostle of God said, "You will certainly follow the customs of those who were before you, span by span, and cubit by cubit, until, if they entered a lizard's hole, you would follow them." It was said, "O Apostle of God, (dost thou speak of) the Jews and Christians?" He replied, "Who else?"'—*Muslim, Al Bukhárí.*

It is related from Ḥudhaifah that, 'The Prophet said, "The hour (of resurrection) will not come until you kill your religious leader, and flog one another with swords, and until the wicked amongst you inherit this world of yours."'—*At Tirmidhí.*

It is related from Abú Hurairah that, 'The Apostle of God said, "When your princes are the best of you, and your rich men the most liberal of you, and your affairs are discussed amongst you, then the surface of the earth is better for you than its bosom.[1] But when your princes are the wicked amongst you, and your rich men the meanest of you, and your affairs relegated to your women, then the bosom of the earth is better for you than its surface."'—*At Tirmidhí.*

It is related from Abú Hurairah that he said, 'When the revelation descended, "And admonish thy near relations," the Prophet called the Quraish, and they gathered together. And he addressed them collectively and individually and said, "O Bani Ka'b bin Luwa, save yourselves from the fire; O Bani Murrah bin Ka'b, save yourselves from the fire; O Bani 'Abdu's-Shams, save yourselves from the fire; O Bani 'Abdu Manáf, save yourselves from the fire; O Bani Háshim, save yourselves from the fire; O Bani 'Abdu'l-Muṭṭalib, save yourselves from the fire; O Fáṭimah, save thyself from the fire, for I cannot gain anything from God on thy behalf, except that I recognise the right of blood-relationship, and will do what I can."'—*Muslim.* And in another tradition from Muslim and Al Bukhárí it runs thus, 'He said, "O people of the Quraish, redeem yourselves, for I cannot suffice you anything against (the punishments of) God; O Bani 'Abdu Manáf, I cannot suffice you anything against (the punishments of) God; O 'Abbás bin 'Abdu'l-Muṭṭalib, I cannot suffice thee anything against (the punishments of) God; O Safiyya, wife of the Apostle of God, I cannot suffice thee anything against (the punishments of) God; O Fáṭimah, daughter of Muḥammad, ask me what thou wilt of my property, for I cannot suffice thee anything against (the punishments of) God."'

[1] That is, the grave.

XXV

THE BOOK OF SEDITIONS

It is related from Abú Hurairah that, 'The Apostle of God said, "By Him in whose hand is my life! the world will not pass away until there come a day to man in which the murderer (will not know why he killed, nor the murdered) why he was killed." It was said, "How will that be?" He replied, "On account of strife. The murderer and the murdered will both be in the fire." '—*Muslim.*

It is related from Thawbán that, 'The Apostle of God said, "I only fear for my people leaders who will lead men astray. And when once the sword is unsheathed amongst my people, it will not be taken away from them again until the day of resurrection." '—*At Tirmidhí, Abú Dáud.*

It is related from Safínah that he said, 'I heard the Prophet say, "The succession of Khalifs will be for thirty years. After that there will be kingships." Then, said Safínah, "I reckon the reign of Abú Bakr as Khalif at two years, and the reign of 'Omar as Khalif at ten years, and that of 'Othmán at twelve years, and that of 'Alí six years." '—*Aḥmad, At Tirmidhí.*

It is related from 'Abdu'lláh bin 'Omar that, 'The Apostle of God said, "There will be sedition involving the Arabs, the slain of which will be in the fire, and in which the (abuse of the) tongue will be worse than the fall of the sword." '—*At Tirmidhí, Ibn Májah.*

It is related from Thawbán that, 'The Apostle of God said, "When the sword is unsheathed amongst my people, it will not be put back again until the day of resurrection; and the hour (of resurrection) will not take place until some tribes of my people join themselves to the polytheists, and until some tribes of my people worship idols. And there will arise amongst my people thirty liars, each of whom will assert that he is a prophet of God; whereas I am the seal of the prophets, and there will be no prophet after me. And a party of my people will certainly continue to victoriously follow the truth. None who oppose them will be able to hurt them until the command of God comes." '—*Abú Dáud, At Tirmidhí.*

It is related from Ibnu'l-Musayyib that he said, 'The first insurrection occurred, that is the murder of 'Othmán, and none of those who were present at (the battle of) Badr remained. Then the second insurrection took place, namely, that of Ḥarrah, and none of those who were present at Ḥudaibah remained. After that the third insurrection took place, and did not come to an end so long as there remained any strength amongst the people.'—*Al Bukhárí.*

Concerning Battles

It is related from Abú Hurairah that, 'The Apostle of God said, "The hour of resurrection will not come until two great tribes shall fight, between whom there will be great battles. Their claims (in Islám) will be one. And the hour will not come until nearly thirty false Christs are sent, everyone of whom will assert that he is a prophet of God; and until knowledge is withheld, and earthquakes multiply, and the time approaches, and seditions appear and rebellions increase, and that is murder. (And the hour will not come) until wealth increases amongst you and abounds, so that the owner of wealth will be concerned as to who will accept his alms and until he pleads with him (to accept them). And he with whom he pleads will reply, 'I have no need of it,' and until man is filled with pride in building houses, and until a man passes by the grave of another and says, 'Would that I were in his place!' and until the sun arises in the West. And when it rises, and men see it they will believe altogether. And that is (a day) when the faith of a soul will not benefit it, which has not believed before, or bestowed good in its faith. And the hour will certainly come when two men have spread out their cloths (for sale), but it will arrive before they have concluded a sale, or folded up the cloth. And the hour will certainly come when a man will have departed to milk his she-camel, but before he has drunk it. And the hour will certainly come when he has gone forth to water his camel at his cistern, but before it has drunk therefrom. And the hour will certainly come when a man has raised the food to his mouth, but before he has eaten it." '—*Muslim, Al Bukhárí.*

It is related from Abú Hurairah that, 'The Apostle of God said, "The hour (of resurrection) will not come until ye fight a people whose shoes are of hair, and until ye fight the Turks whose eyes are small and faces red and noses flat, as if their faces were shields covered with leather."'—*Muslim, Al Bukhárí.*

It is related from Abú Hurairah that, 'The Apostle of God said, "The hour will not come until the Muslims fight the Jews. And the Muslims with kill them until the Jews hide themselves behind stones and trees. And the stones and trees will say, 'O Muslim, O servant of God, this is a Jew behind me; come and kill him. But the tree (called) *gharqad* will not say so, because it is one of the trees belonging to the Jews."' —*Muslim.*

It is related from Náfi' bin 'Utbah that, 'The Apostle of God said, "You will wage war in the Island of Arabia, and God will give you the victory. After that (you will fight with) Persia, and God will give you the victory over it. After that with Greece, and God will give you the victory over it. After that you will wage war with Antichrist, and God will give you the victory over him."'—*Muslim.*

It is related from Abú Hurairah that, 'The Apostle of God said, "The hour will not come until the Greeks come down in Al 'Ámáq or in Dáyak. And an army of the best of the people of the earth will come out to them from Madína on that day; and when they arrange themselves in ranks (for battle) the Greeks will say, 'Leave vacant a space between us and those who made captive some of us that we may fight with them.' But the Muslims will say, 'No, by God! we will not make vacant a space between you and our brethren.' And they will fight with them, and a third of them will be put to flight, and God will never forgive them. And a third of them will be killed: the best of martyrs in the sight of God; and a third of them will be victorious and will never create sedition. And they will conquer Constantinople. And whilst they are dividing the plunder, having hung up their swords on an olive tree, behold! Satan will cry out in their midst, 'Verily the (false) Christ has come amongst your families in your absence.' Then they will go forth—and that will be false—

and when they come to Syria he will come out. And whilst they are preparing for battle and dressing their ranks, when prayers begin, Jesus, Son of Mary, will descend and act as leader. And when the enemy of God sees him, he will melt away as salt melts in water. And if he leaves him alone, he would certainly melt away until he is destroyed. But God will kill him by the hand of Jesus; and he will show them his blood upon his lance." '—*Muslim.*

It is related from Dhu Mikhbar that he said, 'I heard the Apostle of God say, "You will make a peace of safety with Greece and you and they will wage war with your enemies behind you. And you will be given the victory and will plunder and will dwell in safety. Afterwards you will return until you descend to a pasturage on high land. Then a man of the Christians will raise a cross and will say, 'The cross gave us the victory.' Then a man of the Muslims will get angry and will beat him. And just then the Greeks will act treacherously and will gather together for battle." And some of them have added to this, "And the Muslims will rush to their weapons and fight. And God will honour that band of men with martyrdom." '—*Abú Dáud.*

It is related from Abú Bakr that, 'The Apostle of God said, "A people of my followers will come down to low land called Busrah, near the river called the Tigris, over which there will be a bridge. Its inhabitants will be numerous. It will be one of the great cities of the Muslims. And when the end of time comes, the Bani Qantúrá (namely the Turks) will come, broad-faced and small-eyed, until they come down to the bank of the river. And its inhabitants will be divided into three bands. One band will be employed with the tails of their cattle (i.e. in agriculture) and in the desert, and they will be destroyed; and one band will be busy saving themselves and will be destroyed; and one band will place their children behind their backs and will fight and will become martyrs." '—*Abú Dáud.*

CONCERNING THE SIGNS OF THE HOUR OF RESURRECTION

It is related from Anas that he said, 'I heard the Apostle of God say, "Verily amongst the signs of the hour is that knowledge will be taken away, and ignorance will be increased, and adultery will abound, and the drinking of wine will increase, and men will decrease in numbers and women will increase, until there will be fifty women for one man." '—*Muslim*, *Al Bukhárí*.

It is related from Abú Hurairah that, 'The Apostle of God said, " The hour will not come until the Euphrates shall show a mountain of gold, over which men will fight. And of every hundred of them, ninety-nine will be killed. And every man of them will say, it may be that I shall be he who will be saved." '—*Muslim*.

It is related from Anas that, 'The Apostle of God said, " The first sign of the hour will be a fire which will drive men from the East to the West." '—*Al Bukhárí*.

It is related from 'Abdu'lláh bin Ḥawálah that he said, 'The Apostle of God sent us on foot to get plunder; and we returned without having obtained any plunder. And he perceived the fatigue in our faces, and he stood up amongst us and said, " O God! do not entrust their affairs to me, for I am unable to manage them; and do not entrust their affairs to themselves, for they are impotent to carry them out; and do not entrust their affairs to men, for they will choose their own in preference to them." Then he placed his hand upon my head, and afterwards said, " O Ibn Ḥawálah, when thou seest that a Khalíf has come down at the Holy Land, then earthquakes and anxieties and severe happenings will be near at hand; and then the hour will be nearer to men than this hand of mine is to thy head." '

It is related from Ibn Ma'súd that, 'The Apostle of God said, " The world will not come to an end until there reign over the Arabs a man of the people of my house whose name will agree with mine." '—*At Tirmidhí*, *Abú Dáud*.

It is related from Abú Qatádah that, 'The Apostle of God said, "The signs (of the day of resurrection) will come after two hundred (years)." '—*Ibn Májah*.

It is related from Thawbán that, 'The Apostle of God said, " When ye see that black standards have come from the direction of Khorásán, then come to them; for verily with them will be the Khalif of God, Al Mahdi." '—*Aḥmad*.

It is related from Abú Isḥáq that, ''Alí said, as he looked at his son, Al Ḥasan, " Verily this son of mine is a Sayyad, as the Apostle of God named him; and there will come out of his loins a man called by the name of your Prophet, resembling him in disposition, but not in outward appearance." Then he repeated a story that (the promised one) would fill the earth with justice.'—*Abú Dáud.*

On the Signs Preceding the Hour of Resurrection, and Accounts of Antichrist

It is related from Ḥudhaifah bin Usaidu'l-Ghifári that he said, 'The Prophet came to us when we were conversing together and said, "What were ye talking about?" They said, "We were mentioning the hour of resurrection." He said, "It will never come until you see previous to it, ten signs." Then he mentioned the smoke, and Antichrist, and the beast, and the rising of the sun in the West, and the descent of Jesus, Son of Mary, and Gog and Magog, and three eclipses: an eclipse in the East and an eclipse in the West and an eclipse in the Island of Arabia. And at the end of that a fire which will come out from Yeman, and which will drive men towards the place where they will be gathered together for judgment.' —*Muslim.*

It is related from 'Abdu'lláh that, 'The Apostle of God said, "It is not hidden from you that God is not one-eyed. And verily the false Christ is blind in the right eye, as if his eye were a swollen grape."'—*Muslim, Al Bukhárí.*

It is related from An Nawwás bin Sam'án that he said, 'The Apostle of God mentioned Antichrist and said, "If he comes forth whilst I am among you, I will repel him without your help. But if he come forth when I am not in your midst, a man will defend himself; and God is my Khalif over every Muslim. Verily Antichrist is a young man with crisp hair and dull eyes, as if I were likening him to 'Abdu'l-Uzza bin Qaṭan. Then whoever of you comes into contact with him, let him recite (as a protection) against him the opening verses of the Chapter of the Cave, for that will be a protection for you from his seditions. Verily he will come forth on a road mid-way between Syria and 'Iráq and will act corruptly on the right hand and on the left. O servants of God, be firm!" We said, "O Apostle of God, how long will his stay be on the earth"?

He replied, "Forty days, one day being like one year, and one day like a month, and one day like a week, and the rest of his days will be like your days." We said, "O Apostle of God, then in that day which will be like a year, will one day's prayers be sufficient for us?" He replied, "No. Compute its share of it for prayers." We said, "O Apostle of God, what is this hastening on the earth?" He replied, "It is like rain followed by wind; and he will come to a people and call them, and they will believe in him, and he will command the heavens, and they will send rain. And he will order the earth, and it will bring forth herbs. And their herds will come to them in the evening longer in their humps than they were before, and with full udders and extended flanks. Afterwards he will come to a people, and will call them, but they will return his words to him. Then he will depart from them, and they will rise in the morning to find their land smitten with barrenness, and with nothing of their possessions in their hands. And he will pass by ruins and will say to them, 'Bring forth your treasures.' Then their treasures will follow him like male bees follow the females. After that he will call a man of full youth and will smite him with a sword and will cut him into two pieces like the shooting of an arrow at its mark. After that he will call him and he will draw near with gladness of countenance and laughing. And whilst Antichrist is acting thus; God will send Jesus, Son of Mary, and he will descend near a white tower to the east of Damascus, between two cloths of red, placing the palms of his hands upon the wings of two angles. When he will lower his head, it will drop (perspiration), and when he will raise it up, there will fall from him beads like pearls. And it will not be permitted for any infidel touched by his breath to do aught but die. And his breath will reach as far as the eye can reach. And he will search for the Antichrist until he finds him at the gate of Ludd; and he will kill him. After that a people will come to Jesus whom God has preserved; and he will stroke their faces in comfort, and will inform them of the degree of eminence they will attain in paradise. And whilst he is doing that, behold! God will send a revelation to Jesus (saying), 'Verily I have brought out servants of mine, whom it is not possible for any to fight. Then give my servants a refuge in Mount Sinai.' And God will send Gog and Magog, and they will come swiftly from every high land, and the first of them will pass over the Lake of Tiberias; and they will drink up what is in it. Then the last of them will pass over and will say, 'Verily there was at one time water in this lake.' After that they will go on until they reach the mountain of Khamar, which is the mountain of Jerusalem. And they will say, 'We have killed those who were on the earth, then come and let us kill all who are in the heavens.' And they will cast their wooden arrows towards the sky; but God will return them upon themselves dyed with blood. And the Prophet of God (Jesus) and his companions will be prevented (from descending the mount) until the head of an ox becomes better for one of them than one hundred dinars is this day to one of you. And Jesus, the Prophet of God, and his companions will pray, and God will send to them (Gog and Magog) worms in their necks; and in the morning they will be as one dead person. After that Jesus, the Prophet of God, and his companions will go down to the earth, but they will not find in the earth the place of a span that their fat and stench have not filled. Then Jesus, the Prophet of God, and his companions will pray to God, and God will send birds like the necks of camels, and they will carry (the corpses) away and cast them where God wishes." And in another tradition it runs, "They will cast them into Nahbal." And the Muslims will make fires of their bows and wooden arrows and quivers for seven years. After that God will send a rain, and no dwelling of masonry or of hair will escape from it; and it will wash the earth clean until it leaves it like a slippery (surface). After that it will be said to the earth, 'Bring forth thy fruits, and send back thy blessings!' On that day a troop of men will eat from one pomegranate, and will shade themselves with its rind. And the earth will be blessed in the matter of milk until one female camel will suffice for a great multitude of men; and a cow will suffice for a whole tribe of men; and one female sheep will suffice for one clan of a tribe. And whilst they are in this condition, behold! God will send a pleasant wind; and it will take them under their armpits, and it will take the soul of every believer and every Muslim. And the wicked amongst men, who created discord on the earth like the quarrelling of asses, will remain, and the hour (of resurrection) will come upon them." ' —*Muslim.*

It is related from Anas that, 'The Apostle of God said, "Seventy thousand Jews of Ispahan will follow Antichrist; and on them will be robes such as are worn by learned men." '— *Muslim.*

It is related from 'Abdu'lláh bin 'Omar that, 'The Apostle of God said, "I saw myself to-night near the Ka'bah; and I saw a man the colour of wheat, like the best of any wheat-coloured man whom thou hast seen; and he had a lock of hair like the best of the locks of hair which thou hast seen. He had dressed it, and it was dripping with water as he leaned on the shoulders of two men whilst going round the House (of God). Then I said, 'Who is this?' They replied, 'This is the Messiah, the Son of Mary.' He said, 'Then behold! I saw a man with wrinkled and curly hair, blind in the right eye, as if his eye were a swollen grape, like as if he resembled a man whom ye have seen named Ibn Qaṭn. And he was placing his hands upon the shoulders of two men as he went round the house. Then I asked, 'Who is this?' They replied, 'This is Antichrist." '—*Muslim, Al Bukhárí.* And in another tradition it runs, 'He said, with reference to the Antichrist, "He was a man red and corpulent, with a head of curly hair, and blind in his right eye. The man most near to him in appearance is Ibn Qaṭn." '

It is related from Abú Sa'ídu'l-Khudri that, 'The Apostle of God said, "Seventy thousand people of my followers will follow Antichrist, arrayed in black clothes." '—*Sharḥu's-Sunnaḥ.*

It is related from Abú Hurairah that, 'The Prophet said, "Antichrist will come forth on an intensely white ass. The distance between its ears will be seventy cubits." '—*Al Baihaqi.*

The Story of Ibn Ṣayyád

It is related from Náfi' that Ibn 'Omar used to say, "By God! I have no doubt that the Antichrist is Ibn Ṣayyád." '—*Abú Dáud.*

Concerning the Coming Down of Jesus

It is related from Abú Hurairah that, 'The Apostle of God said, "By Him in whose hand is my life! it is certainly on the point of coming to pass that the Son of Mary will descend amongst you as a just judge. And he will break the cross in pieces, and will kill the swine and will set aside the poll-tax. And wealth will abound to such an extent that no one will accept it; and one prostration in prayer will be better than the world and all that is therein." Then Abú Hurairah said, "If you doubt this then (read the revelation), 'There shall be none of the People of the Book, but will certainly believe on him before his death.' "'[1]—*Muslim, Al Bukhárí.*

It is related from Jábir that, 'The Apostle of God said, "A party of my followers will continue to victoriously fight for the truth till the day of resurrection. And Jesus, the Son of Mary, will come down; and their prince will say, 'Come and say the prayers for us.' And he will reply, 'No, verily some of you are princes over others, because of God's honouring this people.'"'—*Muslim.*

It is related from 'Abdu'lláh bin 'Amru that, 'The Apostle of God said, "Jesus, Son of Mary, will descend to the earth, and will marry, and children will be born to him. And he will remain on the earth forty-five years. After that he will die and be buried with me in my grave. And Jesus, Son of Mary, and I will rise in one grave between Abú Bakr and 'Omar."'—*Ibnu'l-Jawzí in Kitábu'l-Wafái'.*

Concerning the Approach of the Hour of Resurrection

It is related from 'Áyesha that she said, 'Some men of the desert Arabs used to come to the Prophet and ask him about the hour of resurrection; and he used to look at the youngest of them and say, "If this youth lives, the weakness of old age will not overtake him until your hour comes to you."'—*Muslim, Al Bukhárí.*

---

[1] Qur'án, Súratu'n-Nisá' (iv) 159.

The Hour of Resurrection will Not come Except on Wicked Men

It is related from 'Abdu'lláh bin Ma'súd that, 'The Apostle of God said, "The hour will not come except upon the wicked of creation."'—*Muslim.*

It is related from 'Áyesha that she said, 'I heard the Apostle of God say, "Day and night will not cease so long as Al Lat and Al Uzza are worshipped." Then I said, "O Apostle of God, I certainly thought when God sent down the revelation, 'It is He who hath sent His Apostle with the direction and true religion, that He may cause it to appear superior to every religion, although the idolaters be averse thereto,' that idolatry would come to an end." He replied, "Such will continue so long as God wills. Afterwards God will send a pleasant wind, and then everyone in whose heart is faith of the measure of a barley grain will be made to die; and those who have no good in them will remain, and will return to the religion of their fathers."'—*Muslim.*

Concerning the Blowing of the Trumpet

It is related from 'Áyesha that she said, 'I asked the Apostle of God concerning the revelation, "The day will come when the earth will be changed into another earth, and the heaven (into another heaven.)"[1] and said, "Where will men be on that day?" He replied, "On the bridge (over hell)."'—*Muslim.*

It is related from Abú Hurairah that, 'The Apostle of God said, "The sun and the moon will be folded up like a turban on the day of resurrection."'—*Al Bukhárí.*

It is related from Abú Sa'íd that he said, 'The Apostle of of God mentioned the blower of the trumpet and said, "On his right will be Gabriel and on his left Mícháel."'

Concerning the Gathering Together

It is related from Ibn 'Abbás that, 'The Prophet said, "Verily ye will be gathered together (at the resurrection) barefooted, naked and uncircumcised." After that he recited the revelation, "As we made the first creature, so will we also reproduce it. This is a promise incumbent upon us. We will

[1] Qur'án, Súratu Ibráhím (xiv) 48.

surely perform it."[1] And the first who will be clothed on the day of resurrection will be Abraham. And verily some men of my companions will be taken to the left (for punishment). And I will say, "My companions! my companions!" But he will say, "Verily they are always turning back on their heels ever since thou separated from them." Then I will say, as did the good servant (Jesus), "I was a witness over them so long as I remained amongst them (but since thou hast taken me to thyself, thou hast been the watcher over them; for thou art witness of all things. If thou punish them, they are surely thy servants; and if thou forgive them, thou art mighty and wise.)" '[2]—*Muslim, Al Bukhárí.*

It is related from Abú Hurairah that, 'The Prophet said, "Abraham will meet his father Azar on the day of resurrection; and on the face of Azar will be blackness and dust. And Abraham will say to him, 'Did I not say to thee, disobey me not.' And his father will say to him, 'To-day I will not disobey thee.' Then Abraham will say, 'O Lord, Thou didst promise me that thou wouldst not disgrace me on the day when men would be raised. Then what disgrace is greater than that my father is the farthest removed (from Thy mercy)?' Then God Most High will reply, 'Verily I have made paradise forbidden for the infidels.' After that it will be said to Abraham, 'Look at what is beneath thy feet.' Then he will look and behold his father will become an animal smeared with mud; and he will be taken by his feet and cast into the fire." '—*Al Bukhárí.*

It is related from Abú Sa'ídu'l Khudri that, 'The Prophet said, "God Most High will say, 'O Adam!' He will reply, 'Here I am at Thy service; and all good is in Thy hands.' God will say, 'Bring forth the army of the fire.' He will reply, 'What is the army of the fire?' He will say, 'From every thousand, nine hundred and ninety-nine.' At this time the little ones of the earth will become young men, and every pregnant woman will miscarry, and you will see men as drunkards, though in reality they are not drunkards; but the punishment of God will be severe." They said, "O Apostle of God, who of us is that one (amongst the thousand)?" He replied, "Rejoice, for verily from you

[1] Qur'án, Súratu'l-Anbiyá' (xxi) 104.
[2] Qur'án, Súratu'l-Má'ida (v) 120.

will be one man, and from Gog and Magog a thousand." Afterwards he said, "By Him in whose hand is my life! I hope that you will be one-fourth of the inhabitants of paradise." Then we said, "God is great!" And he said, "I hope that you will be one-third of the inhabitants of paradise." Then we said, "God is great!" And he said, "I hope that you will be one-half of the inhabitants of paradise." And we said, "God is great!". He said, "You will be amongst men nothing else but as one black hair on the skin of a white ox, or like a white hair on the skin of a black ox." '—*Muslim, Al Bukhárí.*

On the Reckoning, and the Retaliation, and the Scales

It is related from Abú Músá that, 'The Apostle of God said, "When the day of resurrection arrives, God will hand over a Jew or a Christian to every Muslim, and will say, 'This is thy redemption from the fire.'" '—*Muslim.*

It is related from Abú Sa'ídu'l-Khudri that, 'The Apostle of God said, "Noah will be brought on the day of resurrection; and it will be said to him, 'Didst thou make known (the message of God)?' He will reply, 'Yes, O my Lord.' Then his people will be asked, 'Did he make known to you the message?' They will say, 'No warner came to us.' And it will be said (to Noah), 'Who are thy witnesses?' He will reply, 'Muḥammad and his people.'" Then the Apostle of God said, "Then you will be brought, and will bear witness that he has made known the message (to mankind)." After that the Apostle of God recited (the words), "Thus have we placed you an intermediate nation, that ye may be witnesses against the rest of mankind, and that the Apostle may be a witness against you." '—*Al Bukhárí.*

It is related from 'Áyesha that, 'She remembered the fire (of hell) and wept. Then the Apostle of God said, "What makes thee weep?" She replied, "I wept, remembering the fire. Wilt thou remember thy family on the day of resurrection?" The Apostle of God replied, "There are three places at which one person will not remember another: at the scales, until he shall know whether his scales will be light or heavy; at the book, when it will be said, 'Come and read the records,' until he knows where his book will be put, whether in his right hand or in his left behind his back; and at the bridge, when it will be placed over the midst of hell." '—*Abū Dāud.*

It is related from 'Áyesha that she said, 'I heard the Apostle of God saying in certain of his prayers, "O God, take from me an easy account." I said, "O Prophet of God, what is an easy account?" He replied, "That He looks into His book and passes over it. Verily, O 'Áyesha, he from whom an exact account will be taken on that day will perish." '—*Aḥmad.*

It is related from Asmá' bint Yazíd that, 'The Apostle of God said, "Men will be gathered together on one plain on the day of resurrection; and a herald will cry and say, 'Where are those people whose sides removed themselves from the beds (in order to pray at night.)' Then they will stand up; and they will be few in number, and will enter paradise without (giving an) account. After that the rest of men will be ordered to give an account." '—*Al Baihaqi.*

Concerning the Pond and Intercession

It is related from Anas that, 'The Apostle of God said, "Whilst I was going through paradise, behold I came to a river, the two shores of which were domes made of hollow pearls. I said, 'O Gabriel, what is this?' He replied, 'This is (the pond called) Kawthar which thy Lord hath given thee.' And behold its clay was strong-smelling musk." '—*Al Bukhārí.*

It is related from Sahl bin Sa'd that, 'The Apostle of God said, "Verily I will go before you to the pond. Whoever will pass by me will drink; and he who drinks will never thirst for evermore. And certain peoples will certainly be brought back to me whom I will recognize; and they will recognize me. After that something will be placed between them and me, and I will say, 'Verily they are of my people.' And it will be said, 'Verily thou dost not know what innovations they made after thee.' Then I will say, 'Begone! begone! those who changed (my religion) after me." '—*Muslim, Al Bukhārí.*

It is related from Anas that, 'The Prophet said, "The believers will be confined on the day of resurrection, so that they will be filled with anxiety and will say, '(Better would it be) if we had sought the intercession (of some one) with our Lord, and He had taken us from this place of ours.' Then they will come to Adam and will say, 'Thou art Adam, the father of mankind. God created thee with His own hand and caused thee to dwell in His garden, and the angels prostrated before thee and taught thee the names of all things, therefore intercede for us with thy Lord, so that He take us from this place of ours.' Then he will reply, 'I am not worthy'; and he will remember his sin which he committed in eating of the tree when he had been forbidden it. But (he will say), 'Come to Noah, the first prophet whom God sent to the people of the earth.' Then they will come to Noah, but he will say, 'I am not worthy', and he will remember his sin which he committed in asking his Lord without knowledge; but (he will say), 'Come to Abraham, the friend of the Merciful.' Then they will come to Abraham, and he will say, 'I am not worthy,' and he will remember three falsehoods which he spoke; but (he will say), 'Come to Moses, a servant to whom God gave the Taurát and with whom He spake and caused him to draw near in order to impart secret communications to him.' Then they will come to Moses, but he will say, 'I am not worthy,' and he will remember his sin which he committed in killing a soul; but (he will say) 'Come to Jesus, the Servant of God and His Apostle, and the Spirit of God and His Word.' Then they will come to Jesus and He will say, 'I am not worthy, but come to Muḥammad, a servant whose former and latter sins God has forgiven.' Then they will come to me, and I will ask permission of my Lord to enter His house; and permission will be given me for that. And when I shall see Him I will fall down in prostration. And God will leave me as long as He wishes to leave me, and will then say, 'Raise (thy head) O Muḥammad; and speak, and thou wilt be heard; intercede, and thy intercession will be accepted; ask, and it will be given thee.' Then I will raise up my head, and will praise my Lord with praises and adorations which He will tell me. After that I will intercede, and a limit will be fixed for me, and I will go forth. And I will bring them out of the fire and take them into paradise. After that I will return a second time and ask permission of my Lord to enter His house. And permission will be given me for that.

And when I see Him I will fall down in prostration; and God will leave me as long as He wishes to leave me. After that He will say, 'Raise up (thy head) O Muḥammad, and speak, and thou wilt be heard; intercede, and thy intercession will be accepted; ask, and it will be given thee.' Then I will raise my head and praise my Lord with praises and adorations which He will teach me. After that I will intercede, and a limit will be fixed for me, and I will go forth. And I will bring them out of the fire and take them into paradise. After that I will return a third time and ask permission of my Lord to enter His house, and permission will be given me for that. And when I see Him I will fall down in prostration; and God will leave me as long as He wishes to leave me. After that He will say, 'Raise (thy head) O Muḥammad, and speak, and thou wilt be heard; intercede, and thine intercession will be accepted; ask, and it will be given thee.' Then I will raise my head, and will praise my Lord with praises and adorations which He will teach me. After that I will intercede, and a limit will be fixed for me, and I will go forth. And I will bring them out from the fire and take them into paradise, until there remain in the fire none except him whom the Qur'án has restrained, that is he for whom eternal punishment is proper." After that he recited this verse, "Peradventure thy Lord raise thee to an honourable station." '[1] ('Anas) said, 'And this is the honourable station which He promised your Prophet.'—*Muslim, Al Bukhárí.*

It is related from 'Abdu'lláh bin 'Amru binu'l-'Áṣ that, 'The Prophet recited the words of God Most High concerning (the prayer of) Abraham, "My Lord, verily they have led many astray, therefore whoever follows me, he is of me." And Jesus said, "If Thou punish them, verily they are Thy servants." Then (the Prophet) raised his hands and said, "O God, my people! my people!" and wept. Then God Most High said, "O Gabriel, go to Muḥammad—and thy Lord knoweth—and ask him what makes him weep." Then Gabriel came to him and asked him; and the Apostle of God informed him what he had said. Then God said to Gabriel, "Go to Muḥammad and say, 'Verily we will satisfy thee in the matter of thy people, and will not grieve thee.' " '—*Muslim.*

---

[1] Qur'án, Súratu Bani Isrá'íl (xvii) 18.

It is related from Abú Sa'idu'l-Khudri that, 'Some men said, "O Apostle of God, shall we see our Lord on the day of resurrection?" The Apostle of God replied, "Yes. Do ye doubt concerning your seeing the sun at mid-day, when there is a clear sky and no clouds, and do ye doubt your seeing the moon on the night of full moon, when there is a clear sky and no cloud therein?" They replied, "No, O Apostle of God." He said, "Ye will not doubt the vision of God on the day of resurrection any more than ye doubt the seeing of one of those two. When the day of resurrection arrives a herald will call, 'Let all people follow what they used to worship.' Then no one will remain who worshipped idols and images instead of God, but they will, one after another, fall into the fire; until when none remains except those who used to worship God, both the righteous and the wicked, the Lord of the worlds will come to them and say, 'What are ye considering? Every people follows that which it used to worship.' They will reply, 'O our Lord; we left the company of men in the world, though we needed many things of them; and we did not company with them.'"' And in another tradition from Abú Hurairah it runs, 'They will say, "This is our place until our Lord comes to us, and when our Lord comes, we will recognize Him."' And in another tradition from Abú Sa'id it runs, 'He will say, "Is there between you and Him a sign by which you will recognize Him?" And they will say, "Yes," and they will be shown legs. And no one of those who used to worship with desire will remain, but God will give him permission to prostrate himself. And none of those who used to prostrate in fear and hypocrisy will remain, but God will make his back one layer (of bone) so that whenever he wishes to prostrate, he will fall down upon the back of his head. After that a bridge will be placed over hell, and intercession will take place. And they will say, "O God, give safety! give safety!" And (some of) the believers will pass over like the twinkling of an eye, and (some) like lightning, and like the wind, and like birds, and like horses, and like camels. And they will be saved in peace. And some will be scratched and then sent off, and some will be cut with lances, until, when the believers are released from the fire, then by Him in whose hand is my life! there is not one of you more earnest in seeking the lost in truth. It has been confirmed for you from the believers in their prayer to God at the day of resurrection for their brethren who are in the fire. They will say (in their intercessory prayer), "O our Lord, they used to fast with us, and they used to pray and go on pilgrimage." Then it will be said to them, "Bring out whomsoever ye wish." And their countenances will be forbidden the fire, and they will bring out many people. After that they will say, "Our Lord, not one remains in it of those concerning whom Thou commandedst us." Then He will say, "Return and bring out him in whose heart, ye find the measure of one dinar of good." Then they will bring out many people. After that He will say, "Return, and bring out him in whose heart ye find the measure of half a dinar of good." Then they will bring out many people. After that He will say, "Return, and bring out him in whose heart ye find the measure of one atom of good." Then they will bring out many people. After that they will say, "Our Lord, we have not left in it any good." Then God will say, "The angels have interceded, and the prophets have interceded, and the believers have interceded, and there is nothing left except the Most Merciful." Then He will take a handful from the fire and will take out therefrom a people who have never done any good, and who had become like coals. And He will cast them into a river near the doors of paradise, called the river of life. And they will emerge therefrom as a kernel of grain comes out from the husk, and they will come out as pearls. On their necks will be seals. And the inhabitants of paradise will say, "These are those who have been released by the Merciful. He has brought them into paradise without their doing any works or good actions which they had sent before them." And it will be said to them, "The things ye see are for you, and with them are others like them." '—*Muslim*, *Al Bukhárí*.

It is related from Anas that, 'The Prophet said, "Verily the heat of the fire will afflict certain peoples as a punishment for the sins which they have committed. Afterwards God will bring them into paradise by the grace of His mercy; and they will be called infernals." '—*Al Bukhárí*.

It is related from Abú Dharr that, 'The Apostle of God said, "Verily I certainly know the last of the inhabitants of paradise who will enter therein, and the last of the inhabitants of the fire who will come out therefrom. (He will be) a man who will be brought on the day of resurrection, and it will be said, (to the angels), 'Bring forth his small sins, and place them before him, and take away from him the great sins.' Then his small sins will be placed before him, and it will be said to him, 'On such and such a day thou didst so and so, and on such and such a day thou didst so and so.' And he will say, 'Yes,' and will not be able to deny it, and during that time he will be in anxious dread concerning his greater sins, that they will be paraded before him. And it will be said to him, 'Verily there will be (written down) for thee a virtue in the place of every sin.' Then he will say, 'My Lord, I did things which I do not see here.' (Abú Dharr) said, 'And I certainly saw the Apostle of God laugh until his front teeth appeared.' " '—*Muslim.*

It is related from Anas that, 'The Prophet said, "My intercession is for those of my followers who commit mortal sins." '—*At Tirmidhí, Abú Dáud, Ibn Májah.*

It is related from Awf bin Málik that, 'The Apostle of God said, "A messenger came to me from my Lord and gave me an option to choose between half of my people entering paradise, and my intercession (for the whole). And I chose intercession, which is for whoever dies without having associated anything with God." '—*At Tirmidhí, Ibn Májah.*

It is related from Abú Sa'íd that, 'The Apostle of God said, "There are some of my followers who will intercede for a multitude, and there are some of them who will intercede for a tribe, and some of them who will intercede for a small number not exceeding forty, and some of them who will intercede for a single individual until they enter paradise." '—*At Tirmidhí.*

It is related from 'Othmán bin 'Affán that, 'The Apostle of God said, "Three classes will intercede on the day of resurrection: the prophets, then the learned, then the martyrs." '—*Ibn Májah.*

A Description of Paradise and the Inhabitants Thereof

It is related from Abú Hurairah that, 'The Apostle of God said, "God Most High said, 'I have prepared for my righteous servants what eye hath not seen, nor ear heard, nor what hath entered into the heart of man.' Then recite, if ye wish, (the words) 'No soul knoweth the complete satisfaction which is secretly prepared for them (as a reward for that which they have wrought).' " '[1]—*Muslim, Al Bukhárí.*

It is related from Abú Músá that, 'The Apostle of God said, "Verily there will be in paradise a tent for the believer made of one hollow pearl, the length of which will be sixty miles. In every corner of it there will be people. They will not see each other, and the believer will go round from one to the other. And there will be two paradises, the vessels of which and whatever is in them will be of silver. And there will be two paradises, the vessels of which and whatever is in them will be of gold. And there will be nothing between the people and their looking at their Lord except the mantle of majesty on His face in the garden of Eden." '—*Muslim, Al Bukhárí.*

It is related from Anas that, 'The Apostle of God said, "Verily in paradise there is a bazaar to which men come on every Friday. And the north wind blows and shakes musk on their faces and on their clothes; and they are increased in beauty and handsomeness. Then they return to their families being increased in beauty and handsomeness. And their families say to them, 'By God! ye have been increased, since leaving us, in beauty and handsomeness.' And they will say, 'And ye also, by God! have been increased, since leaving us, in beauty and handsomeness.' " '—*Muslim.*

It is related from Abú Hurairah that, 'The Apostle of God said, "Whoever enters paradise will live in ease and see no trouble. His clothes will not grow old, nor his youth fade away." '—*Muslim.*

It is related from 'Utbah bin Ghazwán that he said, 'It was mentioned to us that a stone was cast from the edge of hell, and it fell into it for seventy years and did not reach the bottom. And by God! it will certainly be filled. And it was mentioned to us that what is between the two halves of the door of paradise is a journey of forty years. And a day will certainly come to it when it will be filled with a pressing crowd.'—*Muslim.*

[1] Qur'án, Súratu's-Sajda (xxxii), 17.

It is related from Buraidah that, 'A man said, "O Apostle of God, are there horses in paradise?" He replied, "Verily if God take thee to paradise, thou wilt not wish to be carried in it on a ruby horse which will fly with thee in paradise wherever thou wish, but thou wilt do so." Then a man asked a question and said, "O Apostle of God, are there any camels in paradise?" (Buraidah) said, "He did not say to him what he said to his companion. And he said, 'If God bring thee into paradise, there will be for thee therein whatever thy soul desires and whereby thine eye can be satisfied.'"'—*At Tirmidhí.*

It is related from Abú Sa'íd that, 'The Apostle of God said, "The meanest of the inhabitants of paradise is he who will have eighty thousand servants and seventy-two wives. And he will have a dome made of pearls, chrysolite, and rubies, (in extent) like the distance between Al Jábiya and Ṣan'á'. And they who die, whether young or old, of those who go to paradise, will in paradise all return to thirty years of age. They will never exceed that age. And in like manner the inhabitants of the fire (will return to thirty years of age). And there will be crowns upon the inhabitants of paradise, the meanest pearl of which will certainly light up all that lies between the East and the West. And when a believer wishes for a son in paradise, then his conception and birth and full age will be accomplished in one hour as he wished." And Isḥáq bin Ibráhím said in this tradition, "When a believer in paradise wishes for a son, it will be accomplished in an hour; but he will not wish it."'—*At Tirmidhí.*

It is related from Ḥákim bin Mu'áwiyah that, 'The Apostle of God said, "Verily in paradise there is a large river of water, and a large river of honey, and a large river of milk, and a large river of wine. Afterwards they will divide up (into smaller rivers)."'—*At Tirmidhí.*

It is related from Jábir that, 'A man asked the Apostle of God, "Do the inhabitants of paradise sleep?" He replied, "Sleep is the brother of death; and the inhabitants of paradise do not die."'—*Al Baihaqi.*

Concerning the Vision of God Most High

It is related from Ṣuhaib that, 'The Prophet said, "When the people destined for paradise will enter therein, God Most

High will say to them, 'Do ye wish for anything which I can add to you?' They will say, 'Hast thou not made our faces white! hast thou not brought us into paradise and saved us from the fire!'" (The Prophet) said, "Then a veil will be raised, and they will look at the face of God Most High; and nothing will be given them which will please them more than the looking at their Lord." After that he recited (the words) "For those who do right shall be a most excellent (reward), and a superabundant addition."'[1]—*Muslim.*

It is related from Abú Dharr that he said, 'I asked the Apostle of God, "Didst thou see thy Lord?" He replied, "(He is) a Light; how should I see Him!"'—*Muslim.*

It is related from Al Sha'bí that he said, 'Ibn 'Abbás met Ka'b at 'Arafat and asked him concerning a certain thing. Then he said, "God is great," until the mountains returned the echo. Then Ibn 'Abbás said, "We belong to the Bani Háshim." Ka'b replied, "Verily God Most High divided His vision and His conversation between Muḥammad and Moses. He spoke to Moses twice; and Muḥammad saw Him twice." Masrúq said, "Then I went into 'Áyesha and said, 'Did Muḥammad see his Lord?' She replied, 'Thou hast spoken of something on account of which my hair stands on end!' I said, 'Gently!' Then I recited (the words) 'He certainly saw some of the greatest signs of his Lord.' She said, 'Where are the words taking thee? It was only Gabriel. Whoever tells you that Muḥammad saw his Lord, or that he concealed anything of what he was commanded, or that he knew the five things of which God Most High spoke, that with him is the knowledge of the hour of resurrection, and he sends down the rain, etc., has told a great lie. But he saw Gabriel. He did not see him in his proper form except on two occasions: once near the tree Ṣidrutu'l-Muntaha, and once in Ajyád. He had six hundred wings, and he had closed the extremities (of the heavens).'"'—*Al Tirmidhí.*

A Description of the Fire and the Inhabitants Thereof

It is related from An Nu'mán bin Bashír that, 'The Apostle of God said, "Verily the inhabitant of the fire who is

[1] Qur'án, Súratu Yúnas (x) 26.

least punished is he whose two shoes and their thongs are of fire. His brains boil therefrom as a copper cauldron boils. It will not seem to him as if anyone suffers more severe punishment than he; and yet in reality he is the least punished of them." '—*Muslim*, *Al Bukhárí*.

It is related from Samurah bin Jundub that, 'The Prophet said, "Amongst them will be those whom the fire will take up to the ankles, and those whom the fire will take up to the knees, and those whom the fire will take up to the waist, and those whom the fire will take up to the collar-bone." '—*Muslim*.

It is related from Abú Hurairah that, 'The Prophet said, "The fire of hell burnt for one thousand years until it became red; then it burnt for a thousand years until it became white; then it burnt for a thousand years until it became black. Therefore it is (now) black and dark." '—*At Tirmidhí*.

It is related from Anas that, 'The Prophet said, "O men, weep; and if ye are not able to do so, then make yourselves weep. For verily the inhabitants of the fire weep in the fire until the tears flow down their faces as if they were rivulets, until the tears cease. Then blood flows, until the eyes become ulcers. Then had there been boats which could be placed therein, they would certainly float." '—*Sharḥu's-Sunnah*.

It is related from Ibn 'Omar that, 'The Prophet said, "The inhabitants of the fire will be made of large proportions in the fire, so that between the lobe of the ear of any one of them to his shoulder will be a journey of seven hundred years; and the thickness of his skin will be seventy cubits; and his molar tooth will be like (Mount) 'Uḥud." '

It is related from Al Ḥasan that he said, 'Abú Hurairah informed us that the Apostle of God said, "The sun and the moon are two lights which will be bound and cast into the fire on the day of resurrection." Al Ḥasan said, "What was their sin?" He replied, "I have related it to thee as I heard it from the Apostle of God." Then Al Ḥasan remained silent.'—*Al Baihaqi*.

Concerning the Creation of Paradise and the Fire

It is related from Anas that, 'The Prophet said, "(Men) will continue to be cast into hell; and it will say, 'Are there any more?' until the Lord of Glory puts His foot in it. Then some parts of it will contract into others; and it will say, 'Enough! enough! by Thy honour and Thy glory!' And abundance of room will continue in paradise, until God creates a creation for it and causes them to inhabit the superfluous parts of paradise." '—*Muslim, Al Bukhárí.*

Concerning the Beginning of Creation and Mention of the Prophets

It is related from 'Omar that he said, 'The Apostle of God stood up in our midst and related to us the beginning of creation until the people destined for paradise entered their abodes, and the people destined for the fire entered theirs. He who remembered it, remembered it; and he who forgot it, forgot it.'—*Al Bukhárí.*

It is related from Abú Hurairah that, 'The Apostle of God said, "Abraham did not lie except on three occasions: two of them for the sake of God, when he said, 'I am sick,' and when he said, 'Rather, the largest one of them did it.' " And (the Prophet) said, "On a certain day when Abraham and Sarah came to a great tyrant, it was remarked to the latter, 'Verily there is a man here, accompanied by a most beautiful woman.' Then he sent to Abraham and asked him concerning her (saying) 'Who is this woman?' He replied, 'She is my sister.' Then he came to Sarah and said to her, 'Verily if this tyrant knows that thou art my wife, he will overcome me in order to possess thee. Therefore if he ask thee, tell him that thou art my sister in Islám, for there is not on the face of the earth a single believer except thou and I.' Then the tyrant sent to her, and she was brought. And Abraham stood up to pray. And when she entered in where the tyrant was, he went to put forth his hand to take her, but he was withheld. And it is recorded that he was made to snort (in distress), until his feet began to strike on the ground. Then he said, 'Call on God for me, and I will do thee no harm.' Then she called on God, and he was released. Afterwards he attempted to take her a second time, but was withheld as at the first, or more severely. Then he said, 'Call on God for me, and I will do thee no harm.' So she called on God, and he was released. Then he called one of his attendants and said, 'Verily thou hast not brought me a human being; thou hast only brought me a Satan.' Then he gave her Hagar as a servant. And she came to Abraham when he was standing praying. Then he beckoned with his hand seeking to know her state. She replied, 'God returned the stratagem of the infidel upon his own breast; and he has made Hagar my servant.'"' Abú Hurairah said, 'That is your mother, O children of the water of heaven.'—*Muslim, Al Bukhárí.*

It is related from Abú Hurairah that he said, 'A man of the Muslims and a man of the Jews were abusing each other. And the Muslim said, "By Him who preferred Muḥammad over all the worlds!" And the Jew said, "By Him who preferred Moses over all the worlds!" Then the Muslim raised his hand at that and struck the Jew's face. Then the Jew went to the Prophet and informed him of what had passed between him and the Muslim. Then the Prophet called the Muslim and asked him about the matter. And he told him. Then the Prophet said, "Do not give me precedence over Moses; for verily men will fall down senseless on the day of resurrection, and I will fall down senseless with them. And I will be the first of those who come to their senses, and behold! Moses will be standing near the side of the throne. And I will not know whether he was amongst those who swooned and came to his senses before me, or whether he was amongst those whom God exempted (from the swooning)."'

It is related from Abú Hurairah that, 'The Apostle of God said, "The angel of death came to Moses bin 'Imrán and said to him, 'Accept the order of thy Lord (to die).' Then Moses struck the angel of death in the eye and blinded it. Then the angel returned to God Most High and said, 'Verily Thou didst send me to one of Thy servants who does not wish for death, and he has blinded my eye.' Then God returned his eye to him, and said, 'Return to my servant and say, "Is it life thou desirest? If thou desirest life, then place thy hand on the back of an ox, and thou wilt live in years equal to the number of hairs which thy hand covers."' Moses said, 'And what after that?' He replied, 'After that thou wilt die.' He said, 'Then (let me die) now. O Lord, bring me near to the Holy Land, or within a stone's throw of it.'" The Apostle of God said, "By God! If I had come near it, I would have shown you his grave on the side of the road near a red heap."'—*Muslim, Al Bukhárí.*

It is related from Ibn 'Abbás that, 'The Prophet said, "On the night on which I was taken to heaven, I saw Moses: a man of the colour of wheat, tall and of curly hair, as if he were one of the men of Shanú'ah. And I saw Jesus: a man of medium stature, inclining to red and white, and with the hair of his head hanging down. And I saw Málik, the keeper of the fire, and (I saw) Antichrist." (These were) amongst the signs which God showed to him. Therefore be not in doubt concerning his meeting them.'—*Muslim, Al Bukhárí.*

It is related from Abú Hurairah that, 'The Prophet said, "There were two women, each of whom had a son. And there came a wolf and took away the son of one of them. Then her companion said, 'It has only taken thy son.' But the other said, 'It only went off with thy son.' Then they went to David for judgement. And he gave judgement in favour of the elder woman. Then they went out to Solomon, the son of David, and informed him. He said, 'Bring me a knife, and I will divide the remaining son between you.' Then the younger woman said, 'Do not do so. May God have mercy on thee! He is her son.' Then he gave judgement in favour of the younger woman."'—*Muslim, Al Bukhárí.*

It is related from Abú Músá that, 'The Prophet said, "Many amongst men were perfect; but none amongst women were perfect except Mary, daughter of 'Imrán, and Asiyah the wife of Pharaoh. And the excellence of 'Áyesha over women is like the excellence of bread soup over all other food."'—*Muslim, Al Bukhárí.*

It is related from Jábir bin 'Abdu'lláh that, 'The Apostle of God said, "It has been permitted me to tell you about the one amongst the angels of God who bears up the throne. Verily the distance between the lobe of his ears and his shoulder is a journey of seven hundred years."'—*Abú Dáud.*

It is related from Abú Hurairah that he said, 'The Apostle of God took hold of my hand and said, "God created the earth on Saturday, and he created the mountains on it on Sunday, and He created the trees on Monday, and He created all unpleasant things on Tuesday, and He created the light on Wednesday, and he spread abroad the beasts therein on Thursday, and He created Adam after the afternoon of Friday at the end of the creation, and in the last hour of the day, that is, between the afternoon and nightfall." '—*Muslim.*

It is related from Abú Hurairah that, 'The Apostle of God said, "The length of Adam was sixty cubits and his breadth seven cubits." '

It is related from Abú Dharr that he said, 'I said, "O Apostle of God, who of the prophets was the first?" He replied, "Adam." I said, "O Apostle of God, and was he a prophet?" He replied, "Yes, he was a prophet who was spoken to (by God)." I said, "O Apostle of God, how many apostles were there?" He replied, "Three hundred and a few more than ten—a great crowd." ' And in another tradition from Abú Umámah it runs, 'I said, "O Apostle of God, what is the full number of the prophets?" He replied, "One hundred and twenty-four thousand, of whom three hundred and fifteen were apostles—a great crowd." '

Concerning the Excellencies of the Prince of the Apostles

It is related from Abú Hurairah that, 'The Apostle of God said, "I shall be chief of the sons of Adam on the day of resurrection, and the first for whom the grave will split open, and the first to intercede, and the first whose intercession will be accepted." '—*Muslim.*

It is related from Anas that, 'The Apostle of God said, "I shall have more followers than any other prophet on the day of resurrection; and I shall be the first to knock at the door of paradise." '—*Muslim.*

It is related from Abú Hurairah that, 'The Apostle of God said, "There is no prophet, but was given miracles suitable to his case, so that men believed on him. But that which was given to me was only revelation, which God revealed to me; and I hope that I shall have more followers than they on the day of resurrection." '—*Muslim, Al Bukhárí.*

It is related from Jábir that, 'The Apostle of God said, "I have been given five (qualities) which were not given to any before me. I have been given victory through fear (inspired by me) at a distance of a month's journey; and the world has been made a pure place of prayer for me, so that wherever the time of prayer arrives for a man of my followers, let him pray there; and plunder has been made lawful for me, and it was not made lawful for anyone before me; and I have been given intercession; and (formerly) a prophet was sent especially to his own nation, but I have been sent to all men generally." '—*Muslim*, *Al Bukhárí.*

It is related from Al 'Irbáḍ bin Sáriyah that, 'The Apostle of God said, "Verily I was written down near God as the seal of the prophets when Adam was twisted up in his own clay; and I shall inform you of the first matters connected with me, namely the prayer of Abraham ('Send an apostle from amongst themselves'), and the good news preached by Jesus (of the coming of one named Aḥmad), and the vision of my mother which she saw when she gave birth to me, and there came forth a light for her by which the palaces of Syria shined forth." '—*Sharḥu's-Sunnah.*

It is related from Ibn 'Ábbás that he said, 'Some men of the companions of the Apostle of God were sitting; and he came forth so that when he came near to them he heard them discussing things with each other. And some of them said, "Verily God took Abraham as a friend"; and another said, "Moses talked with God"; another said, "Jesus was the Word of God and His Spirit"; another said, "God chose Adam". And the Apostle of God came out to them and said, "I have heard your words and your surprise that Abraham was the friend of God, and he was such; and that Moses received secret communications from God, and it was so; and that Jesus was His Spirit and His Word, and He was so; and that God chose Adam, and it was so. Beware! I am the Beloved of God, and there is no boasting, and I will be the bearer of the standard of praise on the day of resurrection, and under it will be Adam and all others besides him, and there is no boasting. And I shall be the first intercessor, and the first whose intercession will be accepted on the day of resurrection, and there is no boasting. And I will be the first to shake the door of paradise, and God will open it for me and will take me inside, and with me will be indigent believers, and there is no boasting. And I am the most noble of the first and the last with God, and there is no boasting."'—*At Tirmidhí.*

It is related from 'Abdu'lláh bin Ma'súd that, 'The Apostle of God said, "Verily for every prophet there will be a friend from amongst the prophets; and my friend will be my father and the friend of my Lord (Abraham)." After that he recited (the revelation) "Verily the men who are nearest of kin to Abraham are they who follow him, and this prophet, and they who believe; and God is the friend of the believers."'[1]—*At Tirmidhí.*

It is related from Ka'b that when he was speaking of the Taurát he said, 'We found it written, "Muḥammad, the Apostle of God, my chosen servant, neither bad-tempered, nor rude, nor a crier in bazaars, nor one who returns evil for evil, but one who forgives and pardons. His birth-place Mecca, and his flight to (Madína) the pleasant. His kingdom in Syria, and his followers people who praise much, praising God in pleasure and in sorrow, and in every stopping-place, and extolling his greatness in every high place. They observe the sun, and say their prayers when the time comes. They wear their trousers to their knees, and perform ablutions on their limbs. A crier of theirs calls aloud in the skies. Their ranks in battle and their ranks in prayer are the same. The murmur of their voices at night is like the buzz of bees."'

It is related from 'Abdu'lláh bin Salám that he said, 'A description of Muḥammad is written in the Taurát; and it is (also written) that Jesus, the Son of Mary, will be buried with him.' Abú Mawdád said, 'A place for a grave remains in the house (where Muḥammad was buried).'—*At Tirmidhí.*

On the Names of the Prophet, and His Attributes

It is related from Jubair bin Muṭ'im that he said, 'I heard the Prophet say, "I have various names. I am Muḥammad, and I am Aḥmad, and I am Al Maḥi (the eraser), by whom God will erase infidelity, and I am Al Ḥáshir (the gatherer), to whose feet men will be gathered (on the day of resurrection), and I am Al 'Áqib (the last in succession) after whom there will be no prophet."'—*Muslim, Al Bukhárí.*

---

[1] Qur'án, Súratu Áli 'Imrán (iii) 68.

It is related from Anas that he said, 'The Apostle of God was neither conspicuously tall nor short; nor was he very white or wheat-coloured; nor was he very curly-headed, nor was his hair very straight. God sent him at the end of his fortieth year, and he resided in Mecca (after his call) for ten years, and in Madína ten years. And God took him at the end of his sixtieth year. And there were not in his head and beard twenty white hairs.'

It is related from Abú Hurairah that he said, 'I never saw anything more beautiful than the Apostle of God. It was as if the sun was moving in his face. And I never saw anyone move more quickly in his walking than the Apostle of God. It was as if the earth was folded up for him. Verily we used to exert ourselves (to keep up with him), whereas he was not in the least distressed.'—*At Tirmidhí.*

It is related from Anas that, 'A Jewish boy used to wait upon the Prophet. And the boy fell ill. Then the Prophet came to visit him and found his father (sitting) by his head, reading the Taurát. And the Apostle of God said to him, "O Jew, I ask thee by God who sent down the Taurát upon Moses, whether thou dost find a description of me and of my attributes, and the story of my coming out (from Mecca to Madína) in the Taurát?" He replied, "No." The boy exclaimed, "Yes, by God! O Apostle of God, we do find in the Taurát a description of thee and of thine attributes, and the story of thy going out (from Mecca to Madína); and I bear witness that there is no God but Alláh, and that thou art the Apostle of God." Then the Prophet said to his companions, "Make this (Jew) get up from near his head, and do ye come close to your brother."'—*Al Baihaqi.*

On the Morals and Natural Disposition of the Prophet

It is related from Anas that he said, 'I waited on the Prophet for ten years, and he never said, "Fie!" to me, and never said, "Why didst thou do (so and so)," or "Why didst thou not do (so and so)?"'—*Muslim, Al Bukhárí.*

It is related from Abú Hurairah that he said, 'It was said, "O Apostle of God, call down a curse upon the polytheists."

He replied, "I have not been sent as a curse, but I have only been sent as a mercy."'—*Muslim.*

It is related from 'Áyesha that she said, 'The Apostle of God used to mend his own shoes and sew his clothes and work in his house as anyone of you works in his house. He was a man amongst men. He used to clean his clothes of vermin and milk his goats and wait upon himself.'—*At Tirmidhí.*

It is related from 'Amru bin Sa'íd from Anas that he said, 'I never saw anyone more kind to his family than the Apostle of God. His son Abraham was put out to nurse in a high part of Madína, and the Prophet used to go, and we with him, and enter the house when it was full of smoke, his foster-father being a blacksmith, and the Apostle used to take the child and kiss him. After that he would return.' 'Amru said, 'And when Abraham died, the Apostle of God said, "Verily Abraham my son died whilst at the breast. He will certainly have two nurses in paradise to complete his weaning."'—*Muslim.*

It is related from 'Áyesha that she said, 'The Apostle of God said, "O 'Áyesha, if I wished I could certainly have mountains of gold. An angel came to me, whose waist certainly equals the Ka'bah, and said, 'Verily thy Lord sends His salútations to thee and says, if thou wishest to be a prophet who is (at the same time) a servant (then be so); or if thou wishest to be a prophet who is a king, (then be so).' Then I looked towards Gabriel; and he beckoned to me that I should humble myself."' And in another tradition from Ibn 'Abbás it runs, 'The Apostle of God turned to Gabriel as if seeking a sign from him. Then Gabriel made a sign with his hand that he should humble himself. Then I said, "I will be a prophet who is a servant." ('Áyesha) said, after that the Apostle of God would not eat reclining; but would say, "I will eat as a slave eats, and will sit as a slave sits."'—*Sharḥu's-Sunnah.*

Concerning the Sending of the Prophet, and the Beginning of Inspiration

It is related from Ibn 'Abbás that, 'The Apostle of God was sent at his fortieth year; and he remained in Mecca thirteen years, receiving revelations. After that he was commanded to flee; and he fled and remained a fugitive (at Madína) for ten years. And he died when he was sixty-three years of age.'—*Muslim, Al Bukhárí.*

It is related from Ibn 'Abbás that he said, 'The Apostle of God remained at Mecca for fifteen years. He heard a voice and saw a light for seven years, but saw nothing else. And for eight years he received revelations. And he lived in Madína ten years, and died when he was sixty-five years of age.'—*Muslim, Al Bukhárí.*

It is related from Anas that, 'God caused the Prophet to die when he had completed sixty years.'—*Muslim, Al Bukhárí.*

It is related from 'Áyesha that, 'The first revelations which came to the Apostle of God were true visions in sleep. And he never saw a vision, but it came like the dawn of the morning. After that solitary retirement became pleasing to him, and he used to retire to a cave of (Mount) Ḥirá' and worship therein. And he would worship the whole night before he returned to his family; and he used to provide food for the purpose. After that he would return to Khadíjah, and again provide himself with food as before, until the truth came to him when he was in the cave of Mount Ḥirá'. An angel came to him and said, "Recite!" He replied, "I am not a reciter." The Prophet said, "Then he seized me and squeezed me until fatigue overtook me. Then he let me go, and said, 'Recite!' and squeezed me a second time until fatigue overtook me. After that he said, 'Recite!' I replied, 'I am not a reciter.' Then he seized me and squeezed me a third time, until fatigue overtook me. After that he let me go and said, 'Recite in the name of thy Lord who created, created man from a clot of blood. Recite! thy Lord is the most noble who taught by the pen: taught man what he did not know.'" Then the Apostle of God repeated these words, his heart trembling the while. And he entered in to Khadíjah and said, "Wrap me up! wrap me up!" Then they wrapped him up until the fear went from him. Then he spoke to Khadíjah and informed her of the matter, saying "I certainly feared for my life." Then Khadíjah said, "Never by God! God will never bring thee to shame. Verily thou dost perform acts of mercy, and thou dost speak the truth, and bearest weariness, and dost earn that which is lacking, and thou art hospitable to visitors, and givest help to all men." After that Khadíjah took him to Waraqah bin Nawfal bin 'Amm Khadíjah and said to him, "O my nephew, listen to the son of thy brother." Then Waraqah said to him, "O my nephew, what is the matter?" Then the Apostle of God informed him of what he had seen. Waraqah said, "This is the *námús* which God sent down upon Moses. Would to God that I were young in its time! Would to God that I were living when thy people will turn thee out." Then the Apostle of God said, "Will they turn me out?" He replied, "Yes. No man ever came with what thou hast brought, but he was held in enmity. And if that day of thine should come in my time, I will aid thee greatly." It was not long after that Waraqah died, and the revelations were suspended.'—*Muslim, Al Bukhárí.* And Al Bukhárí has added the following, 'So much so that the Prophet grieved at what had reached us, so that many times in the morning he wished to throw himself from the summit of a high mountain; but as often as he arrived at the summit of the mountain in order to cast himself down from it, Gabriel appeared to him and said, "O Muḥammad, verily thou art the Apostle of God in truth." At that his heart became at ease, and his soul was comforted.'

It is related from 'Áyesha that, 'Al Ḥárith bin Hishám asked the Apostle of God and said, "O Apostle of God, how does inspiration come to thee?" The Apostle of God replied, "At times it comes to me like the sound of a bell, and that is the most difficult for me, and (Gabriel) would leave me when I had remembered what he said. And at times the angel appears to me like a man and speaks to me and I remember what he says." 'Áyesha said, "I have certainly seen inspiration descend upon him on a very cold day, and then leave him with his forehead dripping beads of perspiration."'—*Muslim, Al Bukhárí.*

It is related from Anas that 'One of the teeth of the Apostle of God was broken on the day of (the battle of) 'Uḥud, and he was wounded in his head. And he began to wipe the blood from himself and to say, "How will that people prosper who have wounded the head of their Prophet and broken his teeth!"'—*Muslim.*

Concerning the Signs of Prophecy

It is related from Anas that 'Gabriel came to the Apostle of God when he was playing with some boys, and he seized him and threw him on the ground, and split open his heart, and took out therefrom a clot of blood, and said, "This is Satan's portion from thee." After that he washed it in a golden vessel containing Ẓemzem water. Then he bound it up and put it in its place again. And the boys came running to his mother, that is to his wet-nurse, and said, "Verily Muḥammad has been killed." Then they went near to him, and found that he had changed colour.' Anas said, 'I used to see the marks of the stitches on his breast.'—*Muslim.*

It is related from Anas that, 'The people of Mecca asked the Apostle of God to show them a sign. Then he showed them the moon split into two pieces, until they saw Mount Ḥirá' between the two.'—*Muslim, Al Bukhárí.*

It is related from Abú Hurairah that, 'Abú Jahl said, "Does Muḥammad smear his face with dust (in prostration) amongst you?" It was said, "Yes." He said, "By Al Lat, and Al 'Uzza! If I see him doing that, I will certainly trample on his neck." Then he came to the Apostle of God when he was praying, intending to trample on his neck. But he did not come back to them from the Apostle except by retreating on his heels, and protecting himself with his hands. And it was said to him, "What is the matter with thee?" He replied, "Verily between him and me there is certainly a pit of fire and fear and wings (of angels)." Then the Apostle of God said, "If he had come near to me, the angels would certainly have plucked him away limb by limb." '—*Muslim.*

Concerning the Night-Journey to Heaven

It is related from Qatádah from Anas bin Málik from Málik bin Ṣa'ṣa'h that, 'The Prophet of God related to them concerning the night on which he was taken (to heaven, saying) "When I was in Al Ḥaṭím"—and possibly he said, "I was lying down in Ḥijr—behold! a certain one came to me and split open from here to here"—that is from the opening of his upper chest to his lower hair—"and took out my heart. After that a golden vessel was brought to me filled with faith, and my heart was washed. After that it was crammed full, and then it was put back in its place."' And in another tradition it runs, 'The belly was washed with water of Zemzem, and then filled with faith and knowledge. "After that a beast was brought to me, inferior to a mule, but above an ass (in height). It was white, and was called Al Burāq. It placed its steps at a distance as far as its sight reached. And I was carried on it, and Gabriel went with me, until it came to the heavens of the earth. Then Gabriel asked that the door might be opened. It was said, 'Who is this?' He replied, 'Gabriel'. It was said, 'And who is with thee?' He replied, 'Muḥammad.' It was said, 'Has he been sent too?' He replied, 'Yes.' It was said, 'Welcome to him! His coming is well.' Then the door was opened. And when I arrived (inside) behold therein Adam! Gabriel said, 'This is thy father Adam, therefore salute him.' Then I saluted him, and he returned the salutation. After that he said, 'Welcome to the good son and good prophet.' After that Gabriel ascended with me until he came to the second heaven and asked for the door to be opened. It was said, 'Who is this?' He replied, 'Gabriel.' It was said, 'And who is with thee?' He replied, 'Muḥammad.' It was said, 'Has he been sent too?' He replied, 'Yes.' It was said, 'Welcome to him! His coming is well.' Then the door was opened. And when I arrived (inside) behold John and Jesus, who were sons of their respective maternal aunts. He said, 'This is John and this is Jesus, therefore salute them.' So I saluted them, and they returned the salutation. Then they said, 'Welcome to the good brother and good prophet!' After that he ascended with me to the third heaven and asked for the door to be opened. It was said, 'Who is this?' He replied, 'Gabriel.' It was said, 'And who is with thee?' He replied, 'Muḥammad.' It was said, 'Has he been sent too?' He replied, 'Yes.' It was said, 'Welcome to him! His coming is well.' Then the door was opened. And when I arrived (inside), behold! Joseph. Gabriel said, 'This is Joseph, therefore salute him.' So I saluted him, and he returned the salutation. Then he said, 'Welcome to the good brother and good prophet!' After that Gabriel ascended with me until he came to the fourth heaven; and he asked for the door to be opened. And it was said, 'Who is this?' He replied, 'Gabriel.' It was said, 'And who is with thee?' He replied, 'Muḥammad.' It was said, 'And has he been sent too?' He replied, 'Yes.' It was said, 'Welcome to him! His coming is well.' Then the door was opened. And when I arrived (inside), behold! Enoch. Gabriel said, 'This is Enoch, therefore salute him.' So I saluted him; and he returned the salutation. Then he said, 'Welcome to the good brother and good prophet.' After that Gabriel ascended with me until he came to the fifth heaven. And he asked that the door might be opened. It was said, 'Who is this?' He replied, 'Gabriel.' It was said, 'And who is with thee?' He replied, 'Muḥammad.' It was said, 'Has he been sent too?' He replied, 'Yes.' It was said, 'Welcome to him! His coming is well.' Then the door was opened. And when I arrived (inside), behold! Aaron. Gabriel said, 'This is Aaron, therefore salute him.' So I saluted him; and he returned the salutation. Then he said, 'Welcome to the good brother and good prophet!' After that Gabriel ascended with me until he came to the sixth heaven. And he asked that the door might be opened. It was said, 'Who is this?' He replied, 'Gabriel.' It was said, 'And who is with thee?' He replied, 'Muḥammad.' It was said, 'Has he been sent too?' He replied, 'Yes' It was said, 'Welcome to him! His coming is well.' Then the door was opened. And when I arrived (inside), behold! Moses. Gabriel said, 'This is Moses, therefore salute him.' So I saluted him; and he returned the salutation. Then he said, 'Welcome to the good brother and good prophet.' And when I passed on, he wept. It was said to him, 'What makes thee weep?' He replied, 'I weep because a boy has been sent after me, of whose followers more will enter paradise than will enter of mine.' After that Gabriel ascended with me to the seventh heaven; and he asked that the door might be opened. It was said, 'Who is this?' He replied, 'Gabriel.' It was said, 'And who is with thee?' He replied, 'Muḥammad.' It was said, 'Has he been sent too?' He replied, 'Yes.' It was said, 'Welcome! his coming is well.' Then when I arrived (inside), behold! Abraham. Gabriel said, 'This is Abraham, therefore salute him.' So I saluted him; and he returned the salutation. Then he said, 'Welcome to the good son and good prophet.' After that I was taken up to the (tree called) Sidratu'l-Muntaha, and behold! its lotus fruit was like stone water-pots, and behold! its leaves were like elephants' ears. Gabriel said, 'This is the Sidratu'l-Muntaha. And behold! four rivers, two of them hidden and two of them manifest.' I said, 'What are these, O Gabriel?' He replied, 'As for the hidden ones, they are two rivers in paradise, but the two which are manifest are the Nile and the Euphrates.' After that the house called Ma'múr was raised up for me; and after that a vessel of wine and a vessel of milk and a vessel of honey were brought to me. And I took the milk. He said, 'This is religion. Thou and thy people (will act) on it.' After that prayers were ordered for me: fifty prayers for every day. Then I returned and passed by Moses. He said, 'What hast thou been ordered?' I said, 'I have been ordered fifty prayers for every day.' He said, 'Verily thy followers will not be able to perform fifty prayers every day. By God! I tried men previous to thee and contended with the children of Israel with severe strivings. Therefore return to thy Lord, and ask for some alleviation for thy people.' Then I returned; and He took ten prayers from me. And I returned to Moses; and he spake as before. So I returned; and He took ten more from me. And I went back to Moses, and he spake as before. So I returned; and He took ten more from me, and I was ordered to say ten prayers every day. After that I returned to Moses and he spake as before. So I returned, and I was ordered five prayers every day. Then I went back to Moses, and he said, 'What hast thou been ordered?' I said, 'I have been ordered five prayers every day.' He said, 'Verily thy followers are not able to perform five prayers every day; for verily I have tried men before thee and have contended with the children of Israel with severe strivings; therefore return to thy Lord, and ask from Him some alleviation for thy followers.' Muḥammad said, 'I have asked my Lord until I have become ashamed. But I am satisfied, and I resign (all to Him).' He said, 'Then when I passed by, a herald cried, 'I have given my orders, and have provided alleviation for my servants'.'' '—*Muslim, Al Bukhárí.*

It is related from Thábitu'l-Bunani from Anas that, 'The Apostle of God said, "Buráq was brought to me. He was a white beast, longer and higher than an ass, but not so high as a mule. Its foot came down at a distance as far as its eye could reach. Then I rode on it until I came to the Holy House (at Jerusalem). And I tied him to the ring to which the prophets were wont to tie (their steeds). Then I entered the mosque, and prayed there in two *rak'ahs*. After that I came out and Gabriel brought me a vessel of wine and a vessel of milk; and I chose the milk. Then Gabriel said, 'Thou hast chosen religion.' After that he ascended with us to heaven." After that Thábit related as in the former tradition.'

Concerning the Miracles of the Prophets

It is related from Anas bin Málik that, 'Abú Bakr Uṣ-Ṣiddíq said, "I saw the feet of the polytheists above our heads when we were in the cave, and I said, 'O Apostle of God, if one of them looks towards his feet, he will see us.' He replied, 'O Abú Bakr, dost thou imagine there are but two, when God is the Third of them!'"'—*Muslim*, *Al Bukhárí*.

It is related from Anas that he said, 'Verily the Apostle of God took counsel when the news reached us of the approach of Abú Sufyan (with a Meccan army). Then Sa'd bin 'Ubádah stood up and said, "O Apostle of God, by Him in whose hand is my life! if thou order us to drive them into the sea, we will certainly do it. And if thou order us to smite their livers to Baraku'l-Ghimá, we will certainly do it." Then the Apostle of God exhorted the people. And they travelled until they came down to Badr. Then the Apostle of God said, "This is the place where so and so will be smitten to the ground,"—and he placed his hand upon the earth—"here and here."' Anas said, 'Not one of them passed the place touched by the Apostle's hand.'—*Muslim*.

It is related from Sa'd bin Abú Waqqás that he said, 'On the day (of the battle of) 'Uḥud, I saw two men on the right and left sides of the Apostle of God, clothed in white clothes. They were fighting in a manner resembling the fiercest fighting. I never saw them before nor yet afterwards. I mean they were Gabriel and Michael.'—*Muslim*, *Al Bukhárí*.

It is related from Al Baráí' that he said, 'The Prophet sent a small band of men to Abú Ráfi'; and (one of them) 'Abdu'lláh bin 'Atík entered in upon him in his house at night when he was sleeping and killed him. 'Abdu'lláh bin 'Atík said, "I smote a sword into his belly until it reached his back, and I knew that I had killed him. And I began to open the doors until I reached a flight of steps, and I placed my foot on them and fell in the moonlight night, and my leg was broken. And I bound it up with a turban, and went to my companions. And I reached the Prophet and reported the affair. He said, 'Stretch out thy leg.' Then I stretched out my leg; and he rubbed his hand over it. And it was as if I had never complained of it."'—*Al Bukhârí.*

It is related from Jábir that he said, 'The people became thirsty on the day of Ḥudaibah. And there was a small drinking-vessel before the Apostle of God, and he made his ablutions from it. After that the people drew near to him and said, "We have no water with which to perform our ablutions and drink, except what is in the small drinking-vessel." Then the Prophet put his hand into the drinking-vessel; and the water began to flow from between his fingers like springs. Then we drank and performed the ablutions.' It was said to Jábir, 'How many were you?' He replied, 'Had we been a hundred thousand, it would certainly have sufficed for us. We were one thousand five hundred.'—*Muslim, Al Bukhârí.*

It is related from 'Áyesha that she said, 'The Apostle of God was bewitched until he was made to imagine that he did a certain thing, but he did not (really) do it. Until on a certain day when he was with me, he prayed to God and called on Him. Then he said, "Dost thou know, O 'Áyesha, that God has answered me what I asked Him! There came to me two men; one of them sat at my head, and the other at my feet. Then one of them said to his companion, 'What is the man's pain?' He replied, 'He is bewitched.' The other said, 'Who has bewitched him?' He replied, 'Labíd binu'l-'A'ṣam, the Jew.' He said, 'By what did he do it?' He replied, 'By a comb and by a hair which falls from it, and by the film of a male date bud.' He asked, 'Where is it?' He replied, 'In the well Dharwán.'" Then the Prophet went to the well with some men of his companions and said, "This is the well which was shown to me." And it was as if its water was stained with *hina*, and as if its palm-trees (reflected in the water) were the heads of Satans. Then he took it out.'—*Muslim, Al Bukhárí.*

It is related from Abú Hurairah that he said, 'Verily ye say, "Abú Hurairah has related many (traditions) from the Prophet." By God! there is a time appointed (for the punishment of those who fabricate traditions). The fact is, my brethren from amongst those who flew from Mecca to Madína were kept busy bargaining in the bazaars; and my brethren from amongst the helpers were kept busy by work connected with their property. But I was a poor man and kept close to the Apostle of God, content if only my belly were filled. And one day the Prophet said, "No one of you who spreads out his cloth (for me to pray on) until I finish my words, and afterwards gathers it to his breast, will ever forget anything from my words." Then I spread out a blanket, which was the only cloth I had on me, until the Prophet finished his prayer. After that I gathered it to my breast; and by Him who sent him with the truth! I never forgot any of his words until this day.'—*Muslim, Al Bukhárí.*

It is related from Anas that, 'A famine afflicted the people in the time of the Apostle of God; and whilst the Prophet was giving the public address on a certain Friday, a desert Arab stood up and said, "O Apostle of God, our properties are destroyed and our families are hungry; therefore pray to God for us." Then the Apostle raised his hands, and we did not see in the heavens a single speck of cloud, and by Him in whose hand is my life! he had not taken them down before clouds appeared like mountains. After that he had not come down from his pulpit until I saw the rain falling on his beard. Then we were given rain on that day and on the morrow and on the next day until the next Friday. Then that desert Arab and others stood up and said, "O Apostle of God, our buildings are fallen into ruins and our property is submerged; therefore pray to God for us." Then he raised his hands and said, "O God, send down the rain around us, but not on us." And he did not make a sign towards any quarter where there was cloud, but it ceased. And Madína became like an open space (surrounded by clouds). And the valley of Qanáh flowed for a month; and no one came from any direction, but what he reported an abundance (of rain).'—*Muslim, Al Bukhárí.*

It is related from Abú Hurairah that, 'On the day (of the battle) of Tabúq the people became hungry. Then 'Omar said, "O Apostle of God, call them to bring the remains of their rations and then pray to God for them for a blessing upon it." He replied, "Yes." Then he called for a piece of leather and spread it out. After that he called for the remains of their rations. And some people began to bring handfuls of millet, others brought handfuls of dates, others brought small pieces of food until a small quantity of things was gathered together on the piece of leather. Then the Apostle of God prayed for a blessing, and afterwards he said, "Take it in your vessels." (And they took it) until they did not leave amongst the soldiers a single vessel that was not filled.' Abú Hurairah said, 'And they ate until they were satisfied; and there remained some over. And the Apostle of God said, "I bear witness that there is no God but Alláh, and that I am the Apostle of Alláh. There is no servant who will meet God with these two testimonies, free of doubt, who will be prevented from entering paradise."'—*Muslim.*

It is related from Abú Músá that he said, 'Abú Ṭálib went out to Syria; and the Prophet of God, (then a boy), went with him, together with some old men of the Quraish. And when they came near to a certain monk they alighted and opened their pack-saddles. Then the monk came out to them—and they used, before that, to pass by him; neither was he in the habit of coming out to them—as they were opening their pack-saddles. And the monk began to pass amongst them until he came to and seized the hand of the Apostle of God. And he said, "This is the master of all the worlds; this is the Apostle of the Lord of all the worlds. God has sent him as a mercy to all the worlds." Then the old men of the Quraish said to him, "What knowledge hast thou?" He replied, "When ye drew near to Al 'Aqabah there remained neither tree nor stone that did not bow down in prostration; but these do not prostrate to any, but prophets. And I recognize him by the seal of prophecy which is beneath the cartilage of his shoulder, like an apple." After that he returned and prepared food for them. And when he brought it to them, (the Apostle) was amongst the flock of camels. Then the monk said, "Send for him." And he drew near; and above him was a cloud shading him. And when he came near to the people, he found that they had preceded him to the shade of a tree. And when he sat down the shade of the tree inclined towards him. Then (the monk) said, "Look at the shade of the tree inclining towards him!" And he said, "I adjure you by God, who of you is his guardian?" They said, "Abú Ṭálib." And he continued to adjure him until Abú Ṭálib sent him (*i.e.* Muḥammad) back. And Abú Bakr sent Bilál with him. And the monk provided cakes and olives for his journey.'—*At Tirmidhí.*

It is related from Buraidah that, 'The Apostle of God said, "When we arrived at the Holy House (at Jerusalem), Gabriel made a sign with his finger and therewith perforated a stone. And he tied up Buráq to the stone."'—*At Tirmidhí.*

It is related from Ibn 'Abbás that, 'A woman brought her son to the Apostle of God and said, "O Apostle of God, verily my son is mad. And it seizes him morning and evening." Then the Apostle of God rubbed his hand on the boy's breast and prayed. And he vomited, and there came forth out of his belly a thing like a black puppy running about.'—*Al Dárimi.*

It is related from Ibn 'Abbás that, 'A desert Arab came to the Apostle of God and said, "By what means may I know that thou art a prophet?" He replied, "That I call this cluster of dates from this date-tree to bear witness that I am the Apostle of God." Then the Apostle of God called; and it began to come down from the date-tree until it fell beside the Prophet. Then he said, "Return." And it returned to its place; and the desert Arab embraced Islám.'—*At Tirmidhí.*

It is related from Jábir that a Jewish woman of the inhabitants of Khaibar poisoned some roasted mutton and then presented it to the Apostle of God. Then the Apostle of God took a fore-leg and ate of it; and a small number of his companions ate of it with him. Then the Apostle of God said, "Withhold your hands!" And he sent to the Jewess and called her and said, "Didst thou poison this mutton?" She replied, "Who informed thee?" He said, "This piece of fore-leg which is in my hand informed me." She said, "Yes (I poisoned it). I said 'If he be a prophet, then it will never hurt him; but if he be not a prophet, then we shall be rid of him.'" Then the Apostle of God forgave her, and did not punish her. But his companions who ate of the mutton died. And the Apostle of God was cupped on the shoulder on account of what he had eaten of the mutton. Abú Hind cupped him with a horn and a knife. And he was a freedman of the Bani Bayáḍah of the Helpers.'—*Abú Dáud.*

It is related from Ibn 'Abbás that, 'The Quraish conspired together on a certain night in Mecca. Some of them, referring to the Prophet, said, "When day dawns, then bind him with fetters." Others of them said, "Rather kill him." Others of them said, "Rather turn him out (of the city)." But God disclosed the matter to His Prophet; and 'Alí spent that night on the Prophet's bed. And the Prophet went forth until he reached a cave. And the polytheists passed the night watching 'Alí, thinking that he was the Prophet. Then when the morning dawned, they rushed upon him; and when they saw 'Alí, God defeated their plans. Then they said, "Where is this friend of thine?" He replied, "I know not." Then they followed (the Apostle's) tracks; and when they reached the mountain they were confounded. And they ascended the mountain and passed by the cave. And they saw a spider's web across the entrance, and said, "If he had entered here, the spider's web would not be across its entrance." And he remained in it three nights.'—*Aḥmad.*

It is related from Usámah bin Zaid that, 'The Apostle of God said, "He who pretends that I have said what I did not say, let him make his resting-place in the fire." And that was because he sent a man, and he lied about him. Then the Apostle of God invoked a curse upon him. And he was found dead with his belly split open; and the earth would not receive him.'—*Al Baihaqi.*

Concerning the Miracles of Holy Men

It is related from 'Áyesha that, 'When the King of Abyssinia died, we were remarking to one another that a light continued to be seen over his grave.'—*Abú Dáud.*

It is related from Ibnu'l-Munkadir that, 'Safínah, a freedman of the Apostle of God, lost trace of the army in the land of Greece,[1] or was taken prisoner. And he fled seeking the (Muslim) army. And behold! a lion met him. And he said, "O Abu'l-Ḥárith, I am a freedman of the Apostle of God. Such and such happened to me." And the lion drew near to him wagging its tail until it stood at his side. Whenever it heard a sound (of danger) it went towards it; and afterwards it came near and walked by his side until they reached the army. Then the lion returned.'—*Sharḥu's-Sunnah.*

Concerning the Death of the Prophet

It is related from 'Áyesha that she said, 'One of the benefits of God towards me is this, that the Apostle of God died in my room and on my day (reposing) between my breast and collarbone. And God united my saliva with his near his death. 'Abdu'r-Raḥmán bin Abú Bakr entered in where I was, whilst I was acting as a pillow for the Apostle of God to rest upon, and he had in his hand a stick for cleaning the teeth. And I saw the Prophet looking at the tooth-cleaner, and I understood that he would like it. So I said, "Shall I get it for thee?" And he made a sign with his head in the affirmative. Then I took it; but it was hard for him, so I said, "Shall I make it soft for thee?" Then he made a sign with his head in the affirmative. Then I made it soft; and he rubbed it over his teeth. And there was a small drinking-vessel before him in which was water. And he began to put his hands into the water and wipe his face with them and to say, "There is no God but Alláh; verily in death there are agonies." After that he raised his hand and began to say, "(Give me a place) with the highest companions," until he was taken, and his hand fell down.'—*Al Bukhárí.*

It is related from Anas that, 'When the Prophet was oppressed (with pain) his distress caused him to swoon. And Fáṭimah said, "What agony, O my father!" He said to her, "There will be no agony on thy father after to-day." Then when he died, she said, "O my father! he has responded to the Lord who called him. O my father! whose place is the garden of paradise! O my father! to Gabriel give we the

[1] The word Greece is here used for the Roman Empire.

news of thy death!" Afterwards, when he was buried, Fáṭimah said, "O Anas, are ye happy in throwing dirt upon the Apostle of God!" '—*Al Bukhárí.*

It is related from 'Áyesha that, 'When the Apostle of God died, they disagreed about (the place of) his burial. Then Abú Bakr said, "I heard something (relating to this) from the Apostle of God. He said, 'God takes no prophet, but in the place in which he loves to be buried.' Bury him therefore in the place where his bed is." '—*At Tirmidhí*

It is related from 'Áyesha that she said, 'The Apostle of God, in the illness in which he died, was saying, "O 'Áyesha, I continue to feel the pain from the (poisoned) food which I ate at Khaibar; and this is the hour in which I feel the cutting of my arteries from that poison." '—*Al Bukhárí.*

It is related from Ibn 'Abbás that, 'When the Apostle of God was approached by death, there were some men in the house, amongst whom was 'Omar binu'l-Khaṭṭáb. And the Prophet said, "Come, and I will write for you a writing after which ye will never go astray." Then 'Omar said, "The pain has overcome him, and ye have the Qur'án; the Word of God is sufficient for you." But the people of the house differed about the matter and squabbled. And some of them said, "Bring near (writing materials), so that the Apostle of God may write for you." And some amongst them said what 'Omar had said. And when the clamour and dissension increased, the Apostle of God said, "Get up from me." 'Ubaidu'lláh said that Ibn 'Abbás used to say, "Verily the misfortunes, all the misfortunes which have come to us, between the Apostle and his writing for them that writing, have come on account of their disagreement and clamour.'—*Muslim, Al Bukhárí.*

It is related from 'Áyesha that she said, 'The Apostle of God returned to me on a certain day from a funeral in Baqi'a; and he found me suffering from a headache. And I said, "O my headache!" He said, "Rather, O 'Áyesha, I say, O my headache! What harm is it to thee, if thou die before me, for I will wash thee and shroud thee and pray over thee and bury thee." I said, "I fancy I see thee! by God! if thou didst that, thou wouldst certainly return to my house and co-habit therein with some of thy wives." Then the Apostle of God smiled. After that the pains began from which he died.'—*Al Dárimi.*

It is related from 'Áyesha that she said, 'The Apostle of God never left a single dinar, or a single dirham, or a goat, or a camel; nor did he leave anything by will.'—*Muslim.*

CONCERNING THE VIRTUES OF THE QURAISH

It is related from Ibn 'Omar that, 'The Prophet said, "This office (of the Khalifate) will continue in the Quraish so long as there remain amongst them two persons."'—*Muslim, Al Bukhárí.*

It is related from Jábir bin Samurah that he said, 'I heard the Apostle of God say, "Islám will continue powerful up to twelve Khalifs, all of whom will be from the Quraish."'—*Muslim, Al Bukhárí.*

It is related from Sa'd that, 'The Prophet said, "Whoever wishes for the humiliation of the Quraish, him will God humiliate."'—*At Tirmidhí.*

It is related from Abú Hurairah that, 'The Apostle of God said, "The sovereignty is in the Quraish, and the judiciary power in the Helpers (of Madína), and the office of calling to prayer in the Abyssinians, and faithfulness is in the Azd, namely in Yeman."'—*At Tirmidhí.*

It is related from Abú Hurairah that, 'Ṭufail bin 'Amrul'-Dawsi came to the Apostle of God and said, "Verily the (tribe of) Daws are ruined and have become rebellious, therefore call down the curse of God upon them." And the people thought that he would curse them; but he said, "O' God, guide the Daws to the right path and bring them back."'—*Muslim, Al Bukhárí.*

It is related from Ibn 'Abbás that, 'The Apostle of God said, "Love the Arabs on account of three things: because I am an Arab, and the Qur'án is Arabic, and the speech of the inhabitants of paradise is Arabic."'—*Al Baihaqi.*

ON THE VIRTUES OF ABU BAKR

It is related from Abú Sa'ídu'l-Khudri that, 'The Prophet said, "Verily the one of most benefit to me amongst men in his companionship and his goods is Abú Bakr. If I had taken a friend, I would certainly have taken Abú Bakr as a friend; but the brotherhood of Islám and its love (is established).

Let there not remain in the mosque any window except that of Abú Bakr."' And in another tradition it runs, 'If I had taken a friend besides my Lord, I would certainly have taken Abú Bakr as that friend.'—*Muslim, Al Bukhárí.*

It is related from 'Áyesha that she said, 'The Apostle of God said to me in his illness, "Call Abú Bakr, thy father, and thy brother to me, so that I may write a writing; for I fear that some may desire (the succession) and say, I (am more worthy); but such will not be so. And God and the believers will refuse any but Abú Bakr."'—*Muslim.*

On the Virtues of 'Omar

It is related from Ibn 'Omar that, 'The Apostle of God said, "Verily God has placed the truth on the tongue and heart of 'Omar."'—*At Tirmidhí.*

It is related from 'Uqbah bin 'Ámir that, 'The Prophet said, "Had there been a prophet after me, it would certainly have been 'Omar binu'l-Khaṭṭáb."'—*At Tirmidhí.*

It is related from Anas and Ibn 'Omar that, ''Omar said, "I agreed with my Lord in three things. I said, 'O Apostle of God, if we had taken the place of Abraham as a place of prayer, (it would have been better).' Then the revelation descended, 'Take the place of Abraham as a place of prayer.' And I said, 'O Apostle of God, good and bad men go in where thy wives are; if thou hadst ordered the latter to veil themselves (it would have been better).' And then descended the verse of the veil. And the wives of the Prophet were agreed together in a matter of jealousy. So I said to them, 'It may be that if he divorce you, his Lord will bring in place of you other wives better than you.' Then the revelation came down thus."'—*Muslim, Al Bukhárí.*

On the Virtues of 'Othmán

It is related from Ṭalḥah bin 'Ubaidu'lláh that, 'The Apostle of God said, "There is a companion for every prophet; and my companion in paradise will be 'Othmán."'—*At Tirmidhí.*

It is related from 'Omar that 'The Apostle of God mentioned an insurrection and said, "This man will be killed in it unjustly." (This he said) alluding to 'Othmán.'—*At Tirmidhí.*

On the Virtues of 'Alí

It is related from Sa'd bin ábu Waqqáṣ that, 'The Apostle of God said to 'Alí, "Thou art to me in the relation that Aaron was to Moses, except that there will be no Prophet after me." '—*Muslim, Al Bukhárí.*

It is related from Ibn 'Omar that he said, 'The Apostle of God established a bond of brotherhood between his various companions. Then 'Alí came, his eyes shedding tears, and said, "Thou hast made a bond of brotherhood between thy companions; but thou hast not established such a bond between me and anyone." Then the Apostle of God said, "Thou art my brother in this world and in the next." '—*At Tirmidhí.*

It is related from 'Alí that, 'The Apostle of God said, "I am the house of Knowledge, and 'Alí is the door." '—*At Tirmidhí.*

It is related from 'Alí that, 'The Apostle of God said, "There is in thee a resemblance to Jesus. The Jews hated him until they calumniated his mother. And the Christians loved him so much that they placed him in a position which was not his." ' After that, 'Alí said, 'Two people will be destroyed on my account: one who loves me, and one who acts unjustly towards me. The one will laud me with regard to things which are not in me; and the one who hates me will be led through his hatred of me to calumniate me.'—*Aḥmad.*

On the Virtues of the Ten with Whom God was Pleased

It is related from 'Áyesha that, 'The Apostle of God remained awake on a certain night on his arrival at Madína. And he said, "Would that there was a good man to keep watch over me!" And behold! we heard a sound of arms; and he said, "Who is this?" He said, "It is I, Sa'd." The Prophet said, "What brought thee?" He replied, "Fear fell into my soul on account of the Apostle of God, and I came to keep watch over him." Then the Apostle of God prayed for him, and after that went to sleep.'—*Muslim, Al Bukhárí.*

It is related from Anas that, 'The Prophet said, "The kindest of my followers to my (other) followers is Abú Bakr; and the most strenuous of them in the matters of God is

'Omar; and the truest in shame is 'Othmán; and the one most skilled in the law of inheritance is Zaid bin Thábit; and the best reader amongst them is Ubai bin Ka'b; and the most learned of them in matters lawful and unlawful is Mu'ádh bin Jabal. For every religious sect there is a faithful guardian; and the faithful guardian of this sect is Abú 'Ubaidah binu'l-Jarraḥ." '—*Aḥmad, At Tirmidhí.*

It is related from 'Alí that, 'It was said, "O Apostle of God, whom shall we appoint as prince after thee?" He replied, "If ye make Abú Bakr your prince, ye will find him faithful, indifferent to this world, and eager for the next. And if ye make 'Omar prince, ye will find him strong and faithful, not fearing the blame of detractors in the matters of God. And if ye make 'Alí prince—though I cannot imagine your doing so—ye will find him a guide who is rightly directed, and one who will lead you into the straight path." '—*Aḥmad.*

On the Virtues of the People of the Prophet's Family

It is related from Abú Hurairah that he said, 'I went out with the Apostle of God in a certain part of the day, until we came to Fáṭimah's house. And he said, "Is the boy there? Is the boy there?" meaning Ḥasan. And he did not delay, but came running until each of them embraced his companion. And the Apostle of God said, "O God, verily I love him; then do Thou love him and those who love him." '—*Muslim, Al Bukhárí.*

It is related from Buraidah that he said, 'The Apostle of God was giving the public address (in the mosque) when Ḥasan and Ḥusain came, wearing red shirts. And they were walking and stumbling along. Then the Apostle of God descended from the pulpit and picked them up and placed them in front of him. Then he said, "God spoke truly, 'Your goods and your children are only a temptation.'[1] I looked at these two children walking and stumbling along, and I could no longer contain myself, so much so that I cut short my words and took them up." '—*At Tirmidhí, Abú Dáud.*

It is related from Anas that, 'The head of Ḥusain was brought to 'Ubaidu'lláh bin Ziyád, and it was placed in a basin.

[1] Qur'án, Súratu'l-Anfál (viii) 28.

And he began to violate it, and said something concerning its beauty. I said, "By God! he most resembled the Apostle of God of them all." And the head was dyed with indigo.'—*Al Bukhárí.* And in another tradition from At Tirmidhí, he said, 'I was near Ibn Ziyád, and they brought the head of Ḥusain. And he began to strike it with a stick on its nose, and say, "I have never seen anything so beautiful as this." I said, "Beware! verily he resembled the Apostle of God more than they all."'

On the Virtues of the Wives of the Prophet

It is related from 'Alí that he said, 'I heard the Apostle of God say, "The best of the women of her time was Mary, the daughter of 'Imrán; and the best of the women of her time was Khadíjah, the daughter of Khuwailid."'—*Muslim, Al Bukhárí.*

It is related from 'Áyesha that, 'Gabriel brought her likeness to the Apostle of God on a green, silk cloth and said, "This is thy wife in this world and the next."—*At Tirmidhí.*

It is related from 'Áyesha that she said, 'I was never so jealous of any of the Prophet's wives as I was of Khadíjah, although I had never seen her. But he used to mention her frequently; and often he would slay a goat and cut it up into pieces and then send them to Khadíjah's friends. And often I said to him, "It seems as though there was no woman in the world except Khadíjah!" And he would say, "She was so and so; and I had children by her."'—*Muslim, Al Bukhárí.*

It is related from Abú Músá, that he said, 'No tradition was ever difficult for us, the companions of the Apostle of God, and we asked 'Áyesha, but we found a knowledge of it with her.'—*At Tirmidhí.*

It is related from Músá bin Ṭalḥah that he said, 'I never saw anyone more eloquent than 'Áyesha.'—*At Tirmidhí.*

It is related from Anas that he said, 'When God gave booty to His Apostle from the property of the Hawázin, and he in turn began to give each man of the Quraish a hundred camels, then some men of the Helpers said, "May God forgive the Apostle of God! he gives to the Quraish, and he omits us, though it was our swords which shed their blood." Then their words were reported to the Apostle of God. So he sent to the Helpers and gathered them together in a leathern tent, and he allowed no one else in with them except them. And when they were gathered together the Apostle of God came to them and said, "What is this story which reaches me about you?" Then the wise amongst them said, "As for the sensible among us, O Apostle of God, they have not said anything, but as for certain young men amongst us they did indeed say, 'May God forgive the Apostle of God! he gives to the Quraish, and omits the Helpers; and it was our swords which shed their blood.'" Then the Apostle of God said, "It is true I give to the men who are new in the covenant concerning infidelity in order to attach them firmly (to us). Are ye not content that the men might take the property and that ye may return to your camps with the Apostle of God?" They replied, "O Apostle of God, we are content."' —*Muslim, Al Bukhárí.*

Concerning the Rewards of this People

It is related from Ibn 'Omar that, 'The Apostle of God said, "Verily your appointed time is no more in comparison with the time of the peoples who were before you than what is between the afternoon prayer and the setting of the sun. And the likeness of yourselves and that of the Jews and Christians is like a man who engages workmen and says, 'Who will work for me till mid-day for one *qirát*?' Then the Jews worked till mid-day for one *qirát*. After that he said, 'Who will work for me from mid-day till the afternoon prayer for one *qirát*?' Then the Christians worked from mid-day until the afternoon prayer for one *qirát*. After that he said, 'Who will work for me from the evening prayer till the setting of the sun for two *qiráts*? Are not ye those who work from the evening prayer until the setting of the sun! Are not wages for you twice over!' Then the Jews and Christians became angry and said, 'We have worked more, and yet have received less.' God Most High will say, 'Have I dealt unjustly with you in anything in the matter of your rights?' They will say, 'No.' God Most High will say, 'Verily this is my favour. I bestow it on whom I will.'"'—*Al Bukhárí.*

Published by

Facsimile Publisher
Ashok Vihar, Delhi-110052 (India)
Website: www.facsimilepublisher.com

Distributed by

Gyan Books Pvt. Ltd.
5, Ansari Road, Daryaganj, New Delhi-110002 (India)
E-mail: books@gyanbooks.com, Website: www.gyanbooks.com